Form & Function

American Modernist Jewelry, 1940-1970

Marbeth Schon

Schiffer Publishing Ltd

4880 Lower Valley Road Atglen, PA 19310

Schiffer Books are available at special discounts for bulk purchases for sales promotions or premiums. Special editions, including personalized covers, corporate imprints, and excerpts can be created in large quantities for special needs. For more information contact the publisher:

Other Schiffer Books by Marbeth Schon:
Modernist Jewelry, 1930-1960, The Wearable Art Movement

Library of Congress Control Number: 2008920034

Designed by John P. Cheek
Cover design by Bruce Waters
Type set in Zurich BT

ISBN: 978-0-7643-2976-0
Printed in China

Published by Schiffer Publishing Ltd.
4880 Lower Valley Road
Atglen, PA 19310
Phone: (610) 593-1777; Fax: (610) 593-2002
E-mail: Info@schifferbooks.com

For the largest selection of fine reference books on this and related subjects, please visit our web site at **www.schifferbooks.com**
We are always looking for people to write books on new and related subjects. If you have an idea for a book please contact us at the above address.

This book may be purchased from the publisher.
Include $3.95 for shipping.
Please try your bookstore first.
You may write for a free catalog.

In Europe, Schiffer books are distributed by
Bushwood Books
6 Marksbury Ave.
Kew Gardens
Surrey TW9 4JF England
Phone: 44 (0) 20 8392-8585; Fax: 44 (0) 20 8392-9876
E-mail: info@bushwoodbooks.co.uk
Website: www.bushwoodbooks.co.uk
Free postage in the U.K., Europe; air mail at cost.

CONTENTS

PART IV: MACCHIARINI

PART V: MAKERS' MARKS

ACKNOWLEDGMENTS

Without the kind assistance of many people, this book and its accompanying exhibits would not have been possible. I express my heartfelt thanks to Fred Doloresco; his hard work and continuing enthusiasm for this project have assured its quality and success. Special thanks also to Armand Winfield for his poignant introduction—he lived much of this history!

I am very grateful to The Fort Wayne Museum of Art , Executive Director, Charles A. Sheperd III and Curator, Sachi Yanari-Rizzo for their willingness to present the exhibit, American Modernist Jewelry, 1940 – 1970 with such style and attention to detail and to The School of Creative Arts at the University of St. Francis, Richard Cartwright, Chairman of the Art Department, and Justin Johnson, Gallery Director, for their excellent presentation of The Modernist Movement and Beyond: The Works of Peter and Daniel Macchiarini / Earl Pardon and Tod Pardon.

Much appreciation is due Stanley Lechtzin and Daniella Kerner for allowing me some of their precious time last May during graduation week at Tyler School of Art.

Thank you to Sheila Pamfiloff for her well-researched biography of Mary Kretsinger.

I would also like to thank the following artists, collectors and organizations that consigned pieces for the exhibit and/or photographs for this book: Reme Aldana; The American Craft Council; Wendy Hurlock Baker at the Archives of American Art ; Lilyan Bachrach; Irvin and Bonnie Burkee; Kathy Buszkiewicz; Steven Cabella; Valerie Carberry, Valerie Carberry Gallery; Lisa Cliff, 20th Obsession; Jill Crawford ; Robert Dhaemers; Joanne and Fred Doloresco; Ken Dukoff; Robert Ebendorf ; Kim and Al Eiber; Fred Fenster; David Fine; Rose Foster; Richard Gompf; Daniel Morris and Manuela Zissler-Grenert, Historical Design Gallery; Joe Holdner and Wendy Sacks; Michael Jerry; David Jones; Gayle Kauihou; Juliette Kontor; Terry Kovel; Denise Lassaw; Ed Levin; John Paul Miller; Libby Cooper, JoAnne Cooper, and Marisa McCarthy, Mobilia Gallery; Tom Muir; Stanley Lechtzin and Daniella Kerner; Patricia Riveron Lee; Daniel Macchiarini; Mark McDonald, Tod Pardon; Dwayne Resnick and Paula Superti, 555 Warren Street, Hudson New York.; Munir Meghji; Albert Paley, The Paley Archive, Elizabeth Cameron, archivist and David Burdett, Director, Paley Studios, Ltd; Sheila Pamfiloff, The Glitterbox; Gerald L. Peterson, University of Northern Iowa; Jean Radakovich; merry renk; Alice Seymour; Jane Milosch and Fern Bleckner, Renwick Gallery; Florence Resnikoff; Clayton Roach; Martin Roenigk; Lois Schecter; Mary Schimpff; Alice Seymour; Helen Shirk; Arlene Shrut; Jan Krenke Southern; Kathy Taylor, Indiana University Art Museum; John Titus; Dwight Wallace, Josephine A. Wallace Trust; Lois Franke Warren; Sherrye Webster; Michele Wiener; and Armand Winfield.

Thanks to my editor, Nancy Schiffer, for her patience; to my husband, Andrew Tilden, for his long suffering during the writing of the manuscript; and to my assistant, Shirley Byrne.

FOREWORD

Marbeth Schon is a thorough researcher and an art historian of note. That she has chosen this exciting period of modernist jewelry and writes about it in her clear and meticulous style is a real treat for those of us who are interested in the now collectible jewelry of this era and those who brought these wonderful creations to fruition.

I, fortunately, was an active pioneer and participant in the Wearable Art Jewelry movement, and I am probably one of the few craftsmen of this era still alive (I will be eighty-eight this month—December, 2007). I have a firsthand knowledge of this period and of those who made it famous. I was also one of the founders of Craftsmen's Equity, which flourished in Greenwich Village in New York City for several years from the mid-1940s forward.

When Marbeth asked me to write this Foreword to her manuscript, past memories of an exciting chapter in my life, in the 1940s in Bohemian Greenwich Village, were awakened. I was amazed by the thoroughness of her research as she made the period come alive. She introduces the jewelers and craftspeople as though they were living and describes their work with such verve and detail that I can mentally pick up each piece and examine it and enjoy doing so.

This was a very creative and equally exciting period in the growth of America's contribution to jewelry, and I am happy to relive it with Marbeth. Practically all of my memories have been regenerated, so I can bring to mind the many talented men and women of this period in their studios, as visitors, and many as close friends. Paul Lobel, Julien Goodenow, Arthur King, Zahara Shatz, Pedro Pujol and his very talented brother, Rebajes, Paul Voltaire, Ed Wiener, Arpad Rosti, Sam Kramer, and Arthur Smith all pass by me in fondest memories of this epoch, which Marbeth has made come alive in a way that few have done so well before.

Her unusual and extensive background in art and history has prepared Marbeth well for this creative assignment. I am truly grateful that she chose this era to write about, and I am equally grateful that she chose me to write this Foreword.

Armand G. Winfield
Albuquerque, New Mexico
December 4, 2007

Winfield Fine Art in Jewelry, brooch, watercolor on paper en cased in acrylics, artist: Marnye Reinhart, c. 1946 or 1947, Courtesy of Armand Winfield, photograph by Shirley Byrne.

INTRODUCTION

"It can be a point in the endless ocean of time. Whether it is an attempt to capture the instantaneous emotion or the enigma of eternity, it can be a measure of the significance of man. It is one of the ways he can take to show he passed this way and to make his passing a thing of purpose." (Nat Koffman,* *Art as a Record, the Notebook of Nat Koffman*, Abingdon Square Publications, 1951.)

It is with respect for the great art jewelers of the past that we attempt to define them. We don't necessarily wish to apply labels to their work—this in some way negates their autonomy, their inventiveness. As much as possible, we try to listen to what they have to say about themselves and their work through writings and interviews. To assess a piece of art jewelry without understanding its quality of individuality would be pointless.

Within a broad scope, however, are circumstances of collective creativity; world events and world changes give way to new types of artistic expression that become the "isms" of the art historian. An artist is usually one of the first to give voice to these changes as he is spurred on by his milieu to, in some way, creatively absorb them into his work—to give meaning to the idiosyncrasy of "what is." And when this "modern" work is perceived in a positive light by other artists, they may use it, not as a template, but as a "springboard" to project their own creativity in a new direction.

As an historian of 20th century modernist jewelry, I believe a study of this kind must, through historical perspective, further an understanding of the jewelry, certainly, but also of the creators of the jewelry. It is my desire to in some way make "his [the artist's] passing a thing of purpose."
Marbeth Schon

**Nat Koffman was a Pennsylvania painter who created small works of art for Winfield Fine Art in Jewelry, in Greenwich Village, in the mid-1940s.*

Winfield Fine Art in Jewelry, pendant, drawing on silver foil encased in acrylics, artist: Nat Koffman, c. 1946 or 1947, Courtesy of Armand Winfield, photograph by Shirley Byrne.

Part I
AMERICAN CRAFTS REVIVAL IN METALWORK

Harry Bertoia, necklace, gold, 9" x 8-1/2". *Courtesy of Mark McDonald, 555 Warren St., Hudson, New York, photograph by Bill Hibbs.*

CHAPTER 1
Before and During World War II

The United States was a haven for extraordinary European artists and crafts people during the 1930s. Schools such as Black Mountain College in Ashville, North Carolina, the School of Design in Chicago, and Cranbrook Academy in Bloomfield Hills, Michigan, reaped the benefits of these remarkable refugees.

In the 1920s Paris was the center of "taste and luxury." Wealthy American collectors, art enthusiasts, students, and anyone who could scrape up enough money to travel abroad, went to France where they were exposed to the paintings, sculptures, jewelry and architecture of the "modernists."

The United States lagged behind the rest of the world in artistic innovation. A newspaper article dated February 1922, titled *Is there an American Art?* quotes Cecelia Beaux as saying that "America has no national art and must continue to go to France for inspiration" and British painter C. W. R. Nevinson as saying, "[America's]...idea of art is a well appointed bathroom and [America's] Raphael is the plumber."[1]

The 1925 *Exposition Internationale des Arts Decoratifs et Industriels Modernes*, addressed the principal concerns of the mid-century. The pairing of "modern" and "industrial" integrated the fields of architecture and applied arts through the dramatic and grandiose interiors by Emile-Jacques Ruhlmann, the profligacy of Maurice Marinot's and René Lalique's glassware, and the splendor of Cartier's jewelry and Jean Puiforcat's silver. "Stylistic currents ran the gamut from Louis XVI classicism to cubism, to the exotic of the Near and Far East."[2]

By 1935 the combined effects of the Great Depression and the winds of war brought the extravagance of the 1920s to an end.

The 1930s gave birth to a new idea of modernism, "a rational, architectonic style with a 'reductivist' aesthetic. In 1930 the Deutscher Werkbund staged an important exhibition in Paris at XXe Salon des Artisted Décorateurs; designed by Walter Gropius, Marcel Breuer, László Moholy-Nagy, and Herbert Bayer, it brought home the importance of this new aesthetic. Similar tendencies were revealed in the important exposition held in Stockholm in 1930 as well as the *Monza IV Triennale* in 1930."[3]

The shift in artistic taste between 1925 and 1935 was not only involved with aesthetics, it also had a basis in socioeconomic issues—major social

Peter Macchiarini, *Rakov*, sculpture: bronze, red/brown patina, base: wood, c.1936. *Courtesy of Daniel Macchiarini, photograph by Leslie W. Rabine.*

changes took place. Socialists came to power in the Scandinavian countries: Denmark (1929), Sweden (1932), Norway (1935) and Finland (1937). In Italy, "Il Duce and the Fascists sought a future in which the engineer was the new savior...it was industrial design rather than handcraftsmanship that was being stressed as the new key element of design. Consequently, it was the architect and the industrial designer, rather than the artist or the craftsman, who were promoted as the new heros."[4]

The political tone in Europe by the 1930s was becoming increasingly unsympathetic to free-thinking artists and intellectuals, leading many of them to seek safety in the United States. Among them were Walter Gropius, Meis van Der Rohe, Lazlo Moholy-Nagy, Marguerite and Franz Wildenhain, Anni and Joseph Albers, and Trude Guermonpre—students, teachers, and disciples of Germany's radical-thinking school of the Bauhaus, closed by the Nazis in 1933.

Husband and wife, Joseph and Anni Albers, were hired to teach at Black Mountain College near Asheville, North Carolina (later, Walter Gropius would also teach there). Though neither taught metalsmithing (Anni was a weaver and Josef a painter), the cross-genre Bauhaus-type program they established became a model for future craft programs, including metals, at American colleges and universities.

By the 1940s some of the most enlightened minds of the time were on the faculty at Black Mountain College and it had become a potent paradigm for American experimental education. In later years, during the Second World War, the school experienced difficulties—the draft seriously diminished the number of young male students and its small size kept it from qualifying for wartime programs. The school continued to attract gifted individualists, however, such as artists Arthur Penn, Kenneth Noland, Robert Rauschenberg, James Leo Herlihy, Ruth Asawa. John Cage, Merce Cunningham, Willem de Kooning, Beaumont and Nancy Newhall, and Buckminster Fuller.[5] Black Mountain continued its innovative programs until the mid-1950s when the temperament of society began to change and the school was forced to close.

In 1937, in Chicago, Hungarian born László Moholy-Nagy who had been an instructor at the Bauhaus in Berlin, was hired by industrialist Walter Paepcke to direct an American version of the Bauhaus that would disseminate the tenets of the original school. It was christened "The New Bauhaus" and was housed in a mansion on Prairie Avenue, designed by Richard Morris Hunt for Marshall Field.

Lacking financial support, The New Bauhaus was forced to close in1938, but a year later Moholy-Nagy opened the School of Design that in 1944 became the Institute of Design.

László Moholy-Nagy. *Photograph by Lucia Moholy-Nagy.*

László Moholy-Nagy's experimental programs at the School of Design in the 1940s inspired many of America's foremost modernist jewelers. Margaret De Patta credited this education as the most significant of her life. It was Moholy-Nagy who encouraged her to focus on the potential of "non-objective visual and special concepts in jewelry design."[6] He was a photographer, fascinated by the transmission of light. De Patta transferred this fascination into her jewelry designs—she began to experiment with the way light could be employed as a design element using semi-transparent stones.

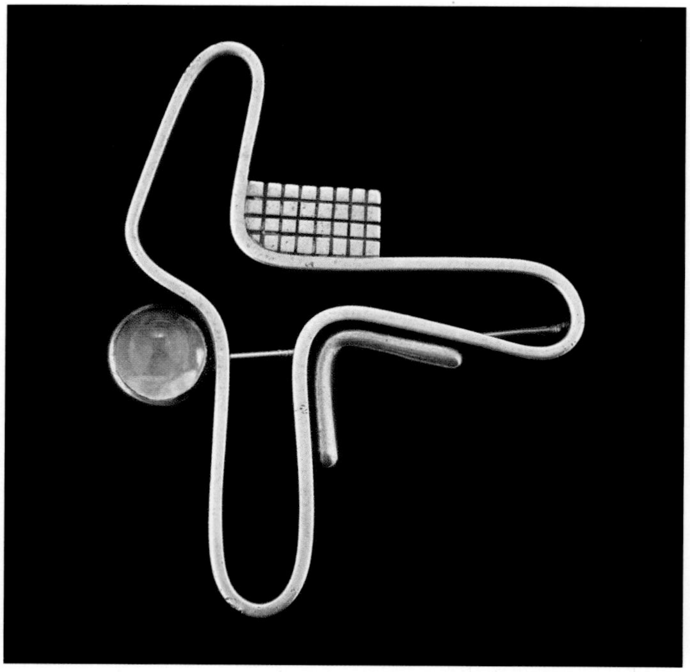

Margaret De Patta, brooch, sterling silver, glass, 3-1/2" x 2" *Courtesy of Mark McDonald, 555 Warren St., Hudson, New York, photograph by Bill Hibbs.*

The early 1930s saw the birth of another school whose curriculum was enlightened by European pre-World War II philosophies. Cranbrook Academy of Art in Bloomfield Hills, Michigan, began as a collaborative effort between Detroit newspaper baron and philanthropist George Gough Booth and Finnish architect Eliel Saarinen. The objective was to train artists and artist/craftsmen to produce "objects to embellish and improve the American environment, and [to form a] community where art would be integrated with daily life to the benefit of all."[7] Something like William Morris's union of aesthetics and social reform—the basis of the Arts and Crafts Movement.

The Saarinen-designed academy drew celebrated artists from all over the world, including Carl Milles, Harry Bertoia, Charles Eames, Maija Grotell, Eero Saarinen and Florence Knoll. Together, these artists and other Cranbrook students and teachers who came later have had a formidable impact on the American crafts movement.

Beginnings of Craft Organizations in America

In 1940 The Handcraft Cooperative League of America opened America House in New York City. In 1942 The American Craftsmen's Cooperative Council was founded and the magazine Craft Horizons began publication. In 1943 the American Craftsmen's Educational Council, Inc. was inaugurated.

The Great Depression had a devastating effect on the production of luxury, one-of-a-kind objects. People bought what they could afford and what they could afford were items of mass production. Craftsmen were unable to find markets for their work and craft programs suffered while most universities changed from teaching crafts to teaching industrial design.

In late summer of 1939 in Shelbourne, Vermont, a small group of representatives from several New England states met to discuss the dilemma of the rural craftsmen. The instigator of this meeting was Mrs. Vanderbilt Webb, a wealthy copper heiress who saw it as her duty to contribute philanthropically to society. In 1932, during the Depression, the hardships she witnessed moved her to organize a crafts cooperative to help create small rural home industries. It was called the Putnam County Products—an effort she later described as "the marketing of 'string beans and eggs." A person of foresight, she realized the importance of strengthening the market for crafts not just locally, but nationally and, because of her vision, the meeting at Shelbourne was the genesis of an organization that would indelibly influence the structure of the American crafts movement from the early 1940s to the present day—the Handcraft Cooperative League of America, the forerunner of The American Craft Council.[8]

In 1940 the Handcraft Cooperative League of America opened America House, in New York City at 485 Madison Avenue. America House was the first significant retail outlet to acquaint the public with the richness and uniqueness of American crafts.

In 1982 in a speech at the symposium, *American Metalsmithing and Jewelrymaking in the 1940s and 1950s*, sponsored by the Renwick Gallery and the Archives of American Art, metalsmith Adda Husted-Andersen praised Mrs. Web, "The tremendous opening of the crafts in America was of course due to Mrs. Webb. When she opened America House a new era began and for all the activities that followed we owe her endless gratitude."

Peter Macchiarini, *Mother and Child*, sculpture, wood, gilded wood frame, 14" x 10-1/4" x ½". *Courtesy of Daniel Macchiarini, photograph by Leslie W. Rabine*.

Adda Husted-Andersen, pendant and neckring, sterling silver with moss agate. Courtesy of The Sarah Bodine & Michael Dunas Archives of 20th Century Jewelry, Tyler School of Art, Temple University,Professor Stanley Lechtzin, Curator of Metals/Jewelry and collection.

In 1942 the Handcraft Cooperative League of America and the American Handcraft Council merged to become the American Craftsmen's Cooperative Council with a mandate to promote both craft education and retail sales of handmade objects. The magazine Craft Horizons (now American Craft) was also published that same year by the ACCC and in 1943 the educational branch of the organization, The American Craftsmen's Educational Council, was established to facilitate exhibitions, training programs for veterans and to provide library services.

In1943 the Board of Regents of the State of New York granted a charter to the organization that became the extant American Craftsmen's Council (now called the American Craft Council).

Early Craft Training Programs

In 1944 the Rehabilitation training Program at Dartmouth College, sponsored by the American Craftsmen's Educational Council, was renamed the School for American Craftsmen in order to focus on the professional craftsman.

Purportedly, the idea for the School for American Craftsmen was born out of a conversation between Mrs. Vanderbilt Webb and a soldier who had recently returned from serving in the Second World War. The subject of the discourse was the American Craftsman and how he was being threatened with extinction by the growth of industrialization. In order to address this crisis, the American Craftsmen's Educational Council and the Dartmouth College Student Workshop united to found the School for American Craftsmen in Hanover, New Hampshire.

The school was organized around five areas of instruction—pottery, woodworking, metals, weaving, and ironworking. Working craftsmen were hired as teachers with the expectation that they would be role models for the students who, acting as apprentices, would learn enough skills to later become practicing craftsmen, able to support themselves with their respective crafts.[9]

The length of the course was originally six months and students and faculty were expected to put in forty hours each week in the shops. In order to insure that each graduate would be able to make a living with his craft, two objectives were expected to be met: the "integration in teaching of design, technique and production" and the "simulation of marketing conditions the student would meet on graduation." When their work was considered adequate for the market, they were expected to produce pieces to be sold at America House in New York City.[10]

In order to fulfill the definition of "good product" the objects produced by the students needed to have the following attributes: "Beauty of design; well executed technically; function—must meet a real need of use or decoration; must be part of a 'line' and so usable with other products; must meet fashion trends; and must be a correct price"[11]

Less than a year after the School for American Craftsmen was founded at Dartmouth it was moved to Alfred University in Alfred, New York, and in 1950 to its permanent home at the Rochester Institute of Technology in Rochester, New York.

Metalsmithing for GIs

Metalsmithing, which proved to be exceptional occupational therapy for GI's returning from World War II, was the justification for new programs in metalsmithing and jewelry making at various American colleges such as Cranbrook Academy of Art in Michigan, the University of Kansas, and Indiana University. Similar "socially commendable" programs were set up at The War Veteran's Art Center and the Museum of Modern Art in New York.

In 1944, while volunteering at the Great Lakes Naval Hospital in Illinois, Kansas jeweler Margret Craver recognized the possibilities of using metalsmithing as therapy for World War II veterans. Later, while in New York on a visit to Handy and Harman (a metal refining and supply company) to inquire about materials for a class she was teaching at the School of the Wichita Art Association, she expressed her ideas to the president of the firm, Gustave Niemeyer, who responded favorably and went on to set up a Hospital Service Program with Withers at the head.

In order to secure approval from the Surgeon General in Washington, Withers made prototypes of coiled wire jewelry that could be fashioned with basic tools and inexpensive materials. She then set up a workshop in the furnace room of the Walter Reed Army Hospital in Washington where injured veterans could learn wire-working techniques as part of their occupational therapy.

> "I saw a lot of GI's," Withers remembered, "... In one hospital there were almost a hundred... And you get to know the GI's and the first thing you know you are thinking about exactly what projects you think they would like...I wanted to do something for the war effort. Instead of trying to learn to knit for the soldiers of World War II, I joined Handy & Harman and set up a pilot program under the watchful eyes of General Kirk, Surgeon General of the United States Army, and the Chief Occupational Therapist." [12]

Margret Craver Withers sketching out a design, 1946. *Courtesy of the Margret Craver Withers papers, 1926 – 1992, in the Archives of America Art, Smithsonian Institution.*

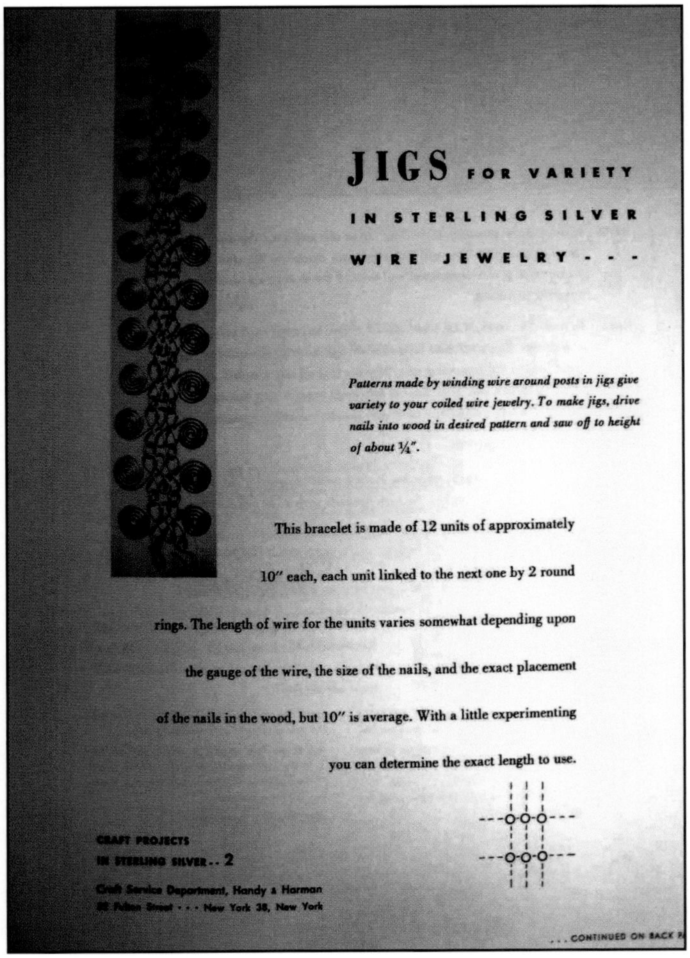

Handy and Harman brochure, *Crafts Products in Sterling Silver. Photograph courtesy of The Sarah Bodine & Michael Dunas Archives of 20th Century Jewelry, Tyler School of Art, Temple University, Professor Stanley Lechtzin, Curator of Metals/Jewelry Archives and Collections.*

Craver went on to establish similar programs for the Army at each of its thirteen Commands and, after the war, was invited to England by the Worshipful Company of Goldsmiths, London's oldest crafts guild (responsible since 1327 for confirming the quality of gold and silver through the hallmarking system), to speak about her experiences. She spoke about this experience in 1982 at the symposium, *American Metalsmithing and Jewelrymaking in the 1940s and 1950s*", sponsored by the Renwick Gallery and the Archives of American Art:

> My recollections of London were fire weed blooming in unearthly craters, great white marble capitals imbedded in streets, their former location still unknown, one third of Goldsmiths' Hall a deep black hole, all buildings surrounding Christopher Wren's Church destroyed leaving it with just the space that he intended for it in the first place. At the same time, I became a member of a two-week refresher course at the London School of Art for their leading designers and teachers who were just back from the service. I was greatly impressed with the amount of work the fifteen of us accomplished.

Craver also established the first crafts department at the School of the Wichita Arts Association, a branch of the Wichita Art Museum where from about 1935 – 1945, she taught metalworking and other craft courses and served as part-time curator.

Craft Students League

For a countless number of Americans and refugees from other countries seeking to become either practicing craftsmen or teachers, the affordable programs offered at the Craft Students League in New York City before and during World War II were an invaluable introduction to metalsmithing and jewelry making.

The following is an excerpt from a speech by jeweler/teacher Adda Husted Andersen in 1982 at the symposium *American Metalsmithing and Jewelrymaking in the 1940s and 1950s*, sponsored by the Renwick Gallery and the Archives of American Art:

> The Craft Students League was started by the New York Society of Craftsmen and the YWCA in the 1930s. It taught the major crafts plus design and painting and sculpture. I became an instructor in Jewelry and enameling not quite from the beginning.
>
> At that time there was very little going on as far as teaching metal work in New York. There seemed to be a need of a school of this kind where anyone could join that could pay a modest fee. The Y paid the overhead. It became the most integrated place one could imagine. We had men and women, young and old, people from all walks of life and all kinds of nationalities and colors—and everyone got along well. They were all craftsmen together although at very various stages of workmanship and the students got exposed to different cultures and viewpoints.
>
> During the war the school was able to serve some GI's by letting them take classes and giving them bench time free of charge.
>
> A Viennese refugee woman came to New York to settle with her husband. She was able to take classes and she was highly creative and a joy to work with. The reason I am mentioning her is that she was in my class for over 5 years.
>
> I had other refugees. I have seen a concentration camp number burned into a student's arm.
>
> In the 50s some young women were brought over from Hiroshima for medical treatments. They were offered free instruction and I had 3 in a class. They worked with their little maimed hands. Before they left they gave us a tea party, we all sat on the floor. The people that brought them back returned with a fan for each of us who had worked with them. They were inscribed: The parents of Hiroshima are grateful. That made one very humble.
>
> I had a Polish woman in my class, also brought over for medical treatment; she had been a prisoner at Buchenwald and subjected to medical abuse. She was a fine jeweler but wanted to do enameling so we were happy to welcome her. She spoke French but could not write it so I lost touch with her.

Adda Husted-Andersen, pendant, sterling silver, 2-7/8" x 1". *Collection of Joanne and Fred Doloresco, photograph by Fred Doloresco.*

CHAPTER 2
After World War II, Late1940s to mid-1950s

Hand-in-hand with the postwar education of young jewelers, academic interest in jewelry as an art form grew.

Craft Exhibitions, Conferences, and Guilds

There were very few national exhibitions that included handmade jewelry and metalware during the depression and hardly any during World War II. The Golden Gate International Exposition in San Francisco took place in 1939 and, though hampered by the lasting affects of the Depression, the Exposition is historically important in that it reinforced the theme of modernism through its architectural exhibits and allowed women prominent roles as organizers and exhibitors.

It wasn't until 1946 that the Museum of Modern Art mounted their seminal and unconventional exhibit, *Modern Handmade Jewelry*. The exhibit mixed jewelry made by artists and sculptors such as Richard Poussette-Dart, Alexander Calder, and Jacques Lipschitz with that of actual working jewelers such as Paul Lobel, Margaret De Patta, and Adda Husted-Andersen. Even weaver Anni Albers participated with a necklace made from a sink drain and paper clips. The exhibit "emphasized innovation over technical perfection, displaying designs of great spirit and vitality that incorporated unusual materials...The works exhibited revealed a strong reaction against the prevalent conventional design of much commercial, costume, and traditional jewelry." Following its New York venue, the exhibit traveled to other places such as the Art Museum at Rhode Island School of Design, Providence.[13]

Alexander Calder, pendant, sterling silver, 2-1/2" diameter. *Courtesy of Mark McDonald, 555 Warren Street, Hudson, New York, photograph by Bill Hibbs.*

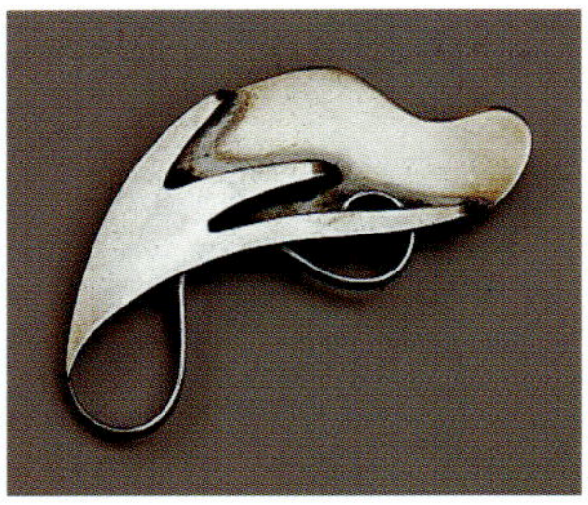

Paul Lobel, brooch, sterling silver, 1-5/8" x 3-3/8". *Collection of Joanne and Fred Doloresco, photograph by Fred Doloresco.*

Art Smith, *Modernette* cuff, brass, 2-1/2" x 2-5/8". *Courtesy of Mark McDonald, 555 Warren St., Hudson, New York, photograph by Bill Hibbs.*

The progressive Walker Art Center in Minneapolis, Minnesota followed with an exhibit in 1948 titled *Modern Jewelry Under Fifty Dollars*. The work of thirty-two innovative artist/jewelers was included and each piece was priced under fifty dollars. Many of the participants of this exhibit had been producing modernist jewelry and metalwork since the 1930s and early 1940s—Margaret De Patta, Sam Kramer, Paul Lobel, Art Smith, Harry Bertoia, Philip Morton, and Adda Husted-Andersen were among them. Some others were Hurst & Kingsbury, Claire Falkenstein, Doris Hall, Walter Rhodes, Caroline Rosene, Zahara Schatz, Pearl Shecter, Winfield Fine art in Jewelry and Bob Winston.

Sam Kramer, pendant, sterling silver, moonstone, 3-1/2" x 2-1/4". *Collection of Jill Crawford, photograph by Shirley Byrne.*

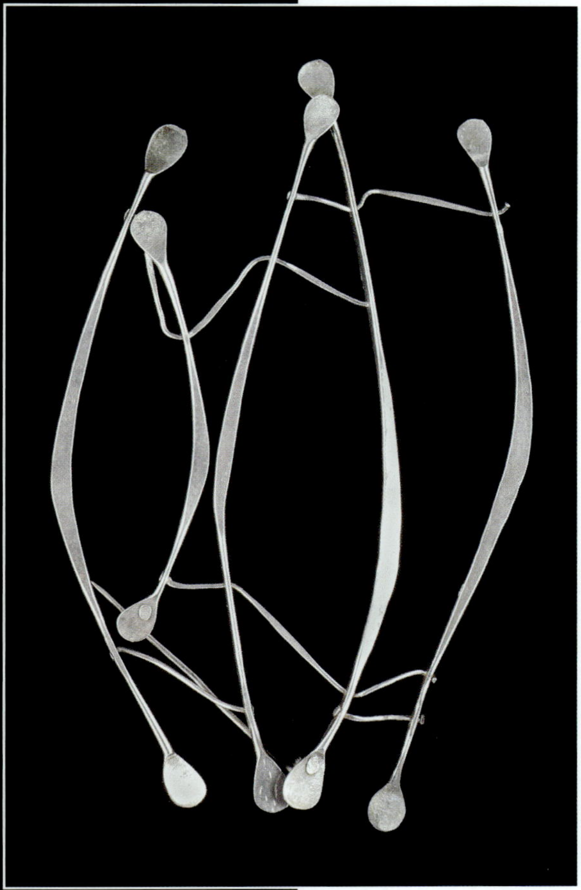

Harry Bertoia, brooch, sterling silver. 4-1/2" x 3". *Courtesy of Mark McDonald, 555 Warren St., Hudson, New York, photograph by Bill Hibbs.*

Zahara Schatz, cuff, Plexiglas, copper, brass, steel wire, Lurex thread, 2-1/4" wide. *Collection of Steve Cabella, photograph by Geoff Turner.*

Hurst & Kingsbury, cuff, sterling silver and amethyst, 1-3/4" wide x 2-1/4" inside diameter, c. 1950s. *Collection of Rose Foster, photograph by Shirley Byrne.*

Winfield Fine Art in Jewelry, brooch, watercolor on paper by Tobias, encased in acrylics, 2-5/8" x 2-1/4". *Collection of Joanne and Fred Doloresco, photograph by Fred Doloresco.*

The Walker Art Center presented two exhibits of contemporary jewelry (on paper), in their *Design Quarterly* publications (issue #33, 1955 and double issue #45 – 46, 1959). The 1955 exhibit of the work of eighty-four jewelers from across the country reflected the burgeoning and broadening interest in metalworking in the mid-1950s.

Some of the exhibitors at the 1955 Walker exhibit included Adda Husted-Andersen, Mildred Ball, Harry Bertoia, Eleanor Caldwell, Betty Cooke, Robert Dhaemers, Virginia Dudley, Robert and Audrey Engstrom, Sam Kramer, Mary Kretsinger, Philip Morton, Caroline Rosene, Earl Pardon, Miriam Smith Peck, Coralyn Pence, Barney M. Reid, merry renk, Florence Resnikoff, Ruth Roach, George K. Salo, Christian Schmidt, Pearl Shecter, Byron Wilson, and Bob Winston.

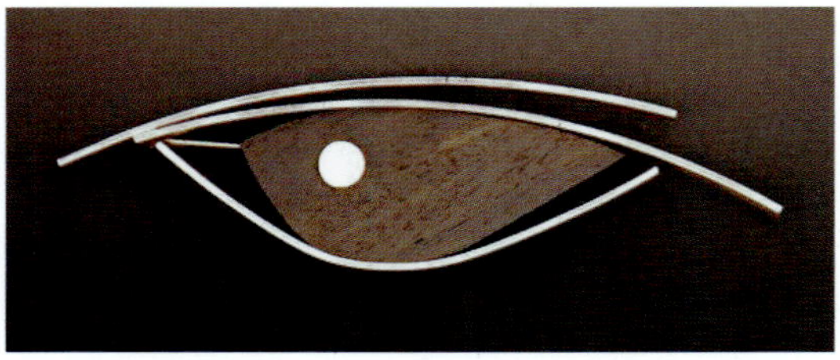

Betty Cooke, brooch, sterling silver, ebony, 1-1/4" x 4-3/4". Collection *of Joanne and Fred Doloresco, photograph by Fred Doloresco.*

Sam Kramer, pendant and chain, sterling silver, glass, taxidermy eye, pendant: 3-1/8" x 2". *Collection of Joanne and Fred Doloresco, photograph by Marbeth Schon.*

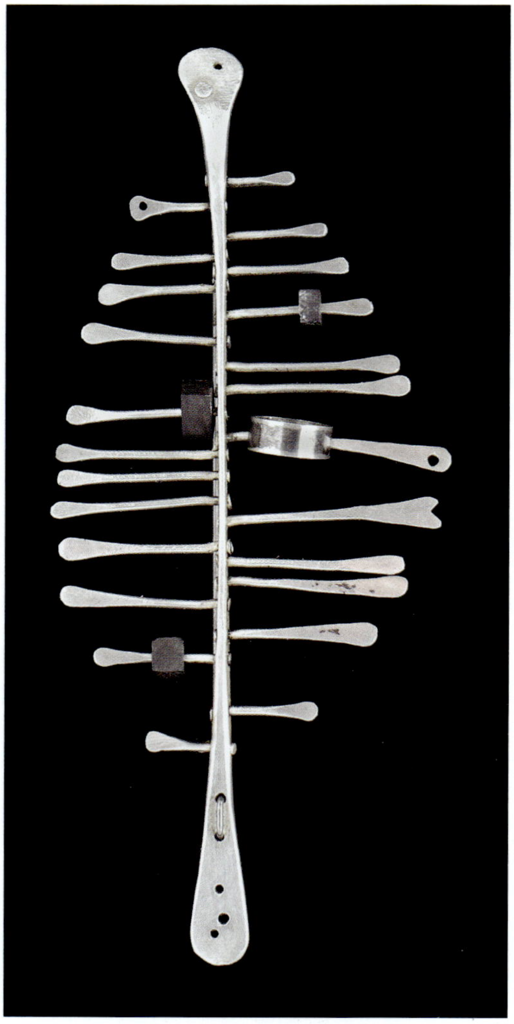

Harry Bertoia, Abacus brooch, sterling silver, ebony, 4-1/4" x 1-7/8". *Courtesy of Mark McDonald, 555 Warren St., Hudson, New York, photograph by Bill Hibbs.*

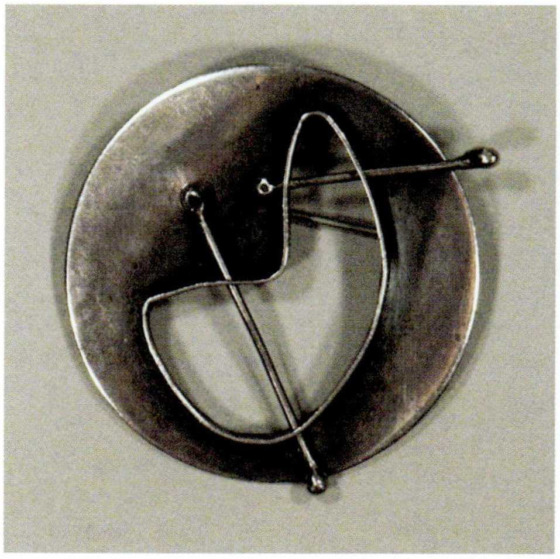

Florence Resnikoff, brooch, sterling silver, 2" diameter. *Collection of Munir Meghji, photograph by Justin Johnson.*

The 1959 Walker Art Center exhibit on paper contained photographs of the work of eighty-eight jewelers but was double the size of the 1955 issue of *Design Quarterly*. Some of the exhibitors included Mildred Ball, Francis Holmes Boothby, Irena Brynner, Eleanor Caldwell, Betty Cooke, Margaret De Patta, Robert Dhaemers, Virginia Dudley, Alma Eikerman, Robert and Audrey Engstrom, Elsa Freund, Richard Gompf, Clifford Herrold, Michael Jerry, Sam Kramer, Earl Krentzin, Mary Kretsinger, John Paul Miller, Philip Morton, Ronald Hayes Pearson, Ruth Penington, Miriam Smith Peck, John Prip, merry renk, Svetozar and Ruth Radakovich, Florence Resnikoff, Walter Rhodes, Ruth Roach, Pearl Shecter, Nancy Sherwood, Mary Schimpff, Christian Schmidt, Byron Wilson, and Bob Winston.

(For a list of the jewelers involved in the exhibits *Modern Handmade Jewelry*, Museum of Modern Art, 1946; *Modern Jewelry Under Fifty Dollars*, Walker Art Center, 1948; and the two exhibits on paper, 1955 and 1959, at the Walker Art Center, see my previous book, *Modernist Jewelry, 1930 – 1960, The Wearable Art Movement*, Schiffer Publishing, Ltd., 2004.)

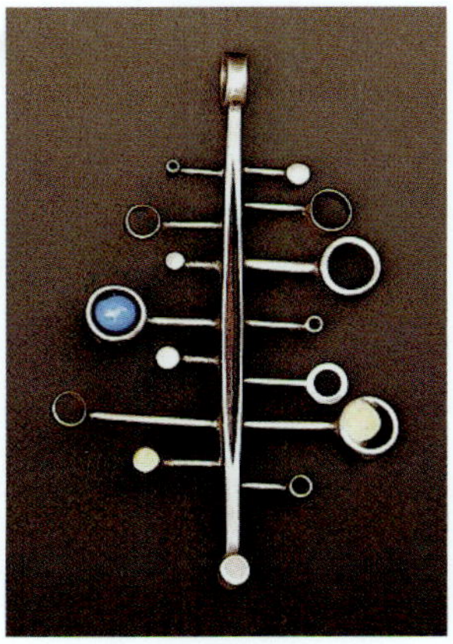

Frances Holmes Boothby, pendant, sterling silver, copper, blue bead, 3"x1-7/8". *Collection of Joanne and Fred Doloresco, photograph by Fred Doloresco.*

Mary Kretsinger, ring, enamel and sterling silver, 1-5/8" 1/2", c. 1958 (Shown in advertisement for Nanny's in San Francisco). *Collection of Munir Meghji, photograph by Munir Meghji.*

Mildred Ball, necklace, sterling silver, 2-3/8" x 1-1/2". *Collection of Joanne and Fred Doloresco, photograph by Fred Doloresco.*

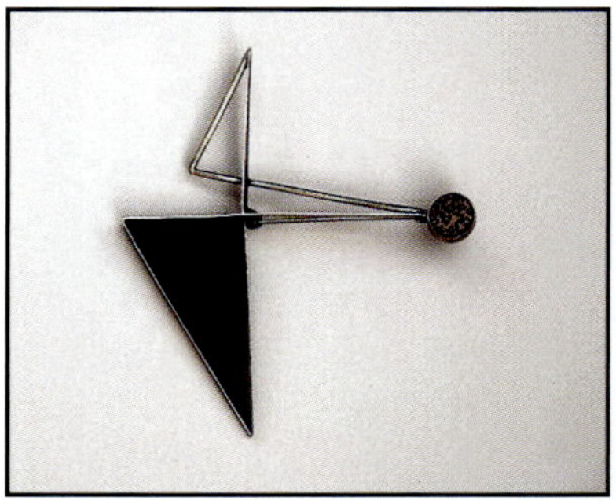

Byron Wilson, brooch, sterling silver, ebony, 5/8 x 3 ¼, c.1944. *Collection of Joanne and Fred Doloresco, photograph by Fred Doloresco.*

Ruth Roach, double cuff, sterling silver, moss agate, 2-1/2" x 1-1/4". *Courtesy of Mark McDonald, 555 Warren St., Hudson, New York, photograph by Bill Hibbs.*

Sam Kramer, brooch, sterling silver, pearl, glass. *Courtesy of Mark McDonald, 555 Warren St., Hudson, New York, photograph by Bill Hibbs.*

Elsa Freund, necklace, sterling silver, glass, 4-1/2" x 4 1/4". *Collection of Joanne and Fred Doloresco, photograph by Fred Doloresco.*

In 1955 the Museum of Contemporary Crafts opened in New York City. The name was changed to the American Craft Museum and is now called the Museum of Arts & Design. The museum has been the "craft center" of the nation, with numerous exhibits of jewelry held since its inception.

The Cleveland Museum of Art's annual May shows, open to any artist or craftsman born or residing in Ohio's Cuyahoga County (later open to artist living in what was called the Western Reserve—thirteen counties in northeaster Ohio), was of particular importance to mid-20th century enamellist/jewelers because it provided them regional and sometimes national recognition and introduced them to techniques and achievements by other artists in their field. Enamellist Doris Hall began submitting her work as early as the 1930s.[14]

Doris Hall, enamel bowl, 5-1/4" diameter x 5/8" high. *Collection of Marbeth Schon, photograph by Marbeth Schon.*

Though during World War II, programs at most museums and galleries had slowed considerably, Hall and her husband Kalman Kubinyi exhibited their work in 1944 at the 1030 Gallery on Euclid Avenue in downtown Cleveland. A Cleveland journalist reported, "With that reverence for the art of the past, isn't it just as important to keep our modern art alive and assure our artists of an audience? Our spirits in war-time need the solace that art can give."[15]

In 1951, because of a commitment to encourage and support working contemporary craftsmen, the St. Paul Gallery in St. Paul, Minnesota, initiated its biennial exhibition, *Fiber, Clay, and Metal.* This was the first major exhibit of crafts on the regional level to take place outside of the eastern seaboard.[16]

One of the exhibitors in the 1954 *Fiber, Clay, and Metal* exhibit was Earl Pardon who won a purchase award.

Earl Pardon, brooch, sterling silver, coral, 3-5/8" x 1-3/4", c. 1952. *Courtesy of Mark McDonald, 555 Warren St., Hudson, New York, photograph by Bill Hibbs.*

After the war in the late 1940s, Margret Craver again made her mark on the American metal arts movement. Because there had been no programs for her when she began her career in metals in the late 1920s and1930s, she was adamant that American metal arts students should now have the opportunity to study. Stressing the need for an educational project that would renew the knowledge and techniques of the craft of silversmithing, she again approached the generous Gustave Niemeyer for help. Craver told Niemeyer that this goal could be partly accomplished through conferences for teachers who would then be motivated to establish their own metalworking programs at American colleges and universities. Neimeyer liked the idea, realizing that conferences for silversmiths would promote the silver industry and, in turn, benefit his company. " It was Mr. Niemeyer," Withers remembered, "and I told him about this and he thought it was great and his acceptance of my wanting conferences for American teachers to get American teachers motivated and going in this country was wonderful!" [17]

Each summer, from 1947-1951, the conferences offered four weeks of silversmithing training to students selected from a pool of mostly young American applicants with degrees in design or art education. The first two conferences were held at the Rhode Island School of Design and the last two at the School for American Craftsmen in Rochester, New York. William Bennett, instructor from the College of Arts and Crafts in Sheffield, England, headed the 1947 conference; Baron Erik Fleming served in 1948, '49, and '51; and Reginald Hill, instructor at the Central School of Arts and Crafts in London, led the Conference in 1950. Many of the participants went on to become well recognized metalsmiths, teachers, and innovators at American universities, including Fred Miller, John Paul Miller, Earl Pardon, and Alma Eikerman.

Earl Pardon, brooch, sterling silver, ivory, ebony, enamel, 4" x 2-1/4" x 1/2", c. 1960. *Courtesy of Mark McDonald, 555 Warren Street, Hudson, New York, photograph by Bill Hibbs.*

The first real craft exhibition at the Metropolitan Museum of Art, *Form in Handwrought Silver*, took place in 1949. The works exhibited were finished pieces made by the participants of the Handy and Harman conference that year.

In 1982, in Washington D.C., at the symposium, *American Metalsmithing and Jewelrymaking in the 1940s and 1950s*, sponsored by the Renwick Gallery and the Archives of American Art, Margret Craver spoke about the first Handy and Harman conference:

> Our small staff was now working overtime when the press got wind of the prestigious Handy and Harman...doing something with designers which meant to them production, which sounded as though we were going into competition with our own customers, Reed & Barton, International, Towle, etc. Here we were lucky again when help came from a public relations firm that had worked interpreting museum type exhibitions—Nathan and Erskin.
>
> Finally opening day of the first conference arrived, all conferees reported in spite of its being such an unheard of project. Mr. Niemeyer came from New York to welcome the twelve, five minutes later Mr. Bennett gave a blocking demonstration and twenty minutes later twelve hammers were at work, miracles beginning. The Providence paper had a photograph of our opening ceremony on its front page before the lunch hour. Our press coverage from then on was one of our best assets.
>
> Our conference breaks were talks by Handy & Harman metallurgists and such people as Edith Halpert of the Downtown Gallery and others who could lead us into understanding the mysteries of the craft or the art field.
>
> ...Results of the conference [were] amazing and a bit like magic. The pieces of contemporary American works were exhibited in many places in New York, a tour of Europe under the State Department, but, of course, the real coup was the exhibition at the Metropolitan Museum of Art. This was an educational type exhibition with conferee pieces and one of John Prips's as the denouement.
>
> One hour before the press conference, Henry Francis Taylor, the Director, was surveying critically—the first [exhibit] sponsored by industry. I rushed ahead to make sure of the lighting on the finished pieces and they were missing! Helen Fauver, my department's business partner, went into action. The museum registrar reported no silver came in [and the] display company reported no silver there because every scrap from this job had been dumped on the sidewalk the night before for trash collection. Helen grabbed a cab, raced to the end of the Island, found one huge barrel still on the walk, offering a young boy leaning against the wall five dollars to find a box in all the junk. He found it and it got installed in the museum case just three minutes before the press arrived. Thus ends one of the hair raising moments, but most of all it describes Helen.

Participants of the Handy and Harman Silversmithing Workshop Conferences:

1947

Gunda Lee Cornell. Wichita, Kansas

Virginia Wireman Cuts, Philadelphia Museum School, Philadelphia, Pennsylvania

Raoul A. Delmare, Iowa University, Iowa City, Iowa

Rufus Jacoby, Calvin Coolidge High School, Washington, D.C.

Bert Keeney, Kansas State Teachers College, Pittsburg, Kansas

Thetis Lemmon, Texas State College for Women, Denton, Texas
Ruth Penington, University of Washington, Seattle, Washington
Carlyle Smith, University of Kansas, Lawrence, Kansas
Dooley D. Shorty, Navajo Arts & Crafts Guild, Window Rock, Arizona
Roy Walker, City College of San Francisco, San Francisco, California

1948
William De Hart, University of New Mexico, Summit, New Mexico
Carlton F. Ball, University of Wisconsin, Madison, Wisconsin
Wiltz Harrison, Texas Western College, El Paso, Texas
Alma Eikerman
Henry J. Kauffman, State Teachers College, Milersville, Pennsylvania
Frederick A. Miller, Cleveland Institute of Art, Cleveland, Ohio
Richard H. Reinhardt, Philadelphia Museum School of Art, Philadelphia, Pennsylvania
Arthur J. Pulos, University of Illinois, Urbana, Illinois
Carl O. Podszus, New York University, New York, New York
Wallace Saunders, Vocational High School, Minneapolis, Minnesota
Frank W. Smith, Sandusky Schools, Sandusky, Ohio
Raoul A. Delmare, Iowa University, Iowa City, Iowa

1949
Veronica Amter, Albans, Illinois
Evelyn Baumann, West High School, Madison, Wisconsin
Martha Brennan, Indiana University, Bloomington, Indiana
Frank W. Clancy, Stockton College, Stockton, California
Leslie Johnson, University of Virginia, Charlottesville, Virginia
Gordon C. Lawson, University of Maryland, College Park, Maryland
Robert MacPhail, Craft Service Department, Handy & Harman
Thomas E. Ryder, Lower Marion Senior High School, Ardmore, Pennsylvania
Herold Stacey, Steuben Glass, Inc., New York, New York
Mary Louise Steinbuchel, Cody High School, Cody, Wyoming
Hazel Willis, Ohio University, Athens, Ohio

1950
Robert R. Coleman, San Jose State College, San Jose, California
Eleanor M. De Pree, Hope College, Holland, Michigan
Mrs. Patricia Hallagan, Lebanon Schools, Lebanon, Indiana
Walter J. Kipp, Pennsylvania Township Schools, Pittsburgh, Pennsylvania
M. Robert Koch, Omaha University, Omaha, Nebraska
Lawrence McKinin, University of Missouri, Columbia, Missouri
Earl B. Pardon, Memphis Society of Arts, Memphis, Tennessee
Caroline Posse, Skidmore College, Saratoga Springs, New York
Aileen Runkle, Contra Costa Junior College, Richmond, California
Wiley Sanderson, University of Georgia, Athens Georgia
Wallace Saunders, Vocational High School, Minneapolis, Minnesota
George Wardlaw, Hayes Academy of Arts, Memphis, Tennessee

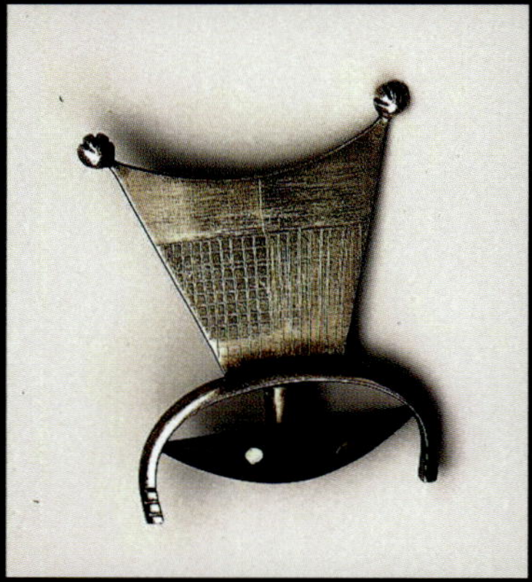

Wardlaw, brooch, brooch, sterling silver, ebony, 2" x 1-5/8". *Collection of Joanne and Fred Doloresco, photograph by Fred Doloresco.*

Lois Franke Warren, ring, sterling silver, 1-1/8" x 5/8", c.1952, *Collection of Joanne and Fred Doloresco*

1951

Howard L. Ackerman, Teacher, Nutley Secondary Schools, Nutley, New Jersey

Merrie K. Auld, Teacher, Hampton Schools, Allison Park, Pennsylvania

Doris M. Collin, Teacher and Student, Cleveland Institute of Art, Cleveland, Ohio

Roland Crookes, Student, Indiana University, Bloomington, Indiana

Lois K. Franke, Teacher, Fairfax High School, Los Angeles, California

John Paul Miller, Teacher, Cleveland Institute of Art, Cleveland, Ohio

Max Nixon, Teacher, Mills College, Oakland, California

Mary R. Parker, Professor, Illinois State University, Normal, Illinois

Margaret Schmidt, Teacher, North Dakota State College, Fargo, North Dakota

Eleanor B. Tinsley, Teacher, University of New Hampshire, Durham, New Hampshire

Robert W. Tomberlin, Assistant Professor, University of Oklahoma, Norman, Oklahoma

Douglas G. Williams (alternative), Student, Indiana University, Bloomington, Indiana

John B. Wilson, Graduate Assistant, Indiana University, Bloomington, Indiana

Helen Corral, Teacher, Reading Public Schools, Reading, Ohio.

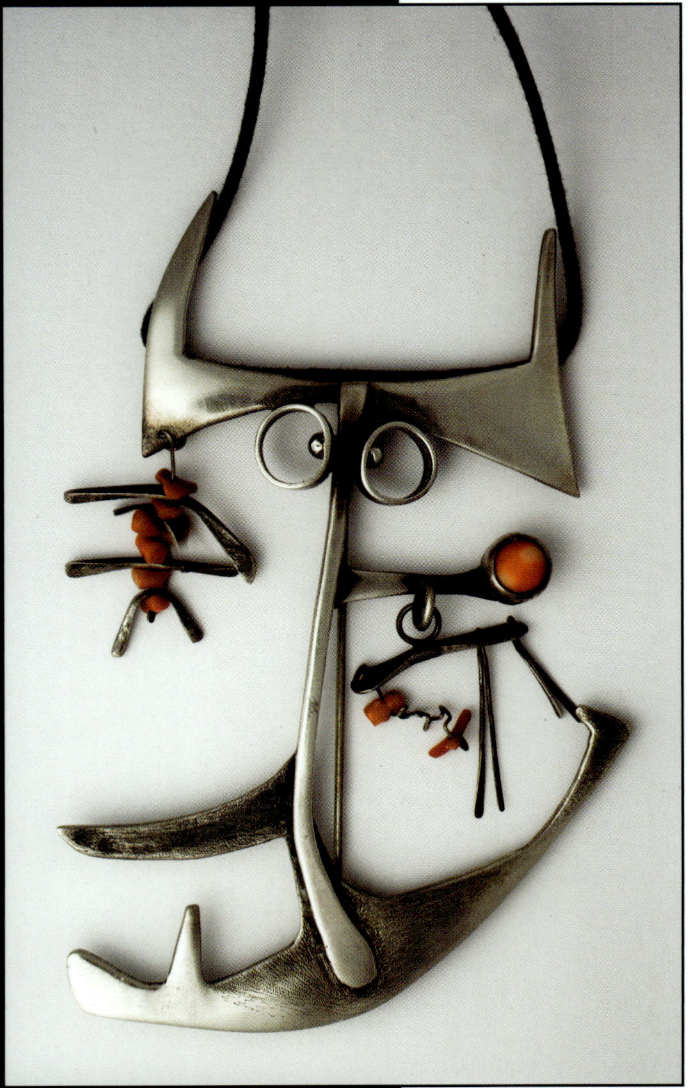

Robert Coleman, pendant, sterling silver, coral, 4-1/4" x 3", c. 1953, *Collection of Steve Cabella, photograph by photograph by Geoff Turner.*

In the early 1950s working metalsmiths began to band together to share their knowledge and techniques. In 1951Byron Wilson, Milton Cavagnaro, Peter Macchiarini, Margaret De Patta, merry renk Florence Resnikoff, Irena Brynner and other Califormia metalsmith/jewelers formed the San Francisco Metal Arts Guild. Byron Wilson, said that the formation of the Metal Arts Guild was a big factor in getting things moving for him and many others.[18]

Byron Wilson, pendant, sterling silver, ebony, 4-1/2" x 1". *Collection of Joanne and Fred Doloresco, photograph courtesy of Mobilia Gallery, Cambridge, Massachusetts.*

Peter Macchiarini, brooch, sterling silver, iconel, brass, copper, ivory, ebony, 4-5/8" x 2-1/4". *Courtesy of Mark McDonald, 555 Warren St., Hudson, New York, photograph by Bill Hibbs.*

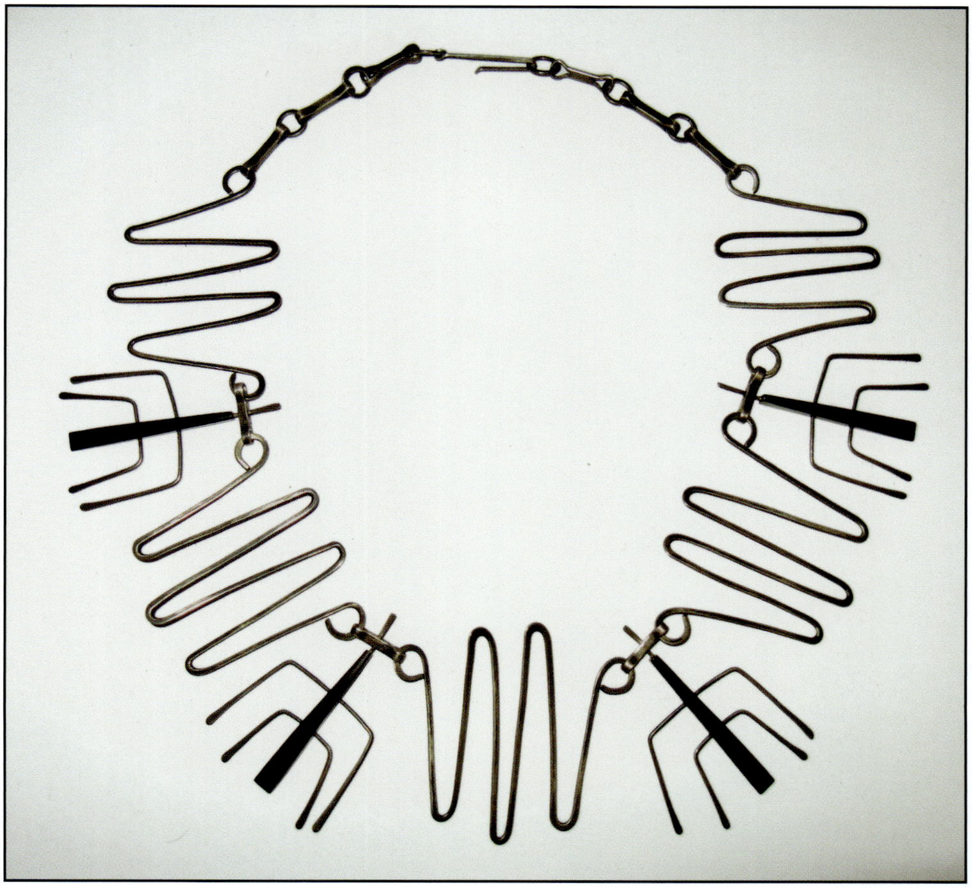

Milton Cavagnaro, necklace, sterling silver and ebony, 17" long, c. 1950s. *Collection of John Titus, photograph by John Titus.*

In the 1980s, Byron Wilson put together the following list of charter members of the Metal Arts Guild. (At the date of this writing, The Metal Arts Guild continues to be an active organization.)

Vera Allison
Irena Brynner
Mable Bush
Milton Cavagnaro
Stella Chen
Jean Crotty
Hal Davis
Lorena Lee Davis
Margaret De Patta
Harry Dixon
Edward Fourtane
Loyola Fourtane
Neal George
Ramona Germishausen
Orran Grossman
Connie Grothkopp
Helen Heick
Leslie Klepper
Barbara Langford
Jean Leslie
Fallie Lind
David Loveless
Peter Macchiarini
Virginia Macchiarini
Rosanne Marden
S. Martin
Byron Menendez
Phyllis Menendez
Josephine Mount
Ruth Phipps
Patricia Pope
merry renk
Florence Resnikoff
Victor Reis
Caroline Rosene
A'leen Runkle
Muriel Savin
Marguerite Segal
Mayer Segal
Patrick Seeler
Francis J. Sperisen
Maggie Stix
Edward Taylor
Byron Wilson

Some others who joined shortly after were:

Claudia Williams
Dr. Robert Coleman
Robert Randolph
Richard Gompf
Martin Strech
Martin K. Webber

merry renk, brooch, *Double Atom*, sterling silver, 2-1/2" x 2-1/2", c.1958. *Collection of Joanne and Fred Doloresco, photograph by Fred Doloresco.*

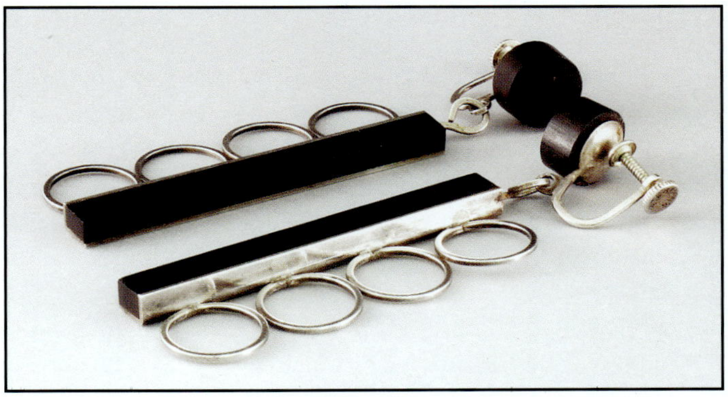

Milton Cavagnaro, earrings, sterling silver, rosewood, each 2-3/8" x 5/8". *Collection of Marbeth Schon, photograph by Shirley Byrne.*

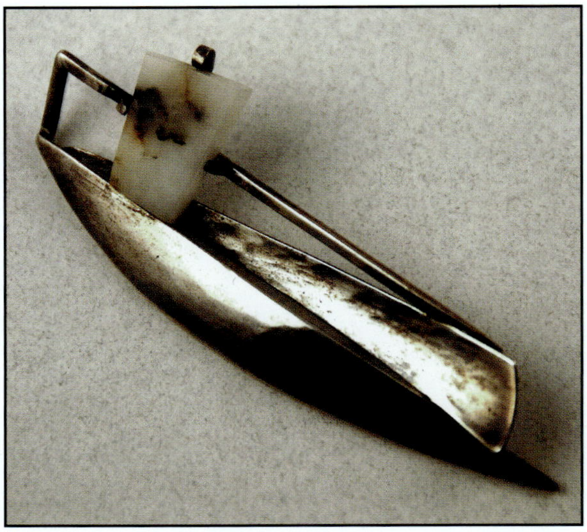

Victor Ries, brooch, sterling silver, agate, 1-1/4" x 3-1/4". *Collection of Joanne and Fred Doloresco, photograph by Fred Doloresco.*

Shops and Galleries for Fine Crafts

In addition to America House, several shops and galleries for the display and sale of fine crafts were established in the 1950s. In San Francisco, Nanny's Design in Jewelry carried the work of about eighty craftsmen, many of them jewelers. One of the most influential outlets for crafts was Shop One in Rochester, New York.[19]

In 1952, in order to create a facility to market fine crafts, four faculty members from the School of American Craftsmen, John Prip, Frans Wildenhain, woodworker Tage Frid and Ronald Pearson founded Shop One. The shop filled an immediate need for retail and exhibition space and also became a popular meeting place for students, teachers and customers who would come long distances expressly to see and purchase the handcrafted items. "So much revolved around it, both professionally and socially," Pearson recalled, "It was something like Black Mountain College."

"Before Shop One," John Prip recalled, "Pearson used to pack his work into his old Buick and cruise up and down the streets of a town looking for a 'contemporary' shop that might buy his work. He could tell which shops sold contemporary goods because they always had an Eames chair and a rubber plant in the window."

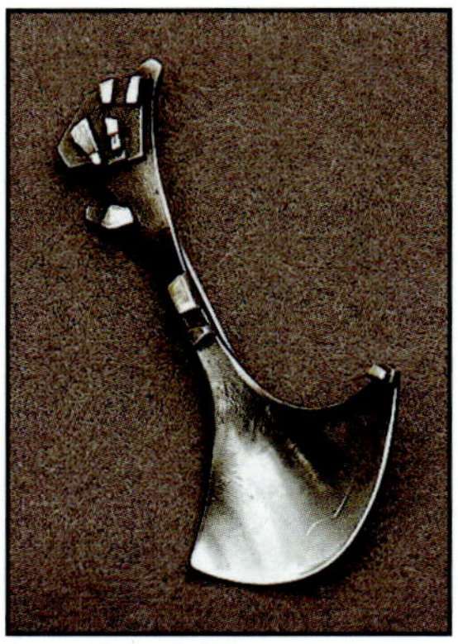

Ronald Pearson, brooch, sterling silver, 2-1/2" x 1-1/4". *Collection of Joanne and Fred Doloresco, photograph by Fred Doloresco.*

Greenwich Village

By the mid-1940s there was an increased number of metalsmiths living and working in the United States. Greenwich Village and other Bohemian quarters of New York City became strongholds for jewelers who had either been educated at art and design schools or were self-taught.

Conditions in the United States after World War II were "ripe" for the ensuing craft revival. Returning GI's, many who had been trained during the war as mechanics, machinists, or engineers found that they could creatively transfer these skills into metalworking. Under the GI bill, veterans had free access to training programs in metals available at several universities, museum schools, and craft centers. Crafts offered a new "way of life"—a less stressful, hands-on life style after the dehumanizing traumas of the war years.

Greenwich Village in the early 1960s, MacDougal Street, showing Paul Lobel's shop and the Jumble Shop. *Photograph by William Acker, from: The Picture Book of Greenwich Village © 1985, by R. Bruce Gaylord, p.48, Courtesy of Joe Holdner and Wendy Sacks.*

Paul Lobel, brooch, sterling silver, 3" x 1-1/2". *Collection of Jill Crawford, photograph by Shirley Byrne.*

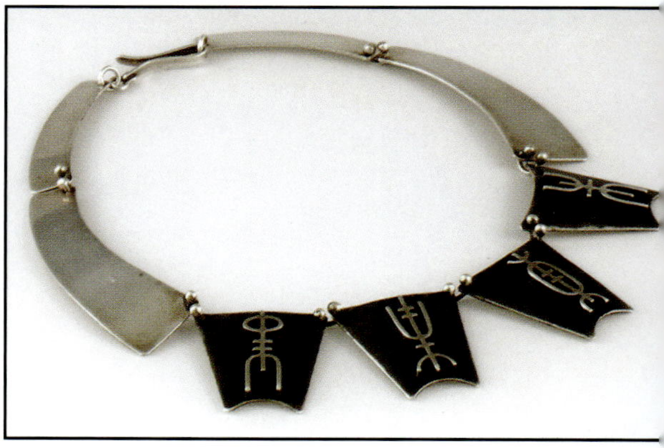

Ed Wiener, necklace, sterling silver, c. 1940s – early 1950s, 16" overall, plaques are each 1-1/4" x 1". *Collection of Marbeth Schon, photograph by Marbeth Schon.*

In the 1940s Greenwich Village, always a haven for artists, was the choice of many emerging metalsmiths. Jeweler Paul Voltaire described it this way:

> After World War II, Greenwich Village in New York was the place to have a little workshop, a storefront where you could sell your wares, and a group of like-minded craftsmen and customers to talk with. Some of the metalsmiths who started their studios in the late 40s were not at all trained in jewelry making—they apprenticed, they learned from each other, and they just did it, developing their individual styles as they went along. At this point there were very few schools where you could learn your craft, so whatever motivated these former engineers, designers, architects, and English Majors to pound on silver and then finally gold was just a desire to do things of beauty with their hands. Paul Voltaire, Paul Lobel, Sam Kramer, Art Smith, Ed Wiener to name a few, were some of the very talented young men to have ateliers in the Village and it was very interesting to see how their work differed. All had very strong individual statements, and all made jewelry that was beautiful use of the medium.
>
> There were a few potters and leather workers, some weavers, and finally they decided to form an organization and the Artists Craftsmen of New York was born. They called themselves Designer-Craftsmen because they both conceived of the piece and fabricated it themselves. They also sold it themselves, and that entrepreneurial combination was pretty much unique to the United States. In Scandinavia architects designed the flatware and jewelry and craftsmen produced it. In many countries abroad you couldn't just open a shop without licenses and permits. So the groundwork was laid for more and more young people who wanted to be involved in the crafts to apprentice, there were now schools which specialized in teaching craftsmen like Alfred University, and organizations were being formed like the American Crafts Council, galleries like America House on Madison Avenue, then opposite the Museum of Modern Art, and juried craft Fairs in various parts of the country that showed the work of hundreds of fine producing craftsmen to hundreds of shops and galleries. A business, a very thriving business was formed.
>
> I got involved in the first Greenwich Village Crafts Fair in 1947 that was attended by 120,000 people. We had decided to charge 10 cents admission just to kept the little children from running in an out and suddenly we found ourselves with $12,000, but we never saw any of it because the treasurer disappeared.
>
> Craftsmen went from doing simple beginning things to becoming highly skilled both technically and artistically. And perhaps because of the openness of fairs and exhibitions and publications, the natural desire of like-minded people to congregate with each other, the ever increasing public awareness of the American Craftsman and the attitude of retailers to take a chance on showing and promoting American crafts, the public began to respond by purchasing this work and soon the American Craftsman was producing some of the most beautiful, varied and well-priced work in the World.[20]

Sam Kramer, brooch, sterling silver, banded agate, carnelian, 3-1/2" x 2". *Collection of Jill Crawford, photograph by Shirley Byrne.*

Some of the more well-known modernist jewelers working in and close to Greenwich Village in the 1940s and early 1950s were Bob and Esta Blood, Arthur King, Sam Kramer, Idella La Vista, Ed Levin, Paul Lobel, Frank Miraglia, Frank Rebajes, George Salo, Art Smith, Henry Steig, Bill Tendler, Paul Voltaire, Ed Wiener, and Armand Winfield.

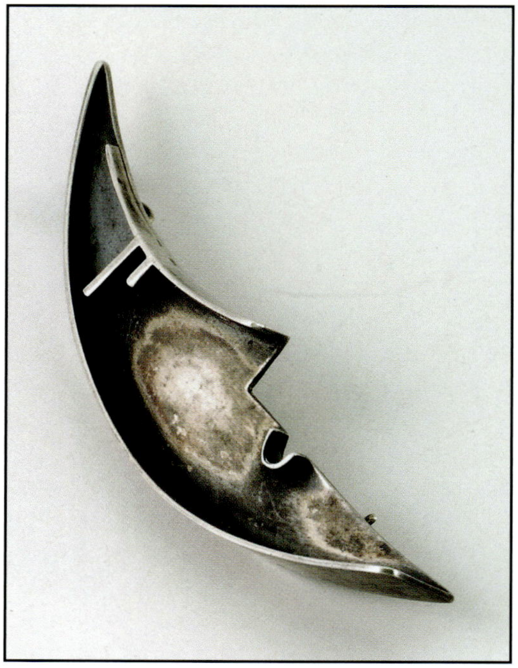

Bill Tendler, brooch, sterling silver, 2-3/4" x 5/16", c. 1950s. *Collection of Marbeth Schon, photo by Shirley Byrne.*

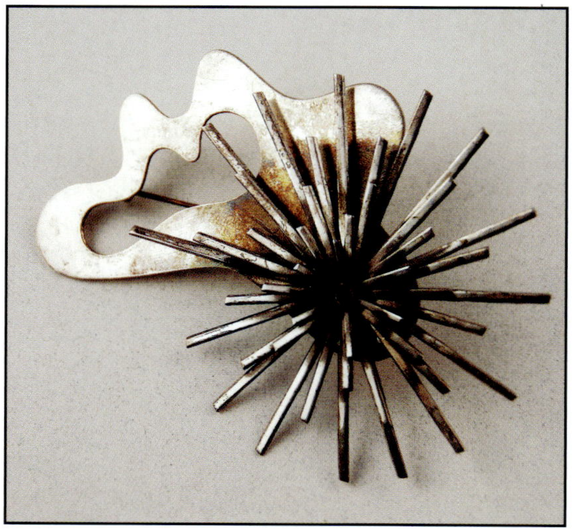

Rebajes, brooch, sterling silver, 3-1/2" x 3". *Collection of Joanne and Fred Doloresco, photograph by Fred Doloresco.*

Bob and Esta Blood, earrings, sterling and ebony, 2-3/8" x 1-1/8", c. 1950s. *Collection of Munir Meghji, photograph by Munir Meghji.*

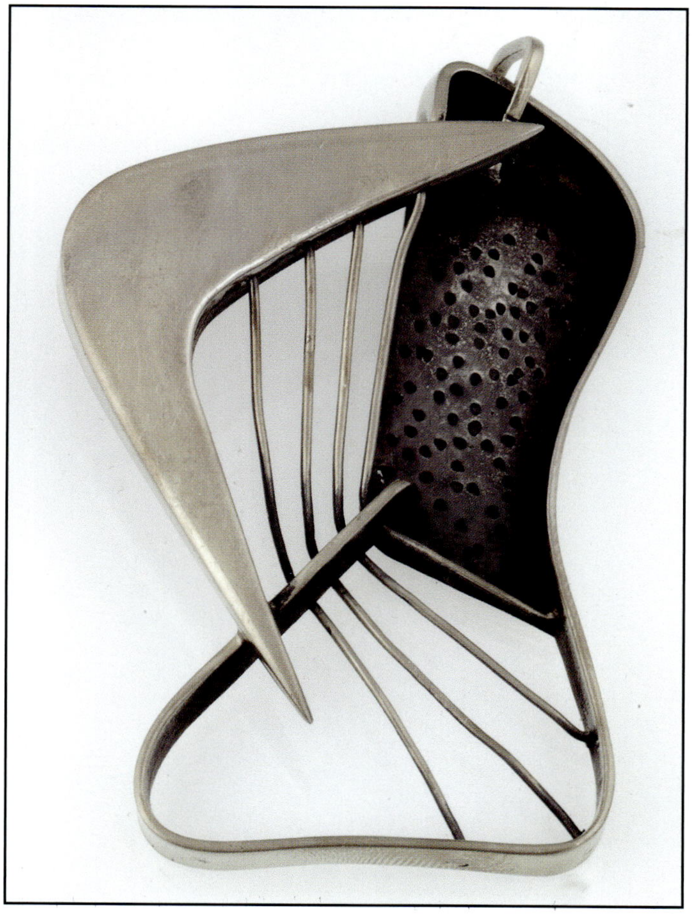

Ed Wiener, pendant, sterling silver, 3" x 2-1/4". *Courtesy of Mark McDonald, 555 Warren St., Hudson, New York, photograph by Bill Hibbs.*

Paul Lobel, cuff, sterling silver, 2-1/4" wide, c. 1950s, *Collection of Lisa Cliff, photograph by Lisa Cliff.*

Art Smith, necklace, brass, 7-1/2" x 7-1/2", *Courtesy of Mark McDonald, 555 Warren St., Hudson, New York, photograph by Bill Hibbs.*

Frank Miraglia, pendant, patinated sterling silver, c. 1950s. *Collection of Jill Crawford, photograph by Shirley Byrne.*

Arthur King, brooch, sterling silver, agate, 2-1/2" x 3-1/4". *Collection of Joanne and Fred Doloresco, photograph by Fred Doloresco.*

University Metals Programs

In the 1950s the crafts movement in metal arts became more university oriented with new courses being offered and some of its more inventive artists turning to teaching.

Critical to the post-war survival of metal arts programs at colleges and universities was their approval for benefits under the GI Bill. American and European teachers were hired to handle the burgeoning interest in metalworking as a profession. Programs teaching metalsmithing and jewelry were expanded as colleges such as Cranbrook Academy of Art in Michigan, the University of Kansas, Indiana University, the Maryland Institute, and Tyler School of Art added new, better equipped metal arts departments.

Jeweler, Betty Cooke was hired by the Maryland Institute to teach metalsmithing to returning veterans. She had classes of sixty to seventy students and taught Design and Materials which included leather, wood, gold, steel, and the basic elements of design as well as welding and soldering. She described her experience in an interview with the author in 2001:

> Well, at that time the Maryland Institute had about 80 students and one of them was a boy and the rest of us were woman. This was during the war. So then all of a sudden (after the war) they had about 300 or so. I had classes of 60 and 70 students and I taught something called design and materials, which was how to work with all kinds of materials like leather, wood, gold, steel, and also the basic elements of design that were necessary. Yes, it was very exciting—it was wonderful.

Betty Cooke, brooch, sterling silver, rosewood, 4" x 2-1/4", c. 1950. *Collection of Jill Crawford, photograph by Shirley Byrne.*

The School for American Craftsmen

In the late 1940s and early 1950s, The School for American Craftsman, true to its founding intentions, was a place where servicemen could go to find a profession that would make their lives more meaningful.[21]

Jeweler Ronald Pearson enrolled in the school in 1947 after serving in the Merchant Marine. He recalled, "It was basically a shop to teach production methods with very little else. You came, and you learned how to do it and to get some kind of stimulation—it was really a first stepping stone, it wasn't intended to do everything for you. This was up to the individual." Pearson studied under metalsmiths Laurits Eichner, Charles Reese and Philip Morton. Eichner and Frances Wright Caroé (daughter of Frank Lloyd Wright and, at that time, director of American House) wanted to keep the focus of the school on preparing students to make a living with their craft. Morton, because of his more esthetic approach, had the greatest influence on Pearson who said, "[Morton] was a fabulous teacher. His emphasis was on design and esthetics. He required his students not only to master technique but to search for the meaning of the forms which were being made."

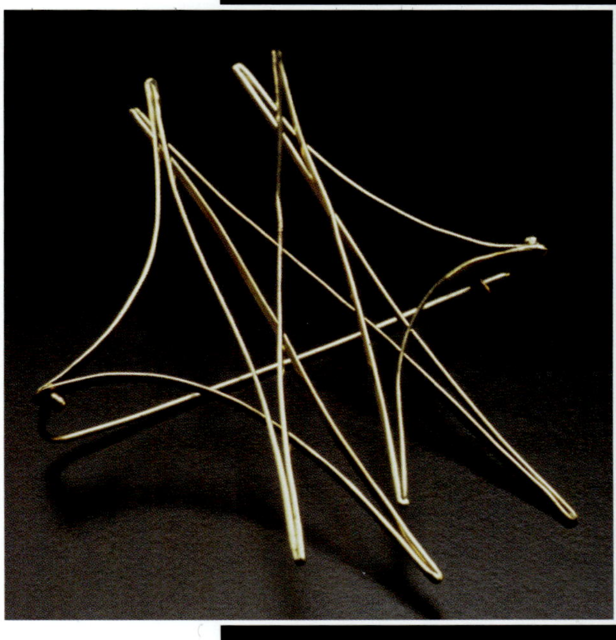

Philip Morton, Fibula brooch, 14k gold, 3-1/2" x 3", c.1960. *Collection of Tom Muir, photograph by Keith Meiser.*

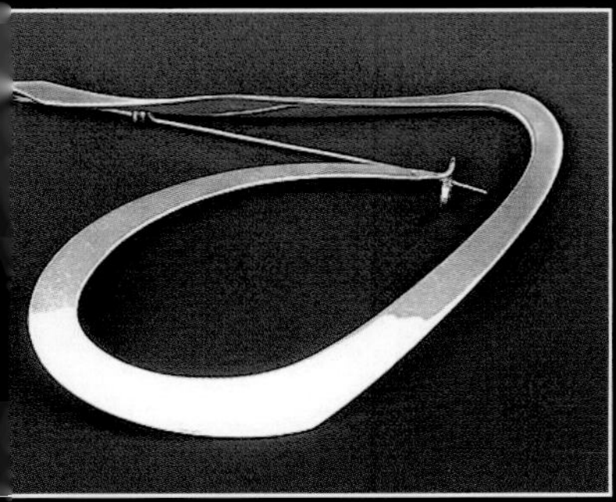

Ronald Pearson, brooch, sterling silver, 2-3/4" x 4". *Collection of Joanne and Fred Doloresco, photograph by Fred Doloresco.*

Morton's less practical approach to metalsmithing did necessarily fit into the rather rigid philosophy of the school at that time so he was asked to resign. In response to Morton's dismissal, Pearson decided to leave the school in order to become a full time producing craftsman. Believing that Pearson would not be able to make it on his own unless he could make jewelry, Morton offered Pearson a month long one-to-one craft course in jewelry making at his apartment.

In the latter 1940s it was a practice for schools with metal arts programs to look to Scandinavia for instructors. In 1948, when Harold Brennan became the director of the SAC, he recruited vigorously in Scandinavia because there were very few master craftsmen in America.

Metalsmith/jeweler Alma Eikerman, who at one time attended the School for American Craftsmen, studied in Denmark and Sweden during the late 1940s. She spoke of this experience, "It was the best place to learn, given the beauty of true designing that existed in the late forties and fifties. Crimping, stretching, Dutch bending, seaming, and forging are the processes which metalsmiths all over the world know. Each factory, all handmade work at that time, may have had a few unique ways of doing a given process, but these are world known processes. They are universal."[22]

Alma Eikerman, necklace and pendant, sterling silver, Australian lapis, 5-1/2" x 1-5/8", c.1967. *Gift of Natalie Hope, Courtesy of the Indiana University Art Museum.*

Margret Craver, who studied with Baron Erik Flemming in Sweden in the 1930s, was also impressed with the Scandinavian craft system, "In this country at the close of the War, optimism abounded and the big silver plants went into full gear, eventually crowding out nearly all the fine, small established shops. When I say this, I think of the wisdom of the Scandinavian countries who saw some of the less attractiveness of an Industrial Revolution in advance. They built displays for permanent exhibition comparing the handmade work with the machine made in quality, design, and price so that no crafts were completely lost."[23]

Arline Fisch who received a Fulbright grant to study in Denmark said, " I really felt passionate about working in metal because I had had some success at it, I certainly didn't feel that I had the skill level to go very far. So applying for a Fulbright was a good thing. I applied to Denmark for two reasons: one, they didn't have a language requirement; and two, Denmark and Sweden were where silver was happening in the fifties."[24]

John Prip was one of the Scandinavian teachers hired by Brennan. He had been born in the United States, but unable to return because of the Second World War. After the war, in 1948, he was informed about the job opening at the School of American Craftsmen through the Danish Society of Arts and Crafts and decided to find out more about his country of birth. He was 26 years old when he joined the faculty.[25]

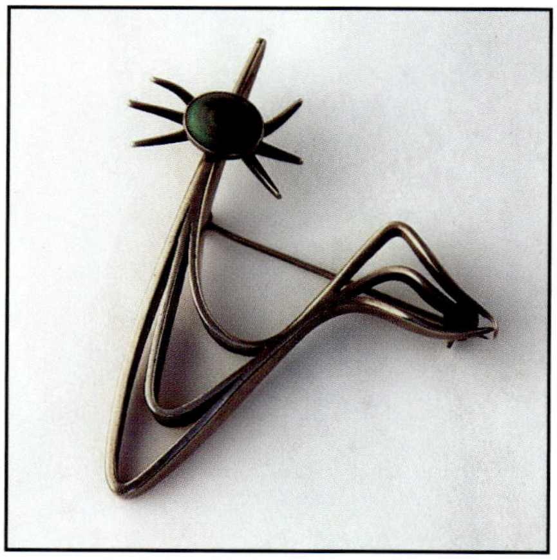

John Prip, brooch, sterling silver, stone, 2-1/2" x 2". *Collection of Joanne and Fred Doloresco, photograph by Fred Doloresco.*

Because he came from a Danish trade background, Prip was aware of what it took to make a living as a producing craftsman. About his philosophy at the time, Prip said, "I never thought in terms of having a philosophy. In Denmark I had a 'philosophy' based on the reality of the situation—you did what you were told. It was very technically oriented.

Though Prip's background was pragmatic and technical, he was immediately impressed with the "freedom and inventiveness of American metalwork." "What was being done in American was more interesting to me (than what was being done in Europe)— the work of Margaret De Patta, Sam Kramer, Paul Lobel, Bob Winston, and Phil Morton. Most had been trained as sculptors or painters or in other design areas. They were self-taught in jewelry. The technical quality of American work wasn't very good, but it was done with spirit and determination and very often with a great deal of imagination."

Finally free to experiment, Prip's forms evolved away from his Danish modern tradition. To Prip, "the spirit that pervaded SAC primarily stemming from the post-war mood of America, was its most impressive asset." "People were tired and disillusioned after the war. Many saw craft as an alternative way of life," he explains. "It was a really vigorous learning situation which everyone accepted wholeheartedly. We worked 'round the clock' seven days a week. If you locked the office, students would come through the chimney. The silver cabinet was always open. The school was loose and free as could be."

In order to strengthen the founding idea that teachers should also be producing craftsmen, salaries for teachers were low. "I had to make things on the side and sell them to survive," Prip said, " It wasn't a question of whether I wanted to make things or make something occasionally to send to the show." Prip loaded his station wagon with student and faculty work once a month and drove to American House in New York City.

In 1950 Bauhaus trained ceramist Frans Windenhain became part of the faculty at the SAC. "He had a stature that other faculty members lacked," notes Ronald Pearson, "he challenged people, made them think." "He was more experienced and more worldly," Prip explained, "I was just scratching around. More than anyone working in metal, Wildenhain served as my mentor." According to Ronald Pearson, Wildenhain began to slowly change the school's primary emphasis from "production of goods to aesthetic concerns."

In 1950 the SAC was relocated to its permanent home at the Rochester Institute of Technology in Rochester, New York perhaps because Mrs. Webb felt that the proximity to cultural activities in Rochester would be advantageous for the school The change was both positive and negative. "Being part of an institute meant we were subject to institutional rules and regulations, " Prip explained, "But because we were in a separate building we were able to maintain our identity. We felt we were different from the rest of the Institute. We weren't institutional people."

On the positive side, the school became part of a bigger and better-financed institution with more opportunities for additional programs.

In 1954 John Prip left the SAC in order to become a full-time producing craftsman and suggested his former associate Hans Christensen, then head of Georg Jensen's model department in Denmark, as his replacement. After much coaxing, Christiansen was finally persuaded to accept the position. In an article in *American Artist* Herold Brennan described Christensen's approach to metalwork, "He insists that the design be practical—that is, it should handle easily, with the forms related to function and the structural means." In the same article Christensen is quoted as saying, "I feel that silver needs little ornament if any. The silver surface with its rich effect of light and shadow...makes decorations superfluous."

Hans Christensen. *Photo credit: Rhode Island School of Design, Courtesy of The Sarah Bodine & Michael Dunas Archives of 20th Century Jewelry, Tyler School of Art, Temple University, Professor Stanley Lechtzin, Curator of Metals/Jewelry Archives and Collections.*

As with Prip, Christiansen's trade background made him a good fit for the SAC's practical approach. "I felt that students particularly in this country, are putting too much emphasis on becoming artists rather than on learning first to be good craftsmen," he said.

Ronald Pearson remembered Christensen as a perfectionist. "He was a wonderful person, but sometimes difficult to work with. In the early years he emphasized design less than technique. He believed in the Danish approach that once students had a firm technical background they could go on to other things."

Pearson returned to SAC as a member of the faculty in 1959, though he continued to work as an independent craftsman with his own workshop.

Sculptor/jeweler Albert Paley joined the faculty of SAC in 1969. His beliefs, greatly influenced by the counter-culture movement of the late '60s, were very different from those of his SAC predecessors." Paley changed the emphasis of the school from hollowware to jewelry. "In the '30s, '40s, and '50s, hollowware was a real social symbol and there was a market for it," Paley explained. "But in the '60s, traditional values changed and hollowware became a symbol of the lifestyle that many were rejecting. Contemporary jewelry, on the other hand, allowed you to express yourself as an individual. It projected an image of nonconformity which was an important aspect of the '60s social revolution."

Paley personified the new role of the craftsman in society. "Prior to the '60s, craftsmen were makers, artists were thinkers," Paley recalled, "I tried to bring crafts more to the level of art by intellectualizing about it—by giving it more of an intellectual context. I resented the image of the humble craftsman."

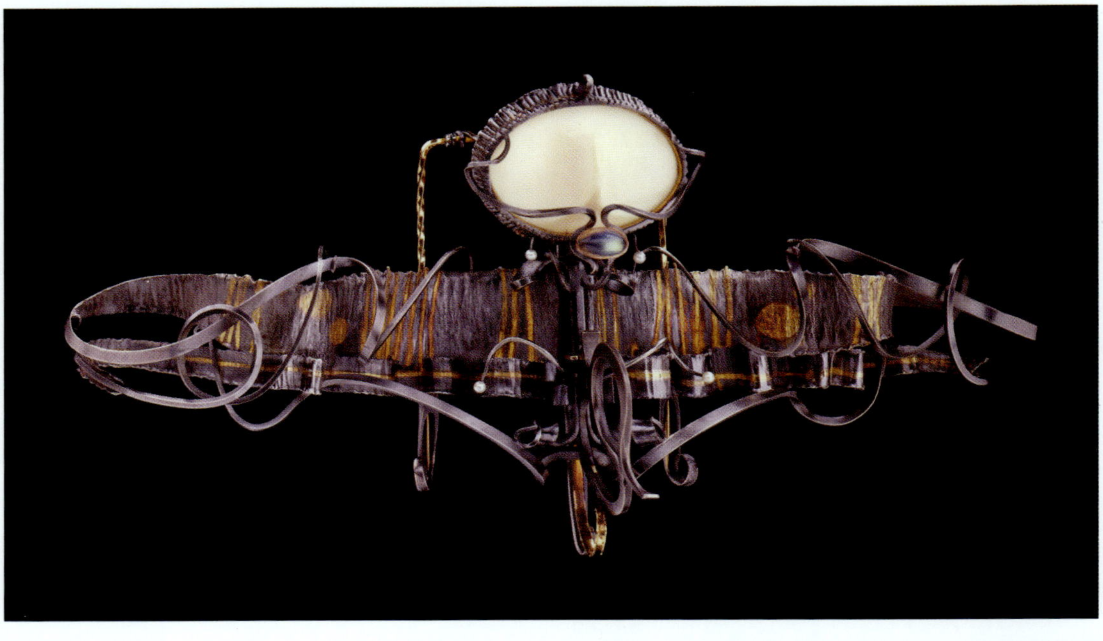

Albert Paley, *Sectional* brooch, silver, gold, ivory, pearls, laboradite, forged, fabricated, fused and carved, c. 1970. *Courtesy of Albert Paley, The Paley Archive, Rochester, New York.*

Over the years, changes in the philosophy, curriculum and guiding principles of SAC's metalsmithing department paralleled those in American metalsmithing in general. Former faculty member John Prip attributed this close relationship between the two histories to the fact that the school and the larger metalsmithing movement changed as society changed.

The importance of the School for American Craftsmen to the History and continuation of American metalsmithing can be attributed to the outstanding metalsmiths who have been a part of the school's history. A very abbreviated list includes faculty members: Philip Morton, John Prip, Ronald Pearson (also attended as a student), Hans Christensen and Albert Paley and alumni: Olaf Skoogfors and Svetozar and Ruth Radakovich and even those who attended very briefly (maybe only a summer course): Fred Fenster, John Paul Miller, and Arline Fisch.

Fred Fenster, choker, sterling silver, 7" long, c. 1976. *Courtesy of Fred Fenster.*

Cranbrook Academy of Art

Of the few American art schools that offered serious study of the crafts after World War II, Cranbrook Academy of Art in Bloomfield Hills, Michigan can be singled out as an institution responsible for turning out exceptional craftsmen and teachers. Whereas The School for American Craftsmen set up a pragmatic curriculum to produce metalsmiths who could make a living at their craft, the metal arts program at Cranbrook was much more experimental and unautocratic.

Fred Fenster (who graduated from Cranbrook in 1960), in an interview with Jan Yager for the Archives of American Art, related:

> ...at the time I went, they were training young artists ...in metal, in ceramics, in textiles, in architecture, in design...We had...a general shop from which all the studios kind of radiated out where you could – anybody could go there and use the facilities. And we had a large sculpture program there at the time. So it was an exciting place to be...although I really stayed mostly in metal, I used to wander around the sculpture studios all the time and go to the lectures. I loved being there. It was a magical place, physically beautiful...I rarely left... once I got to school...I hated going outside the confines of Cranbrook. It was a world of its own in a very posh area of Bloomfield Hills. It's still like that.[26]

In the latter 1940s Richard Thomas, who received his Art Education degree from Indiana State Teachers College, Indiana, Pennsylvania, and who enrolled at Cranbrook to study painting, became the

Harry Bertoia, brooch, gold, 5-1/4" x 2-1/2". *Courtesy of Mark McDonald, 555 Warren St., Hudson, New York, photograph by Bill Hibbs.*

head of the metals department at Cranbrook. The metals program was fairly limited at that time having undergone many changes in leadership. Harry Bertoia had been the director from 1939-1940 and when Thomas was still a student at Cranbrook the German metalsmith who had been directing the program left. Thomas was asked to keep the metal shop open on an informal basis. Upon graduation, Thomas, "who had nurtured his interest in metal through study, experimentation and observation, was asked to join the faculty and develop the metals program.... Thomas admitted that he was not the world's greatest metalsmith but that he was an outstanding tool clerk." Stanley Lechtzin, who, beginning in 1960, studied metalsmithing at Cranbrook, said Thomas basically set up the metals shop and let people work on their own for a couple of years.[27] Lechtzin indicated that this was disconcerting to many of the students, but that overall, it was a program that worked—they learned from each other. Lechtzin says that it was at Cranbrook that he first began to understand and respect the academic community and its goals; he developed a sense of the value of academic freedom and the importance of research.

Richard Thomas. *Photograph courtesy of The Sarah Bodine & Michael Dunas Archives of 20th Century Jewelry, Tyler School of Art, Temple University, Professor Stanley Lechtzin, Curator of Metals/Jewelry Archives and Collections.*

In 1982, in a conversation with Julie Hall for *Metalsmith* magazine, Richard Thomas said, "We were a rather insular body of people at that time, so it became necessary for us to find our own solutions. In many of these instances, we found that we were simply rediscovering ancient techniques!"

Fred Fenster continued:

> ...There were eight of us, I think, in that original class. And they were an odd mixed group of people. Michael Jerry was in there, fortunately for me, because he...made it really good for me to be there. He was patient, he explained things to me, he talked to me. And I also didn't realize how much metalwork background I had until I saw my teacher, Richard Thomas, who was writing a book on metalsmithing [*Metalsmithing for the Artist-Craftsman*; Philadelphia: Chilton Co., Book Division, 1960], and he was dealing with stuff that my junior high school – my junior high school kids knew because I taught it to them. He was dealing with the names of sheet metal stakes, and my kids knew that like the back of their hands. And I thought, I came out here to learn, and this man doesn't know what my beginning metal students do. That was very discouraging to me.... I read like crazy. I spent a lot of time in the library, which I always do, and I spent a lot of time in the studio. I spent every waking hour, seven days a week, in the studio. There was no real teaching that went on. You basically learned by working.... the best thing that happened at Cranbrook was the mix of students, both in the metal studio and outside. The second year Brent Kington came in and Stanley Lechtzin came in, which Stanley's presence was a real boon for me because I got to ask a million questions about jewelry and he answered them. I could ask anything I wanted, and he would give me a really good, comprehensive answer.[28]

Julie Hall in an introduction to her interview with Richard Thomas spoke about the hands-off approach of Thomas:

> During the two years I attended Cranbrook, I do not remember Thomas ever making a positive or negative comment regarding my work—we had no individual or group critiques. While this was occasionally frustrating at the time, I can now appreciate its value. Where else can you be left alone to develop yourself in the stimulating presence of other highly motivated and talented students and still have access to anything you need? Perhaps one could say we were carefully nurtured with benign neglect. Now as a teacher I find it difficult to leave students on their own...

it takes a very wise, mature and intelligent person to provide just the right amount of technical background and instruction to shape creative, independent individuals.[29]

In an interview, Stanley Lechtzin, who is himself an historian who believes strongly in preserving and studying the history of metalsmithing in the United States through its objects and written records, spoke of his respect for Thomas as someone who preserved many of Cranbrook's important early 20th century objects:

> Thomas arrived at Cranbrook just past that point where they had completed the architecture and the art and the artisans and the artists had departed, but it was all very much alive in people's minds and he absorbed that and quickly came to appreciate that history and over his career which spanned close to forty years he watched a lot of that physical history dissipate, remodeling, repurposing, etc., caused many valuable art and artifacts to wind up on the trash heap which... aggravated Thomas. Heating of the various buildings was conducted on that campus from running steam pipes through tunnels between buildings, underground from a central tower facility. One of those tunnels opened up from his office so he went around a visited the refuse piles on a regular basis, when he knew things were being torn down or discarded and he went in and grabbed the things and squirreled them away in the tunnel. Years later, in the early 1990s, Cranbrook woke up to their history and realized that many things that appeared in early photographs...were gone! One day Richard Thomas said, "it is not gone, I have it all!"[30]

Cranbrook's metal arts graduates have gone on to become some of the most influential teachers and metal artists in America. Among them are Stanley Lechtzin, Brent Kington, Heikki Seppä, Eugene and Hiroko Pijanowski, Mary Lee Hu, Fred Fenster, Phillip Fike, Al Pine, Fred Woell, and Lois Betteridge.

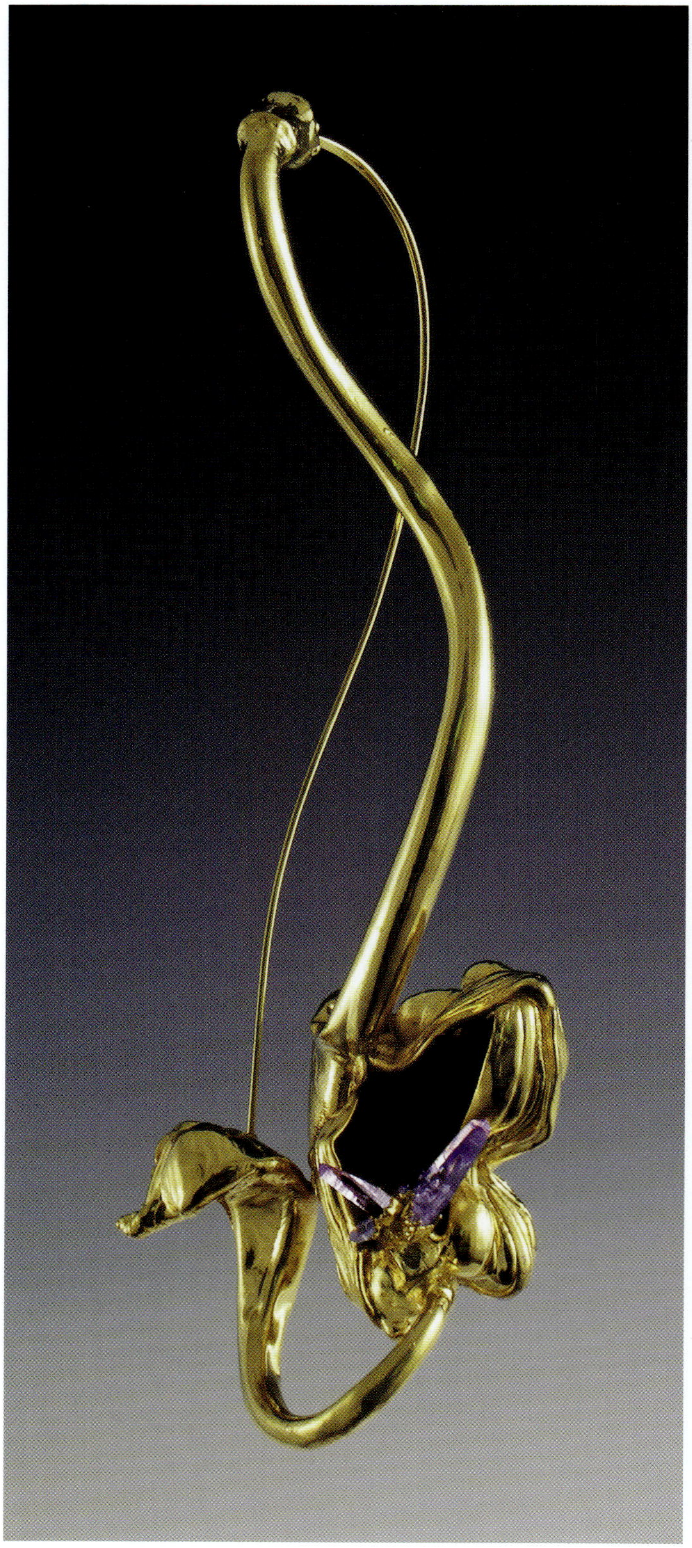

Stanley Lechtzin, brooch, electroformed silver gilt, amethyst, 8-3/4" x 3" x 2". *Courtesy of Stanley Lechtzin.*

CHAPTER 3
The 1960s

The Beginnings of a Dialogue between American and European Craftsmen

A dialogue between American and European artist/craftsmen began in the 1960s; The World Crafts Council was inaugurated in 1964, the exhange of ideas among craftsmen was spawned by international travel and several international craft exhibitions were held.

In 1964, at Columbia University in New York at the American Craft Council's fifth conference, Mrs. Vanderbilt Webb founded the World Crafts Council, a UNESCO affiliate. She served, first as its president and then as an honorary officer. In a speech at that conference, Mrs. Webb said:

Helen Shirk, *Ring for Index Finger*, sterling silver, c. 1967. *Courtesy of Helen Shirk.*

> ...The year 1964, will, we believe, be another landmark in the world history of the crafts—a beginning of great things. If the contemplated World Association of Craftsmen becomes a reality as the result of action on the part of the delegates to the First World Congress of Craftsmen, a wonderful future is opened to the craftsmen of the world. The problems will be many and complicated, for the conception of craftsmanship differs widely in many areas. This solution will come by trail and error, by patience over the years and constant adherence to the ultimate goal. The basic desires of all will be the same as they have been in the U.S.—to provide markets for the work of each country's craftsmen, to educate the people of the world to the value of craftsmanship, and lastly, to bring this about through proper leadership and in a spirit not of competition but of cooperation. In this spirit, craftsmen can move mountains and can lead not only in the practical but also in the spiritual field. Their cooperative attitude can not only help to achieve their own success, but can point the way towards a solution of many problems that beset mankind on this weary but still living and wonderful planet. For craftsmen it is an exciting time to be alive, for the future is theirs for the making. May such a challenge be met with vision and enthusiasm.[31]

The opening of the World Congress of Craftsmen was June 8 –19, 1964. In 1965 Stanley Lechtzin and Olaf Skoogfors traveled to Europe to visit Freidrich Becker, Reinhold Reiling, Claus Bury, Max Fröhlich, Sigurd Persson, Wendy Ramshaw and David Watkins.

In 1969 Benno Premsela, "the prominent designer and applied arts activist, organized *Objects to Wear* which toured the United States bringing Dutch avant-garde jewelry to the attention of Americans. Before that, in 1967, *Tendenzen* had been initiated at the Schmuckmuseum and these seminal exhibitions continued under the direction of Fritz Falk. In 1969 the Smithsonian exhibit *Objects USA* and its corresponding catalog by Lee Nordness was the first major national survey of contemporary American craft.[32]

In 1968 in Chicago, Philip Morton held a meeting with Robert Ebendorf, Phillip Fike, Hero Kielman, Brent Kington, Stanley Lechtzin, Kurt Matzendorf, Ronald Hayes Pearson and Olaf Skoogfors to organize an American guild of contemporary jewelers and metalsmiths. It was the genesis of the Society of American Goldsmiths (SNAG) and in 1970 the

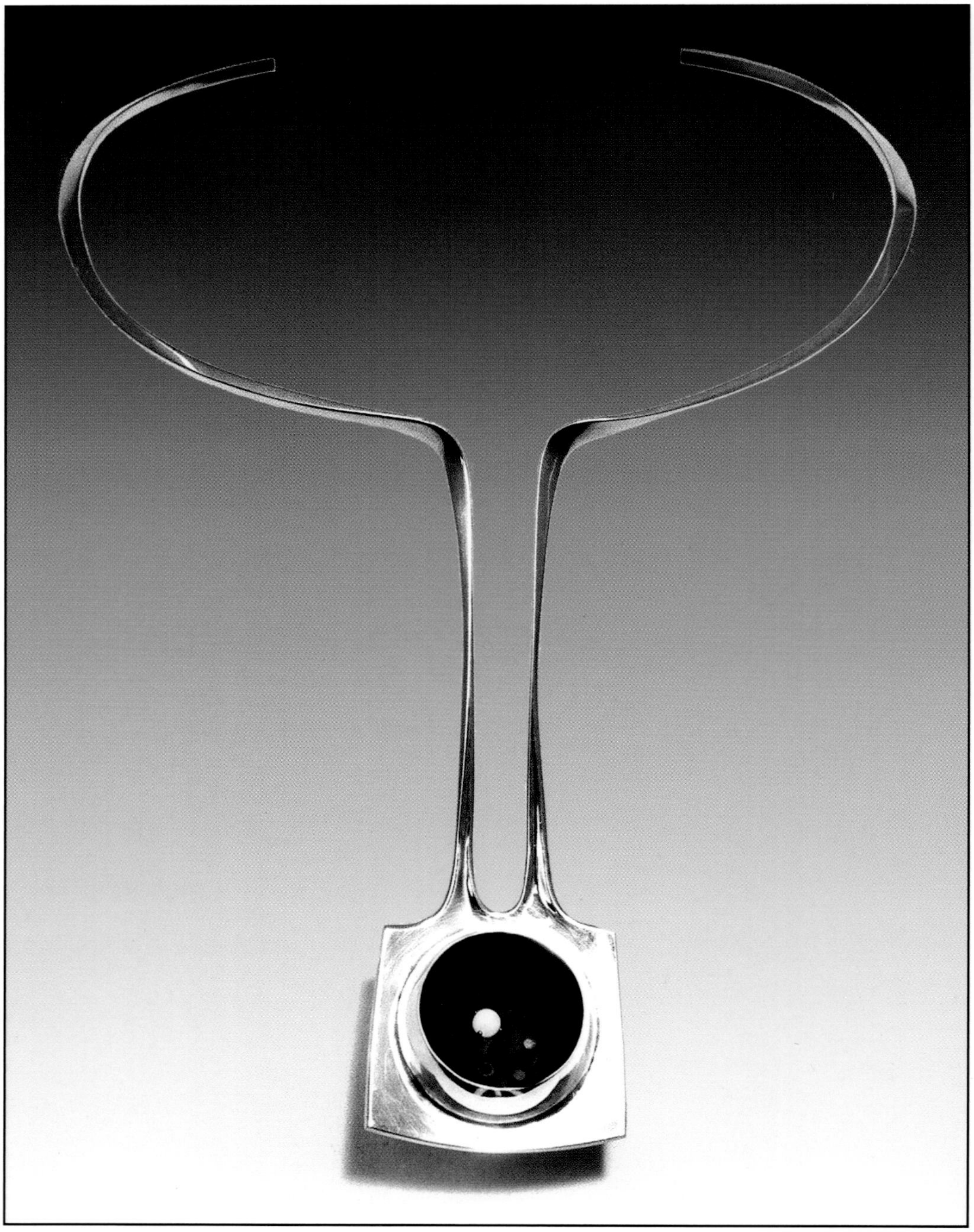

Michael Jerry, necklace, sterling silver, moonstone, 9-1/2" long x 6" wide x 1" deep, c. 1966. *Exhibited in Objects: USA, 1969, collection of the Museum of Art & Design, New York, New York, photograph courtesy of Michael Jerry.*

inaugural exhibition sponsored by SNAG titled *Goldsmith '70,* held at the Minnesota Museum of Art in St. Paul, began a national exchange of ideas.

Changing Definition of "Good Design"

Jamie Bennett, in an article in 1998 titled *"Jewelry Meditating Jewelry"* in *Metalsmith* magazine, wrote about the changes that took place in the 1960s:

> What we saw in the 1960s was a political and economic crisis in the west. The emergence of Third World nations and the women's movement, increasing restrictions in socio-economic life, and ecological destruction all exposed the exclusionary and failing character of humanistic discourse. The impact of these changes should not be underestimated as they all became of interest to post structuralists who would in the mid-to late seventies expose the complicity of the modernist ideal with problems of social and cultural order. [33]

In the 1960s there was a tremendous growth in in the number of art schools and universities with programs in the metal arts. This education was also within the reach of a greater percentage of the population. "This broader cultural and ethnic mix brought with it greater radical expectations from education. In the late 1960s students in America and Europe rebelled against the narrowness of curricula and the stifling effects of authoritarianism in society. This eventually generated a more diversified curriculum with a more liberal approach." [34]

The 1960s saw the beginning of the age of the "individualist." "There appeared a new tendency toward flamboyance rather than conservatism, of political activism rather than apathy. It was the Beatles and the Rolling Stones rather than Doris Day and Pat Boone, Carnaby Street rather than Brooks Brothers, Mary Quant and the miniskirt rather than Christian Dior and the crinoline. The order of the day was permissiveness and the Pill. It was the time of Timothy Leary and bob Dylan, psychedelic drugs, meditation, and gurus, rather than Sunday church and Dr. Norman Vincent Peale"[35]

Modernist studio jewelers, never a part of the mainstream and always somewhat allied with the American counterculture, championed the new art of Pop and Funk. Jewelry became more relevant to contemporary society. Good craftsmanship continued to taught and was important to even those experimenting with non-precious materials, but the era of what *had* been called "Good Design" came to an end.

True art reflects it's time.

David Jones, necklace, sterling silver, old bone buttons, *Three Stooges* lenticular lens pictures (from 1960's plastic rings), 19" long overall. *Courtesy of David Jones, photograph by Shirley Byrne.*

Part II
WHAT IS JEWELRY?

Perhaps the question should be "what is modernist jewelry?" Is it art? Is it sculpture? Is it something to collect or to put on a pedestal or to hang on the wall? Must it be wearable? A piece of jewelry by Sam Kramer or Art Smith, created forty to fifty years ago, still holds special fascination. Why? Because the magic of the artist's imagination turned the material(s) into an object of lasting value.[1]

Contemporary metalsmith/jeweler Bruce Metcalf put it this way, "I have come to believe that Jewelry, more than most other disciplines in the vis++ual arts, is characterized by social and psychological utility. The personal uses to which adornment is put suggests an aesthetic possibility that few observers have noticed: Jewelry has the ability to touch people."[2]

Opposite page and above: Sam Kramer, framed sash buckle with detachable brooch, 20-1/5" high x 9-5/8" wide (overall), frame and background: rosewood, patinated copper, sculpture/buckle: 6-1/4" high x 4" wide, sterling silver, copper, jade, citrine. *Collection of Ken Dukoff, photograph by Paul J. Toussaint.*

CHAPTER 4
Jewelry as Art

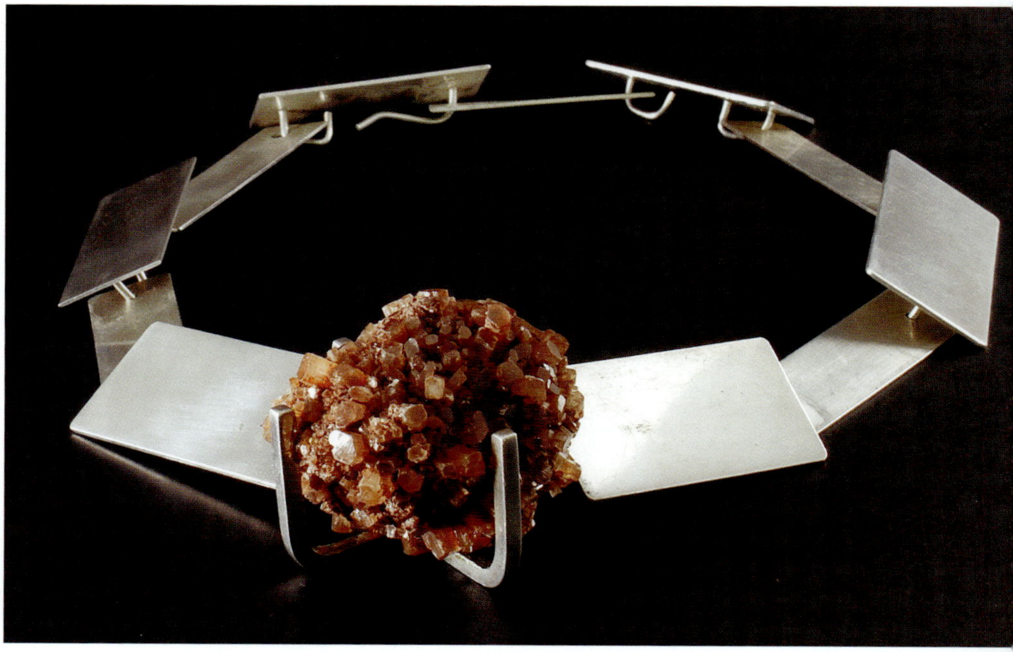

Betty Cooke, necklace, sterling silver, geode, 21" overall x 1" widest link. *Collection of Jill Crawford, photograph by Shirley Byrne.*

The distinctions between "applied" and "fine art" began to be broken down in the 1930s. Even as early as 1929, with the opening of the Museum of Modern Art in New York, the Bauhaus idea of equating painting and sculpture with architecture and design-- the beginning of "the democratization of art"-- was becoming accepted in the United States. In 1931 the MOMA's exhibition, *Recent European Architecture*, featured the work of Ludwig Mies van der Rohe and Gropius from Germany along with that of Le Corbusier and André Lurçat from France and of J.J.P. Oud and Gerrit Rietveld from the Netherlands—all the major protagonists of the new rationalism.[3]

It was not until after the war, in 1946, however that the Museum of Modern Art added jewelry to the list and featured one hundred thirty-five pieces of jewelry by artists making jewelry and jewelers making art jewelry in its exhibit, *Modern Handmade Jewelry*.

Jewelry As Sculpture

Sculptor Ibram Lassaw said, "For me, the desire to make jewelry arises from leisurely, even playful, experimentation with forms and the flow of molten metals; sometimes it is probably a subconscuios preparation for larger works." [4]

Ibram Lassaw, pendant, 3" x 3", copper sheet, bronze, gold plated, *Photograph ©Denise Lassaw.*

There are sculptors who create jewelry and jewelers who envision their work as miniature sculpture. During the war, when "necessity was often the mother of invention," sculptors often turned to jewelry making because of the scarcity of metal for larger projects.

Sculptor Harry Bertoia, for example, resorted to making smaller silver and copper pieces when metal for his large sculptures was not available. His jewelry pieces, like his larger sculpture, were involved with the reflective qualities of metal and how the light played on the surface of highly polished planes. His pieces were often "bone-like, organic shapes...articulated by the play of light and shadow on roughly textured surfaces and the interweaving rhythms of solids and voids." [5]

Greenwich Village sculptor/jeweler Paul Lobel devised jewelry designs to save on materials. These were accomplished by either cutting out areas with care and using such pieces in juxtaposition to the original piece or by creating areas enclosed with space. He believed that jewelry design enters the sculptor's field—"that a person with a feeling for form can create, in jewelry, sculpture that has a use value."[6]

Jeweler Pearl Shecter wrote about her jewelry in the Walker Art Center's 1959 *Design Quarterly Magazine*:

> Preserved by its hardness, jewelry not only survives because of its outer forms but has a curious influence touching the lives of people, and this influence is the creative symbol invented by the artist. As an abstract painter, I am led by my space concepts to problems and exploration of line movement, negative-positive relationships, transparencies, tension, (and) suspension. These are the involvement of the sculptor too. My work in sculptured jewelry is an extension of these directions with a different material—metal.[7]

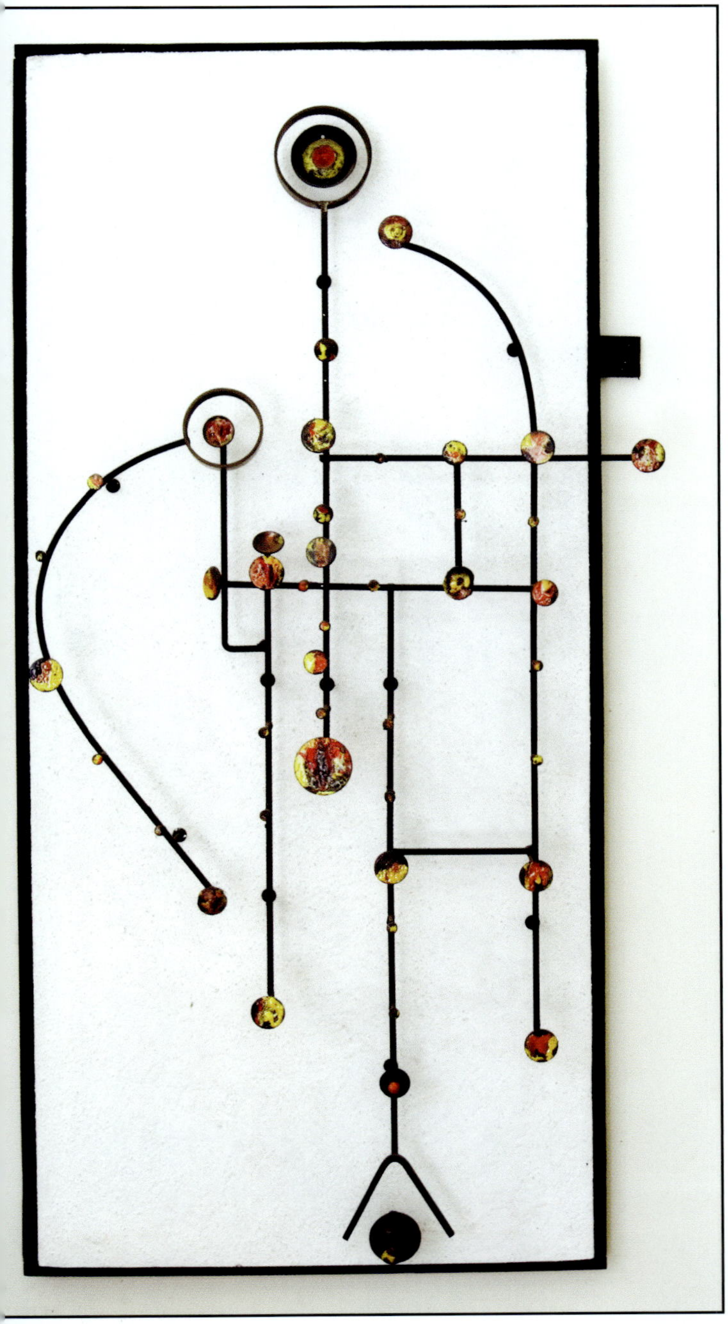

Peter Macchiarini, *Architectural* enamel wall sculpture, iron, enamel, on painted wooden base with sand, c.1950s. *Photograph courtesy of Daniel Macchiarini.*

Pearl Shecter, brooch, *Cyclops*, sterling silver, 2-3/4" x 2-1/8". *Pictured in Esempi di Decorazione Moderna di Tutto il Mondo by Roberto Aloi, Collection of Munir Meghji, photograph by Munir Meghji.*

Sculptor Jose De Rivera was drawn to the work of constructivists Naum Gabo and Antoine Pevsner, whose ideas of negative space as an element of sculpture influenced him to open up the mass of his own work. His jewelry pieces were prototypes for his lager sculptures, though flatter and less three-dimensional because of the necessities of wearability, however his jewelry designs also possess high reflectivity and linear definition.

In 2001, in an interview with the author, Betty Cooke said, "I have a lot of pieces that are very sculptural--that could be reproduced on a different scale. It's hard to define sculpture. Sculpture is (three) dimensional but so is jewelry. I would put design in there also because a lot of sculpture is like Art Smith and a lot of it's like Harry Bertoia. So you have all these in-betweens. Or Noguchi. I think Noguchi has been an influence on everyone, his simplicity and appreciation of nature and all those good things."

Internationally recognized sculptor and jeweler Claire Falkenstein created pieces described as "thorny thickets of welded metal fused with melted glass." Her highly unique and individual jewelry forms, though well designed for the body, have an intrinsic relationship with austere sculpture of the most succinct forms. "When I went into jewelry," she said,"I was just getting into metal, and I treated jewelry as a means of teaching myself how to work metal. I could do little things and have lots of failures, and it wouldn't matter because they were just little things. I could try things out, techniques and forms and shapes. It was all aesthetic development for me, because I began to explore ideas and shape and form and so on through metal." [8]

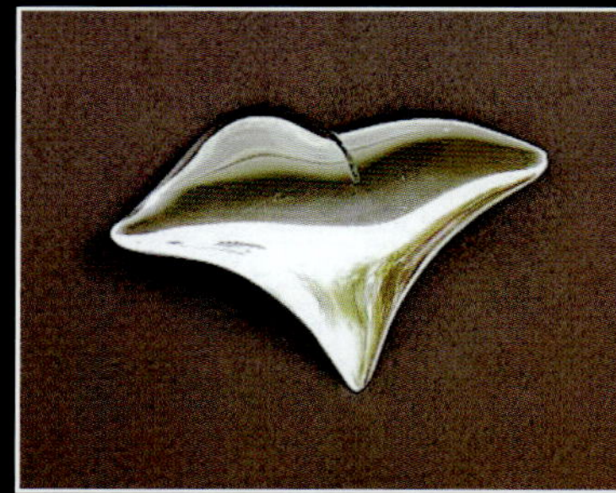

Jose de Rivera, brooch, stainless steel, 2-1/2"x 1 5/8". *Collection of Joanne and Fred Doloresco, photograph by Fred Doloresco.*

Betty Cooke, brooch, sterling silver, 3-1/4" x 1/4". *Collection of Joanne and Fred Doloresco, photograph by Fred Doloresco.*

Claire Falkenstein, brooch, sterling silver, 4" x 3-1/2". *Courtesy of Mark McDonald, 555 Warren St., Hudson, New York, photograph by Bill Hibbs.*

Greenwich Village jeweler Sam Kramer's work was very closely related to the sculpture of the 1950s. "Both had their share of apocalyptical birds, such as Kramer's pterodactyl brooch. Sculpture's tendency to 'negative space' can be compared to Kramer's skeletal pieces, his habit of segregating individual parts on different planes, projecting stones on elongated stems or capturing space in wire. On occasion he used the word 'architectural' to describe this spatial extension." [9]

Though jewelers and sculptors can share exactly the same forms (usually on a different scale) and share the same design elements of negative and positive space, texture, color, patina, etc., unlike sculptors, jewelers face the issue of "wearability." The concept of jewelry not necessarily designed to be worn has been hard to accept by the general public as well as by many jewelers themselves—especially those that have their own studios and galleries and make their living by providing their work directly to their customers. Should jewelry be freed from the restrictions of "wearability"?

Sam Kramer and Peggy Ackerly, made by Peggy Ackerly, *Skeleton Bracelet,* sterling silver, copper, 3" long x 2-3/8" high x 1-5/8" wide, c.1948. *Illustrated: Messengers of Modernism: American Studio Jewelry, Toni Greenbaum, Montreal Museum of Decorative Arts, 1966. Courtesy of Historical Design, Inc., photo ©HD, Inc.*

California jeweler Everett Macdonald who initiated the use of nylon monofilament--strung between the negative spaces of his pendants and earrings recalling the work of sculptors Henry Moore and Naum Gabo--said that his work is never "sculpture to be viewed as an entity on solitary display but is made to be worn and enhance the wearer."[10]

Everett Macdonald, earrings, sterling silver, fish line, 1" x 3/4", *Courtesy of Mark McDonald, 555 Warren St., Hudson, New York, photograph by Bill Hibbs.*

New York jeweler Ed Wiener was enthusiastic about the movements controlling modern art in the early 1950s such as surrealism and Dada, but still uncertain about their application to jewelry, realizing that he related to the modernists aesthetically and ideally, but also understanding that jewelry was an engineering challenge that must be "able to survive in the environment of human activity."[11]

Greenwich Village artist, Art Smith's jewelry, though sculpturally advanced, was not made to stand alone. "A piece of jewelry, he said, is a 'whatisit?' until you relate it to the body...like line, form and color, the body is a material to work with. It is one of the basic inspirations in creating form...(the question is) not how do bracelets go, but what can be done with an arm?"[12]

Ed Wiener, necklace, sterling silver, ebony, 7" x 4-1/2", *Courtesy of Mark McDonald, 555 Warren St., Hudson, New York, photograph by Bill Hibbs.*

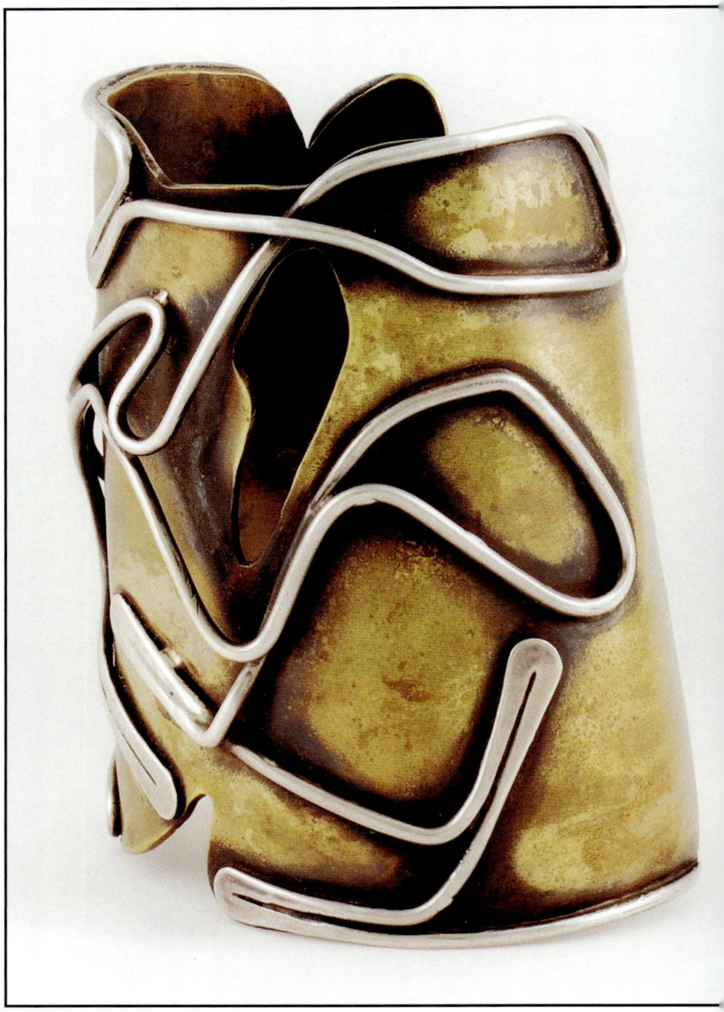

Art Smith, cuff, brass, sterling silver, 3-5/8" x 3-3/4" (inside diameter). *Collection of Jill Crawford, photograph by Shirley Byrne.*

Irena Brynner said that her decision to become a jeweler was based on a piece of jewelry she saw by Claire Falkenstein--a choker with a mobile form suspended on one side—"it was free, it was beautiful, it was sculpture. No compromises to make, just the challenge to scale the sculpture and relate it to the human body, instead of space or architecture."[13]

Brynner, like Art Smith believed that jewelry was sculpture that did not stand alone—it was for the body. "In contemporary jewelry, she said, "there is a greater element of sculpture than ever before. I use all my training as a sculptor in evolving my jewelry forms. I work out the forms spatially keeping in mind that they must have their base on the human body. This relationship of jewelry to the body is all-important. Jewelry must be wearable and must function with and on the body—it must at all times enhance the person. In this way, it becomes subordinate to its base. That is where it differs from sculpture which must rise from its base and dominate it and the space around it." [14]

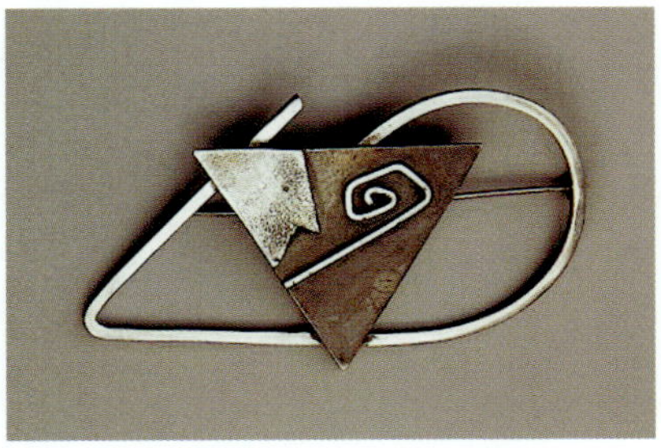

Irena Brynner, brooch, sterling silver: 1-1/4" x 3-1/4". Collection *of Joanne and Fred Doloresco, photograph by Fred Doloresco.*

Claire Falkenstein, *Yolk* necklace, sterling silver, 11-1/2" x 11-1/4". *Courtesy of Mark McDonald, 555 Warren St., Hudson, New York, photograph by Bill Hibbs.*

Margaret De Patta may have been one of the first to coin the phrase "wearable sculptures" when speaking of jewelry but she also spoke of the limitations "imposed automatically upon the [jewelry] designer—limitations as to size, weight of piece, durability of materials and structure, degree of projection from the body, sharpness and organic relationship to the body structure."

Metalsmith Olaf Skoogfors thought of himself as an artist as well as a craftsman. Though he designed for the body, he also thought of his jewelry as sculpture that should and could be able to stand alone as a work of art. His inspirations were everywhere, coming from his interests in "music, film, literature and nature" as well as the traditions of many cultures, including his own Scandinavian/Viking heritage, Benin, pre-Columbian and Celtic.[15]

Ruth Radakovich was involved with sculptural, organic forms in jewelry design; the human body became part of the sculpture--the perspective of the jewelry changed as the wearer moved. "A pin or pendant is not looked on at eye level," she explained, "on the wearer it's looked at below eye level at an angle...you have to pay attention to these things."[16]

Olaf Skoogfors, pendant, sterling silver, constructed, pendant: 5-3/4",11-1/2" x 6"(overall), c.1974. *Courtesy of Mobilia Gallery, Cambridge, Massachusetts.*

Ruth Radakovich, brooch, 18k gold, purple tourmaline, 3" high x 1-5/8" wide. *Collection of Jean Radakovich, photograph by Jean Radakovich*

J. Arnold Frew, *Mobile* earrings, sterling silver, each: 1-1/2" x 2-1/4". *Collection of Joanne and Fred Doloresco, photograph by Fred Doloresco.*

Hans Christensen who came from the more pragmatic school of Scandinavian metalworking, was critical of some of the trends he found in American jewelry:

> I feel that jewelry design today should be questioned...Sometimes the shapes [are] developed—in order to make them visually rich—in such a fashion as to make them a hazard to the wearer and anyone who comes near her! It appears that there has been a too strenuous search for novelty in contemporary jewelry, and the resulting forms are usually suggestive of exaggeration and strain. Jewelry should decorate the wearer, always in character and secondary to her interest and personality...also it should be materially and structurally coherent—not just an aggregate of sculptural shapes reduced to pygmy scale.[17]

Ronald Pearson agreed with Christensen philosophically—he also thought that jewelry should be functional. "Jewelry is for the human form—to compliment it, not to use a person as a pedestal," Pearson maintained.[18]

Robert Dhaemers is primarily a sculptor who interprets his ideas in jewelry. He feels that jewelry should be seen in the round; his pendants are designed to stand on their own as three-dimensional sculpture--all sides having equal importance and usability.

Arline Fisch said in an interview with Sharon Church for the Archives of American Art, "...I try everything on, so all of that has to do with comfort and movability, and flexibility, but the idea that all of what I do is sited on the body gives it a dimension, gives it a scale that I'm comfortable with. I've tried working larger, off the body, and I don't feel as comfortable or as confident there, so I chose not to pursue that. But the idea that what I do goes on the body gives me a destination and a limitation that I like. It has some drawbacks, but it's sort of setting parameters for me that I am very happy to work within.[19]

Robert Dhaemers, pendant and necklace, pendant: patinated bronze, jade, necklace: patinated bronze, pearl, pendant: 6-3/4" x 4-1/2", necklace: 6-3/4" long x 4-1/2" diameter. *Exhibited at Brigham Young University in 1976, Collection of Robert Dhaemers, photograph by Shirley Byrne.*

Movement as a Design Component in Jewelry

When one thinks of movement in sculpture, Alexander Calder's mobiles come to mind. Calder revolutionized the art of sculpture by making movement one of its main components. In 1931 artist Marcel Duchamp was the first to describe Calder's large moving structures as "mobiles."

It was the paintings of Dutch neoplasticist Peit Mondrian that inspired Calder—when looking at the colored rectangles of Mondrian's paintings, he remarked that "he would like to see them move." After experimenting himself with abstract painting, he started making constructions from wire and wood, adding movement with cranks or small motors. "Just as one can compose colors, or forms," Calder said, "so one can compose motions."[20]

Calder's stabiles and mobiles "challenged the prevailing notion of sculpture as a composition of masses and volumes by proposing a new definition based on the ideas of open space and transparency." Perhaps it was his fixation with the science and art of movement that brought Calder back to jewelry making in the 1930s--once jewelry is positioned on the body it becomes mobile.[21]

Many of Betty Cooke's pieces are kinetic — her abstract wooden elements are often made to pivot; in the 1950s she made pieces that would flip from "an ebony side to a silver side, or a gold side to a silver side."

Like Calder, whose innovative mobiles created a constantly changing spatial arrangement among design elements, Margaret De Patta made pieces that could change from dark to light or expand and change shape in order to advance and further strengthen the concepts of space. She designed them with spinning elements, some would also "vibrate or rattle"—a number of pins were designed with moving parts and could be worn in three positions, each position would cover or reveal different stones and therefore alter the color of the design. She also created pieces for children with the same special and innovative qualities.[22]

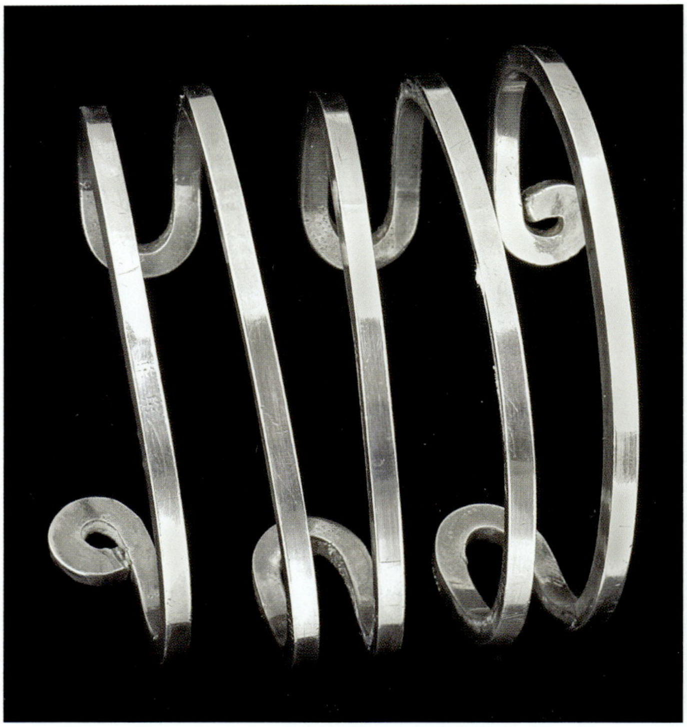

Alexander Calder, cuff, sterling silver, 2-1/2" x 2-1/8". *Courtesy of Mark McDonald, 555 Warren St., Hudson, New York, photograph by Bill Hibbs.*

Betty Cooke, necklace, sterling silver, ebony, 20" long (overall). *Collection of Jill Crawford, photograph by Shirley Byrne.*

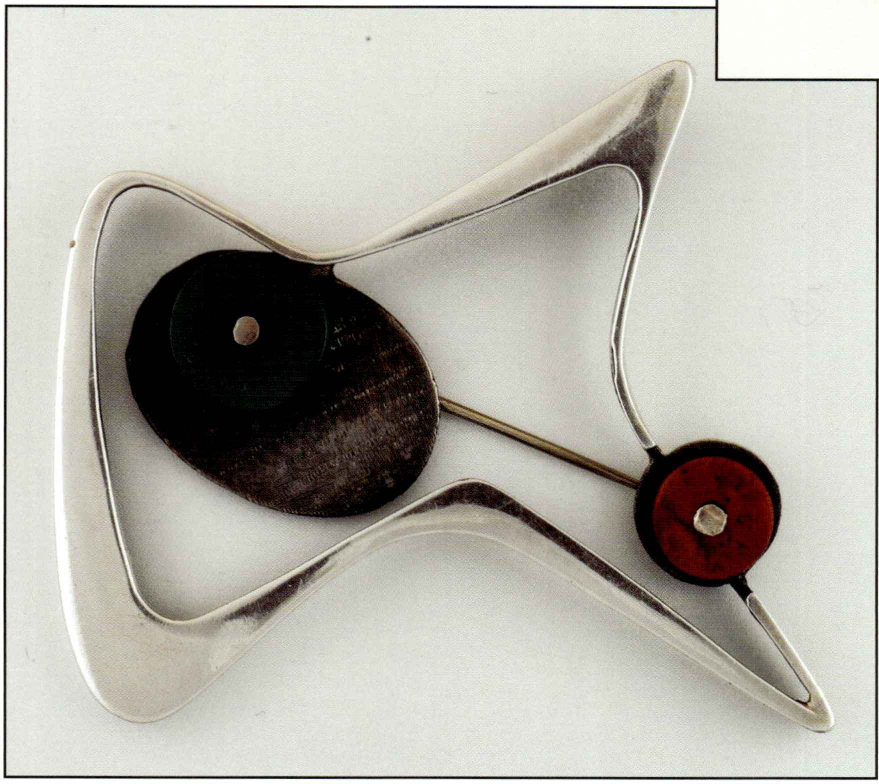

Margaret De Patta, brooch, sterling silver, chrysoprase, carnelian, 3-1/2" long. *Illustrated: Design 1935-1965, What Modern Was, ed. Martin Eidelberg, Le Musée des Arts Décoratifs de Montréal, Courtesy of Historical Design, Inc., photo ©HD, Inc.*

Margaret De Patta said, " Movement of forms is not new to the realm of jewelry, however it is now consciously used by contemporary artists as an important field for experimentation. Movement in itself is visually exciting but when it is used to articulate space and to produce definite positive and negative volume relationships it takes on a new vitality and meaning. Movement has been used in many ways by present day jewelry designers—ingenious methods worked out to allow a pin to reverse its sides so as to change from dark to light or negative to positive or to create a movable form to cover or reveal colored stones and thus change the color accents of the piece—or movement to alter the size and shape of a piece—or to construct movable forms for manipulative pleasure—or to enhance the play of visual effects in transparent stones."[23]

Earl Pardon's early sculptural pieces are masterful constructions; his sterling, wood, and ivory bracelets of the 1950s are playful and kinetic.

By 1954 San Francisco jeweler merry renk was experimenting with movement in her work. She designed a ring, which she called *Rolling Pearl*, a simple elegant form terminating in a pearl that rotated on a silver peg. merry said that she sold a similar ring to an airline stewardess who rolled it so much that she had to replace the silver peg with a stainless steel wire. Her *Sticks* necklace from the same year was developed from the structure of wire earrings "that were suspended from each other making a fringe like motion."

Earl Pardon, bracelet, sterling silver, enamel, ivory, ebony, 2-1/4" x 1/4", c. 1950s, Collection of Lisa Cliff, photograph by Lisa Cliff.

merry renk, *In the Sky*, necklace, sterling, iridescent stones, 12" x 11-3/4. *Courtesy of Mark McDonald, 555 Warren St., Hudson, New York,photograph by Bill Hibbs.*
About the above necklace, *merry renk said, "I designed a large silver wire unique tiara, Sea Water, in 1969 for my New York exhibit at the Lee Nordness Gallery. My first structure was this design pattern. I found the lightness and the open skin composed of the thick and thin lines of metal delightful. I decided to make a necklace in 1971, I began with a single bent wire "V" with pounded ends. I added other radiating wires and constructed my wire necklace 12 inches wide with five repeating patterns. In the center I pegged three long pink biwa pearls. This unique design is named, In the Clouds. In 1972 a client ordered a new version of the necklace with silver and opals. This special design is named, In the Sky."*

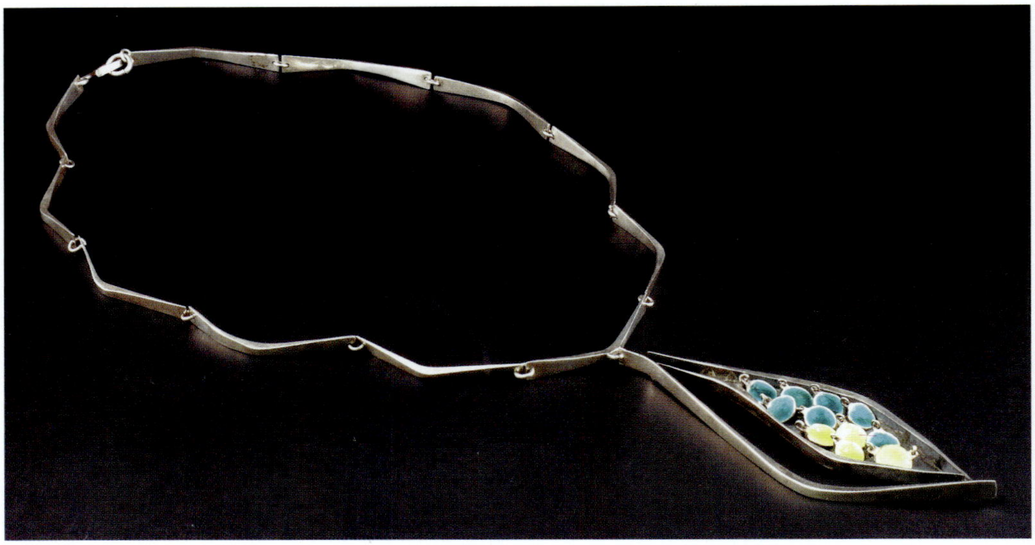

Lois Franke Warren, necklace, sterling silver, green enamel drops, forged chain, chain: 18", pendant: 1-3/8" x 3-1/2" x 1/8", c. 1946. *Illustrated in Handwrought Jewelry by Lois Franke, 1962 by Mc Knight Publishing Company, Title page. Collection of Lois Franke Warren, photograph by Shirley Byrne.*

Interlocking forms were an integral part of renk's designs of the 1950s as well as her later large sculptures. Her *Together* earrings of 1958 are made from 14k gold sheet, which were sawed, and the pieces "interlocked." The sections of the earrings "fly" in space like a flock of birds and the form is reminiscent of a Calder mobile. [24]

Because she thinks of jewelry as sculpture, Lois Franke Warren designs her pieces so they can be viewed from all sides, often incorporating movement or rotation.

The study of flow and movement, structure and rhythm has been continuous for Mary Schimpff as she develops new forms:

I always like triangles and things that sort of "Swish," she said, "I like buoyancy, action—things that flow, plus the interplay of detail in some place—a surprise. I like a piece to look as if it were going to go somewhere. One outstanding difference between a piece of jewelry and all other art forms is that jewelry is viewed in constant motion, as it is seen on an animated being rather than stationary on a wall or pedestal...I am fascinated with reflecting materials that cause ever-changing patterns as the jewelry is worn...Therefore, jewelry, being seen from all angles, must be designed in the round. The designing of a piece of jewelry also has many facets to be considered that are not required by other art forms. As well as aesthetic qualities, one must consider (since jewelry is worn) balance, weight, contour of the body, freedom from sharp points or snagging curves and soundness of structure for durability. [25]

The actual or implied movement in Ed Wiener's jewelry was inspired by the melodic layering and complex rhythms of jazz.

Mary Schimpff Webb, brooch, sterling silver, carnelian, 2-1/4" x 1-1/4". *Collection of Joanne and Fred Doloresco, photograph by Marbeth Schon.*

Ed Wiener, pendant, sterling silver, 1-3/4" x 3/4", *Collection of Munir Meghji, photograph by Munir Meghji.*

Ruth Roach also used movement as a design component. The seven-foot necklace sterling necklace below, titled *Percussion,* "dances" to the syncopation of tiny drums and the beads in her bracelet spin on axes of silver wire.

Ruth Roach, bracelet, sterling silver, 1" x 7-1/2", c.1950, *Collection of Joanne and Fred Doloresco, photograph by Marbeth Schon.*

Ruth Roach, *Percussion* necklace, sterling silver, 7 feet long x 1/4" wide, *Courtesy of Mark McDonald, 555 Warren St., Hudson, New York, photograph by Bill Hibbs.*

Earrings are a natural form in which to include movement as they already "dangle" from the ear.

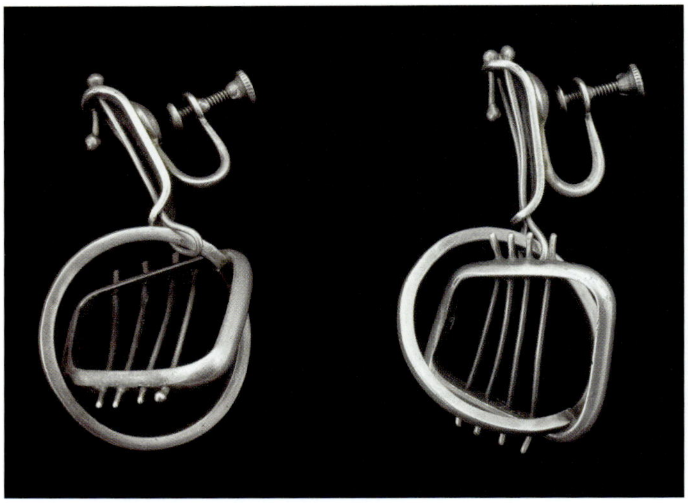

Attributed to Ed Wiener, earrings, sterling, each: 2" x 1", *Courtesy of Mark McDonald, 555 Warren St., Hudson, New York, photograph by Bill Hibbs.*

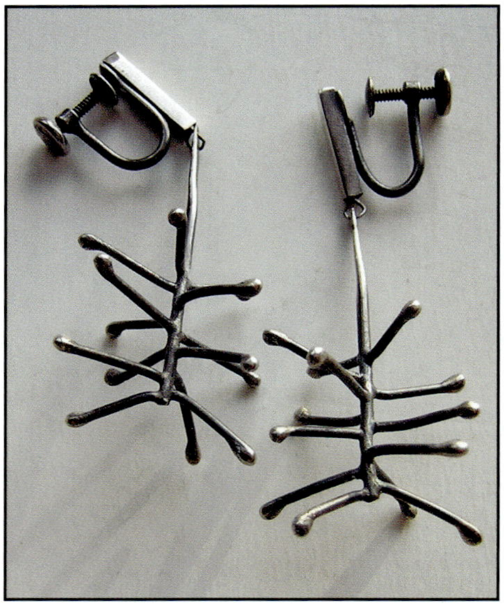

Polly Stehman, earrings, sterling silver, 2" x 3/4". *Collection of Munir Meghji, photograph by Munir Meghji*

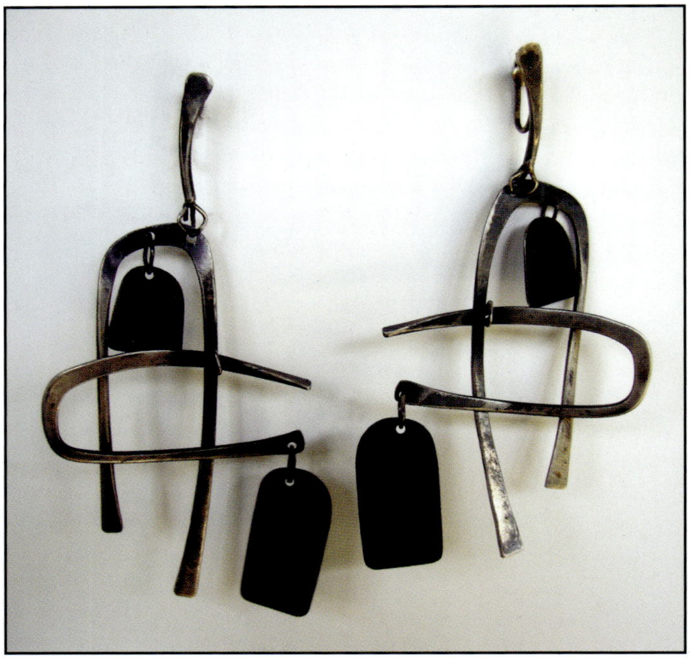

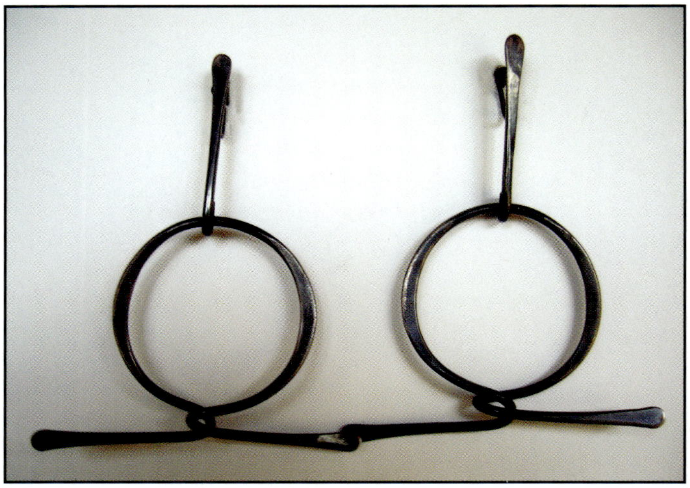

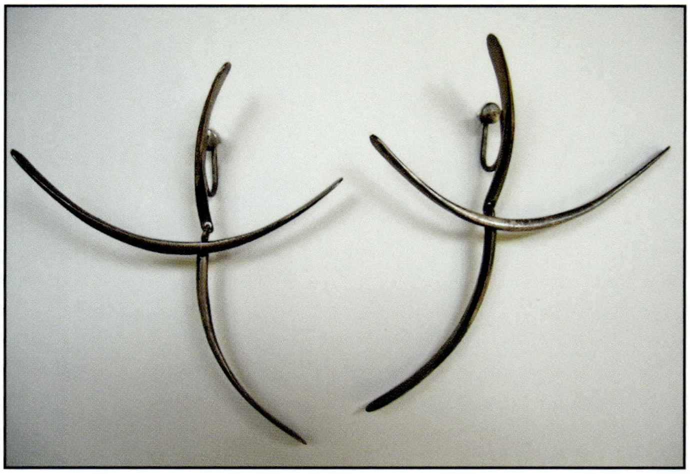

Art Smith, three sets of Mobile earrings, sterling silver, wood. *Collection of Lisa Cliff, photographs by Lisa Cliff.*

Peter Macchiarini, gold and ivory earrings, 2-3/4" x 11/16", c.1940s. *Collection of Munir Meghji, photograph by Munir Meghji.*

The Exploration of Space

One of America's leading Abstract Expressionist sculptors, Ibram Lassaw, was one of the first artists to intentionally create "sculpture to wear." For fifty years, Lassaw created miniature abstract expressionist sculpture for the body. He called them "Bosom Sculptures.[26]

Around 1928 he began to experiment with abstraction in both two and three-dimensional forms. "He came to the conclusion that the sculpture of the future...had to move into three dimensional open space." He was interested in the ideas of Moholy-Nagy and Buckminster Fuller and was familiar with the work of the Cubists, Russian Constructivists and other abstractionists.

Lassaw never doubted his vision that the future direction of sculpture was into "open space."' Lassaw observed that "art" adapted to the latest technologies and materials before the general population and realized that human thought was being redirected into the discovery of Space and the character of nature. It is his open space welded sculptures in bronze, nickel silver, phos-copper, silicon bronze, steel and other alloys that he is most well known for, though he simultaneously worked with other media such as works on paper and canvas with inks and acrylic, lithographs, and welded bronze-gold plated jewelry. Lassaw was doing in three dimensions what Abstract Expressionist painters were doing in two dimensions.

Between 1940 and 1944 Claire Falkenstein worked in wood producing a series of wood sculptures titled Exploded *Volumes*. They were made of interlocking sections that could be moved and combined in different ways by the viewer. "This concept of the importance of the interval," Falkenstein said--"the spaces between-- has always been important to me."[27]

Ibram Lassaw, pendant, gold-plated bronze, amethyst, amber, rose quartz, 3-1/2" (diameter). *Collection of David Fine, photograph by Shirley Byrne.*

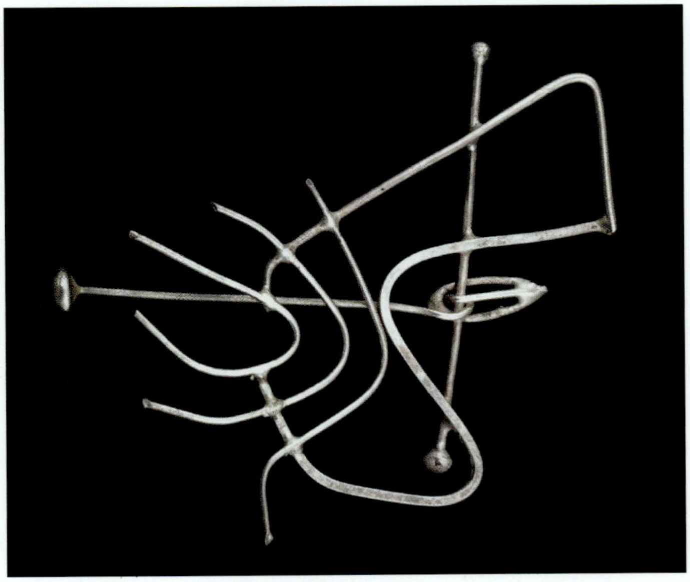

Claire Falkenstein, brooch, sterling silver, 4" x 3-1/2", *Courtesy of Mark McDonald, 555 Warren St., Hudson, New York, photograph by Bill Hibbs.*

In the 1940s, using the experimental approach learned at the Institute of Design, San Francisco jeweler merry renk began to work with enamels on metal and not too long after began to form wire into simple designs for jewelry. Influences of her studies with Moholy-Nagy can be seen in her jewelry from the 1950s many of which are light geometric constructions with generous use of negative space, some with "floating" enamel sections.

Claire Falkenstein also worked within an artistic expression she called *Topology* (a form that connects matter and space, conveying the idea of the continuous void in nature). In 1958 Falkenstein exhibited at the new Galleria Spazio in Rome. Architect, Luigi Moretti wanted her to design a welded stair railing for the gallery. He recommended that she use colored glass that would cast colored light on the floor when the sun shown into the gallery from the street. Falkenstein declined the use of flat panes of glass and instead used fused pieces of colored glass with copper tubing by heating them together in a kiln. This type of bent and welded tubing, hammered flat in places, with pieces of colored glass melted in the crevices, became her uniquely invented medium.[28]

San Francisco sculptor/jeweler Peter Macchiarini explored form through a unique process of fenestration: the internal structuring of metal in multi-layered creations called "Pods." The "exploration of form" was the constant, never ending journey that he began in the 1930s. Peter Macchiarini would carry on long discussions with sculptor Beniamino Bufano about form. Bufano believed that the exterior form was the most important element of sculpture. He liked to compare this concept to what he considered "natures most exquisite sculptural form--the egg." Peter Macchiarini's concepts went a step beyond Bufano's in that he said," You must start with the idea of the egg, yes, but the real journey of discovery is what is inside the egg. " One of the greatest contributions Peter Macchiarini made to the study of metal work and modern design was this constant exploration of depth—the search to find "what was inside the egg."[29]

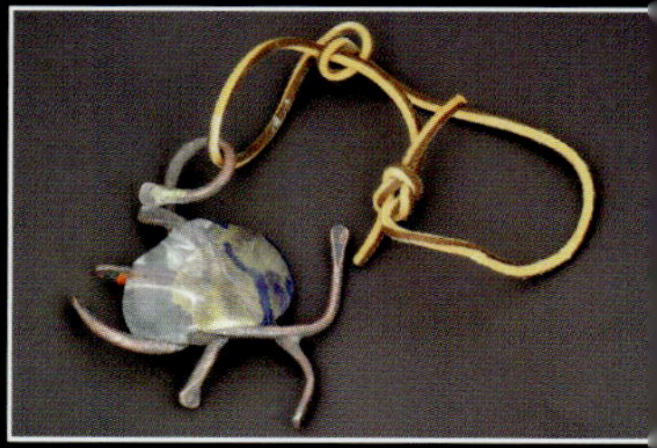

Claire Falkenstein, pendant/ necklace, brass, glass. Courtesy of Mark McDonald, 555 Warren St., Hudson, New York, photograph by Bill Hibbs.

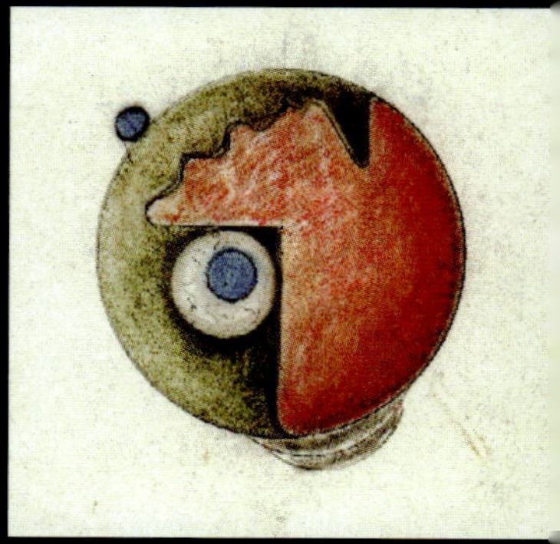

Peter Macchiarini, drawing for *Pod 2. Photograph courtesy of Daniel Macchiarini.*

Peter Macchiarini, *Pod* pendant, sterling silver, brass, wood, copper, patinated copper, 3-5/8" x 3". *Collection of Jil Crawford, photograph by Shirley Byrne.*

"Creating the pods was difficult, painstaking work," Daniel Macchiarini recalled. "He (Peter Macchiarini) used many different layers of metal and patinas to affect depth within the form. In my own work, I have found that if I go far enough into these layers and visual depths, many times I actually return to the outside of the egg—I find another outside on the inside. I am still on this journey and it is hard work, many times I get tired; I struggle very hard to make all the layers and levels of design "right" and find how to make them all work together in a complete form in any given piece. I've never suffered from a single moment of boredom, and that is what keeps me on the journey." [30]

Another area of exploration in Macchiarini's work dealt with concepts of space. For a building at 1422-24 Second Street, Santa Monica, California, Peter Macchiarini created designs for two terrazzo circles at the two entrances using his "Dot Matrix design concept." Macchiarini explained:

> The sizes of the dots in the design field create depth and spatial relationships. In actuality all the dots are the same size but are at different distances from the viewer's eyes. This is the same as stargazing where a certain bright star may look closer but in actuality a smaller, less bright one might be the same size but further away. The designs I have made where lines are integrated into the dots create a more unified entity within a given design field. Historically, I first created this concept in 1955 and I have integrated it into various ring, sculpture, pendant and bracelet designs since then. I am glad that it is now possible that it will be integrated into an architectural building design.[31]

Peter Macchiarini, *Pod* pendant, sterling silver, black pearl , 2-1/2" x 2-1/2". *Collection of Joanne and Fred Doloresco, photograph by Fred Doloresco.*

Peter Macchiarini, three dot rings, sterling silver, brass, copper, ebony, ivory. *Collection of Jill Crawford, photograph by Shirley Byrne.*

Jewelry Inspired By Architecture

Margaret De Patta was intensely interested in jewelry as a structural form and not mere ornamentation; she was profoundly influenced by the study of architecture. For her, the structure of the work was paramount. "...The open steel structures, the cantilevers, the floating structures of contemporary architecture were all aspects which found strong application to her work." She said, "When it is understood that structure encompass[es] the whole field of function it is not difficult to visualize this area as one of absolutely unlimited possibilities and unpredictable findings—the holding of stones in new and ingenious ways, of devising new fastening, catching, and holding forms—are all products of original thinking." [32]

Irena Brynner was profoundly impacted by a show of Gaudi architecture at the Museum of Modern Art in New York. The bizarre, strong, organic structures of Gaudi began to influence her work, which afterward took on a more baroque, organic quality.

Margaret De Patta, ring, gold, sterling silver, gold-flecked stone, top: 1-3/16" x 3/4". *Collection of Jill Crawford, photograph by Shirley Byrne.*

Irena Brynner, earrings, sterling silver, gold, pearls, 1-3/4" x 2-1/4". *Courtesy of Arlene Shrut, photograph by Marbeth Schon.*

Jewelry Inspired By Nature

John Paul Miller, *Octopus*, stickpin, 18k yellow gold, enamel, 2-1/2" high (including pin stem) x 7/8" wide x 1-3/8" deep. *Collection of Kathy Buszkiewicz.*

Jeweler John Paul Miller was fascinated with the paintings of Charles Burchfield who "transformed the sights and sounds of nature into animated fantasies." Miller's work in gold has a strong connection with the forms and structure he sees in nature.[33]

Minnesota jeweler Christian Schmidt wrote of his processes and ideas of design in his book *Encounter with Art* that he co-authored with Reid Hastie, " I purposely juxtapose unlike materials and intermingle different techniques in order to achieve expression of an idea. While exploring and developing a variety of surface qualities inherent in silver, I found many of these adaptable to natural forms. They suggested seeds, plants, marine life, and insects. The vitality of living things is an inexhaustible source of inspiration to me. I find these forms more vital than pure design or manipulation of design elements without content." [34]

One of Schmidt's most successful designs was the "milkweed pod." Schmidt won many awards with this form, which he expressed in several different ways. The intricately formed pod is vital with a surrealistic quality-- tentacles curl out from the interior and a small stone in the center appears to have a tiny face. The reverse, as interesting as the front, has an embossed, textured design that makes the pod look even more creature-like. Schmidt described this design:

> When the designer of jewelry observes a milkweed pod, he is aware of more than a drying, drab, gray shape. He is aware of the overall form of the gently swelling curves and the dynamically changing thrust from the rounded mass to the tapering end which turns upward. He sees the texture change from a pronounced roughness to a smoother surface. He looks for the attachment of the pod to the main stem, along with the others of its own kind. From previous experience he knows that in the tensions caused by drying the pod will burst open forcing the light, feathery seeds up into the air where they are caught by the wind and carried along to another place as the cycle of life in nature moves on. In his imagination, he slices the pod open, replaces the material of the pod with silver and its center with a semi-precious stone.

Christian Schmidt, *Milkweed Pod,* pendant, sterling silver, gold, stone, 4-1/2" x 1-1/8". *Collection of Joanne and Fred Doloresco, photograph by Marbeth Schon.*

Schmidt considered his work to be within the framework of what he termed "the new naturalism'--what is being sought is not the mere effect and outward appearance, but rather the content from which the outward effect derives."

The pod necklace below, by Ruth Roach, relates to the one above, created by her friend and colleague, Christian Schmidt. Both lived and worked in the upper Midwest and were influenced by the native plants of that area.

The dramatic, picturesque landscape of America's northwest coast inspired the jewelry of Ruth Penington. Other influences were northwest coast Native American art and objects, and the art of the Oriental community of that area. Found objects such as upolished beach pebbles and agates were used as well as "spindle whorlds, trade and tomb beads, amulets, feathers." She often combined forms and decorations from differing cultures into one piece. Other influences were the orientalist philosophies of Dow and Fennollosa--she used the archaic and natural forms as a starting point for a modernist esthetic.[35]

Ruth Penington, *Feather Necklace. Photo credit: University of Washington, courtesy of The Sarah Bodine & Michael Dunas Archives of 20th Century Jewelry, Tyler School of Art, Temple University, Professor Stanley Lechtzin, Curator of Metals/Jewelry Archives and Collections.*

Ruth Roach, *Pod,* necklace, sterling silver, 3-1/2" x 1-1/4". *Courtesy of Mark McDonald, 555 Warren St., Hudson, New York, photograph by Bill Hibbs.*

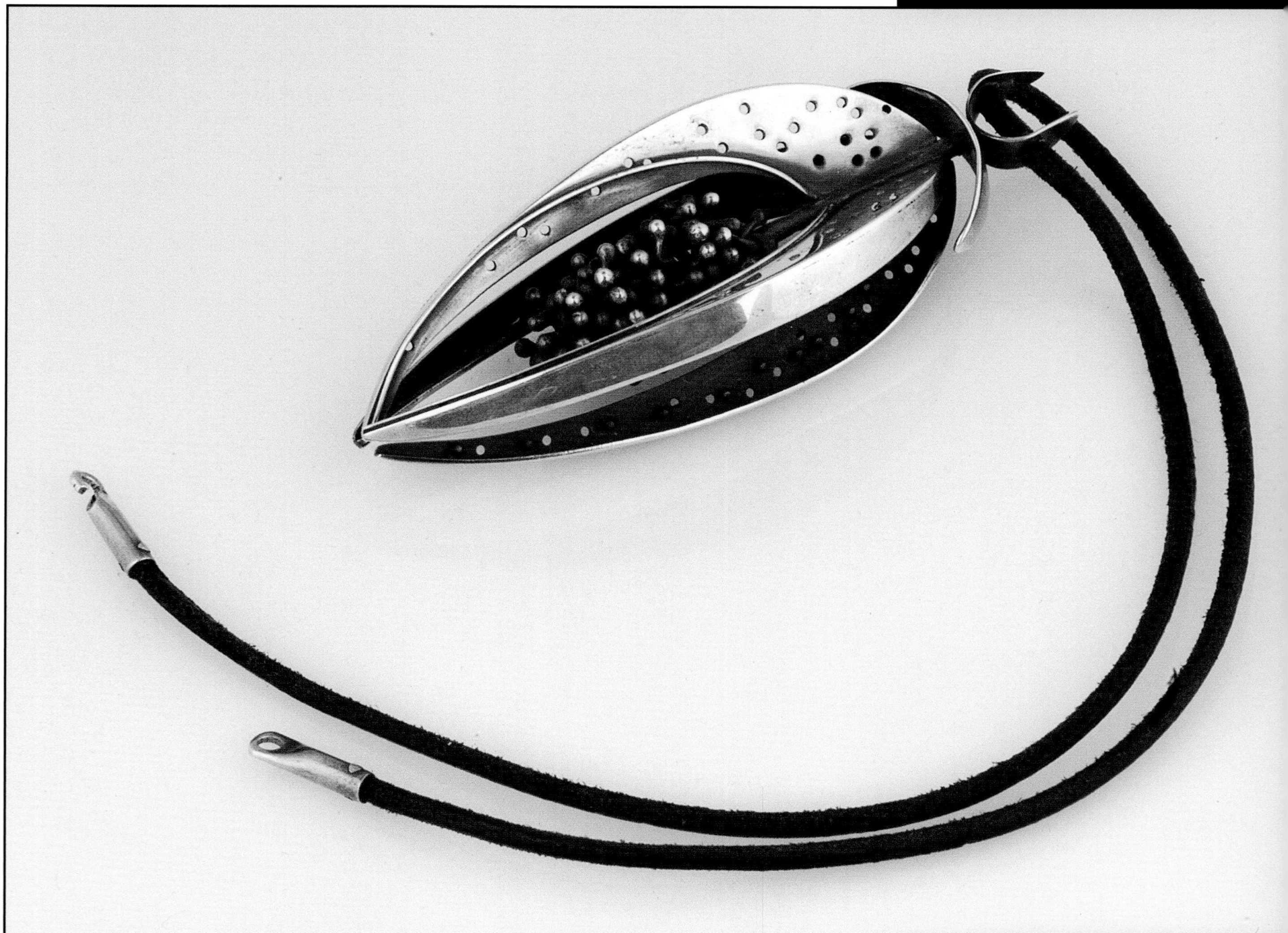

Jewelry That Reflects Art Movements

Bauhaus: Form Follows Function

The pedagogy of the New Bauhaus and the later School of Design in Chicago had a profound influence on the definition of "good design" in the mid-20th century in America. These ideas, closely related to that of the Arts and Crafts movement, that "art should meet the needs of society" and that "no distinction should be made between fine arts and practical crafts" were part of the rationalization for metalsmiths and jewelers to begin to use the term artist/craftsman.

Other tenets of the Bauhaus dealt with the necessity for modern art and architecture to respond to the needs of the "modern industrial world" and that "good design must pass the test of both aesthetic standards and sound engineering. The Bauhaus, and the later International Style, was also identified with the absence of excess ornament, ostentation and harmony between form and function.[36]

Art Smith, ring, sterling silver, stone. *Courtesy of Mark McDonald, 555 Warren St., Hudson, New York.*

Betty Cooke, who was influenced by Bauhaus philosophy, said in an interview with the author in 2001, "My concept of design is extremely important. I think there are a lot of people who are very organic in their approaches to things, but I do like very architectural clean-cut simple things that look as if they are very easy to make. Sometimes they are and sometimes they aren't, but it has to have perfection—they have to be perfect in the design itself. Everything has to be logical and clear. And if it's held together with something it has to be decorative. Nothing is hidden. I guess I judge a lot of people by that, and yet there are a lot of people who do things that are much freer and wilder that I think are wonderful too, but that's not my nature." [37]

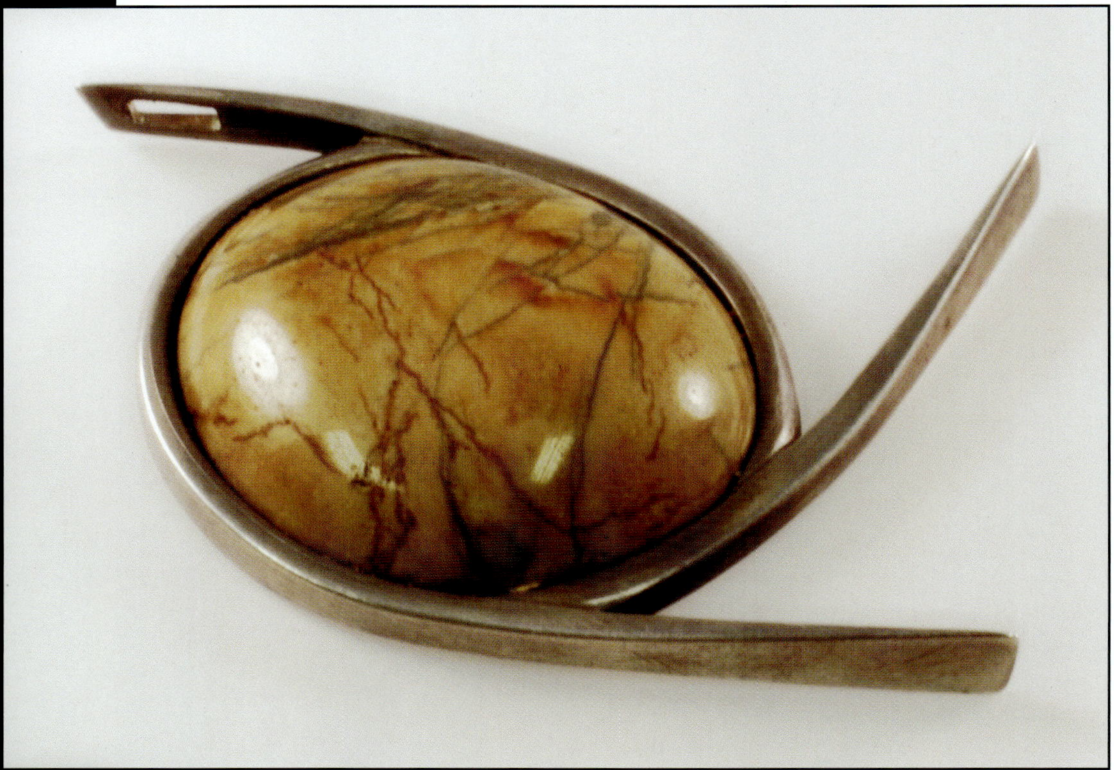

Betty Cooke, pendant, sterling silver, agate, 3" x 3", c. 1950. *Collection of Jill Crawford, photograph by Marbeth Schon.*

In 1941 Margaret De Patta took time out from creating jewelry to attend the School of Design in Chicago to study with László Moholy-Nagy who she knew previously from a summer session at Mills College. Moholy-Nagy recognized that the principals of Bauhaus design were already at work in Margaret De Patta's jewelry. Each new design resulted from years of preparation involving visual and manual experiences and discoveries and numerous sketches that illuminated her concepts as she worked. She was logical, orderly, meticulous, and disciplined. She was also constantly perfecting her techniques. "There were no random or accidental designs; each part of every piece performed a specific function. Every cut of a stone, every element of metal represented the logical working out of a structural or spatial problem. There was nothing in any of her pieces that did not make a vital, relevant contribution toward the total design. Her work appeared dramatically simple and elegant, although it was the result of painstakingly intricate and complex processes." [38]

Philip Morton worked in what he called the "rational mode," based on simplicity and the honest use of materials and tools. In his book, *Contemporary Jewelry, A Studio Handbook*, Morton said, "Simplicity is expressive of the nature of a rationalized milieu which always seeks the simplest, most direct, most effective, and most economical forms...eliminates all nonfunctional elements." This was very close to the Bauhaus credo, but he did not credit it as such.

Philip Morton, pendant, sterling silver, polished flint, 3" x 2-7/8" x 3/8". *Collection of Stephania Frank, courtesy Tom Muir, photograph by Keith Meiser.*

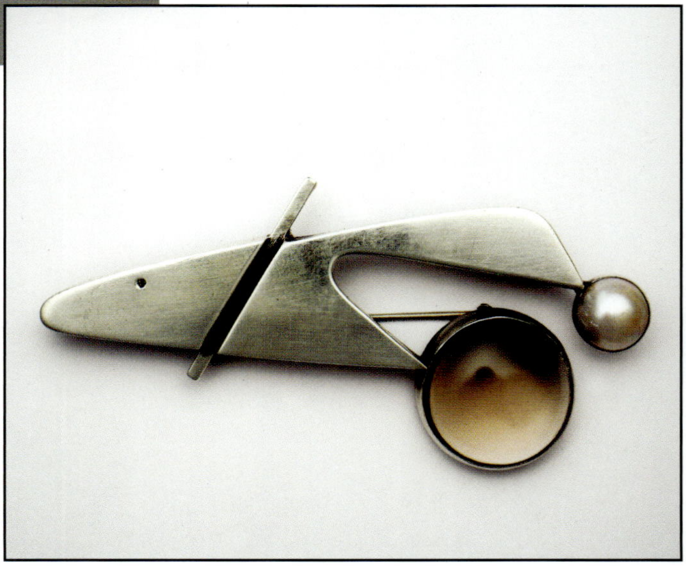

Margaret De Patta, brooch, sterling silver, glass. *Collection of Steve Cabella, photograph by Geoff Turner*

Cubism/Primitivism

Ralph Turner in his book, *Jewelry in Europe and America, new times, new thinking*, said, "The lack of goldsmithing traditions in the United States meant that jewelry there developed in a polarized way that was independent from activity in Europe (there had always been an exchange of influences between European countries). This relative isolation in the US prompted individual innovation which in the 1940s and 1950s aligned itself with surrealism, constructivism, and primitivism.[39]

Ed Wiener, brooch, sterling silver, cinnabar, 3-1/4" x 2-1/4". *Collection of Joanne and Fred Doloresco, photograph by Fred Doloresco.*

Attributed to Byron Wilson, cuff, sterling silver, ebony, 2-5/8" wide x 2-5/8" (inside diameter). *Collection of Jill Crawford, photograph by Shirley Byrne.*

Cubism, another movement which offered a break from the traditional visual perception of art, was lead by George Braque and Pablo Picasso who fragmented and analyzed objects in their paintings and sculptures, presenting the parts simultaneously or re-placed within the designs—rhythmically syncopating the elemental planes like the musical compositions of jazz.

Peter Macchiarini, necklace, brass, wood, 13" overall, each pendant: 2-3/8" long x 7/8" wide. *Collection of Jill Crawford, photograph by Shirley Byrne.*

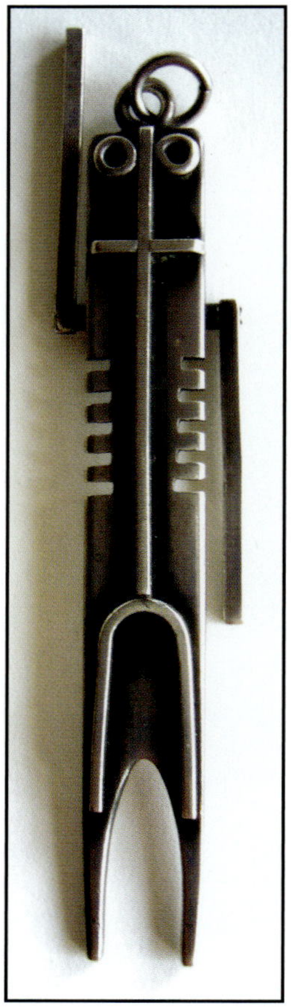

Irvin and Bonnie Burkee, pendant, sterling silver, 2-7/8" long, c. 1950s. *Collection of Lisa Cliff, photograph by Lisa Cliff.*

An additional facet of cubism was the abandoning of the actual representation of an image, substituting, instead, a symbol, which might or might not retain some reminiscence of the original object. This was influenced in large part by the primitivism of African art, which, instead of evolving artistically throughout the ages, was created in a traditional style evoking certain religious or practical purpose. African masks had a significant effect on artists such as Derain and Picasso. American 20th century modernist jewelers also were influenced by the primitive art of Africa as well as by Native American and pre-Columbian art.

Michael Jerry's neckpiece of 1968 combines ivory and sterling in a symmetrical form; the piece is evocative of African or pre-Columbian symbolism. Jerry said he was beginning to work with iron at this time and though it is silver, the design and patina of the metal resembles ironwork.

Mark Rothko remarked in a radio program broadcast in 1943, "If we profess kinship with the art of primitive man, it is because the feelings they expressed have a particular pertinence today in these times of violence." [40]

Though not primitive in the over simplified style of other jewelers, Sam Kramer's shells, tusks, quills, and natural stones evoke an emotional response similar to that of African and Native American art. "Some people may say work like this is disquieting and has a quality deep-rooted and uncivilized, like fetishes and amulets," he said, " Well, why not? It is just another aspect of the new medium of jewelry that offers the artist one of the richest and most rewarding environments for his own kind of expression." [41]

Michael Jerry, neckpiece, sterling, ivory, 9-1/2" long x 5-1/2" wide x 5" deep, c.1968. *Collection of Michael Jerry, photograph courtesy of Michael Jerry*

Sam Kramer, earrings, sterling silver, glass taxidermy eyes, 2-1/2" x 1-1/4", *Courtesy of Mark McDonald, 555 Warren St., Hudson, New York, photograph courtesy of Bill Hibbs.*

California jeweler Byron Wilson, a mostly self-taught metalsmith, preferred primitive forms, often based on pre-Columbian motifs. He worked in natural materials such as wood, ivory, turquoise and obsidian combined with silver.

Earl Krentzin who lists his influences as Paul Klee, Picasso and Salvador Dali, speaks of his creations in silver as capturing the "essence" of things—"essence of bird, essence of a person, essence of animal—they are primitive in that sense, " he says, "...closer to primitive and folk art objects." [42]

The bent and twisted wire jewelry of Alexander Calder in which he sometimes used found objects such as bone fragments, uncut stones, and glass was based partly on the primitivism of African art.

Frank Rebajes' designs, loosely based on modernist theory, were, for the most part, a mixture of constructivist technique and a sort of stylized cubism. His one-of-a-kind jewelry was often ornamented with non-precious stones or branches. The motifs of his production jewelry were based on primitive masks, musical instruments, ethnic characters, leaves and flowers, artists' palates, and geometric shapes.

Byron Wilson, pendant, sterling silver, ebony, ivory, 5" x 1-1/2". *Collection of Joanne and Fred Doloresco, photograph by Fred Doloresco.*

Earl Krentzin, brooch, sterling silver, 2" x 3/4", *Collection of Marbeth Schon, photograph by Shirley Byrne.*

Francisco Rebajes, ring, sterling silver, 1-1/4" x 5/8". *Collection of Joanne and Fred Doloresco, photograph by Fred Doloresco.*

Alexander Calder, belt buckle, brass, 6" x 2-5/8". *Courtesy of Mark McDonald, 555 Warren St., Hudson, New York, photograph by Bill Hibbs.*

Francisco Rebajes, cuff, sterling silver, Musanga wood, 1-1/4" wide, 2-3/8" (inside diameter), c. 1940s. *Collection of Rose Foster, photograph by Shirley Byrne.*

Much of Peter Macchiarini's oeuvre exhibits elements of cubism; his African-inspired masks, musical instruments and other geometric, abstract pieces exhibit the type of symbolism used by Picasso and Braque.

The pendant by Cantanzaro (below) illustrates a direct use of the imagery of primitivism.

Peter Macchiarini, brooch, sterling silver, copper, brass, ivory, 4-3/8" x 1-1/4". *Courtesy of Historical Design, Inc., photo ©HD, Inc.*

Peter Macchiarini, pendant, sterling silver, copper, brass, ebony, ivory, black woven twine, 6" x 2-1/8". *Courtesy of Historical Design, Inc., photo ©HD, Inc.*

Peter Macchiarini, brooch, sterling silver, brass, copper, ebony, ivory, 4-7/8" x 1-3/8". *Courtesy of Historical Design, Inc., photo ©HD, Inc.*

Peter Macchiarini, silver, wood, brass, ivory, 3-1/4" x 1-1/4". *Collection of Jill Crawford, photograph by Shirley Byrne.*

Cantanzaro, pendant, sterling silver, 2-1/2" x 1-1/4", Collection of Joanne and Fred Doloresco, photograph by Fred Doloresco.

Constructivism

"Constructivism" describes the modernist movement of abstract or nonobjective art that began after the Russian Revolution of 1917. Within the tenets of constructivism, elements of works of art are "constructed" or assembled from different materials; iron, tin, wood, glass, plaster, and other materials were used to "bridge the gap between everyday life and art." It was also called "production art" early on because one of its ideas was to create artist-engineers in order to revolutionize industrial design. Antoine Pevsner and Naum Gabo were instrumental in bringing constructivist principles to light in the United States. Other tenets of constructivism were dynamism and the integral use of space.

In jewelry, constructivism or constructivist design has come to describe work that is hand-built--assembled, but it also can describe kineticism, the creative use of positive and negative space, and the "structuring of space through (the use of) obliquely intersecting lines, planes, and geometric shapes," as seen in the work of American studio jewelers Margaret De Patta and Peter Macchiarini.

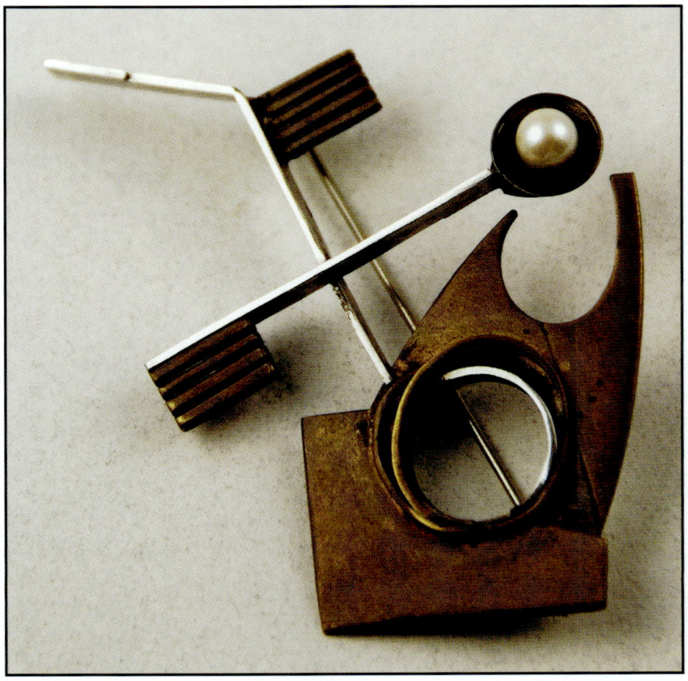

Peter Macchiarini, brooch, copper, brass, sterling silver, pearl, 3" x 2". *Collection of Joanne and Fred Doloresco, photograph by Fred Doloresco.*

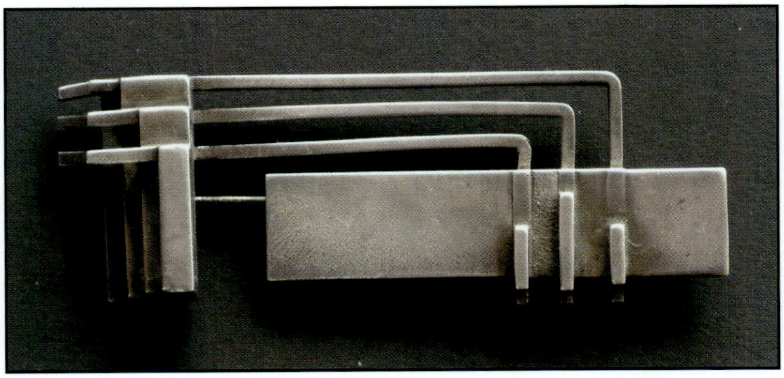

Peter Macchiarini, brooch, sterling silver, 4" x 1-1/4" x 1/2". Courtesy of Mark McDonald, 555 Warren Street, Hudson, New York, photograph by Bill Hibbs.

Peter Macchiarini, brooch, sterling silver, copper, brass, carnelian, 3-1/2" x 1", *Collection of Joanne and Fred Doloresco, photograph by Fred Doloresco.*

Probably the most influential jeweler to begin working in the modernist tradition within the decade of the 1930s was Margaret De Patta. In 1929, already influenced by constructivist ideas, she decided to turn to metals after discovering, while searching for a wedding ring, that conventional jewelry lacked the principles of good contemporary design. She decided to make her own wedding band, realizing that metal held exciting possibilities for working in the constructivist style. [43]

Margaret De Patta, ring, sterling silver, top: 1-1/8" x 3/4". *Collection of Jill Crawford, photograph by Shirley Byrne.*

Abstract Expressionism

Abstract expressionism flourished in America after the Second World War until the beginnings of Pop Art in the 1960s. In the fine arts, it was also called The New York School and was the first significant modernist art movement established in the United States—a movement that facilitated the acceptance of the United States as a world art center.

Abstract expressionism originated from other earlier 20th century art movements such as cubism and surrealism that endorsed abstract rather than representational art. In it's pure form, Abstract Expressionism is expressed only through the use of color and form—completely non-representational and non-objective. [44]

Ibram Lassaw, pendant, 3.5" x 2.5", bronze, gold plated. *Photograph © Denise Lassaw.*

In the latter 1940s Ed Wiener was inspired by the intellectual art colony at Provincetown, Massachusetts, where he had a shop and spent his summers. There were art schools teaching Social Realism and their primary challengers, the Abstract Expressionists, as well as numerous galleries and craft shops. Wiener identified with the latter group of artists, many of whom became his customers. He said that the best part about summers in Provincetown was the "talk," from which he learned about negative space, silhouette, scale and containment, texture, shading, volume, etc., qualities that were already part of his work but unknown to him in terminology. At that time, Provincetown artists would work in the mornings and have long discussions on their decks in the afternoons. Wiener reveled in the education he received from his customers, who included such notables as Hans Hoffman, Harry Engel, Adolph Gottlieb, Barnett Newman, Peter Grippe, Chaim Gross, and Ward Bennett. [45]

In 1948, recognized for her wire sculpture and jewelry, Claire Falkenstein acquired a teaching position at the California School of Fine Arts. The faculty also included Abstract Expressionists Clyfford Still and Richard Diebenkorn. Still became her close friend and she was greatly influenced by his ideas.

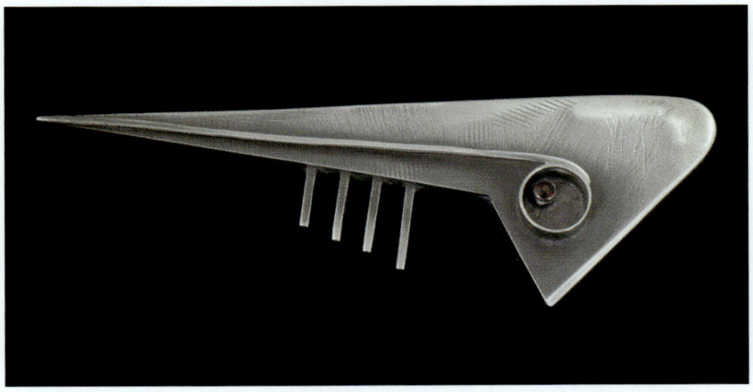

Ed Wiener, (attribution), brooch, sterling silver, red stone, 3-1/2" x 2-1/4". *Courtesy of Mark McDonald, 555 Warren St., Hudson, New York, photograph by Bill Hibbs.*

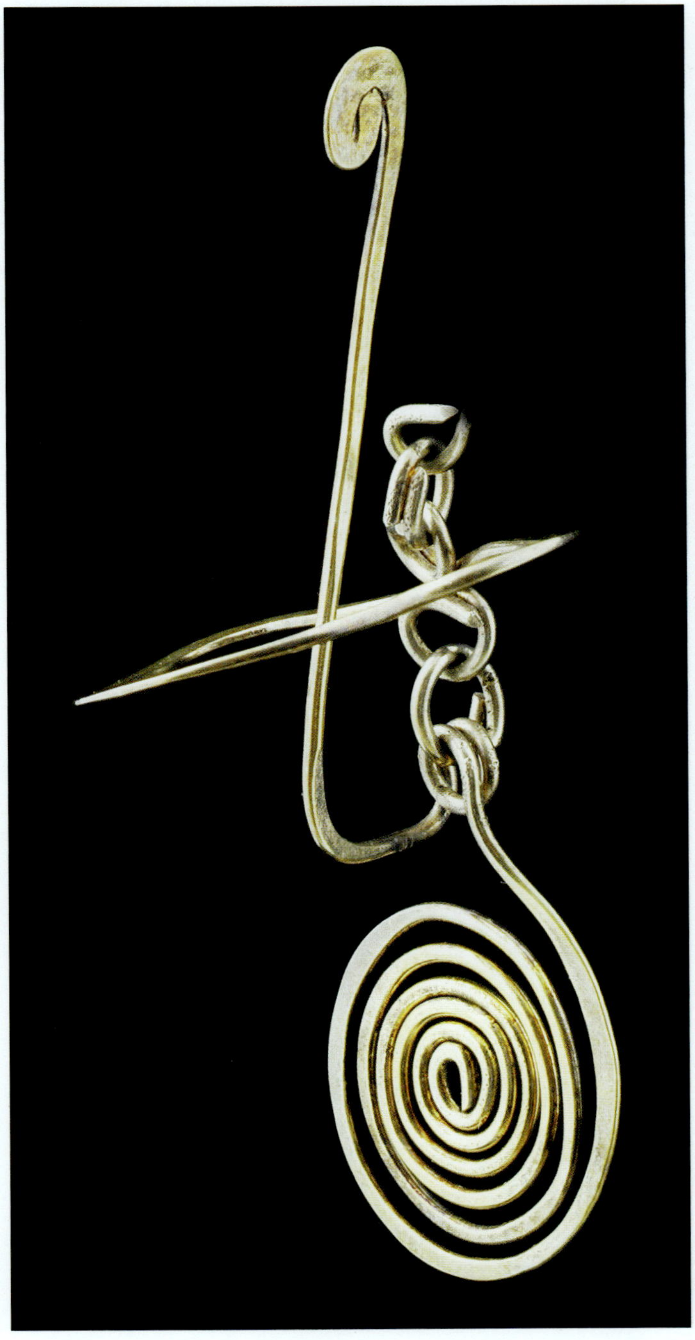

Claire Falkenstein, *Erotic* brooch, brass, 4" x 2- 3/8". *Courtesy of Mark McDonald, 555 Warren St., Hudson, New York, photograph by Bill Hibbs.*

Surrealism

A successor to Dada, surrealism was a strong undercurrent in European modernist design in the early 20th century, but was antithetical to the ordered rationalism of the Bauhaus. Dada was a word that originally had no meaning in its application to art but was picked randomly from a dictionary. The controversial credo of Dada was, "everything the artist spits is art." Devotees of this movement used the found object to create art as well as ascribing artistic qualities to the ready-made object. Dada artists made use of the techniques of collage and montage.

Surrealism is expressed in some of the same forms as Dada, but is more based in the unconscious. Philip Morton, in his book *Contemporary Jewelry, A Studio Handbook*, described these movements, "Surrealism and Dadaism celebrate, not the aspects of existence which stand forth in the illuminating light of the mind, but those subterranean relationships which have their movement behind the bright face of nature, in the half-light and shadow of uneasy mystery and uncertain meaning." [46]

Sam Kramer, considered one of the first American modernist jewelers, created surrealist-inspired jewelry as early as 1936. Many of Kramer's pieces evoke mysterious dreamlike qualities and he was known for incorporating glass taxidermy eyes into his designs—the eye, a theme in surrealist work, is also seen in the works of its proponents Dali and De Chirico.

At the time when "Herman Mueller's glass modes of microorganisms were exhibited at the Museum of National History, when those celluloid celebrities—the pod, the blob, and the thing appeared in popular culture, Kramer was combining glass eyes, semiprecious stones and shells into his jewelry for both an esthetic and emotional effect." [47]

Kramer's mark included the symbol of a mushroom which he said he used because "a mushroom grows in dark, gloomy places and my jewelry is often eerie and mysterious." [48]

Sam Kramer, ring, sterling silver and taxidermy eye, 1-1/4" x 1-1/2". *Collection of Munir Meghji, photograph by Munir Meghji.*

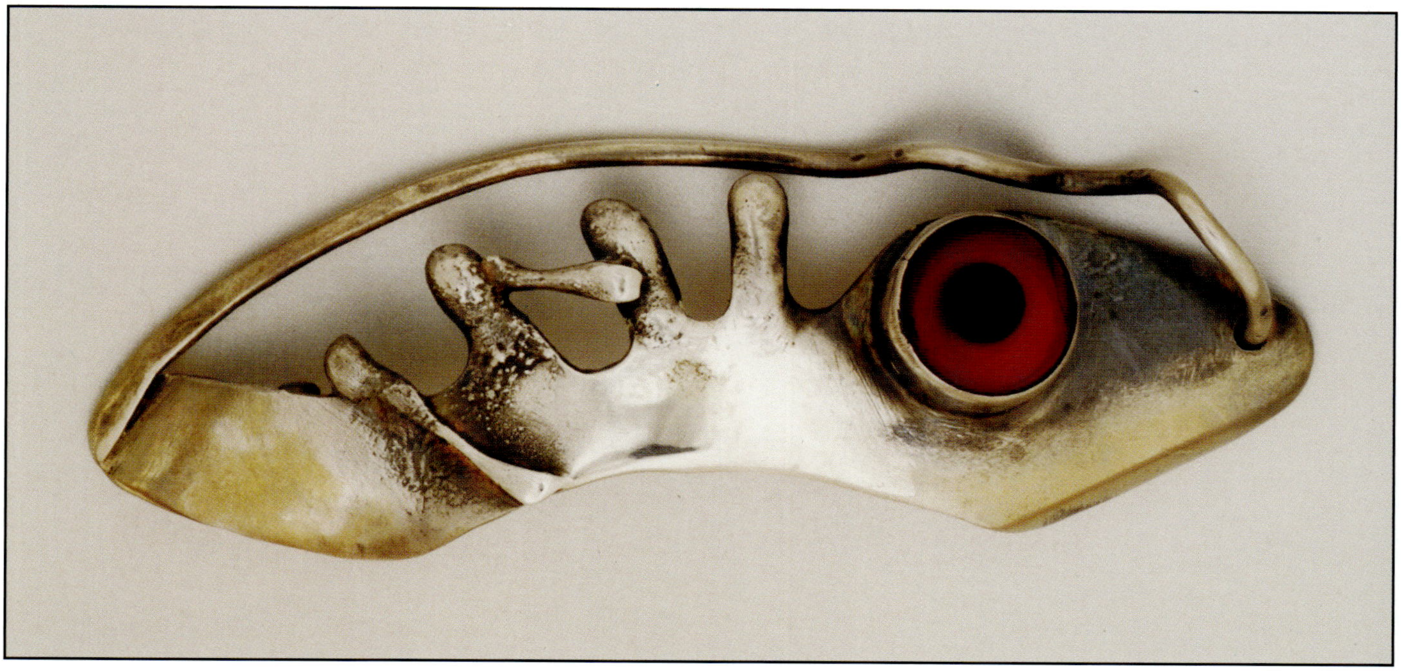

Sam Kramer, *Eye* brooch, sterling silver, glass taxidermy eye, 3" long x 1" high. *Courtesy of Historical Design, Inc., Photo ©HD, Inc.*

From his studies at the University of Southern California with potter Glen Lukens, Kramer learned about the art of the accidental. "To Lukens...the crackled, dripped or pooled glaze was an asset. Even the most mundane tasks could be vitalized by opening them to the psyche...the accidental made normative: The prosaic imbued with process." This appealed to Kramer who believed that experimentation was the life flow of jewelry as a creative expression.[49]

Sometime later he applied the accidental to his work in metals. " One time, working by trial and error in the fireplace (a convenient place for such experiments)," he related, "I was trying to evolve a new casting technique. When silver is molten, it flares and dances like mercury. Suddenly a sputtering bubble of liquid silver squirmed out of the ingot-mold and cooled in an odd shape on the hearth. This piece, this accident of spilled metal, vaguely resembled a duck's head. And it started me thinking about how silver and gold could be blasted by flame until it ran almost fluid, then controlled, built-upon and fused again until it resulted in small sculptures with the texture and all the flame-like movement of this kind of primal ordeal by fire."[50]

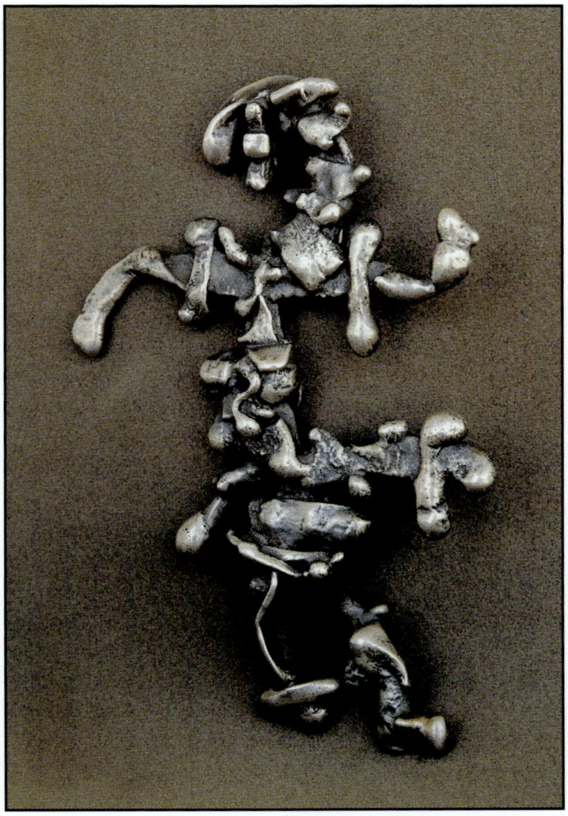

Sam Kramer, brooch, sterling silver, 3-3/4" x 2-1/2", *Collection of Joanne and Fred Doloresco, photograph by Marbeth Schon.*

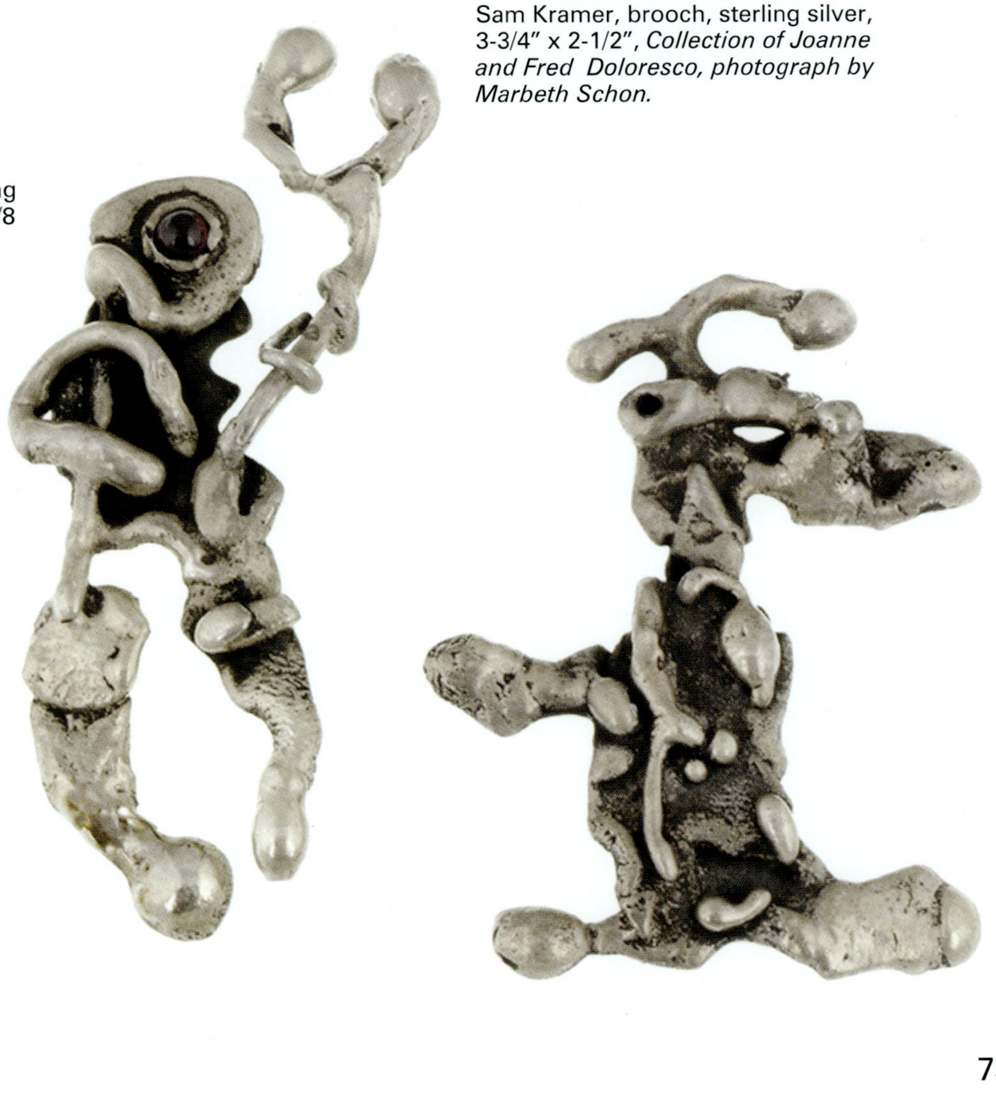

Sam Kramer, two brooches, sterling silver, glass, left: 2 3/8 x 7/8, r: 2 1/8 x 1-1/2" *Courtesy of Mark McDonald, 555 Warren St., Hudson, New York, photograph by Bill Hibbs.*

Biomorphism

The contours of surrealism gave impetus to the designs of the 1950s that were concerned with the imagery of vital forms termed, "biomorphism." In Biomorphism the sculptor releases the "vital force" hidden within the materials. The organic object released from the materials develops naturally into a "form that is appropriate to both its formation and its ultimate use." In theory, biomorphic forms are both "beautiful and appropriately functional"--often defined by sensuous curves suggestive of the human body or amoeboid shapes. [51]

Biomorphism in its truest form can be seen in the sculptural jewelry of mid-20th century artist Art Smith. Though his layered biomorphism recalls the work of Miro, Smith's shapes are more instinctual, more related to the natural movements of vital forms and dance. "Things should really play with each other, he said, "and they should play with the body. It should be fun; it should be exploitation. It should be an investigation. A good piece of jewelry literally caresses the body and fondles it and as I say, plays with it... it enjoys itself and it enjoys you and you enjoy it." [52]

The amoeboid shapes of Sam Kramer's pieces are also biomorphic, referencing living organisms.

Art Smith, Lava Cuff, brass, copper, 6" x 2-5/8". *Courtesy of Mark McDonald, 555 Warren St., Hudson, New York, photograph by Bill Hibbs.*

Art Smith, brooch, copper, brass, 3-3/8" x 2-1/2", *Collection of Jill Crawford, photograph by Shirley Byrne.*

Sam Kramer, brooch, sterling silver, copper, beach glass, glass taxidermy eye, 3-3/4" x 1". *Collection of Jill Crawford, photograph by Marbeth Schon*

Pop Art

By the late 1950s the art of the Abstract Expressionists was fast becoming replaced by Andy Warhol's representations of soup cans and Roy Lichtenstein's "homage to the comic strip."[53] In the 1960s, a decade when traditional boundaries in the arts and crafts were crossed, Pop Art was born.

Purportedly, British critic Lawrence Alloway used the term "mass popular art" in a 1958 article for *Architectural Design* entitled *"The Arts and the Mass Media"* and, thereafter was credited with being the first to discuss "pop art," but he did not use the exact term. Though the beginnings of pop art were in England, it was fully embraced in New York in the late 1950s and early 1960s. Its brash and sardonic character appealed to young jewelers who began to make three-dimensional "art" out of the commonplace—and in some cases, the detritus: the disposable matter of society.

What was expressed in the 1960s was "a new brand of American pragmatism—whatever works for you should be pursued"...Nothing was outside the metalsmith's purview: sex, religion, politics, plastics, paper, leather. The definition of jewelry was: "What works in today's society with an audience of your own choosing." [54]

The story of Christian Schmidt's *Medal of Honor*—his account of "the hoax that failed" serves as a paradigm for understanding the deep psychological and ideological changes in the way crafts, including the metal arts, were perceived in the 1960s.

In 1964 Schmidt was chosen to be a juror at the St. Paul Gallery's biennial *Fiber, Clay, and Metal* exhibit. The following is taken from Christian Schmidt's account of this event in his book "Encounter with Art:"

> Since there were four jurors any decision on a two-to-two deadlock was awarded to the expert in the field under consideration. After being outvoted on a particular wall hanging, which.... was so poorly fabricated that it was virtually falling apart, I made the mistake of asking my colleagues to justify their choice. This brought an immediate outburst, "What's there to talk about, you gotta feel it in your guts or it doesn't have it!"

During the rest of the day we completed the fiber section. One jury member preferred to judge most fabrics from the reverse side because "they were more exciting that way." Any attempts on my part to question function, craftsmanship or design were rejected...

The judging of pottery added to my confusion. It seemed to go according to the rule that "if it's been done before—it's not any good!" This automatically ruled out most functional wheel-thrown pots because of their general similarity...

On the last day we were to judge metal—my area. The events of the previous two days seemed like a nightmare. The situation was discussed with my family the last night... It occurred to us perhaps we could shock this jury back "to reality" by some ridiculous joke. We hit upon the idea of creating a monstrous piece of jewelry for this purpose. We swung into action with gusto, beginning with the outer shell of an old rusted fly-fishing reel. My sons began donating their prize possessions for the lark. A homemade sheriff's badge was placed in the center of the reel, an imitation cameo was clamped to the star, rough turquoises were crudely bound on with iron binding wire, and other dime-store trinkets were dangled from the base. This was suspended from a crude "dog chain" that my six-year-old son had handcrafted some years before and which had decorated the scarecrow in our raspberry patch until this fateful night. The "thing" was tagged with an official entry blank and entitled *Medal of Honor* and attributed to the artistry of the fictitious Abraham Isitshit.

I could visualize the scene on the following day when someone would discover it and begin laughing—showing it to everyone as a big joke! Then, I would agree with them and after our big laugh could begin the serious business of drawing a parallel between this piece of junk and the other 'junk" that we had been accepting for the show. What could better prove the point? Then, I hoped that we would return to work inclined to use our intellect as well as emotion in making decisions.

There was no problem slipping my "entry" among the other work the next morning. When the jury arrived we began circulating among the work preparatory to judging. After a bit of browsing, my creation was discovered. Someone held up the pendant for all to see—I was choking with mirth and only hoped that the craftsman could remain anonymous until the situation could be thoroughly enjoyed. But! They like it! "It turned them on!" ....

When I had regained my composure and saw that my little joke was being taken seriously, I decided to see how far it would go. The gallery staff was rather perturbed because the master entry blank could not be found and there was no record of the entry fee. We were told that it could not be judged with the other objects, but if it was found to be a fraud the gallery was not obligated to display it.

When the "Medal of Honor" was considered by the jury it was hailed as a "delightful satire" and a valuable expression in terms of the pop art movement.

The rest is history. Needless to say this was a most controversial show. After coverage in "Craft Horizons," using a half-page illustration of the "Medal of Honor," the controversy raged through letters to the editor for months.

...During ensuing discussions with artists and art critics, those who were fascinated by its brazen statement defended it stoutly against my protests that it was but worthless tripe—their argument being that I was a victim of my own talent and incapable of doing something worthless. This was not only amusing but highly speculative as well. However,

Christian Schmidt, *Medal of Honor,* pendant, mixed media, c.1964. *Photo credit: Janet Schmidt, courtesy of The Sarah Bodine & Michael Dunas Archives of 20th Century Jewelry, Tyler School of Art, Temple University, Professor Stanley Lechtzin, Curator of Metals/Jewelry Archives and Collections.*

Robert Ebendorf, *Portable Souls* (to carry in your pocket), daguerreotype case, mixed media, open: 6-1/2" x 3-3/8", closed: 3-1/4" x 3-5/8". *Courtesy of Robert Ebendorf.*

> operating upon their thesis of infallible talent, it should be pointed out that the "Medal of Honor" was a completely conscious repudiation of everything that I believe. It was a hoax that failed. [55]

In the 1960s, Robert Ebendorf went from creating traditional objects from silver to using "found objects, industrial products, paper, shells and street debris." In about 1969, he created a series titled "Portable Souls." "This collection of three leather cases with daguerreotypes demonstrates his visual language of complex surface design and alternative materials. He saw the ghostly metallic images as 'lost souls' and began to question American spiritual values."[56]

Jewelry Influenced By Philosophies

Post-war New York was fertile ground for the "cross-pollination of artistic and philosophical influences." Together with his strong interest in the natural and physical sciences, Ibram Lassaw studied philosophy with a special interest in the mystical branches of Christianity and Buddhism. "He heard Buckminster Fuller speak in the Village, and was intrigued by the writings of Carl Jung." He joined a class on Zen Buddhism in 1953, which he continued for many years. "The study of Buddhism, mythology, and especially science had a great influence on the way Ibram thought about his sculpture and his own place in the cosmic organism which is how he began to understand existence."[57]

On the other side of the country, in Seattle, Washington, Ruth Penington was profoundly influenced by the theories of Dow and Fenollosa—a philosophy somewhat like that of William Morris who believed that art raised the quality of society and that "the future depended upon a deeper appreciation of art in everyday life." Good design was not only to be sought after, but was necessary for the total betterment of mankind. Art was "the expression of the highest form of human energy, the creative power which is nearest to the divine."[58]

Dow also supported "the ideal of democratic access to things of beauty" and like the tenets of the Arts and Crafts Movement, he believed in reconnecting with the work of the hand. He classified himself as a "modernist' who emphasized structure over representation and rebelled against accepted and traditional trends, though he insisted that nothing was really new and that modernism had its roots in ancient, past epochs.

Ibram Lassaw, brooch, gold plated bronze, 2-1/2" x 3-3/4". *Collection of Joanne and Fred Doloresco, photograph by Fred Doloresco.*

Ruth Penington, cuff, sterling silver, agates and Mexican opals, 1-1/4" (at widest section), *Collection of Munir Meghji, photograph by Munir Meghji.*

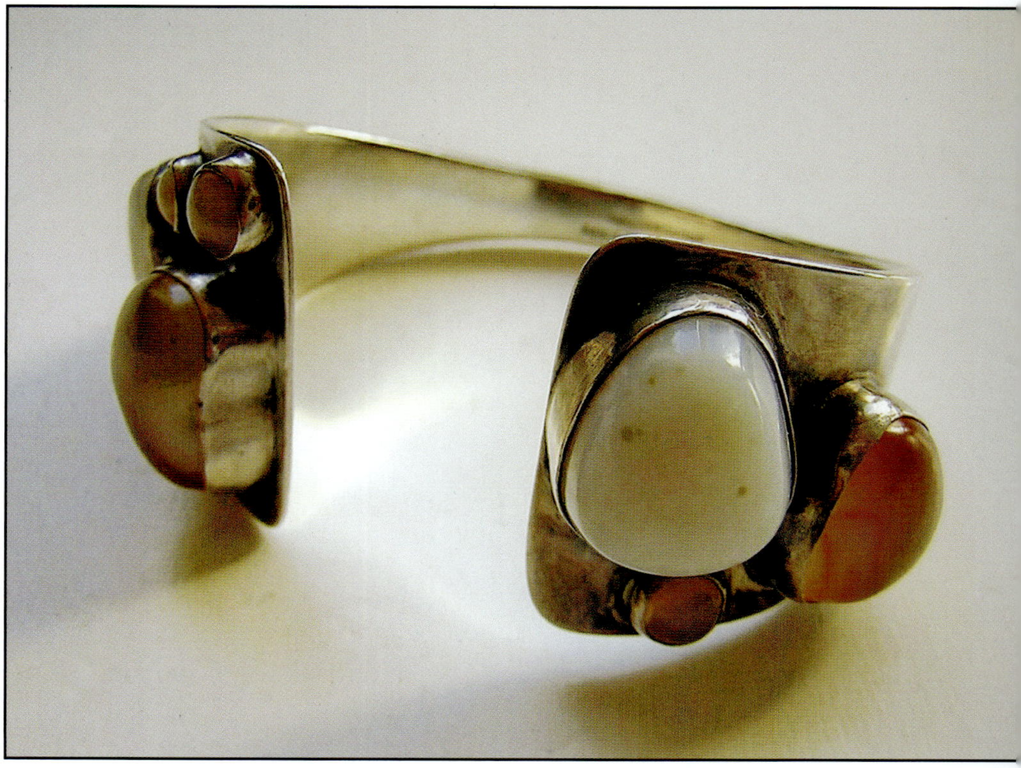

Many of Penington's works, even the smallest physically, were marked from the beginning with a monumental feeling, as if she were thinking architecturally and expansively in the planning stages—large flat and simple areas related to other large flat and simple areas all contained in very large form. The insistant striving for the larger elements of truth in painting the figure corresponds exactly to the broad beginnings of Dow's students in design except that the student in painting class strives to record those truths as he sees them before him while the design student is usually trying to create forms. But in each case the work must unfold from large forms into smaller parts.

Penington was a leader in the direction of monumental scale in jewelry—so much so that her work was sometimes juried out of competititve exhibitions because it was "too big to be wearable." Something the jurors may not have known was that Penington's way of working was to include all the problems in the final solution. Although her jewelry is usually large, it is still comfortable to wear. "A work should be designed all the way through," she explained, "not just on the surface, the material, the techniques, the scale of the wearer, the functional aspects, all dictate the approach. If you know all of this and are sensitive to your surroundings and to your feelings, expression is easy enough. But, maybe you don't have anything to say."

Within the whole of art (especially abstract art) is the question of whether or not the work presents an actual idea or meaning or relegates the process of finding "the meaning" to the viewer. German modernist, Joseph Bueys said, "Freedom equals self-determination equals man...Art is at its most effective and scientific when expressed with a question mark."

Earl Pardon, belt buckle, sterling silver, 2-1/2" x 1-1/2", c. 1958. *Collection of Munir Meghji, photograph by Munir Meghji.*

Of Earl Pardon it was said (at least of his wall sculptures) that the expression of a particular motif within his work is ambiguous. "There was no intention of conveying symbolic meaning by any of the multitude of irregular-shaped metal pieces," he said, " The spectator may read many meanings into the form, thereby participating in his own interpretation of the work. This is not only desirable, but a necessity for communication between the artist and the spectator." [59]

Adversely, Christian Schmidt seems to have wanted to be understood. He said, "The process begins as the artist looks at this world, and abstracts what he perceives to be the essence. With the tools of his craft he gives form to his perceptive vision, and if he is successful, the viewer sees and understands the artist's expression." [60]

Christian Schmidt, pendant, sterling silver, stone, *Collection of Clayton Roach, photograph by Marbeth Schon.*

Ed Wiener developed a concept he called "myriad associations". For example, his "five pointed star" motif of that era which was made into both brooches and earrings, could evoke a bird, a dancer, or other responses depending on the viewer.[61]

Pearl Shecter's star-shaped pendant/brooch may also be considered an example of "myriad associations." In 1957 it was featured in *Religious Arts in American Today* with the caption: "Abstraction, particularly affords unlimited freedom of interpretation as is exemplified in the reproduced brooch by the New York silversmith, Pearl Shecter. Those of Jewish faith might see it as the "Star of David" while Christians will find in it the symbols of the Passion, the crown of thorns, the twisted lash and cross." [62]

Ruth Penington said, "The beholder of the work must do homework, too...to let this particular statement present its own vision. The real work of art is not about something, it simply is." [63]

"I like to give what information I think is necessary," explained Svetozar Radakovich, "and leave room for the viewer's imagination to be part of the seeing..."

Ed Wiener, brooch, sterling silver, tiger's eye, 3-1/2" x 3". *Collection of Jill Crawford, photograph by Marbeth Schon.*

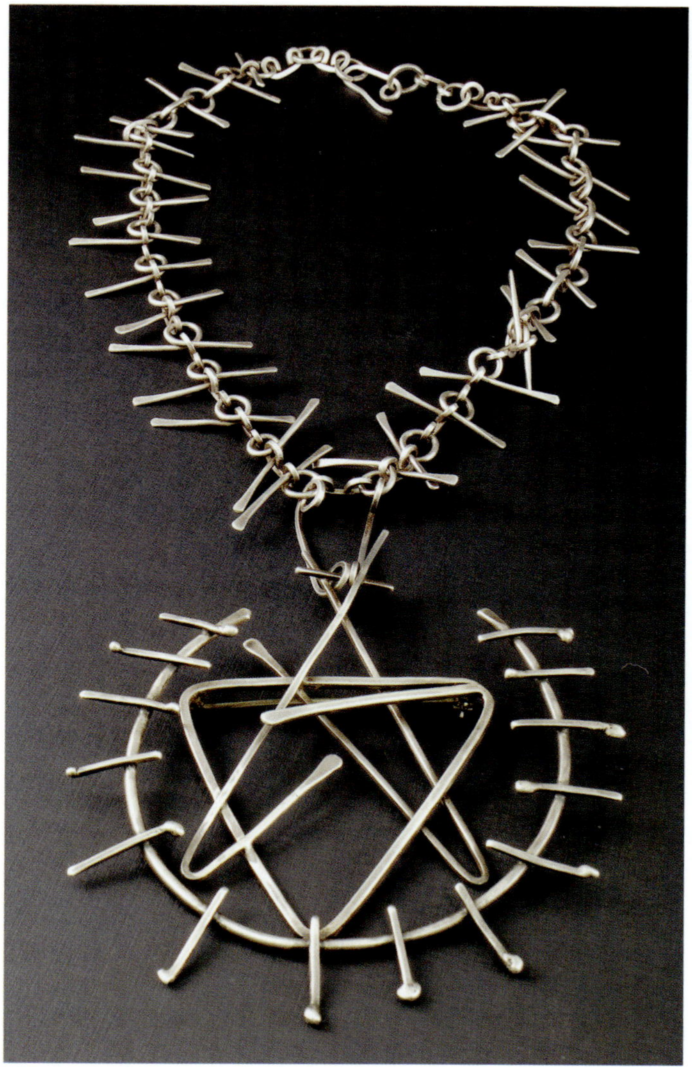

Pearl Shecter, pendant/brooch with chain, sterling silver, pendant/brooch: 3-1/4" x 2-3/4", chain: 23-1/2" long. *Courtesy of Lois Schecter, photograph by Shirley Byrne.*

CHAPTER 5
Materials

Elsa Freund and Robert Ebendorf, *Collaboration Necklace*, sterling silver, glass, resin, mixed media, 7" x 11-1/2". *Courtesy of Martin Roenigk.*

Speaking of materials, Margaret De Patta said she did not believe in preserving the "sacred cows" of the past. If a material could be used to obtain more freedom in design and structure and be made to fit within the requirements of good design she would not hesitate to use it. She realized that each had a specific aesthetic quality that, when used to its best advantage, would create beautiful results.[64]

Stones

One of the single most important contributions made to jewelry design by Margaret De Patta was her work with transparent stones. Influenced by Moholy-Nagy's fascination with the transmission of light, she studied the nuances of light as it passed through stones and, working with the San Francisco lapidary Francis Sperisen, she originated unique cuts to increase transparency and visual range. For centuries, stones had been faceted to produce the optimum amount of brilliance and sparkle. De Patta's stones were transparent "windows" through which the light could pass, enhancing the view of the structure or color of the material behind them. Sometimes she created visual excitement by adding other transparent or semi-transparent materials over or behind the stones to add texture, magnification, or distortion such as her pin that combines crystal and stainless steel wire screen." In a single piece she would make use of light and shadow, transparency, translucency, magnification and multiplication, in a virtuoso development of total visual and spatial concept." [65]

Margaret De Patta, ring, sterling silver, special-cut clear quartz, faceted blue stone, top: 7/8" diameter. *Collection of Jill Crawford, photograph by Shirley Byrne.*

Margaret De Patta, brooch, sterling silver, beach stones, 2-3/4" x 2-1/2" x ½, c. 1960. *Courtesy of Mark McDonald, 555 Warren St., Hudson, New York, photograph by Bill Hibbs.*

When De Patta freed her stones from the bezels and the prongs of the past she also developed ingenious methods of attaching them so they would appear to be free or floating. She found that backings could be attached to stones in a "blind spot" created by the curvature of the cabochon making the attachment invisible from the front of the design. In many of her pieces, the stones appear to float, some within each other.

Margaret De Patta was also one of the first to use diamonds, not for the prestige but because of their color, reflective qualities, and to enhance her compositions. She liked to use semi-precious stones and crystals and was one of the first 20th century jewelers to realize the beauty and inherent modernism of rutilated crystal from Brazil. The stones could be manipulated by angle and placement so the hair-like inclusions became part of her designs.

Her use of stones was revolutionary, opening up new ideas for jewelry design. "The fascination of looking into or through an object of material is boundless," she stated, "And the excitement of optical effects such as magnification, reduction, multiplication, distortion and image reflection and the function of the gem stone in jewelry becomes one to stimulate the ingenuity and imagination of the designer." "Catch your stones in the air," Moholy-Nagy had said to her in Chicago, "Make them float in space, don't enclose them.' And this indeed was what she managed to do."

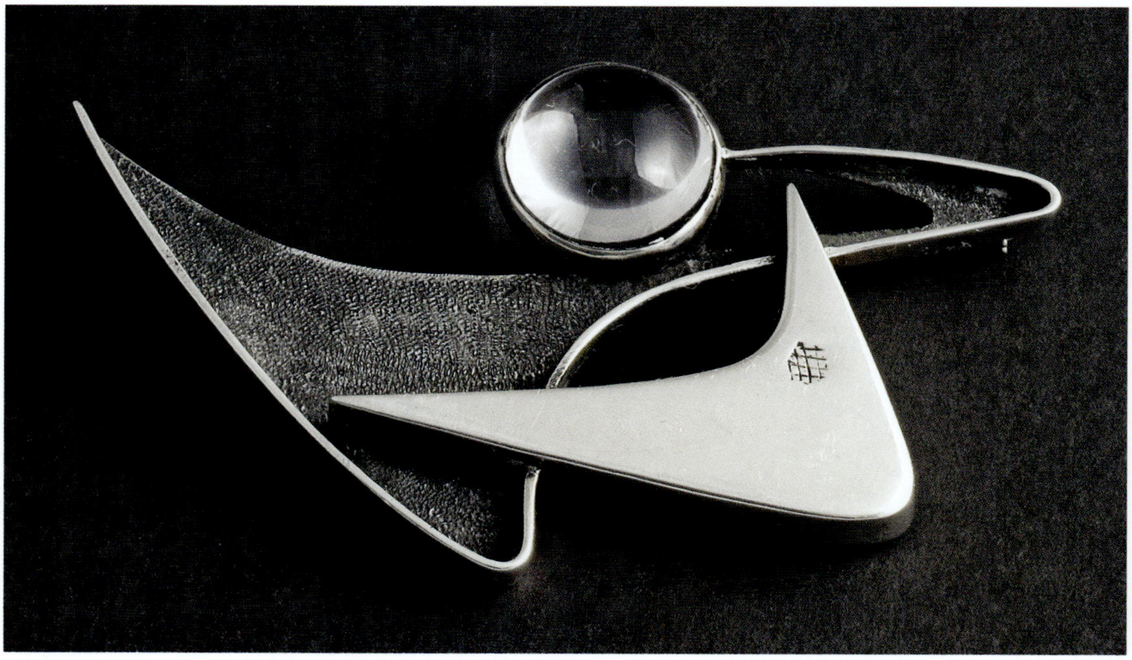

Margaret De Patta, brooch, sterling silver, glass, 3-1/2" x 2", *Courtesy of Mark McDonald, 555 Warren St., Hudson, New York, photograph by Bill Hibbs.*

De Patta spoke about transparency and its relationship to stones:

> One of the major contemporary concepts is that of transparency, it is evidenced in architecture, in our new transparent building materials, in fabrics, furniture, furnishing, films, science, painting and sculpture. Traditionally, the transparent gemstones were cut in cabochon and faceted shapes designed to reflect light and enhance depth of color. When thinking became concentrated on the 'quality' of transparency it became obvious that the new types of stone cuts were necessary and another vast area of exploration opened to the pioneer. An analysis of the possible visual and optical effects produced the following list—transmission, reflection, magnification, reduction, multiplication, distortion, illusion, area of invisibility, visual perspective and space enhancement. At times combinations of two or more of these ideas have been incorporated in one of these 'opticuts.' Development of the space concept among jewelers has brought into use a fascinating stone material that hitherto was only very slightly known—this material is clear quartz with natural inclusions of hair like lines called rutiles or in some cases inclusions of materials such as black tourmaline, iron pyrites or other minerals. [66]

Alan Adler also had semi-precious stones cut in unconventional shapes to become integral parts of his jewelry designs. He hired lapidary George Huston to cut them for him. They were a huge success and he called them "freeform." Mrs. Gary Cooper had one of the first ones and she said that she loved it above all of her other jewelry.[67]

Sam Kramer was fascinated by the "color, sensuousness, and mystery of gems and semi-precious stones." Though not interested in using stones as the primary focus of a piece of jewelry, where the metal was simply a setting for a stone, he believed that the stark, functional, geometric forms of early abstract jewelry lacked imagination and that metal better lends itself to the fluidity of biomorphic shapes. He said:

> When handmade jewelry began to be called 'contemporary' it appeared likely for a brief period that gems and semiprecious stones might disappear from the scene entirely...Jewelry began to reflect the art movements, especially cubism. Surface decoration vanished along with naturalized forms...Complex designs were taboo...jewels and stones were eliminated as a matter of course. With this change, jewelry tended to grow stark and functional looking. The design was in the construction and construction was reduced to a minimum. Clean, sterile areas of metal, devoid of nuances and unusually simple forms somewhat mechanical in implication were the aims of the craftsman in jewelry.
>
> However, jewelry without color...without even the intricacy of unique craftsmanship, could neither stimulate nor satisfy. People refused to surrender one of the few remnants of magic left to them. And so jewels crept back into jewelry. But now, stones were used in new ways and new meanings developed around their usage; they made their impression on jewelry design.[68]

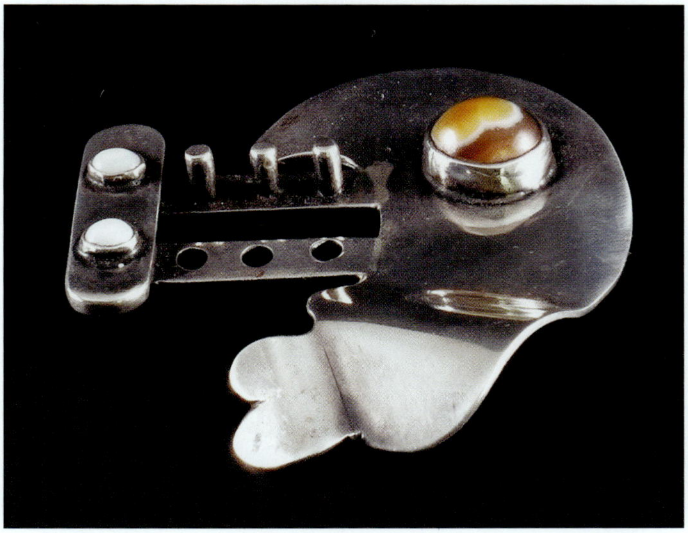

Sam Kramer, brooch, sterling silver, agate, opals, 2-3/4" x 2-1/2". *Collection of Jill Crawford, photograph by Shirley Byrne.*

Earl Pardon's necklace below is an interesting and colorful combination of a semi-precious stone and tiny glass beads within a beautifully complex, abstract composition.

Earl Pardon, necklace, sterling silver, agate, glass beads, 4-3/4" x 3". *Collection of Joanne and Fred Doloresco, photograph by Fred Doloresco.*

The designing of finger rings was an interesting challenge for Art Smith. His rings were ingeniously constructed to mimic and conform to the contours of the hand and the finger. He preferred the term "hand decorations," even creating a special three-part ring that could be worn without pain for a customer with arthritis. His rings often contained stones, almost always semi-precious, often many in one ring, which he sometimes referred to as "families" placed together because of the effect of the juxtaposition of colors and shapes. Like other modernist jewelers, he rarely used precious stones such as diamonds unless commissioned to do so."[69]

Ed Wiener combined colored gems of varying shapes and sizes into bracelets, rings, pins, and necklaces. He thoughtfully juxtaposed colors, textures, and stones--dark against light, cloudy against clear, faceted against cabochon, subjugating the stones and their color to the design (In his own mind, this was the closest he ever came to painting). He later would change the designs by removing the stones or some of the stones to accentuate elements of positive and negative space.[70]

Art Smith, ring, sterling silver, moonstone, garnet. *Collection of Jill Crawford, photograph by Marbeth Schon.*

Art Smith, ring, sterling silver, turquoise, amethyst, rose quartz. *Collection of Jill Crawford, photograph by Marbeth Schon.*

Ed Wiener, ring, sterling, turquoise. *Collection of Lisa Cliff, photograph by Lisa Cliff.*

Milton Cavagnaro, pendant, sterling silver, ebony, 2-1/2" x 1". *Collection of Joanne and Fred Doloresco, photograph by Fred Doloresco.*

Milton Cavagnaro was skilled at combining natural materials such as wood, bone, or shell with silver. He used various woods like many jewelers use stones; ebony, because of it's close-grain is beautifully contrasted with silver. He also used black walnut and vermillion woods. Wood is sometimes the dominant element; the metal (aluminum, brass, or silver) serves as an accent or an inlay. At other times the silver and wood make equal statements. He uses bone in a similar way to wood though it has totally different form and texture.

Elsa Fruend's "stones" are a skillful combination of pottery and glass. She started to work with jewelry in the latter part of the 1940s with a group of students who were attending the summer art school she and her husband had opened in Eureka Springs, Arkansas. "I was teaching weaving and fabrics and several of the crafts" she recalled, "but jewelry had not entered my mind at all." Nor had ceramics, but her students wanted to study the medium. "Why not?" Elsa said, "We'll simply go out and get native clay and see what we can do with it."[71]

Searching the surrounding hills, Freund and her students found a good source of clay in a nearby cave. Back at the school, they pinched off bits of the clay and fired them. When the bits of clay blew up in the kiln, Freund said she "learned a good lesson from the child approach." Because she also knew nothing about glazes, she and her students pulverized glass and fired it with the clay. This first experiment was the basis for her later jewelry; "the beauty of the glass, translucent and fractured on the clay base", inspired her.

Elsa Freund, pendant, sterling silver wire, ceramic/glass "stones", 3" x 1-5/8". *Collection of Jill Crawford, photograph by Shirley Byrne.*

Charles Loloma, cuff, sterling silver, gold, turquoise, 2-7/8" wide x 2-1/4" (inside diameter). *Collection of Jill Crawford, photograph by Marbeth Schon.*

Mary Schimff, two rings, right: 14k gold, lapis, turquoise, pearl, left: sterling silver, 14k gold, hand-cut amethyst, coral, peridot. *Courtesy of Mary Schimff, photograph by Marbeth Schon.*

Though Charles Loloma's jewelry is deeply rooted in his Native American background his expressive use of stones, wood, ivory, and other materials set him apart from others working in that tradition. He was a modernist responsible for "the renaissance and diversity of styles of Native American jewelry in the second half of the 20th century."[72]

Desiring to learn to cut her own stones, Mary Schimpff traveled to Germany to study silversmithing and stonecutting. While there, she was inspired by master stonecutter, Bernd Munsteiner. Schimpff wanted to create odd, unusual designs in stone that would enhance the designs she made in metal. She now cuts many of her own stones, assembling the shapes like a sculptor and juxtaposing the colors like an abstract expressionist painter.

Part of Peter Macchiarini's genius was his ability to combine and assemble a variety of materials into complex jewelry constructions. Like Margaret De Patta, he also designed the shapes of his stones to enhance his designs in metal and had them cut by San Francisco lapidary Francis Sperisen.

Daniel Macchiarini, pendant, sterling silver, 14k gold, opt-cut rutilated quartz mounted in Peter Macchiarini-designed saddle bezel, Australian turquoise, moonstone. *Collection of Marbeth Schon, photograph by Marbeth Schon.*

Byron Wilson used many of the same materials as Peter Macchiarini, combining ivory, wood, and bone in mostly abstract forms.

Stanley Lechtzin's electroformed jewelry from the 1960s combines highly textured three-dimensional surfaces with crystals and slices of agate that work within his structures without the interference of prongs and bezels.

In the jewelry of Svetozar and Ruth Radakovich, stones were used as Toza (Svetozar) said like "a bit of salt on the food." They were a "touch" not used for intrinsic value but because they enhanced the design of the jewelry.[73]

Byron Wilson, necklace, sterling silver, ebony, walrus ivory, 8-3/4" x 8- 7/8" x 1/4"deep, c. 1960. *Courtesy of Mobilia Gallery, Cambridge, Massachusetts.*

Stanley Lechtzin, brooch, electroformed silver gilt, agate, 96 Biwa Pearls, 6-1/2" x 3" x 1-1/4". *Courtesy of Stanley Lechtzin.*

Svetozar (Toza) Radakovich, brooch, 18k gold, aquamarine, 2-11/16" wide x 1-5/8" high, forged, c. 1963. *Collection of Jean Radakovich, photograph by Jean Radakovich.*

Enamels

Enameling, fusing a glass-like coating onto a metallic base, is closely related to the study of ceramics (glazes) and painting. As early as the 13th century, artisans were fusing enamels to gold rings. Modernist jewelers create miniature abstract compositions with enamels on various metals and sometimes frame them in silver or gold. Enamels, like stones, are also used for emphasis and color.

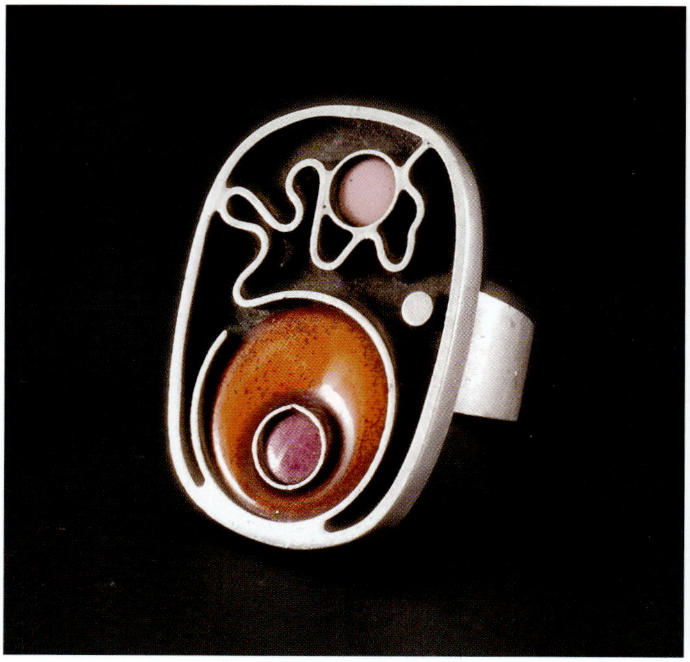

James Parker, ring, sterling silver, enamel, top: 1-3/8" x 1". *Collection of Jill Crawford, photograph by Shirley Byrne.*

James Parker, ring, sterling silver, enamel, top: 7/8" x 1". *Collection of Jill Crawford, photograph by Shirley Byrne.*

James Parker, ring, sterling silver, stone, top: 7/8" diameter. *Collection of Jill Crawford, photograph by Shirley Byrne.*

Master enamellist Karl Drerup approached the medium as a painter—he studied graphic arts under Hans Meid at the Academy in Berlin in 1926 and painting with Felice Carena in Florence, Italy. While visiting the Whitney Museum of Art in 1937 he was impressed by the enamels of Edward Winter. He later met Hungarian-born ceramicist Francis J. von Tury from whom he learned about glazes and artist/ designer Tomi Parzinger who encouraged him to explore enameling on metal. Drerup's work is mostly narrative and/or based on nature, but the style of his painting is closely related to cubism.[74]

Doris Hall's beginnings as a painter are evidenced in her enamels. They are at once figural and abstract—freeform and colorful, at times referencing the decorative paintings of Viennese Secessionist painter Gustav Klimpt.

Karl Drerup, brooch, enamel on sterling silver, 1-3/4" x 3-1/8". Collection of Joanne and Fred Doloresco, photograph by Fred Doloresco.

Doris Hall, bracelet, earrings and ring, enamel on sterling, *Collection of Lisa Cliff. Photograph by Lisa Cliff.*

Mary Kretsinger, *Butterfly* pendant, 18k gold, *cloisonné* enamel, opal, pendant: 4" x 3-1/8", cord: 20", c. 1986. *Courtesy of the Josephine A. Wallace Trust, photograph by Sheila Pamfiloff.*

In the *cloisonné* technique of enameling, strips of gold, silver, copper or brass are attached to the metal base to form a network of small raised cells--a border to hold in the enamels. Layers of enamel are built up and fired separately until the enamel is thick enough so that the cloisons are only visible as a network of wires. Then the surface is ground smooth so the enamel is level with the tops of the *cloisons*. The techniques of *cloisonné* enameling pre-date 4000 BC when the ancient Egyptians set semi-precious stones into jewelry by cold cementing, such as in the gold mask of Tutankhamun.

Mary Kretsinger is renowned for her experimental approach to enameling. She worked mainly in silver and brass combined with enamels in a type of *cloisonné* work. She said that she liked using enamels in small areas so that their "preciousness" was not lost. Her complex forms in gold and silver with added stones and granulation create an almost Byzantine effect.[75]

Earl Pardon joined his love of painting and metalsmithing in his colorful enamel work. His later jewelry designs and large installations were mostly works in enamels and silver or enamels with a combination of other metals such as bronze and copper. Pardon worked with a combination of techniques including cloisonné, fabrication, and inlay.

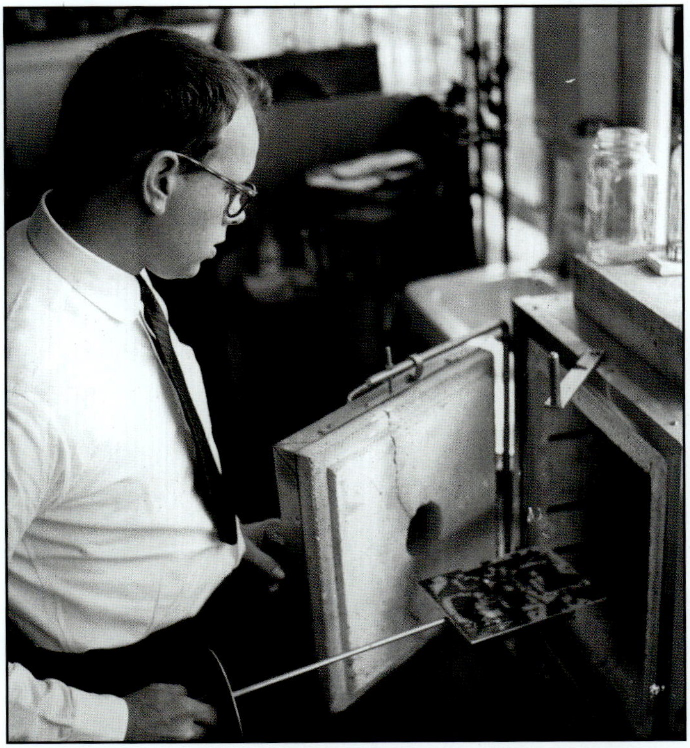

Earl Pardon at his enameling kiln, c.1957. *Courtesy of Tod Pardon.*

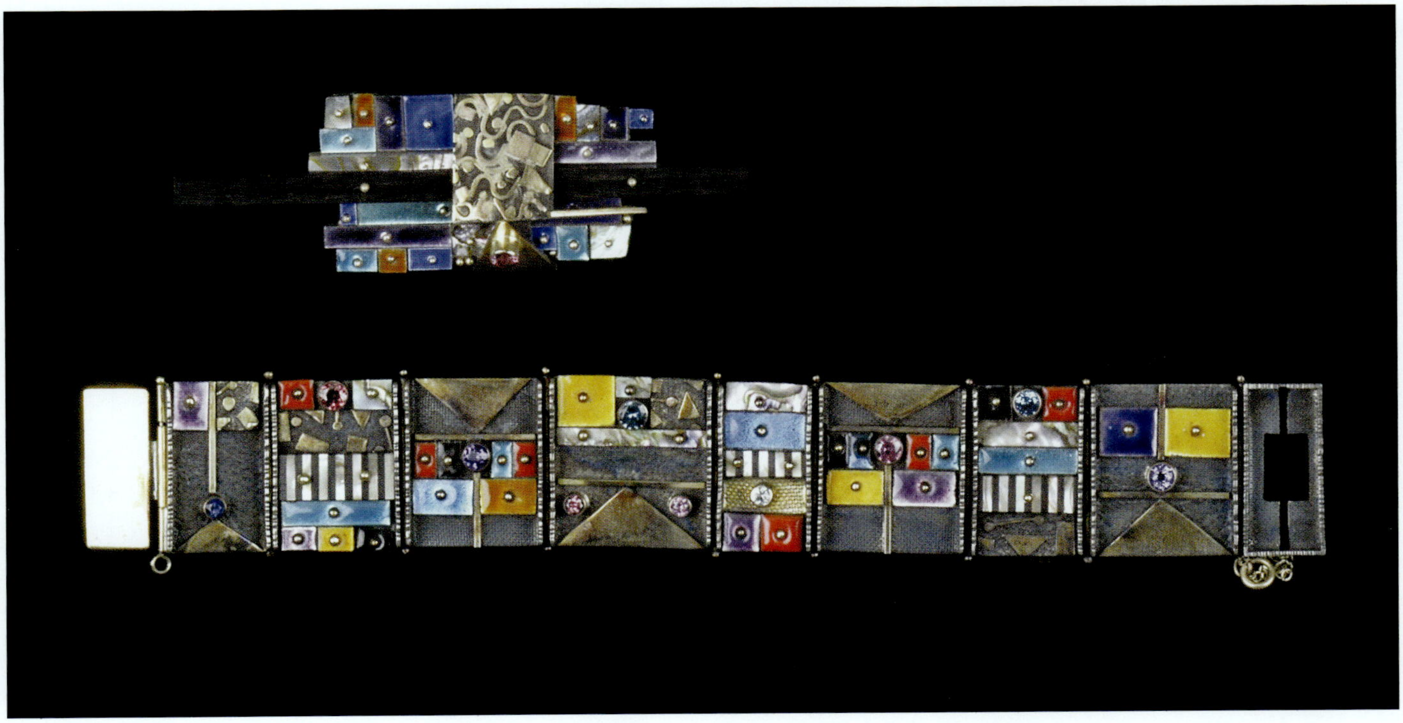

Earl Pardon, brooch and bracelet, sterling silver, 14k gold, enamels, semiprecious stones, brooch: 3-1/2" x 1", bracelet: 6-1/2" x 1", *Courtesy of Mark McDonald, 555 Warren St., Hudson, New York, photograph by Bill Hibbs.*

merry renk, hair comb, *Once Upon a Time,* sterling silver and *plique-a-jour* enamel, 7" x 6", *Collection of Marbeth Schon, photo by Shirley Byrne.*

Doris Hall while showing it in the 1940s in her Chicago gallery, 750 Studio. "All three of us (renk and her two partners Mary Jo Slick and Olive Oliver) had been trained as painters, more or less, that was…our interest, I guess. And seeing [that] enamel was a fantastic, brilliance of color, and such a possibility…we were all very excited about it."

In the same interview merry relates how she discovered the technique of "plique a jour" by accident:

> …One day I was working with this kiln that we had built ourselves, and I had a sheet of copper with a wire that I twisted into a spiral and laid it on top and then covered with some transparent enamel. We had used a fork…so this particular piece, I put in the kiln and we carried it in on a firebrick, which can be put in high heat of about 1,500 degrees. And it has little holes and you have a…long handled fork, and the brick in there with the copper, with the enamel powder that is dried very carefully on top of it and gently set it in, and then you watch it through a little peephole because it has orange red heat in there. So you look in and you see the piece is showing a gloss. So you open the door of the kiln…and you take your fork in and you get it back into the holes in the little brick and you bring this hot brick out. Well, as I was doing that on this piece, I bumped the side of the kiln and the metal wire slipped off the sheet and slipped forward, halfway off the metal. And I brought it out and set it down and it cooled. And there I had metal separation with a clear window, the enamel happened to be red, and it had a transparency that you looked through…like a stained-glass window.

renk went on to create numerous unique, richly hued pieces using wire work with *plique a jour* enameling.

Both merry renk and Florence Resnikoff have used the ancient techniques of *plique-a-jour*. Resnikoff also worked in champlevé enameling.

In champlevé enameling, recesses are created in metal, either by casting, chasing, or engraving and then filled with opaque colored enamels.

It is thought that the *plique-a-jour* technique of enameling was first used around the 13th Century. In *plique a jour*, translucent or transparent enamels form a span across a network of cells without a metal backing. The enamel becomes the structure of the piece and is supported only by the network of metal cells. Finished pieces have the look of a stained glass window.

In 2001, in an interview with Arline Fisch for the *Archives of American Art,* Smithsonian Institution, merry renk talks about being inspired by the work of

Plastics

Margaret De Patta said, "Jewelry of today uses all conceivable materials from wood, bone, pebbles, leather, ceramics, to the time honored precious metals, plus some new materials such as steel, aluminum, a variety of metal alloys and some composition plastic materials. The best designers using these materials handle them directly, boldly and in a manner to emphasize the particular characteristics of the material."[78] In today's world, the ubiquitous overuse of plastics has become the bane of environmentalists—blight on our ecosystem. In the mid-20th century, however, plastics were just beginning to become a part of popular culture and their use held innumerable possibilities for industry and also for artists.[76]

In the 1940s the use of plastics was relatively new and experimental within the sphere of artistic design; plastics distinctive properties created unique challenges for the designer—a sheet of plastic has no natural form or texture, it's only original attributes being color (unless clear), transparency or opaqueness, and reflectivity, yet the medium could be molded and shaped at will.

Armand Winfield, internationally known for his innovations in plastics, was one of the first to work out a commercial embedding process in acrylics in 1945. In order to procure funds to continue his experiments in plastics in 1946, he turned to his brother, Rodney Winfield, who was an art student at the Cooper Union in New York. Together they came up with an idea of getting art students and teachers to create original miniature works of art that Armand could then embed into plastics. The finished pieces could be worn as jewelry or simply kept as indestructible art objects. Armand would supply all the raw materials for the artists and pay each a commission when their work was sold.[77]

On January 20, 1946, the Winfields showed the first pieces at the RoKo Gallery and later they rented a small shop at 184 West 4th Street in Greenwich Village.

Materials used by the artists to make the jewelry were pure gold, fine silver and gems. The findings and accessories were also made of precious metals. Artists were given the materials and tools they needed. Tools included styli for raising designs on the metal shims, tiny scissors and jeweler's pliers. In addition to the gold and silver and both precious and semi-precious gems, gold and silver wires, uncut stones and a variety of less precious metals and wires including copper, brass, and phosphor bronze were provided. Winfield described the process:

> To this list, the artist would add such items as milkweed floss, broken glass and mirrors, colored waxes, bark, sand, stones, colored string, or yarn, colored papers, and/or tissue, canvas, clay, silver foil, glitter, feathers, and fabrics, or whatever else struck the artistic fancy...Often the artist would choose to indicate an outline for an outside shape...Together, we often decided whether a piece was to become a pin or a pendant or an embellishment for a case or compact. The beauty of the process was that we could take a piece of metal and highly polish it. Once embedded, the shine was locked in permanently with no chance of oxidation. Tiny gold and silver wires, thinner than a human hair could be manipulated into equally tiny sculpture which would collapse if touched, yet inside the clear acrylics sheath was ever protected and could be handled and worn. Silver repousse, burnished copper, and tiny oil paintings, watercolors, prints, and etchings found long life and permanence through the medium. Waxes would melt during processing but would solidify in situ, providing color and textures unlike any seen before. Certain fabrics took on new depth dimensions inside the acrylic cover...Some of our jewelry was pictorial; miniature paintings and sculpture, others were abstract--Art Deco in feeling, some dealt with nature, others were religious or spiritual; still others were mythical or mystical. Some were allegorical, some had childlike innocence, others were humorous. Some pieces combined several ideas and styles; some were even grotesque.

The body of art produced by Winfield Fine Art in Jewelry within the two and a half years of its existence, represented almost every mid-20th century design innovation or movement, including montage, collage, assemblage, abstraction, surrealism, cubism, minimalism and biomorphism. Many of Winfield's artists were already exhibiting at major museums and galleries and a number of the young Cooper Union students whom Rodney and Armand persuaded to join this project later became famous painters, sculptors, writers and designers.

Winfield Fine Art in Jewelry, brooch by Lilly Ascher, red beads, wire and other materials encased in acrylics, 2-1/2" x 1-3/4", c. 1947-1948. *Collection of Armand Winfield, photograph by Shirley Byrne.*

Palestinian native Zahara Schatz, whose father founded the Bezalel Art School and Museum in Israel, worked in plastics, laminating the material with bits of wire, sequins, and colored materials. Her fascination with plastics began in the late 1940s and early 50s when she began making small Plexiglas pendants and wide bracelets with arrangements of miniature metal shapes. She later worked with trays, bowls, lamp bases, screens, murals, layer paintings, and sculpture. Her work was done exclusively in Plexiglas, a thermoplastic substance (polymethyl methacrylate) that retains its shape after being molded with heat.[78]

Schatz was excited about the components she couldn't completely control. Her collages created space and new textures of their own when pressed by the lamination process. Plastic sculptures, because of their transparent qualities, would change when the light shone through or on them at different angles. She strove to create abstract designs out of the natural materials she collected; an exercise she admitted was extremely difficult. "Design, she said, must be an organization of many elements: space, line, texture, chiaroscuro, planes and forms."

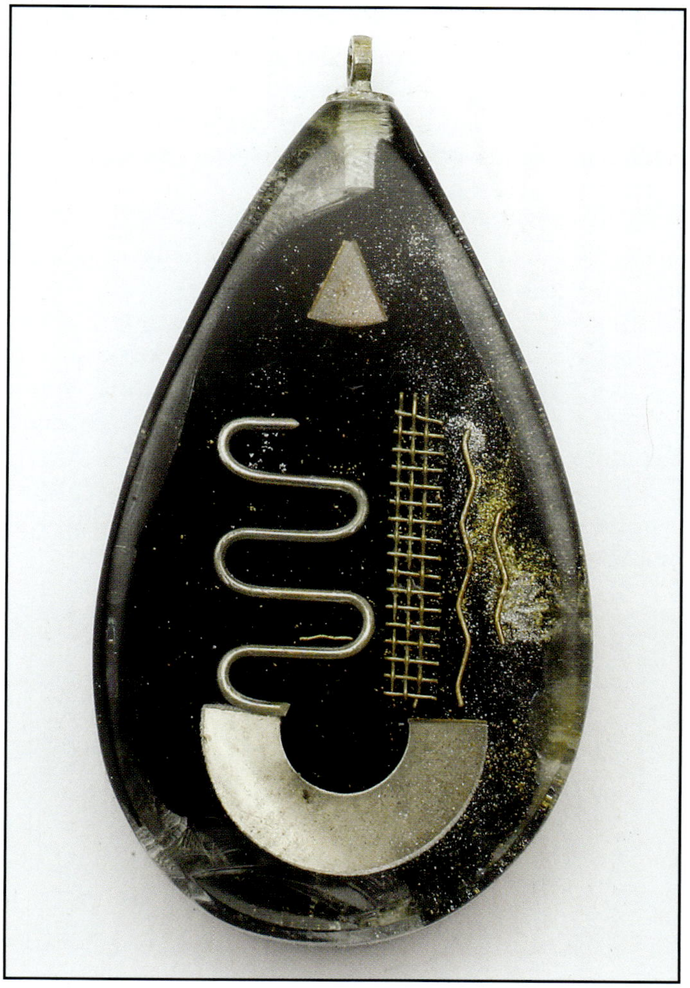

Glass

Another material that added the dimension of transparency to jewelry was glass.

Donald-Brian Johnson, in an article for *Modernism* magazine entitled *"Frances Higgins House of Glass,"* describes one of Frances Higgins' pastimes as a little girl in rural Haddock, Georgia. She liked to make "flower viewers." She dug shallow holes at random spots along Georgia byways, lined each with the heads of colorful wildflowers, then covered the holes with pieces of clear glass. After she had smoothed earth over the edges of the glass, her flower viewers were complete." [79]

This idea of seeing "into a design" was used by Michael and Frances Higgins in their fused glass objects and also their jewelry, though jewelry was actually a small percentage of their total output.

Part of the magic of Higgin's glass is that it is formed from ordinary windowpanes using the art of glass fusing—essentially the creation of a "glass sandwich' that had its origins in ancient times. Higgin's multi-colored creations in fused glass are made by first producing a mold with a highly calculated artistic design, next an original pattern is created upon a piece of glass upon which a matching piece of glass is then placed. "Both go into the mold, then into a kiln where the two pieces of glass are fused into one--thus the combined beauty of form, design and color is imprisoned forever." [80]

Frances Higgins, necklace, glass, brass, 14" (circumference) x 1-1/4" wide. *Collection of Joanne and Fred Doloresco, photograph by Fred Doloresco.*

Zahara Schatz, pendant, Plexiglas, brass screen, copper wire, stainless steel wire, washer, 1-1/2" x 3/4". *Collection of Steve Cabella, photograph by Geoff Turner.*

CHAPTER 6
Techniques

Bob Winston, brooch, sterling silver, pearl, 1-3/8" x 2". *Collection of Joanne and Fred Doloresco, photograph by Fred Doloresco.*

Casting

Most jewelers use some form of casting to create certain parts or the totality of their forms.

Bob Winston was one of the first jewelers to experiment with the lost-wax method of casting by centrifuge. In 1942 he began teaching at the California College of Arts and Crafts in Oakland and by 1945 this process had become an integral part of his teaching program. He was chiefly responsible for the implementation of the lost-wax method by such artist-jewelers as Irena Brynner, Robert Dhaemers and many others. The lost-wax casting course created a great deal of interest; it was the first time the subject had been included in the curriculum of an institution of higher learning. The emphasis of the course was on developing designs that were possible only with the lost wax casting technique.

Robert Dhaemers credits Bob Winston as the inspiration for his work in lost wax casting which is the process he perfected to produce his sculptural forms. Dhaemers creates textures in the negative plaster mold from which he obtains his wax piece in the positive. The wax is then further embellished before casting. Dhaemers also uses actual seedpods, which he casts in the lost wax process to create fascinating naturalistic metal forms with intricate negative and positive spatial relationships. He works with a variety of metals including brass, copper, steel, and vari-colored gold and he prefers to use synthetic stones because, unlike natural stones, they do not change color or fracture during the casting process.[81]

Robert Dhaemers, necklace, patinated bronze, synthetic ruby, pendant: 5-1/2" x 2-1/2", neckring: 8" diameter, c. 1964, exhibited at the Museum of Contemporary Crafts "Creative Casting" in 1964. *Collection of the artist, photograph by Shirley Byrne.*

Olaf Skoogfors created many of his more sculptural forms using the lost wax casting process, introduced to him by Ruth and Svetozar Radakovich. He often added reticulation and chasing and sometimes fused textures. His jewelry designs were strong statements of abstraction imbued with a sense of naturalism. He juxtaposed smooth and textured surfaces and used stones like "exclamation points within his visual statements."[82]

Svetozar and Ruth Radokovich worked with both forged and casting techniques, sometimes combining both within one piece. When their work was entirely cast it was done in very small series and finished by hand. Ruth said that she did as much work on each cast piece as she did on the original. Their work was sold through Shop One in Rochester and also a gallery called Nanny's in San Francisco as well as the Lee Nordness Gallery in New York. The Radakovichs' approach to forged and cast jewelry in the late fifties had a distinct impact upon the younger generation of artists beginning to work in this art form.

Olaf Skoogfors, belt buckle, bronze, silver, *Photograph courtesy of The Sarah Bodine & Michael Dunas Archives of 20th Century Jewelry, Tyler School of Art, Temple University, Professor Stanley Lechtzin, Curator of Metals/Jewelry Archives and Collections.*

Svetozar (Toza) Radakovich, bracelet, gold, turquoise, 2-1/4" high x 2-1/2" diameter, forged, with cast elements, c. 1960s. *Collection of Jean Radakovich, photograph by Jean Radakovich.*

Arline Fisch, brooch, sterling silver, ebony, ivory, wood, 2-1/4 x 2-1/2. *Collection of Joanne and Fred Doloresco, photograph by Fred Doloresco.*

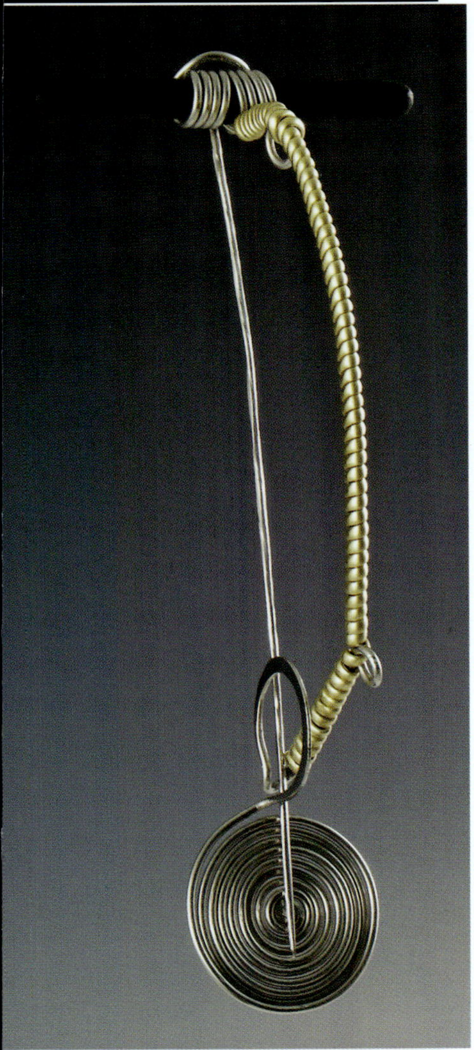

Phillip Fike, *Fibula* brooch. *Courtesy of Daniella Kerner and Stanley Lechtzin.*

The Influence and Revival of Historical Styles and Techniques

In 2001, in an interview with Sharon Church for the Archives of American Art, Smithsonian Institution, Arline Fisch spoke about her enjoyment of studying historical objects:

> I try, when I go to museums, to do two things. One, to appreciate what I'm looking at, just to see it, but then to isolate a few pieces that I really look at in detail. I study and I draw not with any purpose in mind. I mean, I don't go looking for specific things. I just try to be open-minded and keep my eyes open. It's interesting that every time I go back to the same place, I see something different. I've probably spent more time at the Metropolitan in the Egyptian collection than most people, and I still see a new thing that I didn't see before, every time I visit. I'm surprised, delighted, inspired...I don't go looking for specific things, but I go with an open mind. And again, I've probably looked at the pre-Columbian gold at the Metropolitan in their treasury in the Michael Rockefeller wing hundreds of times, but I still love looking at it, and I still notice something new that I didn't notice before..."

Robert Ebendorf is also inspired by ancient objects:

> I've learned much about form, metal, and the uses of materials by going to museums; they have been like research centers for me. I can see the heritage the goldsmiths and silversmiths have handed down, and I feel I'm part of it. It surprises me that today I'm using many of the same tools and some of the same techniques that were used in the Middle Ages. Going to museums has thus helped me better understand what early craftsmen did, I've learned how to use their techniques in my work. [83]

In the latter 1950s and into the 1960s, many metalsmiths that were held in especially high regard were associated with the pioneering or revival of specific techniques. For example, Phillip Fike mastered niello and the fibula form, John Paul Miller revived the technique of granulation, Margret Craver reinvented en résille enameling, and Stanley Lechtzin began the use of electroforming to create jewelry. [84]

These dedicated artist/craftsmen were responsible for expanded thought and experimentation in techniques and esthetics in metal arts both on a studio level and in universities. The techniques of the past were articulated in fresh forms and expressions.

"An artist often does not set out consciously to make a specific contribution. The serious metalsmith certainly does not; rather he is captivated by an idea, a material, a technique, a process of some historical influence." [85]

Philip Fike's romance with the fibula began in 1964 in Rome where he became interested in the bronze and gold pins of the Etruscans, who gave them the name of "fibula' "The fibula was not only a spiritual object which reflected a culture, but was also an artistic sculpture which solved the problem a clasp does." Fike said that the "modern safety pin reflects our distance from potential variety and meaning inherent in the ancient clasp. It functions automatically without concern for pride of display." Fike was able to achieve unity of the mechanical and the decorative.

Fike also experimented with the process of niello. While studying applied art under Arthur Vierthaler at the University of Wisconsin in Madison under the GI Bill, Fike found the book *Silver and Jewelry* by Henry Wilson with an introduction to niello (a technique of metal ornamentation which uses an alloy of sulfur with copper, silver or lead that turns silver a blue-black color). Fike experimented with the process and began to use it in his work. [86]

John Paul Miller's exquisite and painstaking work with granulation created an astoundingly intricate and beautiful body of work in jewelry.

John Paul Miller at his workbench, photograph from an article titled *John Paul Miller, The Complete Artist* by Francis Taft, Cleveland Institute of Art. *Courtesy of The Sarah Bodine & Michael Dunas Archives of 20th Century Jewelry, Tyler School of Art, Temple University, Professor Stanley Lechtzin, Curator of Metals/Jewelry Archives and Collections.*

Phillip Fike at his work bench, *The Mad Professor*. Photograph by Phillip Fike. *Courtesy of The Sarah Bodine & Michael Dunas Archives of 20th Century Jewelry, Tyler School of Art, Temple University, Professor Stanley Lechtzin, Curator of Metals/Jewelry Archives and Collections.*

Phillip Fike with torch in his workshop, photograph by Phillip Fike. *Courtesy of The Sarah Bodine & Michael Dunas Archives of 20th Century Jewelry, Tyler School of Art, Temple University, Professor Stanley Lechtzin, Curator of Metals/Jewelry Archives and Collections.*

The technique of attaching tiny beads of gold to a gold surface without the use of solder had been perfected by the ancient Romans, but lost after the fall of the Roman Empire. "In 1940 I happened to come across photos of granulation by Elizabeth Treskow in a German art magazine called *Die Kunst*," Miller recalled, "I couldn't understand the German and I knew nothing about granulation - including its name - but the work fascinated me."[87]

After much trial and error, Miller discovered that he could attach gold granules to gold without solder by causing copper to oxidize on the surface of the granules and then heating the gold--in the presence of copper, gold melts at a lower temperature than usual so the presence of the copper allows the adhesion of the gold granule. Later experimentation with the process allowed him to create larger shapes and designs in gold that show no visible joints.

John Paul Miller, pendant/brooch, *Plant Form*, pure and oxidized gold, c. 1960s, exhibited at the 1974 May Show at the Cleveland Museum of Art. *Collection of Terry Kovel, Photograph and information courtesy of Terry Kovel.*
About this piece, John Paul Miller said it was a favorite and one of the most difficult he had ever made. He had been doing granulated gold pieces by heating the 18k gold granules and then "gluing" them to the 24k pieces by heating them in an oxygen reduction kiln. This piece was made with gold chips of 18k and 24k gold. He heated the piece, melting and oxidizing the 18k gold. He then chased the surface because he did not like a regular shiny surface.
An atomic scientist saw the piece and asked him to make a similar one. He did. These are the only two he made by this method.

In 1950, fascinated by old world techniques, Margret Craver reinvented the intricate seventeenth-century enameling technique called *en résille*. Some fifteen examples of this fragile sixteenth-century French technique exist in museums of the Western world. The Victoria and Albert Museum labels its few as very rare and the literature on the process is limited to a few sentences and pertains to only one piece now owned by the British Museum" [88]

In *en resille* enameling, depressions formed in thin pieces of glass are lined with gold foil, filled with enamel, and fired in a kiln. Withers cut her glass from windowpanes. "I had to cut it and fix it...myself," she said, "Once you start working with a material you have to do the whole thing!" It was very difficult to keep the glass from cracking and warping, but through much trial and error, Withers managed to create several exquisite examples, which she framed in beautiful raised and soldered gold bezels. "It took forever," Withers says, " because this was such an ancient technique and no one knew a darn thing about it and I had to know, but since there was no way to think about how to get that information from a museum or anyone who owned a piece of it, I had to just start out and do it myself and I was pretty good at inventing and going after a way to do something because I wanted to do it. It was a challenge and I was good at looking." [89]

Craver's designs in *en resile* are technically and artistically exquisite—she has used an ancient technique to create designs that are decidedly modern.

Margret Craver Withers, pendant, e*n resille* enamel, 18k and 22k gold, *Courtesy of Mobilia Gallery, Cambridge, Massachusetts.*

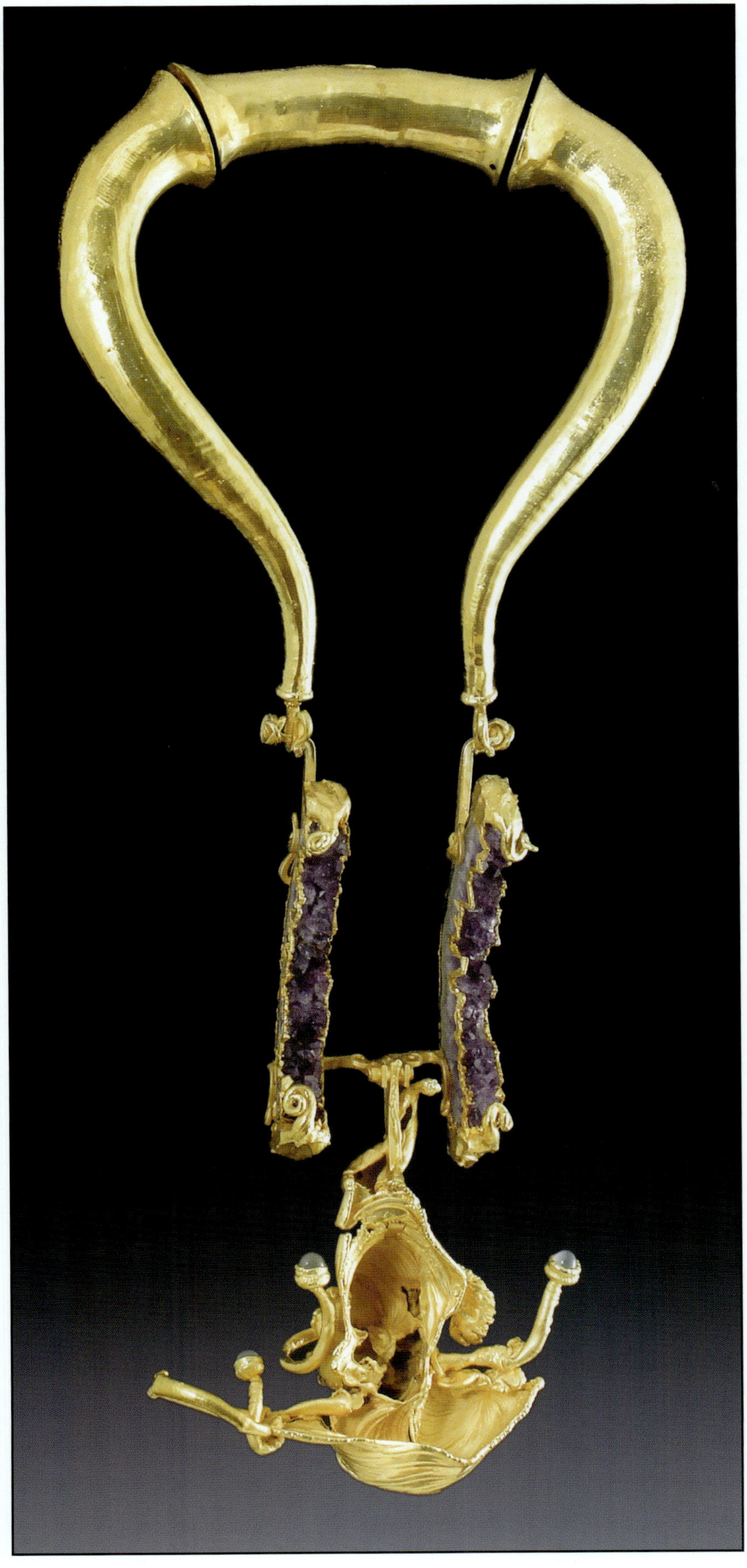

After graduating from Cranbrook Academy of Art, Stanley Lechtzin applied for teaching positions on college campuses. He was offered the opportunity to be a partner in a jewelry business, but instead accepted a teaching position at Tyler School of Art, Temple University in Philadelphia, Pennsylvania. At Tyler, he taught ceramics for two years and developed the jewelry and metalsmithing department.[90] After five years at Tyler, Lechtzin opened the graduate program in metals. His postgraduate work was involved with researching the possibilities of large, lightweight, wearable jewelry. He studied electroforming processes, which he initiated into the metalsmithing field. Lechtzin was one of the first craftsmen to experiment extensively with electroforming in jewelry making. Although the technique dates back to industrial uses in the early nineteenth century, it was not until the 1960s that it was used in the arts. As well as enabling the formation of large, lightweight structures, Lechtzin stated that electroforming opened other form and structural possibilities that he would not have predicted before beginning his work in that technique. Later studies in plastics led him to the successful use of both electroforming and plastics in this field. Lechtzin's electroformed jewelry from the 1960s is powerful and three-dimensional with a rugged quality as if it were "broken" from some natural highly textured surface like bark or fractured stone and at the same time, ethereal—otherworldly—a dichotomy that clearly sets it apart from other jewelry of its time.

Stanley Lechtzin, *Torque*, electroformed silver gilt, amethyst, moontones, 8" x 18". *Courtesy of Stanley Lechtzin.*

Florence Resnikoff also used the process of electroforming to create jewelry. She received a fellowship from the National Endowment for the Arts to study electroforming techniques and their application to jewelry and metalsmithing and enrolled in a graduate workshop conducted by Stanley Lechtzin at Tyler School of Art. She then set up her studio to probe its potential with the related processes of electrotexturing.

Resnikoff finds little need to remain fixed in the techniques and materials of the past. She also believes that we can learn and enjoy the contributions of other cultures without borrowing extraneous symbols--"we can learn from them and our own cultural past without having to romanticize their methodologies."[91]

Production vs. Handmade

One of the most passionate, ongoing debates within the metal arts community is between craftsmen that produce only one-of-a-kind objects and those that are involved with the mass or limited production of objects.

In the early 1950s Peter Macchiarini and Margaret De Patta, both members of the San Francisco Metal Arts Guild, had opposing philosophies on the subject of mass production. The major art design schools, as well as some metal artists, including Margaret De Patta, thought that mass production did not, in and of itself, affect their work. The demand for De Patta's work far exceeded the supply at the time she decided to begin production of her jewelry--the value of her work had risen to the point where it could only be purchased by those who could afford luxury prices and this was a problem for her philosophically. "I had become aware of the contradictions between my social viewpoints and my method of work, " she wrote. It was distressing for her to contradict the Bauhaus philosophy of social integration. "It seems to me that a creative artist has a social responsibility to produce not the single highly priced handmade article for extremely limited consumption," she stated, "but to produce the best possible in design, workmanship and materials to give pleasure to the largest number of people possible."[92]

Peter Macchiarini strongly believed, in opposition to Margaret De Patta, that when an artist began to design so that a machine could mass manufacture his work, the design integrity was compromised and the work stopped being art. In Peter's words, "The development of the artist will stop with his attempts to curb his designing to the machine." He also held that machine mass production destroyed the positive relationship between the consumer who used and purchased it. Macchiarini alleged that jewelry, when designed well, was in actuality "wearable sculpture," and that the consumers who bought it and used their person as the vehicle of displaying the work were saying as much about themselves and the emotions of their personal aesthetics as the artist was in creating the work to begin with. "This intimate connection between creator/artist and consumer/displayer is completely destroyed by the interference of mass production. Not only is the individuality of the work eliminated, but also the uniqueness, spontaneity and creativity of the production process....This tremendous gap from the first onslaught of the Industrial Revolution to the beginning of the 20th Century, amongst other things, brought to the attention of the more romantically inclined that while it was true that a design could be made for the machine to produce a superior cooking utensil or a better pail...it did not speak for the soul." [93]

Peter Macchiarini, brooch, sterling silver, brass, copper, 3-5/8" x 1-3/8". *Courtesy of Historical Design, Inc., photo ©HD, Inc.*

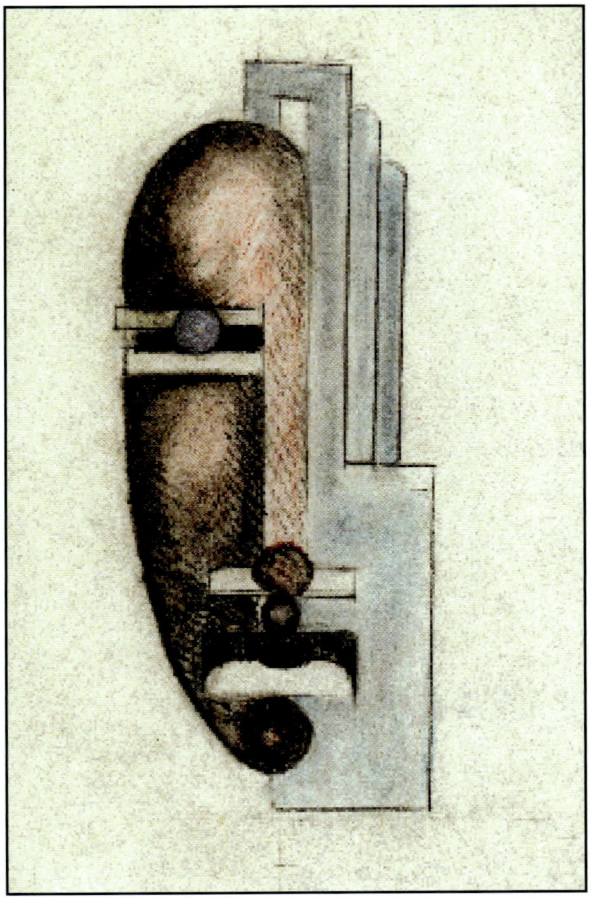

Peter Macchiarini, mask design #1.
Courtesy of Daniel Macchiarini.

Peter Macchiarini, hinged bracelet, sterling silver, brass, rutilated quartz 7/8″ wide x 3″ wide x 8″ long. *Collection of Jill Crawford, photograph by Shirley Byrne.*

Greenwich Village jeweler, Idella La Vista, in harmony with the views of Peter Macchiarini, said, "...The designer-craftsman...creates, or should create, unique objects and designs that are beautifully made and functional as well. At the risk of sounding mystical, for me, the work of a craftsman has soul; it has individual touch. He has worked and shaped his material, he struggled with it, has given it time, care and love, and has created something beautiful for the world, and has, at the same time, given artistic expression to himself. It is this quality of work which mass production rarely achieves."[94]

Robert and Audrey Engstrom spoke of their lives as working craftsmen, "We have made few concessions either to production or starvation...Somehow the forms that lend themselves to duplication become by this very fact sterile and uninteresting... We are proud of being craftsmen in the sense of doing everything ourselves—casting, stone setting, finishing, babysitting, typing, housework, and tree pruning." [95]

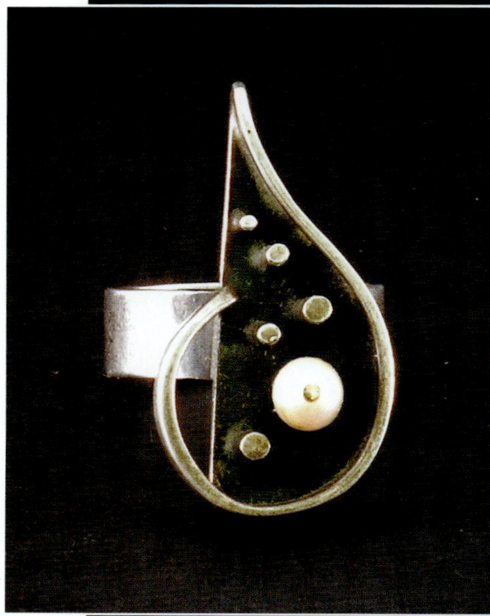

Idella La Vista, ring, sterling silver with pearl, 1-1/8" x 5/8", c. 1950. *Collection of Marbeth Schon, photo by Shirley Byrne.*

Robert and/or Audrey Engstrom, pendant, enamel on copper, 2-5/8" x 1-1/2". *Collection of Munir Meghji, photograph by Munir Meghji.*

Commercial success was not a negative factor in Robert Pearson's approach to a piece of jewelry. "Certain restrictions, such as economic feasibility for commercial manufacturing, are part of the rationale for a design," he said, "These are no more restrictive than restraints encountered because of material limitations." [96]

Ronald Hayes Pearson, pendant and neck ring, sterling silver, agate, pendant: 4-1/4" x 1-1/2", neck ring: 16" overall. *Collection of Rose Foster, photograph by Shirley Byrne.*

Christian Schmidt, who created both cast and hand-constructed jewelry said:

Whether we like to admit it or not, our products on the market are in competition with machine-made articles. The jewelry designs of the large manufacturers are dictated by the limitations of the machine, the prime factors being cost and speed of production. I believe the craftsmen should avoid designs which can be done better by machines and should devote his efforts to work which best exploits and displays his individual artistry and workmanship.

In view of the increasing competition in the handcrafted field, I feel that a craftsman is placing himself at a disadvantage if he does not duplicate those designs which prove to have appeal and salability. Only a relatively few of the top workers survive on custom work alone. If a craftsman's outlets are widespread, a few copies can be sent to each and the "exclusive quality", an important factor to many buyers will be preserved.[97]

Christian Schmidt, *Fish* brooch, sterling silver, red stone. *Collection of Clayton Roach, photograph by Marbeth Schon*

The studio jeweler, who continues to produce one-of-a-kind, handmade pieces, develops close relationships with customers and galleries that purchase his/her work and an awareness of "wearability" and market appeal. To many, such as San Francisco jeweler Daniel Macchiarini, they are satisfying relationships that he would not change:

I will carry on creating pieces that are unique, speak to the world about sculptural modernism... (and) generate a sense of personal uniqueness in those that buy the work I create. They wear it or put it up in their houses and project something positive to the world about themselves, how they view design and art. This would get lost if I went into mass production. The soul and chemistry between the artist and the consumer is destroyed when the machine makes the work. Good design is lost to the machine when an artist is forced to consider the machine in terms of the mass production of the design. The machine takes over. This is OK for cars, furniture, boats, beds and beer cans, but it is not all right for visual art which must come from within the soul and out of the hands of the artists if it is to be true to the creative spirit who originates it.[98]

Daniel Macchiarini, ring, sterling silver, copper, brass, ivory, ebony, top: 2-1/2" x 1-3/8" x 3/16". *Collection of Jill Crawford, photograph by Shirley Byrne.*

In the *Penland School of Crafts Book of Jewelry Making*, Robert Ebendorf speaks about production from the perspective of the university student, "... In a university atmosphere a student can design and make the kind of forms he wants, without caring about whether they will sell. He makes a form because he believes in it. But there is a different audience outside the university with different demands. A craftsman must realize who this audience is and how to deal with it."[99]

CHAPTER 7
Reaching Into The Future

Jeweler Bruce Metcalf, in his essay *On the Nature of Jewelry*, speaks about a new type of jeweler who "feels responsible to concepts and ideals alongside of the economic demands of making a living. Many jewelers insist that their production be completely divorced from the marketplace. To some, jewelry has become a pure expression of thought and feeling, and less connected to the traditional roles of ornament. Stripped of the familiar codes and functions, jewelry has become a modern art form."[100]

[Many] art jewelers of today are "connected with metals programs in college and university art departments and are exposed to the intellectual environment of a university, which develops aesthetically literate artists, who are well aware of the historical, philosophical, social, an psychological bases of artistic expression," explains Arline Fisch, "This education teaches the artist to be both articulate and self-critical. Another benefit, is the pursuit of technical research and experimentation...a serious commitment to the investigation of materials and processes, both old and new." [101]

Academia leads more to experimentation and a cross-fertilization among departments "that is design, painting, textiles, metals, etc.," which contributes "significantly to the look of metalsmithing bearing little resemblance to the past." [102]

In the late 1970s Staley Lechtzin started to look to computers and computer aided technologies as a new way of making jewelry. He believes that artists are the "cultural antenna" of society and in that role address the issues of contemporary society; unique objects have and will continue to maintain importance in society. Reaching into the future, he is engaged in an exploration of how metalsmithing and craft communities are changing to fulfill the continuing need for unique objects in society as well as what the objects will be and how they will be made.[103]

Conclusion

My hope is that jewelry as an expression of art and human emotion will evolve brilliantly and dynamically and without restrictions; that this peculiarly personal form of art may outpace other craft-like media and also forge still farther ahead of the rest of the world, which is still unaware of what is happening in jewelry here. Surely it can be achieved! But only by means of exploration and knowledge, by inspriation and work, by sensibility and wit—and certainly not by throwing away the tools, forgetting the skills, and abandoning all insight into the behavior and spirit of metal itself.[104]—Sam Kramer, 1960[104]

Sam Kramer. Pendant, sterling silver, moonstone, garnet, 2-3/4" x 2". Collection of Jill Crawford, photograph by Marbeth Schon.

Part III
ARTISTS' BIOGRAPHIES

CHAPTER 8
103 American Artist/Jewelers

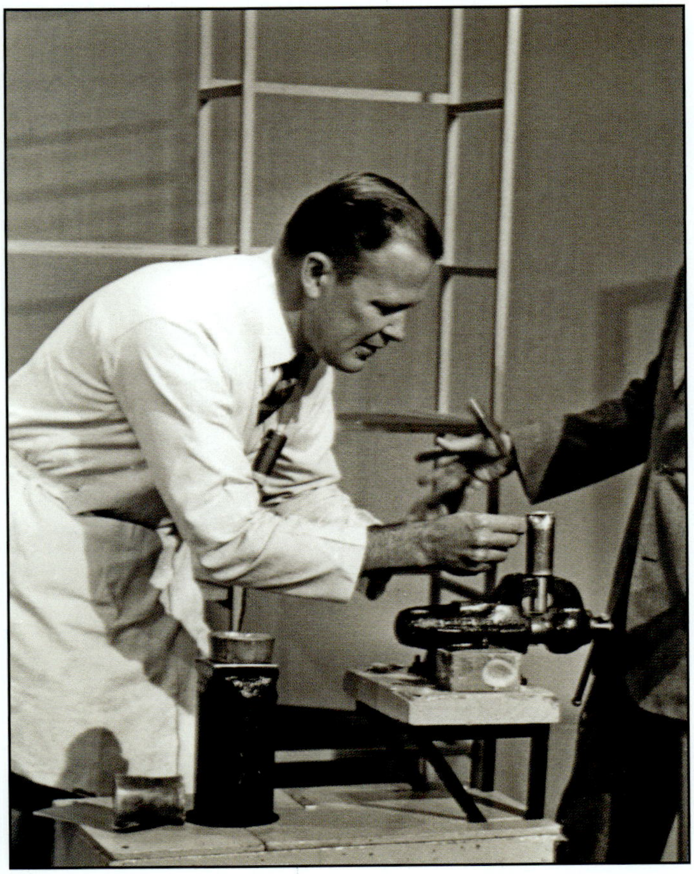

Allan Adler in his workshop about 1956. *Courtesy of The Sarah Bodine & Michael Dunas Archives of 20th Century Jewelry, Tyler School of Art, Temple University, Professor Stanley Lechtzin, Curator of Metals/Jewelry Archives and Collections.*

Allan Adler

"I strive for simplicity and believe that simplicity is beauty and that a thing of beauty lives forever." —Allan Adler

Allan Adler (1916-2002) was a master silversmith who worked in the Arts and Crafts tradition, but expressed himself in the simple clean lines of modernism. He was born in Missoula, Montana but spent his childhood in Burbank, California. He married Rebecca Blanchard (Porter Blanchard's Daughter) in 1948. Since Porter Blanchard had no sons, he persuaded Adler to work for him and learn the fine craft of silversmithing. When Blanchard decided to retire from the retail business, Adler took over the store on Sunset Boulevard. In 1980, after a fire destroyed his shop, he opened a new workshop in the San Fernando Valley as well as La Jolla, Corona del Mar, and San Francisco.

Adler is known primarily for his designs in holloware, but he added jewelry to his repertoire during World War II. The designs of his jewelry, like his hollowware, are usually clean and modern. [1]

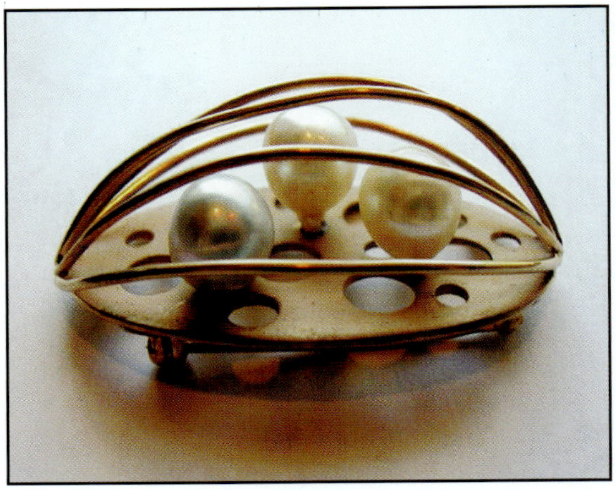

Allan Adler, brooch, 14k gold, pearls, 1-3/4" x 1-1/8". *Collection of Juliette Kontor, photograph by John Kontor.*

Adler's hollowware, jewelry, and especially his flatware became popular among the rich and famous of Hollywood. He also received many important commissions including a silver coffee urn made for a John F. Kennedy presidential campaign fund-raising event. A set of flatware was made for California Governor Pat Brown and a silver hairbrush for Winston Churchill.

Adler was one of the few latter 20th century silversmiths to devote himself full-time to creating silver jewelry and objects for sale from his own shop. He considered himself a member of an endangered species.

Allan Adler's shop about 1956. *Courtesy of The Sarah Bodine & Michael Dunas Archives of 20th Century Jewelry, Tyler School of Art, Temple University, Professor Stanley Lechtzin, Curator of Metals/Jewelry Archives and Collections.*

Adler was awarded a *Living Treasure* proclamation from the state of California legislature and a *Good Design Award* from the Museum of Modern Art in New York. He designed the crowns for Miss Universe and Miss U.S.A in 1953 and the famous silver "shoe" campaign pin for Adlai Stevenson's presidential race in 1959 as well as pins for the first seven American astronauts in space."

Vera Allison

Vera Allison (1902-1993) was born in San Francisco, California on December 5, 1902. After earning her B.A. at the University of California, Berkeley, she worked as a commercial artist art for billboard company, Foster & Kleiser. In 1929, following her marriage to artist George Gaethke, she lived in Berkeley where she worked mostly in gouache (painting local scenes), and made jewelry. In 1949 she exhibited at Gump's in San Francisco. [2]

Vera Allison, earrings, sterling silver, 2 1/4" x 3/4". *Collection of Joanne and Fred Doloresco, photograph by Fred Doloresco.*

Vera Allison, brooch, sterling silver, wood, 2" x 4". *Collection of Steven Cabella, photograph by Geoff Turner.*

Allison was a member of the San Francisco Arts Association, San Francisco Women Artists, and was one of the founders of the San Francisco Metal Arts Guild. In 1967 she moved to Mill Valley where she remained until 1986. She died at her daughter's home in San Cristobal, New Mexico, on August 20, 1993.

Adda Husted-Andersen

"For the many years on 1st Avenue and at Craft Students League, I want to say: Thank you, America." —Adda Husted-Andersen (From a speech in 1982 at the symposium, *American Metalsmithing and Jewelrymaking in the 1940s and 1950s*, sponsored by the Renwick Gallery and the Archives of American Art)

Adda Husted-Andersen (1898-1990) was a native of Denmark. She began working in metal in Copenhagen where she was awarded a medal by the Gold and Silversmith Guild. She later studied at *Badishe Kunstgewerbeschule* in Pforzheim, Germany, and with Jean Dunand in Paris. During World War II she worked at Georg Jensen, Inc. in New York City, and during the three decades following she created jewelry, hollowware, enamels, and flatware in her shop near the United Nations in New York. She was president of the New York Society of Craftsmen for several years and taught jewelry and enameling at the Craft Students League. [3]

Many jewelers, including Pearl Schecter, Walter Rhodes, Mary Kresinger and Alice Zimmerman, studied and were influenced by Husted-Andersen. She worked in platinum, gold and silver. Some of her work was done in free-form wire with added stones and some in cutout geometric silver shapes with wire accents or enamels.

Adda Husted-Andersen, brooch, sterling silver, enamel, 1-1/2" x 1-1/4", *Collection of Marbeth Schon, photograph by Shirley Byrne.*

Lilyan Bachrach

"From my father I learned to inspect what we made, always looking for any faults. His favorite question was, 'Can you make it better?' I still look at my own work in almost the same way. If there is a fault, it is the first thing I spot. If the piece holds together, then I know it is acceptable." [4] —Lilyan Bachrach

Lilyan Bachrach, brooch, enamel on sterling silver, 1-3/8" diameter. *Collection of Joanne and Fred Doloresco, photograph by Fred Doloresco.*

Lilyan Bachrach, brooch, cloisonné enamel, sterling silver, gold foil, gold wire, 2-5/8" x 2-1/8". *Collection of Marbeth Schon, photograph by Shirley Byrne.*

Lilyan Bachrach is a remarkable, versatile enamellist whose oeuvre includes jewelry, wall pieces, plates, bowls, mezuzahs, and switch plates. Her work flows easily between floral and abstract designs; she is equally adept at both. She was born in New Haven Connecticut in 1917, later moving with her family to Lowell, Massachusetts, where her father opened a curtain and drapery store.

In 1934 Bachrach enrolled at Boston University where she studied to be an interior decorator. About that time she met her future husband, Sam Bachrach, who was studying at Tuft's Medical School.

While raising her family, she decided to renew her interest in the arts by taking lessons in various media such as sewing, tray painting, oil painting, silversmithing and jewelry. "I even tried pottery," she said, "but that did not fit in with my life style…it took too long to clean up. When I discovered enameling in 1955, it was just right. With a smock over dress clothes, I could turn off the kiln and leave my work bench within five minutes."

Lilyan was studying silversmithing at Worcester Craft Center in 1955 when her instructor decided to teach enameling. The instruction was non-inspiring, however, so she went back to silversmithing. A friend, who also had taken the class, decided it would be less expensive to get a group together and set up a home workshop. They found eight other housewives, put in forty dollars each, ordered equipment and supplies and set up a workshop in a member's basement. About this time, Doris Hall announced that she would give demonstration lessons. Lilyan and four other members drove to Boston to her studio once a week for about 6 weeks. Doris Hall handled enamels as a painter's medium and Lilyan was attracted to the medium because of the infinite range of colors and their tactile quality. Shortly after, Lilyan studied the technique of cloisonné with Joseph Trippetti for two years and, at his urging, taught enameling for four years to the adult classes at the Worcester Trade School.

By the time Lilyan's fourth child was six years old, she had enough help at home to go back to school. She was accepted as a full time student at the School of the Worcester Art Museum. Throughout the years she studied enameling and/or silversmithing with Bill Kurwacz, Fiometta Shieh, Mary Kretsinger, Charles Jeffrey, Curtis LaFollette, and Tim McCreight in addition to short workshops with Kenneth Bates, June Schwarcz, Earl Pardon, and Margaret Seeler.

Lilyan uses pure copper and fine silver for her enamels. She says that fine silver is primarily used for jewelry "because of its cost, color, and the advantage of not producing a firescale coat like copper does when it is fired." She usually domes the jewelry, which she fabricates from twenty-six gauge or twenty-eight gauge fine silver or oxygen-free copper. "Doming the thin gauge metal gives it added strength and keeps the piece of jewelry, especially pins, from being too heavy. " Lilyan uses both fine silver and fine gold wire to create her intricate, abstract cloisonné enamels.

Since 1970 her "Bachrach Art Enamels" have been exhibited in museums and galleries across the United States including Worcester Center for Crafts, the Worcester Art Museum, Danforth Museum, DeCordova Museum, Fitchburg Art Museum and the Palo Alto Cultural Center. Shops that carried her work included Gumps, Skera, Appalachian Spring, Voltaires, and others.

Her commission work has ranged from cloisonné pins to architectural panels and religious objects. She recently wrote two books on enameling, entitled *Enameling with Professionals* and *Contemporary Enameling,* in which she teaches the materials and techniques of enameling and takes the reader into the studios of other leading enamel artists who discuss their own techniques.

Mildred Ball, necklace, enamel on sterling silver, 17" circumference x 3/4". *Collection of Munir Meghji, photograph by Munir Meghji.*

Mildred Ball

Mildred Ball (1902–1997) was born in Harrison County, West Virginia. She attended Columbia University and taught jewelry making at the Community Art Center in Winston-Salem, North Carolina and Salem College. She was one of the founders of the Arts and Crafts Association in Winston-Salem (now the Sawtooth Center for Visual Arts) and a charter member of the Piedmont Craftsmen, Inc., for ten years. She worked with various materials and techniques using enamel, ceramics, and sterling silver, creating jewelry and hollowware. She also created enamels depicting some of the buildings in Winston-Salem.[5]

Harry Bertoia

Harry Bertoia, brooch, sterling silver, 1-1/8" x 2-5/8", c. 1943. *Collection of Munir Meghji, photograph by Munir Meghji.*

"The urge for good design is the same as the urge to go on living." —Harry Bertoia

Sculptor, designer, and jeweler Harry Bertoia (1915–1978) was born in San Lorenzo, Udine, Italy. When he was fifteen he traveled to the United States, to Detroit, to visit his older brother. He decided to enroll in Cass Technical High School (one of the few high schools at the time with a strong crafts program—Stanley Lechtzin also attend Cass at a later date). It was there that Betrtoia first studied design and jewelry making. He began studies at the Art School of the Detroit Society of Arts and Crafts (now known as the College for Creative Studies) and in 1937 received a scholarship to study at Cranbrook Academy of Art in Bloomfield Hills, Michigan. There he was indelibly influenced by Walter Gropius, Edmund N. Bacon, Eliel and Eero Saarinen, and Ray and Charles Eames (for whom he made wedding rings).[6]

In 1939 Bertoia opened Cranbrook's metalworking shop and taught there until 1943. Later, out of necessity (during the war, materials were scarce), he created highly sculptural jewelry forms.

Beginning in 1943, Bertoia worked with Charles and Ray Eames in Venice, California—a collaboration that would lead to the development of molded plywood furniture.

Harry Bertoia, brooch, sterling silver, 1-3/4 x 2-7/8. *Collection of Joanne and Fred Doloresco, photograph by Fred Doloresco.*

His jewelry and sculpture were widely exhibited. He showed monoprints in 1943 as well as jewelry in silver, brass, and gold in a one-man show at Nierendorf Gallery in New York City. He continued to provide the gallery with prints and jewelry until 1947. He also exhibited at the Fairweather Harden Gallery in Chicago. In 1947 he created his first welded sculptures and began to receive commissions for large-scale work in that medium.

He was given a gold medal by the Architectural League of New York (1955-56), the Fine Arts Medal from the Pennsylvania Association of the American Institute of Architects (1963), and an honorary doctorate from Lehigh University in Bethlehem, Pennsylvania (1976).

Robert Alvin Blood
Esta Damesek Blood

Bob and Esta Blood, 1950s. *Courtesy of Munir Meghji.*

Robert Blood (b. 1924) and Esta Blood (b. 1933) met in New York City in the 1950s. Bob's interest in Esta was spurred on by seeing one of her paintings based on the modern opera "Wozzeck." They were married in 1953. [7]

At one time Bob worked for Morley Crimi (who produced commercial copper jewelry) with the intent to learn how to cast metal. He also studied at the Pennsylvania Academy of Fine Arts.

Esta Damasek was a painter. Bob and Esta started to experiment with jewelry making in the early 1950s. Eventually they produced sterling silver and brass jewelry in combination with exotic woods such as Macassar ebony, Brazilian rosewood, cocobolo, zebrawood and tulipwood.

They sold their jewelry through gift stores such as the Palmer House Hotel in Chicago; The Willow in Philadelphia; The Artshop at the Munson-Williams-Proctor Institute in Utica, New York; and street fairs such as the "The Greenwich Village Outdoor Fair."

Between 1953-1959 they made jewelry for the general public. Around 1960 they moved to Schenectady, New York where Bob became an artist-in-residence at the Schenectady Museum of Art. He taught sculpture and did his first public commissions there. Esta began a career in music; she took advanced piano lessons and started to compose music based on the folk dancing of the Balkan countries such as Macedonia and Bulgaria.

In 2002 the Schenectady Museum had a retrospective exhibition of Robert Blood's works. He continues to produce sculpture to this day.

The Bloods sought inspiration from musical instruments, the human figure, constellations, the Sputnik launch, the biomorphic sculpture of Henry Moore, etc. In most cases, Esta would conceive the form and Bob would execute the design. Most of their work was collaboration. Their "Wishbone" earrings appeared in an advertisement in *Craft Horizons*, Jan/Feb 1959.

Bob and Esta Blood, necklace, sterling and ebony, 15" (circumference). *Collection of Munir Meghji, photograph by Munir Meghji.*

Francis Holmes Boothby

Frances Holmes Boothby was a graduate of Iowa State College. She taught art and physical education in the Waverly, Iowa public schools and at the Metairie Park Country Day School in New Orleans, Louisiana. She was a jewelry instructor at Emma Willard School in Troy, New York and at the Fletcher Farm Crafts School in Ludlow, Vermont. After 1955 she taught jewelry making at the Birchkill Arts and Crafts Guild in Troy. Her own work was done mostly in silver or gold with exotic woods and/or semi-precious stones as well as brass and plastics.[8]

Boothby is also known for making small, whimsical, animal-shaped brooches with wire legs. Boothby sold her work from her workshop in Weston, Vermont.

Frances Boothby, brooch, sterling silver, 2-1/4" x 2-1/8". *Collection of Joanne and Fred Doloresco, photograph by Fred Doloresco.*

Frances Boothby, *Owl,* brooch, sterling silver, 1-3/8" x ¾", *Collection of Marbeth Schon, photograph by Marbeth Schon.*

Jules Brenner

Jules Brenner (1917-1991) was born in New York City. His first art classes were private instruction in painting and sculpture. In the late 1940s he went to Provincetown were he worked for a while with Ed Wiener creating "large, functional objects hammered from copper and brass." Probably noticing that sales for Wiener's jewelry were better than they were for his platters, he turned to jewelry as his main focus and in 1951, he and his wife, Lee, opened a summer shop in the art-minded resort town of Woodstock, New York. [9]

In 1953 Brenner moved back to New York where for nine years he operated a store in Greenwich Village at 127 MacDougal Street. At that time Brenner worked mostly in silver using simple biomorphic shapes with added wire and sometimes semiprecious stones.

In 1963 he again changed New York locations, opening up at 828 Lexington Avenue where he began to work in gold in a more naturalistic style using a combination of direct handwork and lost-wax casting. He made one-of-a-kind as well as limited production pieces.

In 1956 Jules and Lee returned to Provincetown where they opened a shop to sell his jewelry and other paintings and art objects. Brynner continued to operate a New York store for most of the year, but spent his summer months in Provincetown. In 1974 he closed the New York location and moved permanently to Provincetown where he and his wife continued in business until his death in 1991. Jules Brenner was a civic-minded person who shared his time and talents in numerous political and cultural endeavors.

Jules Brenner, brooch, sterling silver, glass, beads, 2-3/8" x 1-1/2". *Collection of Joanne and Fred Doloresco, photograph by Fred Doloresco.*

Jules Brenner, cuff, sterling silver, 1" x 5- ¼". *Collection of Joanne and Fred Doloresco, photograph by Fred Doloresco.*

Irena Brynner

Irena Brynner, c. 1955-56. *Photo credit, Van Nes, Ramon Rosario. Permission to use this photograph, published in* Craft Horizons, *September/October 1956, is granted by the American Crafts Council.*

Irena Brynner (1917-2002) was a skilled sculptor, painter, musician, and most importantly, one of the most celebrated American jewelers of the mid-20th century. She openly shared her techniques of jewelry making and stories about her fascinating life through two books, *Jewelry as an Art Form*, 1979, and *What I Remember*, 2002. [10]

She was born in Vladivostok, Russia on Dec. 1, 1917 of Swiss and Russian parents. In 1928 she and her family moved to Manchuria in Northern China where she attended school until leaving in 1936 for the University and Art School in Lausanne, Switzerland. She returned to China in 1940 where she studied Chinese painting. In 1942 Brynner's father, who had been the Swiss consul general in Dairen, China, died and in 1944, when he was posthumously suspected by the Japanese of being a spy, Irena and her mother fled to Beijing. In 1946 they immigrated to San Francisco, leaving behind all their possessions.

Irena continued her art studies in San Francisco where she met sculptor Ralph Stackpole from whom she learned stone cutting along with an appreciation for modern art.

One of her first jobs in San Francisco was with potter/jeweler Franz Bergmann. She worked on his jewelry while he devoted his time to ceramics. Bergmann recognized Irena's talents and encouraged her to make her own jewelry and in 1950 Brynner started on her own to create jewelry using an old ironing board for a soldering table, a Bunsen burner and a polishing motor that came from an old washing machine. Excited by the design challenges of jewelry making, she created three original pieces that she offered to Fraser (one of the only shops in San Francisco that carried studio jewelry at the time). They selected a pair of cufflinks and when they asked her if she had more, she quickly ran home and made them.

Irena's early work was constructed of wire and silver sheet or screen. Her jewelry was, from the beginning, abstract and three-dimensional, referencing her work as a sculptor. Her earrings were sometimes influenced by Calder's mobiles—"sculpture suspended from the ear."

Brynner, together with Margaret De Patta and Peter Macchiarini, helped to organize the first San Francisco Open Air Art Festivals. The Metal Arts Guild eventually grew out of that organization.

In 1956 Brynner traveled to New York to find a place to show her jewelry. An article about her in *Craft Horizons* preceded this visit and was a boost to her acceptance. She met Greta Daniels at the Museum of Modern Art who helped her connect with the exclusive Walker and Ebeling Gallery where she had her first New York Show.

Irena Brynner, earrings, sterling silver, 1-3/4" x 5/8". Collection of Marbeth Schon, photograph by Marbeth Schon.

Irena Brynner, serpentine ring, gold. *Courtesy of Arlene Shrut, photograph by Marbeth Schon.*

In 1957, determined to live in New York, she and her mother took an apartment at 46 West 55th Street. They rented the entire fifth floor and had room for a small studio. Irena began working almost exclusively in gold and precious stones such as black pearls, emeralds, opals, jade, sapphires, and diamonds. Like Margaret De Patta and Peter Macchiarini, she designed the shapes of her stones to enhance her designs in metal and had them cut by San Francisco lapidary Francis Sperisen.

In order to create a clientele for her jewelry, Irena rented the front space in the lobby of the brownstone where she lived. It had showroom windows on the street and her friend David Campbell, the director of the Museum of Contemporary Crafts, designed the shop with walnut wood and mirrors. At that time Brynner was experimenting with casting and working with wax to achieve openwork designs in gold. She made spectacular gold filigree necklaces, pins, bracelets, and rings set with pearls and diamonds. "Irena hammered gold into varying linear patterns...knowing just how to manipulate the temper and flexibility of the metal to make it work on a spring principle. Her necklaces wind around the neck rather than hang, achieving a modern exoticism that has a kin-ship to ancient Etruscan embellishment."

In 1959 she had a one-woman show at the Museum of Contemporary Crafts, received a gold medal from the Bavarian State *Handewerschmesse* and, along with Arp and Braque, was invited to participate in the exhibit, *Twenty Five Worldwide Known Artists*. In the early 1960s Irena was offered a teaching position in the adult education department at the Museum of Modern Art –a position she kept for seven years until the department closed.

In the mid-1960s Brynner worked on welded sculpture. Her first work, *Requiem to the Earth,* consisted of a sphere that opened up into the center with many hollow and filled spaces. She said it was her idea of what the earth will look like "when we finish playing with (it)."

Between 1965-67 Irena and her mother returned to Europe and the Soviet Union to revisit their birthplace and renew old friendships. In 1967,when they returned to New York, a series of happenings including the death of a dear cousin, caused Irena and her mother to consider another move. Irena described the end of the 60s and beginning of the 70s as difficult years--living alone with her mother in their brownstone, having jewelry stolen from the shop and, by necessity, surrounded by alarm buttons. Their rent was raised, diminishing their income. Though Irena loved New York and found it extremely difficult, they moved back to Switzerland where her mother died not long after.

In 1977 Brynner returned to New York, rented a room and studio space and again began to work and take orders for jewelry. In 1978 she went to Japan to visit, was the honored guest of a jewelry organization and was interviewed on Japanese television.

In 1978, when back in Geneva, she was asked to display her jewelry and sculpture at the Ariana Museum after which she was offered a retrospective show at the Museum of Watches and Enamel—their first with a contemporary artist. The show was in 1979 on her thirtieth anniversary as a professional goldsmith. In December of that year, the show opened at the Renwick in Washington, D.C. Irena traveled to Washington for the opening and was honored as an international designer. After Washington she had a seven-month visit in New York and realized she had "come home." She went back to Geneva for a short period, returning to the U.S. to conduct workshops in Vancouver, Canada as well as slide lectures in San Francisco and Seattle. In 1984 she made the decision to return to New York permanently, finding a studio apartment overlooking the Hudson and beginning teaching at the Craft Students League at the YWCA.

Irena Brynner died in 2002. Her work is in the permanent collections of museums throughout the world including the Smithsonian, the Louvre, and the Hermitage.

Irvin Burkee & Bonnie Burkee

Irvin and Bonnie Burkee are a husband and wife team who followed parallel paths of learning and teaching before making a joint decision to "abandon it all" to fulfill their dreams, working as artist/craftsmen high in the Colorado Mountains. [11]

Irvin studied painting at the School of the Art Institute of Chicago with Boris Anisfeld from 1938 to 1945. Bonnie began her studies at the School of the Art Institute of Chicago in 1941. She was president of the Arts Students League and an assistant photography instructor as well as the official school photographer. In 1945 Irwin and Bonnie married and then traveled through Mexico on Irvin's fellowship.

From 1946 to 1953 Irvin taught art classes at the University of Colorado and Stephens College in Columbia, Missouri where he introduced classes in jewelry and lithography. In 1946 Bonnie established a photography studio in Columbia and became the official photographer for the college as well as an art instructor at the University of Missouri.

About 1949 the Burkee's built a cabin in the mountains near Blackhawk Colorado, established a studio and workshop and founded Burkee Jewelry Studio. In 1950 they had their first child—two others followed in 1953 and 1954. As well as creating one-of-a-kind pieces in their studio, the Burkees went into limited production of their jewelry designs, obtaining and setting up all the necessary equipment for casting. The jewelry was marketed through various craft galleries throughout the U.S., earned many awards and was included in national exhibitions.

In order for their children to go to school, it was necessary for Bonnie and Irvin to move from their isolated home near Blackhawk. In 1957 they settled in Aspen, Colorado, relocating their studio and business operations. It was there that Irvin began to work with metal on a larger scale, accepting commissions for several monumental murals for public buildings. Bonnie assisted with his architectural commissions in metal and gave birth to their fourth child in 1960. In 1961 they were included in Robert Von Neumann's book, *The Design and Creation of Jewelry*.

Irvin and Bonnie Burkee, working as a team, have for years maintained themselves as producing jewelers. In order to do so they have developed limited-production techniques unique in that nothing of the priceless individuality of each work is lost through reproduction. In addition they have created numerous thoroughly unique works incorporating many of the approaches and materials of sculpture using, not only silver and gold, but also wood, stone, ivory and bone.

Irvin and Bonnie Burkee, pendant, sterling silver with leather cord, 3-1/2" x 1-1/4". *Collection of Joanne and Fred Doloresco, photograph by Fred Doloresco.*

Irvin and Bonnie Burkee in front of a mural by Irvin. *Courtesy of Irvin and Bonnie Burkee.*

In 1972 Irvin was awarded a travel grant from Colorado Mountain College after which both Irvin and Bonnie began working in bronze sculpture. In 1978 they moved to Verde Valley, Arizona where they again set up a workshop, this time focusing on sculpture. In 1992 Irwin was elected to the National Sculpture Society and in 2000 he installed his copper, silver, and bronze mural, *Wild Birds of the Rocky Mountains* for the Aspen Center for Environmental Studies, Aspen, Colorado. In 2002 the Colorado Historical Museum in Denver acquired Irvin's multiple metals mural, *The Human History of Colorado—1st Century to the 20th Century* and that same year his bronze sculpture, *The Javelina* was placed in the Frederik Meijer Sculpture Gardens, Grand Rapids, Michigan.

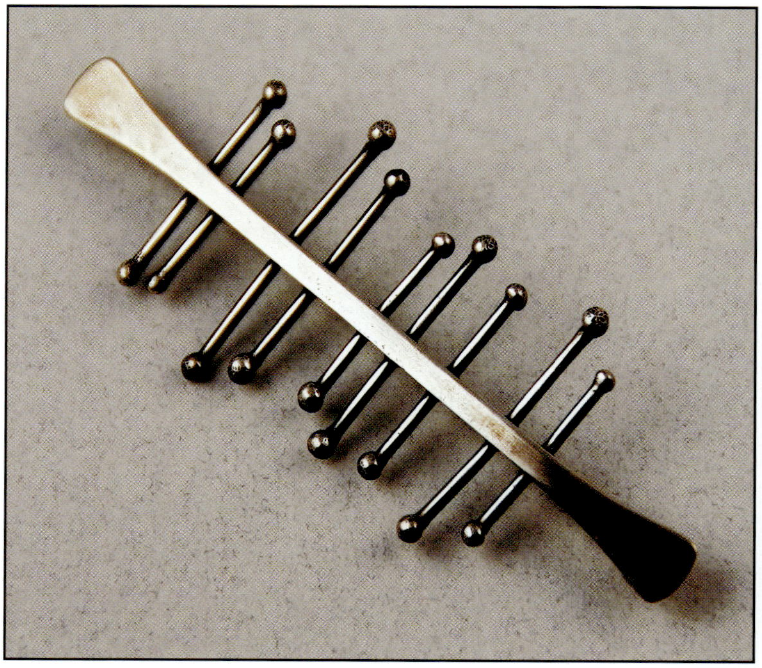

Irvin and Bonnie Burkee, brooch, sterling silver. *Collection of Joanne and Fred Doloresco, photograph by Fred Doloresco.*

Bonnie and Irvin have been able to express themselves successfully in a variety of media including painting, photography, printmaking, jewelry, and sculpture. Their jewelry creations are extraordinarily fluid modern designs often incorporating Constructivist elements such as the intentional use of negative space and balance between linear and solid forms. Natural influences are almost always apparent whether the form is totally abstract or representational and many of their designs have elements of humor or whimsy.

Their work is in many collections throughout the United States and in several books including *Design by Discovery* by Marjorie Elliot Beflin and *Walls, Enrichment* by David Van Dommelsen.

Irvin and Bonnie Burkee, pendant and chain, sterling silver, copper, pendant: 2-1/8" X 1-1/4", chain: 20" (overall). *Collection of Rose Foster, photograph by Shirley Byrne.*

Alexander Calder

"Much of the imagery in my work has been derived from forms found in our environment, visually simplified through careful design. As a jeweler, the making of a work of art involves sensitivity, perception, technical knowledge and superb craftsmanship. The pursuit of these qualities gives meaning to my life." —Alexander Calder

Alexander Calder, brooch, brass, silver, 3-1/2" x 5". *Collection of Joanne and Fred Doloresco, photograph by Fred Doloresco.*

There is no actual "founding father" of American modernist jewelry, but one of the earliest and most influential sculptor/jewelers was Alexander Calder (1898–1976). [12]

Alexander Calder, born in Philadelphia in 1898, grew up among artists; his father and grandfather were sculptors who worked within the academic traditions of their eras. He originally trained to be a mechanical engineer, but in 1922 he took evening classes at the Art Students League in New York in order to learn to draw. His earliest experiments in sculpture were wire figures and toys made in 1925, though he admitted that his first jewelry was made from wire for his sister's dolls when he was eight years old. While in Paris, during 1926-1931, he set up a miniature wire circus that included acrobats, clowns and dancers that revolved around a small ring. Piet Mondrian, Theo Van Doesburg, Jean Arp, Ferdinand Leger and Joan Miro, each a recognized leader in the modernist movements in Paris, came to see his circus. This was probably his first real connection with the Dada and Surrealist artists of his day. About this time also, he produced a series of mobile toys and whimsical animals that were exhibited at the *Salon des Huoristes*.

It is his colorful mobiles that most people consider Calder's most important contribution to the development of modern art. Around 1930 his wire sculptures were becoming more abstract and he was using wire or metal rod links to hold clusters of forms that were balanced in order to create movement when they were suspended from the ceiling. As early as 1931 he added motors to his constructions and by the mid-1930s, he was creating stabiles--large sculptures made from abstract forms of metal similar to his mobiles but fixed in place.

Wire, which was an important element in his sculptures, was also his preferred material for jewelry. He worked mostly in silver or brass in a simple, primitive mode, twisting or hammering the metal to achieve strong forms without using solder. Each hammer mark had a purpose to the whole composition and his fastenings were consistent with and suitable to the form of the piece.

Calder was quite prolific, producing about fifteen hundred original pieces of jewelry in his lifetime. His jewelry was never mass-produced and most of his pieces were made as gifts for family and friends. Some pieces contain found objects--bits of bone, natural stones, and glass. His pieces have a simplicity and integrity that has influenced a great number of jewelers, some who were his contemporaries and many who came later.

Eleanor Caldwell

Eleanor Caldwell, who currently lives and works in Arizona, has had a very successful career as both artist/craftsman and teacher. One of her earliest teaching positions was as an instructor in handcrafts and jewelry at Fort Hays Kansas State College.

She attended Southwest Missouri State College where, in 1948, she received a B.S. in education. She received her M.A. from Columbia University and worked in the Education Department at Columbia University Teachers College. She was an art instructor at the high school level in Waterloo, Iowa, and at Southwest Missouri State College. During the 1959 summer session she taught enameling and weaving at Columbia University Teachers College. [13]

A distinguished member of the Society of North American Goldsmiths since 1974, she has participated in four of its international exhibitions.

Caldwell was a professor of art at Northern Illinois University where she was also chairperson of the Department of Crafts/Sculptures. For fourteen years she was director of the annual *Oakbrook Invitational Crafts Exhibition*, sponsored by Urban Investment and Development, Inc., of Chicago. During her summers she also served as a professor at the Arrowmont School of Arts and Crafts at the University of Tennessee.

In 1984 her work was exhibited in a show at the Michener Library, University of Northern Colorado, titled *Caldwell & Davis: Exceptional Women.* At that time she was focusing on jewelry to adorn the neck. Her pieces were mostly sterling with hand-wrought chains.

She primarily used silver, gold and ebony as well as enamel, stones, plastic, vermilion, walnut and amaranth woods. Her work is exceptionally well crafted and has simplicity of design derivative of cubism and primitivism as it relates to the abstraction of natural forms.

Eleanor Caldwell, earrings, sterling silver, Plexiglas, 3" x 1". *Courtesy of Mark McDonald, 555 Warren St., Hudson, New York. photograph by Bill Hibbs.*

Virgil Cantini, compact, enamel, brass, wood, 4" x 4" x 2", c. 1960s. *Courtesy of the Glitterbox, photograph by Sheila Pamfiloff.*

Virgil Cantini

Virgil Cantini was born in Italy in 1919 and came to the US in 1930, to Pittsburgh. He attended Manhattan College and Carnegie Mellon University (on a football scholarship). During WWII he served as a sergeant in the Engineering Corps in Africa, Europe and the Pacific. In 1948 he received his Master's Degree from the University of Pittsburgh where he became a Professor in the Henry Frick Fine Arts Department. [14]

He was introduced to enameling through the silversmith Frederick Claytor when, drawn to an enameled panel in his studio, Cantini decided that enameling would become his primary form of expression.

In 1948 Cantini's work received immediate national exposure when his enamel *Masquerade* was juried into the *Thirteenth National Ceramic Exhibition* in Syracuse, New York. In 1949 and 1950 his work was again included in the Syracuse exhibits. In 1949 he participated for the first time in the *Wichita Art Associations' Decorative Arts and Ceramics Exhibition,* submitting three works. Two years later he submitted an impressive panel, *Saint Francis*, to the 1951 Wichita exhibition that was purchased for the association's collection. In 1950 the Department of Fine Arts at the University of Pittsburgh organized an important exhibition entitled *History of Enamels: VII – XX Century* in which Cantini was represented by nine works.

His later work was abstract and mostly non-objective. He combined painterly elements with a color field approach in a body of work called "Opus." His enameled jewelry is richly colored in deep blues, reds, oranges, yellows, and sometimes gold.

In 1952 an interview with Cantini conducted by Dorothy Sterling appeared in the December issue of *American Art*--a rare honor since the magazine featured enamellists on only two other occasions. This article brought national recognition to Cantini's work and in Time Magazine's 1953 Poll he was named as one of the *Hundred Leaders of Tomorrow.*

Virgil Cantini, bracelet, enamel on sterling silver, 8" x 1-1/2". *Collection of Marbeth Schon, photograph by Shirley Byrne.*

Josephine Catanzaro
& Antoinette Catanzaro

Josephine Catanzaro (1913 -1988) and Antoinette Catanzaro (1914 - 2003) were sisters from a large Sicilian family living in Buffalo, New York. The Cantazaros grew up in an artistic environment; their grandfather was a cabinetmaker, their mother did embroidery and their younger sister Catherine Catanzaro Koenig became a well-known regional artist.[15]

In the 1950s, through a course in jewelry making, the sisters discovered a lifetime passion for metalworking. Thereafter they created their own jewelry in both copper and silver in a home workshop.

In 1959 they opened a shop called the House of Crafts in Buffalo, New York where they had an onsite studio/workshop for forged, hammered and soldered jewelry of their own design in silver and gold. The sisters sold their own works along with handmade ceramics, textiles, woodworking and glassware by nationally known craftsmen.

Josephine (Jo) and Antoinette (Toni) exhibited their jewelry in craft shows in many locations including Ithaca, New York, Buffalo State College and the Smithsonian Institution in Washington DC. and sold their work through retail craft outlets in New York City and Boston. Antoinette also taught jewelry making at the Buffalo Museum of Science. In the 1970s Antoinette branched out into making metal wall sculptures and mobiles. While Josephine's work was characterized by bold, clean designs, Antoinette's work was more detailed, experimental and whimsical.

The Contanzaros lived and worked together throughout their lives and traveled extensively to Europe, China, South America, and Mexico. The House of Crafts closed in 1987. Josephine died in 1988, and Antoinette continued to create jewelry at her home workshop throughout the 1990s.

Cantazaro, necklace and earrings, sterling silver, pendant: 3-1/4" x 3-1/2", earrings: 2-1/2" x 7/8". *Collection of Joanne and Fred Doloresco, photograph by Fred Doloresco.*

Cantanzaro, pendant, enamel on sterling, 1-1/2" x 1-3/4". *Collection of Joanne and Fred Doloresco, photograph by Fred Doloresco.*

Milton Cavagnaro

"Jewelry should be something you can handle and want to touch." —Milton Cavagnaro

Milton Cavagnaro (1913-1993) began his career as an industrial designer. He taught at the California School of Fine Arts and San Jose State College and spent much of his spare time experimenting with wood, fascinated its textures and surfaces. With a pocketknife and a file he began to work with wood, combining it with metal to make jewelry. His first attempts were primitive figures resembling Native American forms. [16]

In 1949 Cavagnaro and his family moved to Mill Valley, California. He continued to teach until he became established as a jeweler and found he could support himself with his craft; *Arts and Architecture* published an article about him, he had a one man show at the Legion of Honor in San Francisco, a show in Texas and won a *Good Design Award* from the Museum of Modern Art in New York for a pair of wood and stainless steel salt and pepper shakers.

His work is distinctive in its skillful use of silver in combination with natural materials such as wood, bone, or shell. Cavagnaro used wood like many jewelers use stones; ebony, because of it's close-grain is beautifully contrasted with silver. He also uses black walnut and vermillion woods. Wood is sometimes the dominant element; the metal (aluminum, brass, or silver) serves as an accent or an inlay. At other times the silver and wood make equal statements. He uses bone in a similar way to wood though it has totally different form and texture.

Cavagnaro made only one-of-a-kind pieces and did not cast metal or set stones. He made few rings and bracelets. Much of his work requires inlay and Cavagnaro invented his own techniques and materials; he developed an enamel substitute, which hardens to a black matte finish without heat.

Milton Cavagnaro, earrings, sterling silver, wood, piano wire, epoxy beads, 2-1/2" x 1/2", c. 1950. *Collection of Steven Cabella, photograph by Geoff Turner.*

Betty Cooke

"If your house looks good and your clothes look good then your jewelry should all tie in with it." —Betty Cooke

Betty Cooke (b.1924), still vitally interested in her craft, continues to make jewelry that is unmistakably her own, continuing the exploration of the principles of "good design" she adopted over fifty years ago. [17]

She was born in Baltimore, Maryland, where she received her B.F.A. at the Maryland Institute of Arts and Johns Hopkins University. After World War II, in 1946, she was hired by the Maryland Institute to teach metalsmithing to returning veterans.

Cooke's earliest pieces were made from brass, then mostly silver and now she works in both silver and gold which she enjoys combining in her designs. "I like the combination," she said, "I like the different colors. I used to do the Mexican technique of married metals, the gold and silver though it used to be brass and copper and it was subtle and wonderful."

She does not feel that she was influenced by any particular jeweler, inspired instead by well-designed forms of many disciplines and her "inner voice." "I know whom I respected," she said," but I don't know how they would influence me. I don't know where that comes from, what you do. It's just your inner expression and obviously you relate to people who do things that are related to you. Like I like Eames chairs with the wire legs and all that because I like wire and I like the forms that he would come up with. I thought a lot of Harry Bertoia. But, I don't know that it influenced me. Margaret De Patta I thought was quite good and she was."

Sketching is the essential first step of creation for Cooke. "I do a lot of drawing," she explained,"It's spontaneous where as metal work is not spontaneous. It has to look spontaneous. I guess I draw a lot for myself because you just start drawing and, you know, one little dot starts the whole process going and you end up with 50 things and then you have to edit it to one that you make. But often it goes on and on and on and a lot of those things I'll never get to make, but I'm glad that at least I drew them because they're complete in my mind and I know exactly what they will look like-- but I'll never have time to make them all."

The circle has been an ubiquitous element in Betty's jewelry designs. "One year I was sort of involved with the American Craft Council," she said, "and they wanted me to do an exhibition so I thought I would do something with just circles, everything would be circles, but you could spend years on just that, the variety--I mean slicing them, wedging them, twisting them-- all the great things you could do with circles."

In 2001, in an interview with the author, she reminisced about the excitement of having her jewelry accepted into national exhibits. She and her friend camped across the country with a "little box of jewelry," which she presented to museums like the Walker Art Center." I went to the Walker Art Center and they were just putting the show together," she related," and it just fell in line so they included about six or eight pieces of mine in their show...I had a box of jewelry and went in and introduced myself and that was it."

She also thought that more stores and modern galleries should carry modernist studio jewelry. "Actually, what I was really trying to do at that time," she said, "--there were some very handsome showrooms for fur-

Betty Cooke in front of her jewelry at the Store, Ltd., 2001. *Photograph by Marbeth Schon.*

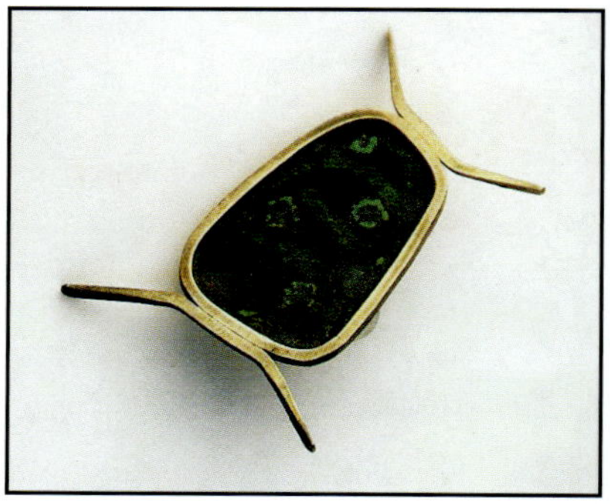

Betty Cooke, brooch, enamel on sterling silver, 1-3/4" x 2-1/4". *Collection of Joanne and Fred Doloresco, photograph by Fred Doloresco.*

Betty Cooke, *Dots* ring, sterling silver, 1-7/8" x 1-1/4". *Collection of Jill Crawford, photograph by Marbeth Schon.*

niture, for Knoll and Eames and all these wonderful people, and I had a series of stores that I thought should carry contemporary jewelry and I was trying to talk them into display cases and having a section of jewelry which was very related to the furniture and the lighting and the whole design revolution because there were no jewelry stores that would sell that (kind of jewelry)-- there wasn't anything except maybe the American Craft Council in New York. And there weren't galleries at that time that would take it..."

She participated in many national shows and has received numerous accolades for her jewelry including the De Beers Diamonds Today Award in 1979 and in 1981. In the 1970s she designed jewelry to accent the clothing of Geoffrey Bean.

Betty Cooke sees art all around her and is inspired. Her unwavering dedication to the principles of "Good Design" absorbed from and expressed within the modernist credos of the Bauhaus have kept her designs continually fresh and modern.

Margret Craver (Withers)

Margret Craver Withers working in her studio with a torch in 1946. *Courtesy of the Margret Craver Withers papers, 1926 – 1992, in the Archives of America Art, Smithsonian Institution.*

"Well, I think that when you do something no one else has done, it attracts attention and when people feel that you know what you are doing and they want to know or they have a school who wants to know it develops. I think it's a wonderful thing in this country that you can learn this way. Because obviously in Europe, you know, you would have been an apprentice and you would have had a labored life and I just bubbled out...and most of my life has been open. And when I say open, I mean that there are no controls...you are on your own... it's your own life. I was a Kansan. People from Kansas did what they wanted to do!" [18]

"I feel like the turtle on top of a fence post when it heard a passerby comment, 'He did not get there by himself.'" —Margaret Carver

Margret Craver was born in Pratt, Kansas, in 1907. She was raised in the community of Copel and was attracted to metalsmithing by an introductory course in the subject while attending the University of Kansas in the late 1920s. By the 1930s programs supporting traditional techniques taught by institutions such as the Rhode Island and the Massachusetts Normal Schools had shifted their focus to industrial design and there were very few courses or university programs in metalwork so Craver was left to design her own program. Each summer she journeyed from Kansas to New York and other centers to study with various metal artists. She studied tool making in 1932 with Leonard Heirich, arms and armor conservator at the Metropolitan Museum of Art and learned traditional techniques in metalworking from Wilson War, jeweler for Tiffanys. She became a part-time teacher at Wichita Art Association in Kansas where she set up the first craft department. During the summer of 1936 Craver studied with Arthur Neville Kirk at Cranbrook Academy of Art, Bloomfield Hills, Michigan. In 1938 she went to Sweden to study with Baron Erik Fleming, silversmith to the King. [19]

Margret Craver Withers, brooch, sterling silver, blue enamel. *Courtesy of Mobilia Gallery, Cambridge, Massachusetts.*

By1938 Craver was gaining national recognition for her jewelry and hollowware. The Philadelphia Art Alliance gave her an award and she exhibited at the Golden Gate International Exposition in San Francisco.

Beginning in 1944, during World War II, she headed a Hospital Service Program funded by the metals supply company, Handy and Harman, to provide occupational therapy in metal working for returning GI's. After the war, in 1946, Craver, again with the backing of Handy and Harman, was able to set up metal working conferences for teachers with backgrounds in art and design headed by well-trained European instructors.

As well as organizing the Handy and Harman Workshops, Margret Craver wrote several technical and instructional booklets on jewelry making and silversmithing. In 1950 Margret married the president of Towle Silversmiths, Charles Withers. She worked as a consultant with Towle as well as maintaining her own studio. Fascinated by old world techniques, she reinvented the intricate seventeenth-century enameling technique called *en résille* in 1950.

In 1988 Margaret Craver retired from metalsmithing and her tools, hallmarks, notes, and correspondence became part of the Archives of American Art, Smithsonian Institution, Washington, D.C.

Margret Craver Withers with her tools in her Boston workshop in 1970. *Courtesy of the Margret Craver Withers papers, 1926 – 1992, in the Archives of America Art, Smithsonian Institution.*

Margaret De Patta

Magaret De Patta (1904 -1964) is probably the most seminal figure ever to work within the modernist tradition of jewelry design during the mid-20th century. She began her art career as a painter studying at the Academy of Fine Arts in San Diego, California; the California School of Fine Arts in San Francisco; and the Art Students League in New York.

In 1929 she decided to turn to metals, studying first with Armenian-born artisan Armin Hairenian. By 1935 she had her own studio/workshop in her home and was selling jewelry through a craft gallery, Amberg-Hirth, in San Francisco. [20]

Margaret De Patta at her workbench in 1948. *Photograph by George Straus, Courtesy of the Margaret De Patta papers, 1944-2000, Archives of American Art, Smithsonian Institution.*

Margaret De Patta, brooch, sterling silver, 3" x 2 ¼". *Collection of Joanne and Fred Doloresco, photograph by Fred Doloresco.*

In 1941 she enrolled at the School of Design in Chicago (originally the New Bauhaus, now the Institute of Design) to study with László Moholy-Nagy whom she knew previously from a summer session at Mills College.

Moholy-Nagy's fascination with the transmission of light stimulated De Patta to experiment with the nuances of light as it passes through stones and, working with the San Francisco lapidary Francis Sperisen, she originated unique cuts to increase the transparency and create new visual effects with her stones.

De Patta used materials that had not been previously used in jewelry making. She was one of the first to find uses for stainless steel, jeweler's bronze, stainless steel screening, plastics and epoxies. Her work was based soundly on the principles of the Bauhaus and constructivism. Each new design resulted from years of preparation involving visual and manual experiences and discoveries and numerous sketches that illuminated her concepts as she worked.

In the early 1940s, while attending the School of Design In Chicago, she met and married design instructor, Eugene Bielawski. The Bielawskis moved to the rolling hills of Napa, California in 1951 where they renovated an old farmhouse. They were hoping to establish a school of design based on the Bauhaus. This did not come to fruition, however, and they focused their efforts instead on production work.

De Patta was certain that her production pieces were comparable in quality to her handcrafted pieces and was pleased to show the two types of jewelry together. "It delights me, she said, "to display a group of these things and see the baffled frustration on the faces of the 'handcraft for handcraft seekers' as they realize their inability to distinguish one group from the other." She only released a limited number of pieces of a certain design in a given area so that the design would not lose its ability to interest buyers because of over familiarity.

After only a few years, the Bielawskis found the details of running their business were too time-consuming. Desiring more time to continue the design and experimental work they enjoyed, they decided to discontinue production work to return to only creating objects by hand.

De Patta was one of the founders of The Metal Arts Guild, formed in the early 1950s when fifty metalsmiths met as a group in San Francisco with the objective of providing a place where metal artists could share their knowledge and techniques, as well as publicly discussing and debating issues that affected their work as metalsmiths.

De Patta's work received more awards than probably any other American studio jeweler working during her lifetime; she was nationally and internationally recognized as one of the foremost modernist jewelers. The British Museum purchased a crystal and diamond pendant in the 1950s and in 1958, her work was included in the American exhibition at the Brussels World's Fair. She had numerous solo exhibitions and two major retrospectives, one at the Museum of Contemporary Crafts (Now the Museum of Arts & Design) in 1965 (a year after her death), and the second in 1976 at the Oakland Museum.

Margaret De Patta passed away on March 19, 1964.

Robert Dhaemers

Robert Dhaemers was born in Luverne, Minnesota, in 1926. He was Assistant Professor in Crafts at the California College of Arts and Crafts, Oakland, California and taught for ten years at Mills College. His exhibitions at the Museum of Contemporary Crafts in New York City include *Creative Casting Thirty Craftsmen*, and *The Art of Personal Adornment*. [21]

Robert Dhaemers, earrings, c. 1940s, sterling, agate. Collection of Joanne and Fred Doloresco, photograph by Marbeth Schon.

Dhaemer's treats jewelry as sculpture—to be seen in the round. His patinas are "premeditated" so that the natural wear from the effects of friction, etc, becomes a part of the design. He does not believe in "artificial maintenance" of a polished surface and purposely engraves deeply into the areas where the jewelry will receive the most wear. He uses silver, gold, brass and bronze with gemstones, often synthetic.

Dhaemers credits Bob Winston as the inspiration for his work in lost wax casting, the process he uses to produce his jewelry and sculpture.

Jose de Rivera

"I was interested in the structural aspects of plastic form...of course, by this time you were aware of Brancusi. You see his Bird. You go to museums. You pick up a little booklet on Vontongerloo. You go to an exhibition of Leger, you know. So you begin. You meet people. You get stimulated." —Jose de Rivera

"Jose de Rivera fashions stainless steel brooches—really studies for large reliefs—whose mirror-bright surfaces reflect the slither of light." [22]

José de Rivera (1904–1985), an internationally recognized sculptor in the modernist tradition, worked mostly in wrought metal including stainless steel. He was of Creole heritage; his mother a Spaniard and his father, Colonial French. As a young man he worked as a blacksmith and machinist on the Louisiana plantation near Baton Rouge where his father was a sugar mill engineer. This training was invaluable to his later work of manually forging, welding, grinding, and polishing the metals he used to create his sculptures.

In 1922, just out of high school, Rivera traveled to Chicago to live with his brother. He supported himself by working in tool and die shops. In an interview with Paul Cummings for the Smithsonian Institution's *Archives of American Art*, de Rivera mentions going to the Field Museum in Chicago where he was inspired by Egyptian sculpture. He had an aptitude for and an interest in the arts, so enrolled in evening classes at the art school of the Art Institute of Chicago, first studying lettering and later drawing with mural painter John W. Norton who encouraged him to work in three dimensions, noticing the strong sculptural quality of de Rivera's work.

By 1930 he was making mostly figural sculpture, which was the norm for commercial work at that time. In 1931 he went to Paris with aspirations to become a professional artist, but his travels took him to Egypt, and North Africa, enabling him to study ancient and historical sculpture.

When he returned to the United States de Rivera moved to New York City where he opened his first real studio on East 39th Street. He said he became aware of the "limitations of the figure" while working on a marble statue of a cavalryman for the Federal Arts Project.

In1938, while working for the Works Progress Administration, de Rivera created an aluminum sculpture for the Newark Airport, an abstract bird suggesting "flight." Much of his sculpture from the late 1930s through the early 1950s was involved with what he referred to as shell shapes"--free-form sheets of aluminum hammered into curves that were painted with primary colors on both sides. He used a mathematical formula he called "plastic geometry" to bring forth a three-dimensional object from a two-dimensional sketch. Eventually he opened up his work with perforations to create relationships between space and mass. His later forms in the 50s were constructions of highly polished stainless steel or bronze tubes. It was this later work that brought him to maturity as an artist and established him as an important figure among American sculptors.

His jewelry making began in the 1940s, when he began to create small, sleek stainless steel prototypes--studies for his larger sculptures. His jewelry was flatter and less three-dimensional than his sculpture because of the necessities of wearability, though the jewelry designs also possessed high reflectivity and linear definition. The Grace Borgenicht Gallery in New York City sold his brooches during the 1950's Christmas Holidays, later offering them on a regular basis. He never had an exhibition exclusively devoted to his jewelry.

In 1958 de Rivera created sculpture for the United States Pavilion at the Brussels Worlds Fair and was the subject of a major retrospective exhibit at the Whitney Museum of American Art in New York City. He was commissioned to create a large work for the New York World's Fair in 1964 and received the American Iron and Steel Institute Award in 1965 for a sculpture that was presented to the Museum of Modern Art in New York City. His most famous work, *Infinity*, a giant revolving Mobius strip, was placed outside the Museum of History and Technology in Washington, D.C. The La Jolla Museum of Contemporary Art in California and the Whitney Museum of American Art jointly organized another retrospective of his work.

José de Rivera, *Construction #5B,* stainless steel, c. 1955, 11" high. *Provenance: Estate of the Artist, to Joseph Ruiz, II. Exhibition History: Jose de Rivera: Sculpture Paintings, Works on paper, Valerie Carberry Gallery, Chicago, November 1, 2002- January 3, 2003, exh. cat. #11, illus. p. 22.*

Florence Dixon

Florence Dixon was a painter and metalworker who lived and worked in Northern California. She specialized in copper jars and bowls, jewelry and found objects assembled and welded into whimsical animal forms. Her entire estate was given to the Sonoma County Museum in Santa Rosa, California.

Florence Dixon, brooch, sterling silver, 1" x 3-1/4". *Collection of Joanne and Fred Doloresco, photograph by Fred Doloresco.*

Karl Drerup

Karl Drerup (1904-2000) was born in Borghorst, Germany. He studied graphic arts under Hans Meid at the Academy in Berlin in 1926. After receiving his master's degree he studied painting with Felice Carena in Florence, Italy. Because of the political climate at that time he did not return to Germany, but he and his wife, who was Jewish, went instead to Madrid and the Canary Islands in 1934 and finally to New York City in 1937.[23]

In New York, Drerup lived with his brother and later settled in Rockville Center, a small community east of New York City, on Long Island where he lived and worked from 1938 to 1946.

In 1937 Drerup visited the Whitney Museum where he had his first encounter with the work of enamellist, Edward Winter. Later he developed a friendship with Hungarian-born ceramicist Francis J. von Tury who was the ceramics engineer at the Fords Porcelain Works in Perth Amboy, New Jersey. Von Tury had trained at the Meissen porcelain factory in Germany and had an extensive knowledge of glazes that he shared with Drerup. A friendship developed and the two combined skills to produce a large body of work in clay that they sold at Rena Rosenthal's gallery and exhibited at the 1937 World's Fair as well as the 1938 National Ceramic Exhibition in Syracuse.

Another chance meeting, this time with designer R. Tommi Parzinger, convinced Drerup to begin in earnest to explore the medium of enameling on metal.

In 1940 Drerup received an honorable mention for his enamels at the Ceramic National from which the Metropolitan Museum of Art purchased a bowl. The following year Drerup submitted a large-scale composition, *Enchanted Garden*, to the Ceramic National.

During World War II, when metal became increasingly scarce, Drerup produced a variety of small objects that he sold through art galleries in New York such as Georg Jensen, Orrefors, Hudson Walker, and Karl Nierendorf. During this period he was also an art instructor at Adelphi College on Long Island.

In 1941 the Arts and Crafts Club of New Orleans organized an exhibit of over fifty of Drerup's earliest enamel plaques, plates, bowls, boxes, and other objects.

In the early 1940s Drerup worked in his home studio in Rockville Center. At one of the Ceramic Nationals arts promoter David Campbell (later director of the American Craft Museum) and ceramists Edwin and Mary Scheier, encouraged him to visit them in New Hampshire. He agreed and was so impressed by the bucolic landscape of the area that he and his wife decided to purchase a home and studio in Thornton, New Hampshire. There he was re-energized by his proximity to nature; he became absorbed in creating enamel work and began to sell his work privately.

In 1946 Drerup became a member of the League of New Hampshire Arts and Crafts and, after teaching a workshop in enameling at Plymouth State College, was appointed to the position of Professor of Fine Arts. In 1986 the college named its art gallery the *Karl Drerup Art Gallery* and acknowledged his work with an Honorary Doctorate. In 1995 Drerup became a Fellow of the American Crafts Council and in 1989 became a recipient of New Hampshire's Living Treasure's Award. Karl Drerup died at the age of 94 on November 22, 2000.

His works are in many permanent collections throughout the world including The Museum of Fine Arts in Boston, The Currier Gallery of Art in Manchester, The Museum of Fine Arts in Dallas, the State of New Hampshire's Living Treasures Collection and museums in Los Angeles, Wichita, Newark and the Smithsonian Institution.

Virginia Dudley, brooch, enamel on copper, 1-3/4" x 2-1/2", c.1950. *Collection of Joanne and Fred Doloresco, photograph by Fred Doloresco.*

Virginia Dudley

Virginia Dudley's aim was to create beautiful and functional objects that would beautify people's homes and enrich their lives. She was a gifted artist whose incredible oeuvre includes paintings in watercolor and oils, lithography, photography, sculpture and enameling on copper for jewelry and large mosaic plaques.[24]

She studied at the University of Chattanooga, the Art Students League, the New School for Social Research in New York, and at Stanley William Hayter's *Atelier 17* in California. She received her Master of Fine Arts degree at the Claremont Graduate School and in 1943, on the basis of her painting and printmaking, was awarded a Julius Rosenwald Fellowship to tour the southern states sketching, painting and taking photographs. Around 1944, during World War II, two of her prints tilted *Tenement Children* were shown at the Metropolitan Museum of Art's *Artists for Victory* show.

It was also in 1944 that she and her first husband, Oscar McElhaney (who died the same year), built the first room of their home on Lookout Mountain.

Between 1945-46 Dudley was Supervisor of Portrait Artists, for the Art Department, at the American Photograph Corporation in New York. While studying with noted artists such as Will Barnett, Harry Sternber, Vaclav Vytlacil, Ossip Zadkine, William Zorach, and Stanley W. Hayter at the Art Student's League she met her second husband Joseph Spencer Moran whom she married in 1946.

At the 14th annual National Ceramic Exhibition of the Syracuse Museum of Fine Arts she sold an enamel on copper piece to Millard Sheets, chairman of the art Department of Scripps College. During the 1940s her work was exhibited at the Metropolitan Museum, New York City; Brooks Memorial Gallery, Memphis; Southern States Art League, New Orleans; San Francisco Museum of Art; and Albright Museum, Buffalo, N.Y. In 1943 Virginia Dudley was given a one-woman show at the University of Chattanooga.

In 1949 she was awarded a scholarship to attend Scripps College in Claremont, California. She obtained her master's degree at Scripps in 1950.

Although derived from various sources, the imagery of Dudley's work is unique and the execution inventive and masterful. She produced plaques, plates, jewelry, and large-scale mural-like works, much of which was sold through dealers, shops, and in particular, the Southern Highland Handicraft Guild." Her work *Symbols of Affirmation* was added to the Syracuse Museum of Fine Arts' collection in 1956. Her work was also included in the traveling exhibition *American Craftsmen, 1953*, organized by the University of Illinois, Urbana. In 1959 five works were included in the seminal *Enamels* exhibition at the Museum of Contemporary Crafts in New York. Additionally, Dudley's work was exhibited at the Metropolitan Museum of Art, the San Francisco Museum of Art, the Albright Museum, Buffalo and other institutions. "[25]

Robert Ebendorf

Robert Ebendorf, *Courtesy of Robert Ebendorf*.

"I'd rather have you say 'Oh it's so ugly.' than to say it's just another piece of jewelry," he said, holding up a bracelet made of bent, rusty nails and antique silver charms.[26]—Robert Ebendorf

Robert Ebendorf is known, not only for his fine work in jewelry, but also for his intense professional energy and the rich content of his ideas.

Born in 1938, in Topeka, Kansas, Ebendorf says that his introduction to jewelry was in high school as a member of that general crafts class that always seems to be "filled with 'hard to teach' students--I made the typical copper pin and other small copper forms." He went on to attend the University of Kansas where he received his B.F.A. in 1960 and his M.F.A. in 1962, after which he received a Fulbright grant to study in Norway at the State School for Arts and Crafts.[27]

Ebendorf says that in Norway he "learned many new ways of working with metals and new materials" and also "how to handle tools and how to take care of them, and a great deal about the importance of precision in gold and silversmithing." Later, on a Louis Comfort Tiffany grant, Ebendorf returned to Norway where he worked in a small production studio. About that experience, he said, "For one year all I did was file and solder, file and solder. This experience taught me a lot about how to make a living from my craft if I would ever want to live entirely from my work."

In 1968 Robert Ebendorf was involved in the initial meetings in Chicago of a distinguished group of jewelers and metalsmiths who founded the Society of North American Goldsmiths (SNAG). Following Brent Kington's term as President of SNAG, Ebendorf took office and moved the organization ahead at incredible speed. His energy seemed limitless as he initiated the first of a series of four National Student Metal Invitation catalogs and served to bridge the communications gap between metal students and instructors around the country.

During his term as President of SNAG, *Gold Dust*, a mimeographed newsletter became the full-fledged illustrated *Goldsmiths Journal*.

Ebendorf uses a combination of solder techniques and cold connections that has helped him to open up the possibilities of different types of construction in his work. He works not only in silver and gold, but combines many different materials such as ebony, amber, wood, ivory, bone, copper and semi-precious stones as well as found objects of myriad types. "Strongly influenced by the ideas and imagery of the German metalsmith Claus Bury, Ebendorf's work reflects his own vision and personal energy." [28]

Since 2004 Ebendorf has been inducted into the Metalsmiths Hall of Fame, named *Master of the Medium* by the Renwick Alliance, honored for leadership and achievement by New York City's 92nd Street Y Art Center, and has participated in the Smithsonian's *Archives of American Art* oral history program. He has also been appointed to a three-year visiting professorship at the Bristol School of Art, Media, and Design in England.

Other professional honors include an American Crafts Council Fellowship and being named the Carol Grotnes Belk Distinguished Professor at East Carolina University's School of Art and Design. His works are held by thirty-eight museums internationally. The Museum of Fine Arts, Boston, recently acquired a gift of his work from a private collection and the Smithsonian, the Mint Museum of Craft + Design and two other institutions have requested a bequest of his archives.

Alma Eikerman, *Photograph by Steve Golden. Courtesy of The Sarah Bodine & Michael Dunes Archives of 20th Century Jewelry, Tyler School of Art, Temple University, Professor Shirley Lechtzin, Curator of Metals/Jewelry Archives & Collections.*

Alma Eikerman

"The true function of jewelry is to decorate, to ornament and thus command attention and admiration. In this sense the ornament must reveal form that is worthy and expressive of its time." —Alma Eikerman

Alma Eikerman (1908–1995) was born in Kansas where she grew up on a farm with six siblings. During the Depression she attended Kansas State College in Emporia Beach, Kansas where she earned a liberal arts degree in history, language, and literature--all of which remained strong influences throughout her life. After graduation she became a teacher in public schools in Pratt and Winfield, Kansas. [29]

She began graduate studies at Kansas University at Lawrence where she studied design and painting and took her first jewelry course. From Kansas University she transferred to Columbia University in New York where she completed her graduate degree in painting, design, art history, and metalsmithing. After moving back to Kansas Eikerman accepted a position at Wichita State University teaching beginning and advanced general design and jewelry design. During this period she developed her skills as a metalsmith and moved further away from jewelry design. During World War II Eikerman served in the Red Cross in Italy, an experience that brought her in touch with Florentine jewelers.

In 1947 Indiana University offered Alma Eikerman a teaching position that included design, watercolor painting, drawing and jewelry. In the jewelry and metalsmithing courses she taught ten to twelve undergraduates and three to four graduate students.

In 1948, during the second Handy and Harman workshop at the Rhode Island School of Design, Eikeenmann studied with silversmithing instructor Baron Erik Flemming, court silversmith to the King of Sweden. From Flemming, Eikerman learned stretching and raising techniques.

Supported by sabbatical leave and funding from Indiana University, in addition to grants from the Ford Foundation and the National Endowment for the Arts, Eikerman took one year of sabbatical leave to go to Europe, particularly Denmark and Sweden, to research these traditional techniques.[30]

In Denmark she was drawn to the designs of Karl Gustav Hansen and after reviewing her portfolio, which at the time consisted of three photographs, Hansen accepted Eikerman into his Kolding factory. Eikerman studied in Hansen's factory for four and a half months under deaf -mute master craftsman, Henrick Boesen. "I didn't know Danish, and he couldn't talk, so we got along very well," she explained.

Eikerman's role in the factory was to learn traditional silversmithing techniques and to experiment. Hansen was available to Eikerman for technical and aesthetic questions. Her most significant and ambitious piece from her time in Hansen's shop was a teapot. It embodied her control of the crimping technique and her ability to successfully assemble multiple units with complex soldering operations. In 1948 Eikerman left for Stockholm to work with Baron Erik Fleming. He had extended an invitation to participants in the Handy and Harman workshops to visit his atelier to do the same type of work as his factory apprentices; thus becoming familiar with all of the processes and operations of production metalsmithing. There she raised an asymmetrical pitcher. Once again Eikerman had the fortunate experience of being surrounded by master craftsmen. From Stockholm she visited Michael Wiler in Munich, to learn granulation and later traveled to Paris where she studied under Cubist sculptor Ossip Zadkine.

Due to her perserverence as an artist and teacher, Eikerman has received numerous awards and honors and her work is collected internationally. In 1976 Alma Eikerman received Indiana University's *Distinguished Teacher* award and in 1978 retired as a *Distinguished Professor Emeritus*. In 1981 the college of Arts and Sciences Graduate School Alumni presented its first awards to distinguished teachers--Alma Eikerman was among them.

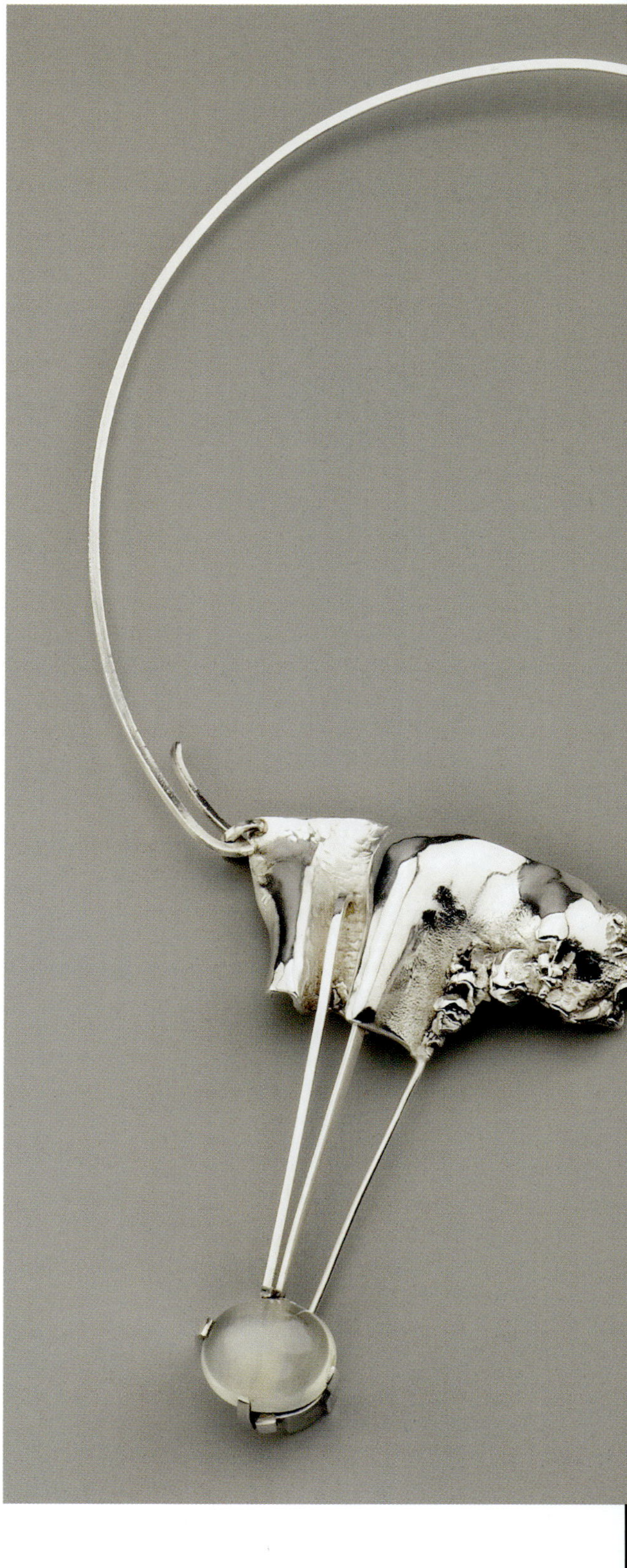

Alma Eikerman, pendant with collar, sterling silver, moonstone, c. 1970. *Gift of Dr. John H. and. Kate Hevner Mueller, photograph courtesy of Indiana University Art Museum.*

Robert Engstrom & Audrey Engstrom

Robert Engstrom. Courtesy of *The Sarah Bodine & Michael Dunas Archives of 20th Century Jewelry, Tyler School of Art, Temple University, Professor Stanley Lechtzin, Curator of Metals/Jewelry Archives and Collections*

"With the present wealth of "how-to" books and classes in jewelry making for all ages and inclinations, it is hard to equate what it meant in the 1950s to be a self-taught jeweler. There wasn't much to help you. The advantage in learning by yourself was being original, not only in developing techniques, but in working out fresh ideas. " —Robert Engstrom

Robert (d. 2003) and Audrey Engstrom were a husband and wife team who worked independently of each other showing distinctly different styles and approaches to jewelry making. Robert took graduate credits at Alfred University, New York, and Michigan State College. He sometimes made a hundred sketches of a single piece before achieving a final design. He worked with metals and precious stones, striving to create unusual and beautiful objects that were also comfortable to wear. [31]

Audrey Engstrom studied ceramics as an undergraduate at Michigan State. Most of her jewelry was done in silver. She often worked on several pieces at the same time; she felt changing activities renewed her spontaneity and she found it more practical to group operations like sawing, soldering, or casting. She was fond of working with enamels.

The Engstrom's studio/home-workshop was located in a 40-acre wood near Rockford, Michigan where they raised "three daughters, Christmas trees, and a herd of deer." They also supplied materials for enameling and handmade jewelry, largely by mail order. Robert Engstrom retired in 1984 after serving 27 years on the faculty at Western Michigan University teaching jewelry making, elementary metalwork and gemology as well as ceramics, three-dimensional design and art history. One of his specialties was Scandinavian art; he lived for a time in Norway and co-authored a book on the history of Scandinavian metalwork.

Robert Engstrom died Jan. 25, 2003 in Kalamazoo, Michigan.

Robert and/or Audrey Engstrom, cufflinks and tie bar, sterling silver, cufflink: 1-1/4" x 3/4", tiebar: 1/4" x 1-1/2". *Collection of Joanne and Fred Doloresco, photograph by Fred Doloresco.*

Claire Falkenstein

"This concept of the importance of the interval--the spaces between--has always been important to me." —Claire Falkenstein

Claire Falkenstein (1908–1997) was an internationally recognized sculptor and jeweler. She was born in the tiny community of Coos Bay, Oregon in 1908. As a child she would ride her horse along the beach among the shells, rocks, seaweed, and driftwood. These natural forms would later influence her sculpture. [32]

Falkenstein graduated from the University of California at Berkeley in 1930 majoring in art with a minor in philosophy and anthropology. She had her first one-woman show at the East-West Gallery in San Francisco before graduation. She received a grant to study with Russian modernist Alexander Archipenko at Mills College in Oakland, California in 1934. During that time she created abstract, textured ceramic sculptures from interwoven strips of clay. Between 1940 and 1944, she worked in wood producing a series of wood sculptures titled *exploded volumes*. They were made of interlocking sections that could be moved and combined in different ways by the viewer.

Claire Falkenstein made her first jewelry about 1944 or 45. "On the

Claire Falkenstein, *Erotic* necklace, sterling silver, 12" x 5 3/4".*Courtesy of Mark McDonald, 555 Warren St., Hudson, New York, photograph by Bill Hibbs.*

occasion of her winning an international award for wallpaper design given by the Association of Interior Design, she decided to wear a knitted, turban-like hat to the award ceremony and desired an ornament for it. To that end, she forged a three-dimensional brooch incorporating two circular shapes and measuring about five inches long."

From 1948 to 1950 Falkenstein taught at the California School of Fine Arts in San Francisco where she was influenced by Abstract Expressionist, Clyfford Still.

While living in Paris, about 1950 until 1952, Falkenstein made mostly jewelry, lacking both space and the resources needed to purchase materials for large sculptures. She began to weld with the cheapest material she could find, stovepipe wire. However, out of this adversity came complex open structures, with individual spatial components, the beginnings of the style for which she became famous.

About 1953 the director of the design department of the Museum of Modern Art in New York, Edgar Kaufman, Jr., saw Falkenstein's jewelry in Paris and a short time later purchased two pieces from Betty Parsons for The Museum of Modern Art's *Art for Use* traveling exhibition. Her jewelry was also shown at the *Werkbund* in Berlin in 1952, the Institute of Contemporary Art in London in 1953, *Galleria Montenapoleone* in Milan in 1954, and *Galleria Spazio* in Rome in 1954, 1955 and in 1959.

Claire Falkenstein, *Erotic* earrings, brass, 3-1/4" x 1-1/2". *Courtesy of Mark McDonald, 555 Warren St., Hudson, New York, photograph by Bill Hibbs.*

Princess Pignatelli commissioned Falkenstein to create welded gates for her sea villa and in 1960 she made gates of metal webbing accented with chunks of glass for Peggy Guggenheim's villa-museum on the Grand Canal in Venice. Guggenheim dubbed them *The New Gates of Paradise*. In these works, for the first time, Falkenstein used the concept of " the never-ending screen"-- a single module is repeated, attaching in all directions to form a continuous field that looks as if it could go on infinitely.

Falkenstein's jewelry is not merely decorative, but related visually and conceptually to her sculpture. Her jewelry was exhibited at Goldsmith's Hall in London in 1961 at the *First International Exhibition of Modern Jewelry*, and in 1967 at *Jewelry by Painters and Sculptors* at the Museum of Modern Art in New York City.

In 1963 Falkenstein moved back to the United States after spending thirteen years abroad and opened a studio in Venice, California.

During the years following her return to the U.S., she created some of her most ambitious public commissions: a fountain for California Federal Savings and Loan in Los Angeles, fountains and sculptures for Fresno and Coos Bay shopping malls, a fountain for the San Diego Art Museum, and a screen for the Seattle Art Museum.

Falkenstein completed her monumental commission for St. Basils Cathedral on Wiltshire Boulevard in Los Angeles in 1960; fifteen stained glass windows, some as high as one hundred fourty-four feet that "reiterate her concept of the never-ending screen"[33]

In 1997 Claire Falkenstein passed away, in Venice, California.

Fred Fenster

"One of the reasons that I'm interested in function is because there's this awful sentiment out there expressed by visual artists that if it's functional, it isn't art...I've heard this ever since I've been in this field...I've chosen to do functional things because these same people who make that statement collect ethnic artifacts which *are* functional. They'll collect ladles, they'll collect bowls, they'll collect all kinds of things that they just love and they're functional objects...I don't understand how they can draw the line...in other cultures they don't do that...In Western culture we do it, European cultures...often do that. But in the Eastern cultures, they don't do that...everybody's involved in it and they don't draw a line between the functional object and the aesthetic object--the art object. It irritates me and it seems so senseless to me that they would do that." [34]

Fred Fenster, photograph by Marylu Raushenbush. *Courtesy of The Sarah Bodine & Michael Dunas Archives of 20th Century Jewelry, Tyler School of Art, Temple University, Professor Stanley Lechtzin, Curator of Metals/Jewelry Archives and Collections.*

Fred Fenster (b. 1934) was born in the Bronx in New York, of immigrant parents: his father from Austria and his mother from Warsaw, Poland. About his parents, Fenster related, " My mother was a homemaker. My father was a floor coverer. He was known as 'Charley the linoleum man,' and I grew up putting down flooring because I was his helper when I was a kid. I was his helper even after I was married. I would go home – even after I was a professor at Wisconsin [University of Wisconsin, Madison], I would go home to New York and we would end up putting down flooring in peoples' homes. He was a one-man contractor, so we worked all over Westchester County north of New York City."

In 1956 Fenster received a B.S. degree in education and taught in the New York City public school system for a short time before enrolling in Cranbrook School of Art where, in 1960, he received his M.F.A. in metalsmithing.

In 1962 he was hired by the University of Wisconsin to teach design, jewelry, and art.

Fenster has also taught jewelry and metalsmithing and has given workshops on the same at schools such as Penland, Haystack, Peter's Valley and Arrowmont. Fenster relates:

> My teaching philosophy was to give the students as solid and as comprehensive a grounding in as many facets of metal work as I could...I had the industrial art background, ...I had a very logical way of teaching it. If you talk to any of my students, they'll tell you that...I cover things very carefully--I demonstrate everything. I never talk about things that I don't do. I do it while they're watching. If I teach soldering, I'm soldering. I'm talking about it, I'm explaining it, I'm doing it, I'm giving handouts on it--...I'm showing slides. And that's what I try to do--to cover it in as many ways and [in] as comprehensive a way as I can. And to work individually with the students...I'm not a factory turning out students who are competent, but I'm trying to get to you as an individual so you can put your own particular twist on things.

Fred Fenster, ring, 14k yellow gold, citrine, cast and fabricated. *Collection of Fred Fenster.*

Fenster's work is in many private and public collections including the Milwaukee Art Museum, the Renwick in Washington, D.C., the Detroit Art Institute, Yale University Art Museum, the Skirball Museum of Judaica in Cincinatti, and the National Museum of Contemporary Art in Seoul, Korea, and others.

He works mostly in silver, pewter, and iron, but also in copper, brass, and bronze and creates both jewelry and hollowware. About his work he says:

> I usually do a lot of sketching and so ideas come from many sources. Many ideas come from the work process itself...When I'm working on one piece I'll think, well, I could do a whole bunch more of these and try out some of the different ideas I had...I will sometimes make paper models and then I begin the piece. And I work in pewter because it's very fast and I can realize my ideas in a short time and because I'm so familiar with the material I'm not afraid of messing it up or making a mistake ... It took me a long time, but now I really have begun to trust my decisions in a different way...Instead of figuring out the rim or the handle or something...I'll have a general idea for it and...I'll figure it out as I do it. And every one of the handles and rims comes out differently because of that.
>
> Silver is a much more demanding material and I'll do more drawing for that--it's a much more exacting...difficult material.

In 1955 Fenster was elected a Fellow of the American Craft Council and in 2002 he received the third *Hans Christiansen Memorial Silversmithing Award.*

In 2005 Fenster retired from teaching but continues to teach workshops and is actively producing metalwork in his own stuido.

He holds the title of *Profesor Emeritus* from the University of Wisconsin, Madison and in 2006 he received a gold medal from the American Craft Council for his work with crafts.

His work has been included in numerous books and publications.

Phillip Fike

Phillip Fike in his workshop, sawing a design. *Photograph by Phillip Fike, Courtesy of The Sarah Bodine & Michael Dunas Archives of 20th Century Jewelry, Tyler School of Art, Temple University, Professor Stanley Lechtzin, Curator of Metals/Jewelry Archives and Collections.*

Phillip Fike (1927-1997) is remembered as one of the most influential metalsmiths of the later 20th Century. He was born in Baraboo, Wisconsin. His interest in crafts came naturally; his grandfather was a woodcarver and violinmaker; his cousin, Norman Harms, a painter and a sculptor; and his friend's father, Fred Ward, was a master stone carver. At the age of ten he had already attempted metalworking by minting a counterfeit fifty-cent piece using the iron forge at his grandfather's farm. [35]

In the early 1940s a class in metal crafting was part of the curriculum at his high school and he was able to cast a silver ring, raise a pewter bowl and learn to engrave metal. Through his teacher, Miss Bauman, he also learned about the modern techniques and designs of Scandinavian silversmithing.

Immediately after high school, in the spring of 1945, Fike enlisted in the U.S. Navy and was stationed at the Naval Air and Technical Training Command in Lakehurst, New Jersey. Working with the fabrication, testing and rigging of experimental parachutes, he discovered a passion and aptitude for mechanics.

After leaving the Navy in 1946, Fike traveled to Massachusetts to visit his cousin Norman Harms, a sculptor who surrounded himself with other artists, poets, and writers. Fike realized for the first time that it was with these people he belonged—he felt "at home" in the art world.

Fike enrolled at the University of Wisconsin in Madison under the GI Bill, to study applied art under Arthur Vierthaler. While looking for a suitable research topic for Vierthaler's class, he found the book *Silver and Jewelry* by Henry Wilson with an introduction to niello (a technique of metal ornamentation which uses an alloy of sulfur with copper, silver or lead that turns silver a blue-black color). Fike experimented with the process and began to use it in his work. When he received his Master of Science degree from the University of Wisconsin in 1951, his graduate show included "niello work, engraving, fine wire work, carved and inlaid ebony brooches, pendants, and small sterling silver castings."

Fike worked at Liberty Powder Defense Corporation in Badgerville, Wisconsin for two years after graduation from college. Each evening he would work at home, in his small bathroom studio, creating metalwork and jewelry which he hoped would further his desired career in metalsmithing and qualify him for a teaching position in a college or university. He obtained that position in 1953 at Wayne University (now Wayne State University) in Detroit, Michigan. He said that this proved to be "the right place;" he stayed for forty-five years establishing one of the premier metal arts programs in the country.

Phillip Fike, Niello ring, c.1955, Courtesy of The Sarah Bodine & Michael Dunas Archives of 20th Century Jewelry, Tyler School of Art, Temple University,Professor Stanley Lechtzin, Curator of Metals/ Jewelry and collection, photograph by Phillip Fike.

Fike won half of the Hikok Company's award for men's accessories with a pair of cufflinks in enamel and silver at the exhibit, *American Jewelry and Related Objects* in 1956. His idea for this design came from a job where he used a lathe to cut jigs and fixtures for the U.S. Air Force's B-52 bomber. He acquired his own lathe and applied this process to the creation of his "Cavex Cuff Links." Fike's cufflinks were a one-piece design that resembled buttons when worn. He used silver, gold, niello and exotic woods and made numerous variations of design before arriving at his most widely acclaimed lathe-turned pair, comprised of discs of 14k gold and ebony or sometimes granadilla wood. Each slice was graduated in size, drilled, tapped, and stacked one on top of the other onto a threaded gold shaft forming a catenoid or double ended funnel." This incredibly complex process created a stunningly simple, beautiful design that won many awards throughout the 1950s.

His passionate study of the ancient fibulae (a clasp) was a lifetime pursuit. It began in Rome in 1965 where he became interested in the bronze and gold pins of the Etruscans, who gave them the name of "fibula." (See Chapter six for a more detailed discussion of the fibula.)

Arline Fisch, collar, c. 1985, machine knit coated copper, gold, fine silver, 18" diameter x 7-1/2" wide band. Courtesy of The Sarah Bodine & Michael Dunas Archives of 20th Century Jewelry, Tyler School of Art, Temple University,Professor Stanley Lechtzin, Curator of Metals/ Jewelry and collections, photograph by Wm. Gulette.

Fike finally got another chance at an iron forge in 1974 at a workshop in Colorado. Shortly after that experience he established a working forge at Wayne University from which he began producing fascinating iron jewelry.

Fike used wood in the same way as metal--stacking, inlaying and laminating it along with metal to create "striped, tiled, diamond, and spinal cord type formations." He thought of himself as a "structuralist," allowing the form and the surface of a piece to reflect the process used in its making."

Fike's work has been widely exhibited museums such as the Renwick Gallery and the Gallery of the American Craft Council as well as in exhibitions in Asia, and South America. He was a member of the College of Fellows of the American Craft Council and received numerous awards and prizes. He was also instrumental in founding the Society of North American Goldsmiths.

Arline Fisch

"...Mine is purely decorative; it's intended to decorate the person in a positive way, to attract the public -- a little bit like birds with beautiful feathers. Why are some birds beautifully colored? It's because it has this particular attraction within nature. And I like that metaphor also, the idea of the butterfly or the bird having this beautiful garb that is purely for attracting some kind of visual response." [36]—Arline Fisch

Arline Fish went to public school in New York City. From the time she was a child, she liked working with her hands. "Working with my hands was something I had done since I was quite small. I'd been a Girl Scout. My mother was a Girl Scout leader. We made baskets, I made my own clothes. I was very comfortable making things," she said, "I don't know that there's a great history of jewelry in my family. There isn't. It wasn't anything that I knew anything about. I simply admired it, not contemporary stuff, but ancient material. I was drawn to the Egyptian stuff. I was drawn to feathers. And I spent a lot of time in a natural history museum. As a Girl Scout, that's something you do a lot of."

Fisch lived on Long Island, in Bayside, Queens and was able to take art classes in High School, after which she attended Skidmore College where she concentrated on painting and art education. For her graduate studies, she decided on the University of Illinois in Champaign.

Fisch spoke about her education:

> I went thinking that I would study art education, which I did, but that I would concentrate in painting. Right away, I knew I wasn't going to do that. This was in 1952, and the graduate students, all of them, were mostly male, and they'd all been in the Second World War, so they were older.
>
> I was 20 years old when I started graduate school, and I just didn't feel that I had anything to say in painting. The paintings I had done before were all flowers and abstractions, and so on, but there wasn't a lot of content. These guys were really heavily into content, and I just didn't feel I could measure up in that arena. So I took courses in ceramics, and I took courses in metal, and I worked in both of those things all through graduate school.

After graduating from Skidmore she accepted a position at Wheaton College, Norton, Massachusetts, where she taught painting, printmaking, and drawing. Wheaton is in Norton, Massachusetts, close to Attleboro and Taunton, which are the jewelry centers of the United States. Fisch admitted that she probably wouldn't be a jeweler except for that circumstance. While looking for a studio in that community she found several jewelry studios, because, she said, "All of the people who worked in industry, or many of them, had their own little private workshops where they worked on weekends and at night... So just down the road...I found a workshop with a very nice gentleman who said, 'Oh please, come and use my studio, and here's a key.' I could go there anytime and work, and he was there in the evenings to help me if I needed help. And it became what I wanted to do. "

Arline Fisch, two bracelets, sterling silver, ebony, each about 3" diameter x ¼" deep. *Collection of Gayle Kauihou, photograph by Steve Aldana.*

Because of her desire to further her knowledge of metalsmithing, Fisch applied and received a Fulbright grant to go to Denmark. After a year of intense apprentice-type work she returned to the United States and began teaching at Skidmore College. The position required that she also teach weaving and, in preparation, she studied at a special workshop with Jack Lenor Larsen and Ted Hallman at Haystack Mountain School of Crafts. Her interest in weaving grew and the rich integration of textile techniques in metal has become one of the distinguishing features of her work.

From 1961 to 2000 Fisch was Professor of Art at San Diego State University in San Diego, California.

Fisch has also made important contributions through her service on the World Crafts Council, the Society of North American Goldsmiths and the American Crafts Council.

She is now Professor of Art (Emerita), San Diego State University. She has won numerous awards including a Gold Medal from the American Craft Council, a *Lifetime Achievement in the Crafts* award from the National Museum of Women in the Arts in Washington, D.C., and has been declared a *Living Treasure of the State of California*. Her work can be found in prestigious galleries and museums throughout the United States and many other countries.

Elsa Freund

"As I see it, there are two ways to approach jewelry making, one is to give a precious stone a proper setting (and) the other is to give something of no particular value a worth by making it a thing of beauty. Of the two methods, I prefer the latter."

"You know, people ask me if I was influenced by the work of Calder or by the kidney shapes of the fifties, but it is these," she says, caressing ocean-tumbled fragments of tile, "that have been my inspiration...I always said that if someone gave me a small diamond, do you know what I would do with it? I would fire it in the kiln to see what would happen and everybody's horrified that no man ever gave me a diamond." —Elsa Freund

Elsa Freund, painting in her studio. *Photograph courtesy of Martin Roenigk*

Elsa Freund (1912 - 2001) was born and raised near Branson, Missouri on a fifteen thousand acre game preserve managed by her father. Elsa spent her childhood exploring the natural beauty of the Ozarks, walking three miles to school among wild elk, deer and turkey.[37]

Freund graduated from high school in 1929 with a certificate to teach at rural schools. She taught all eight grades at her former school for one year "earning seventy dollars a month which included ten dollars payment for cleaning the school."

She had odd jobs during the Depression, one of them operating a crafts shop in the Ozarks making and selling novelties. It was there that she met a WPA painter, Louis Freund, who in 1939 became her husband .

Fruend started to work with jewelry in the latter part of the 1940s with a group of students who were attending the summer art school she and her husband had opened in Eureka Springs, Arkansas.

After some initial trials, firing clay with pulverized bits of glass, she enrolled in a ceramics class which motivated her to experiment in earnest—shaping clay into small shapes, breaking window or colored bottle glass with a hammer and firing clay and glass together.

She had not studied metalsmithing or mounting techniques for jewelry so she "bound, mounted, and wrapped the 'stones' using a little bit of everything: raffia, copper and brass wire, and aluminum clothesline" making her experimental creations into pins, pendants, and rings

Elsa and Louis Freund. *Photograph courtesy of Martin Roenigk.*

In 1949 Elsa and her husband moved to Florida as artists in residence at Stetson University in Deland. When on vacation in Key West in 1953 Freund decided to find shops that would sell her jewelry--she located the one she thought was most suitable and they began to sell her work. "Freund's earrings eventually sold for twenty-five dollars a pair, of which she received half—the most she received for showpiece necklaces was one hundred dollars."

Her work was later carried by other small select shops in Fort Lauderdale, Sarasota and St. Armand's Key, Florida as well as Aspen, Colorado and the esteemed America House in New York, known for showcasing the best in contemporary American crafts. Fruend's most lasting relationship was with an old friend, Jane Hershey, who had sold Freund's earliest pieces in her shop in Branson, Missouri. Hershey carried Freund's jewelry for over thirty years when she opened her shop in Florida—"her detailed inventory shows sales of over ten thousand pieces."

Freund was an intuitive modernist, a regionalist who was not aware that her experiments with jewelry were similar to those of studio jewelers in other parts of the country such as Sam Kramer in New York who was combining materials such as non-precious stones and odd objects (including taxidermy eyes) with metal in unconventional ways. Her concept of the use of materials was instinctive and progressive.

As she continued her craft, Elsa Freund became a major figure in the studio jewelry movement of the 1950s. Her jewelry is now in the permanent collections of many major museums throughout the U. S. and abroad including The Cooper-Hewitt Museum in New York, the Los Angeles County Museum of Art, the Boston Museum of Fine Arts, the *Musee des Arts Decoratifs* in Montreal, and the Victoria and Albert Museum in London.

Elsa Freund, pendant and neck ring, silver, glass, ceramic, pendant: 3-3/4" x 3-1/2", neckring: 21" overall. *Courtesy of Mark McDonald, 555 Warren St., Hudson, New York, photograph by Bill Hibbs.*

Arnold Frew

"I get rather disgruntled at the whole artistic bit. I make my living from my art." —Arnold Frew

Arnold Frew lived and worked in Arcadia, California, in the 1950s. He had a studio in a vine-covered tract community in a tiny shop beside his swimming pool, behind his house.[37] Many of his customers were California millionaire celebrities. "They have enough money," he said.

Frew never cared to enter craft shows because he said, "I've never won a first prize in a craft show and I used to be crushed until I discovered the first prize winners were starving to death." Most of his business was devoted to the development of special-order business by word of mouth and the rest to ready-made jewelry through five contemporary craft-type stores: The Balinese Shop in Pasadena; Contempo in Glendale; The Gallery in Birmingham, Michigan; Nanny's in San Francisco; and Walter Wright at the Farmers Market in Los Angeles.

Frew's jewelry is modern, smooth and mostly undecorated, with interest arising out of its many interlocked planes and contours. He was sure that such jewelry, in which the form of metal is as important to the design as the stones, is here to stay and thought that within a few years, it would replace for good, the outmoded, but still popular Tiffany-type jewelry.

His inspiration came from "organic shapes like tree forms, natural rock formations, even the pattern that the ocean or rain makes in sand."

Frew used the lost wax process for most of his pieces. " Originals of new designs were executed first in wax and cast in metal like silver, which he polished so that soft rubber molds can be made from them. A professional jeweler then casts his piece in wax from the rubber molds and makes duplicate investing compound molds of each wax matrix. Then the molds are cast centrifugally, the wax first burned out and the molten metal brought to a specific temperature for the moment of actual casting. The caster uses a "tree" that casts as many as 100 small objects at once." Frew received the rough casts from his caster, polished them up and set his stones—"I spent five years in a production shop learning how," he said.

Frew, who studied jewelry making at Pasadena City College, had this to say about the use of machinery in hand-made jewelry, "There are so many attachments for the machine I use that I just can't see any reason for hand grinding the final form the way a lot of jewelry craftsmen do. It's so much easier to use a fine rubber wheel with an abrasive 'grog' in it."

Frew said that he made jewelry for women because women buy it—"and you'd be surprised how many women buy a hundred-dollar ring for themselves and a four-dollar tie tack for their husbands," he said.

"I love making jewelry," he confessed, "It's fun knowing how to do it well enough to break the rules. When you like it like I like it and you do it well, you wind up better off financially than if you were doing something you didn't like to do."

Arnold Frew, earrings, sterling silver, wood, 3-1/4" long. *Collection of Lisa Cliff, photograph by Lisa Cliff.*

Sammy P. Gee

Sammy P. Gee worked as a jeweler in San Francisco in the late 1950s. He began in Berkeley with a shop on the corner of Bancroft Avenue and Telegraph. He later moved to North Beach on Upper Grant Avenue, near Peter Macchiarini. He worked, together with Peter Macchiarini, with the San Francisco Outdoor Crafts Festival.

His work was mostly constructed of silver, sometimes with stones, beads and wire.

Sammy P. Gee, pendant, sterling silver, steel wire, trade beads, 3-5/8" x 2-1/2", c.1955. *Collection of Steve Cabella, photograph by Geoff Turner.*

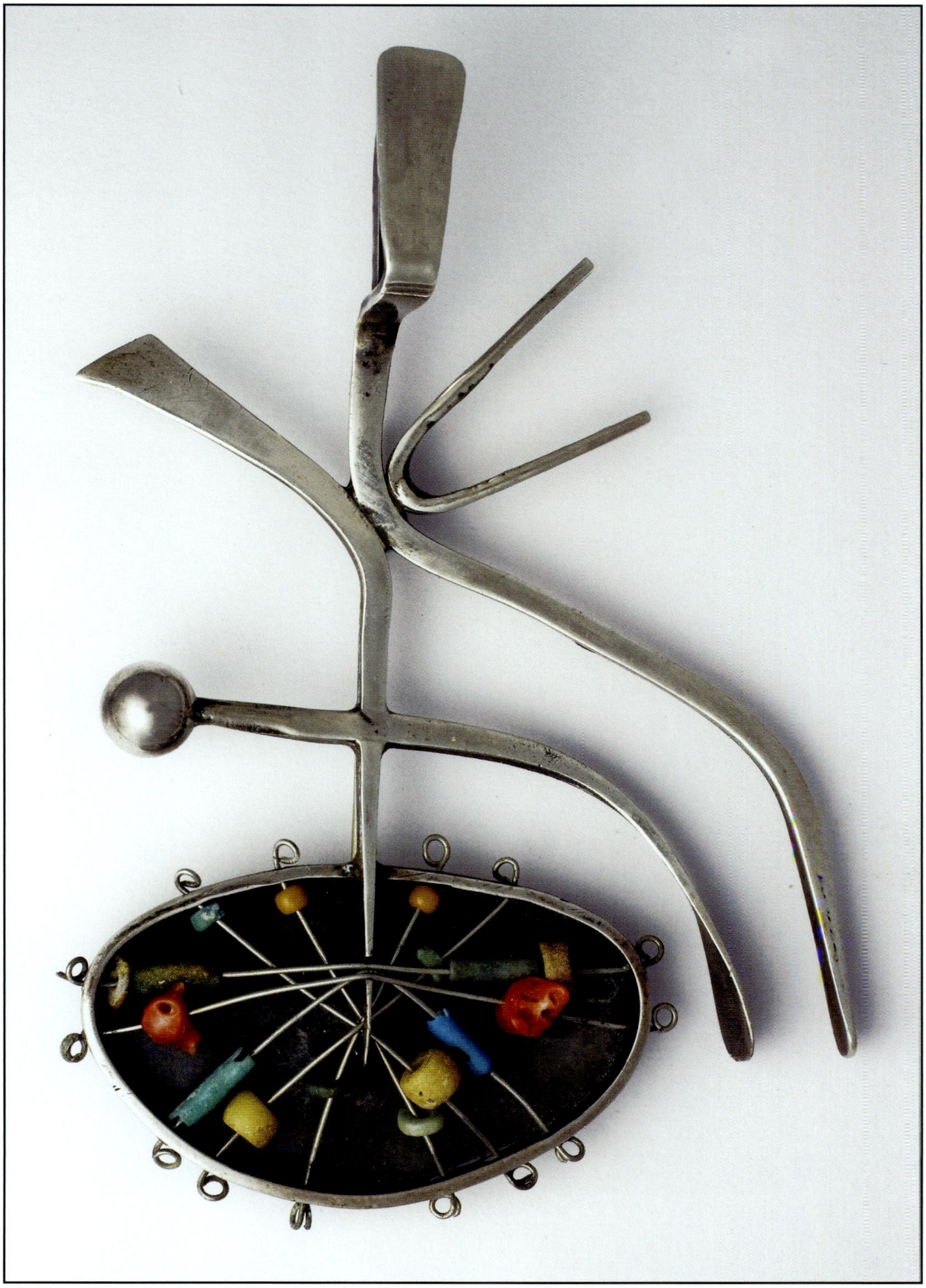

Sammy P. Gee, pendant, sterling silver, Indian trade beads, steel wire, 3" x 1-5/8". *Collection of Joanne and Fred Doloresco, photograph by Fred Doloresco.*

Richard Gompf

Richard C. Gompf was born in Council Bluffs, Iowa. He attended North Dakota Agricultural College in Fargo; Moorhead State Teachers College, Moorhead, Minnesota; University of Minnesota in Minneapolis; and the California College of Arts and Crafts in Oakland. He taught at grade schiool and high school levels in Grand Forks, North Dakota, as well as graduate classes at the University of Minnesota and Wisconsin State University in Superior, Wisconsin. From 1960-1969 Gompf was a jewelry and ceramics teacher at Miramonte High School in Orinda, California.[39]

Gompf first became interested in jewelry in 1952, while studying at the University of Minnesota with Philip Morton, further developing his craft in 1956 at the California College of Arts and Crafts under the direction of Margaret De Patta. Most of his jewelry is made by the sand casting and lost wax processes, which he says "keeps the designs clean and simple" and allows for concepts and forms that are three-dimensional.

His work has been included in numerous national and international exhibitions and museum shows since 1949 including *Young American Craftsmen*, New York, 1958; Notodden, Norway, 1959; Ibiza, Balearic Islands, Spain, 1959; Metal Arts Guild two year traveling show beginning in 1961; Palace of the Legion of Honor, San Francisco 1962; M.H. de Young Memorial Museum, San Francisco, 1963; San Francisco Museum, 1964; Oakland Art Museum, Oakland, California, 1965; and the Invitational Crafts Show, St. Cloud State College, St. Cloud, Minnesota,1968.

Gompf, a member of the Metal Arts Guild (president from 1961-63), exhibited his work with the guild in juried shows at the San Francisco Art Festival for eighteen years. He also demonstrated sand casting while exhibiting his jewelry at the American Craft Council Southwest Region Fairs between 1977-1986. His gallery shows include the Velvet Da Vinci Gallery in San Francisco and Eclectic Gallery in Winnipeg, Canada where he had a one-man-show.

Richard Gompf, flatware, gold, sterling silver, c. 1960. *Photograph courtesy of Richard Gompf.*

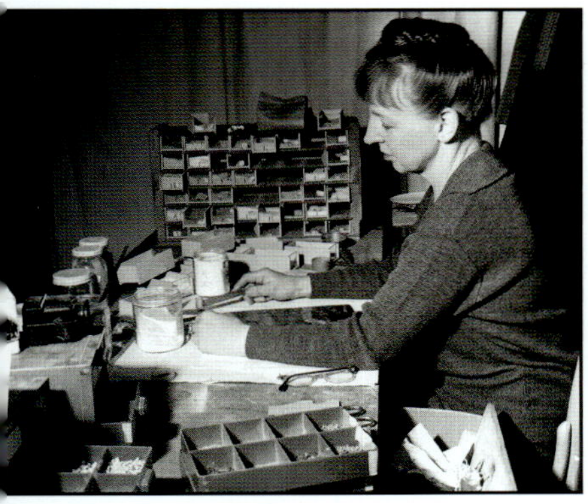

Doris Hall developing a plaque, sifting enamel, "The sifter in Doris Hall's hand was designed and made by Kalman Kubinyi before 1955." *Courtesy of Lilyan Bachrach, photograph by Oppi Untracht.*

Doris Hall

Doris Hall (1907–2000) began her artistic career as a painter. Born in Lakewood, Ohio, she studied at the Cleveland Institute of Art, graduating in 1928. She also studied printmaking with Kalman Kubinyi, founder of the Cleveland Print Makers Club and later director of the Cleveland Arts Project of the Works Progress Administration. (Hall married Kubinyi in 1933.) By the 1940s she had developed a significant regional reputation as a painter.[40]

Her first experiments with enamels were in 1941--she produced her first piece of enamel work on December 7, 1941, the day Pearl Harbor was bombed. "It was so colorful and really quite beautiful," she explained, "and that was the beginning of my career in enameling." Because of scarcity of materials during that time Hall's earliest enamels were jewelry and small functional forms.

Hall began to sell her work at local fairs and shops in Cleveland and by 1944, "both Hall and Kubinyi began exhibiting their works—including paintings, prints, and enamels—at the 1030 Gallery on Euclid Avenue in downtown Cleveland. The work they exhibited was subsequently shown at the Fine Arts Association in Boise, Idaho."

Doris Hall, bowl, enamel on copper, 5-1/4" diameter x 1" high, *Collection of Marbeth Schon, photograph by Shirley Byrne.*

In the 1930s Hall was gaining a regional reputation through the Cleveland Museum of Art annual May Shows. In 1942 she was awarded an honorable mention for her first submission to the May Show--enameled jewelry and an enameled plaque.

At the end of World War II copper was more readily available and she was able to work on a much larger scale, producing wall-mounted enamel plates and chargers.

In 1946 the Kubinyi's had the good fortune to be introduced to stationary and gift store owner H. George Caspari who, after seeing a pair of Hall's enameled earrings at a party, was determined to "track down the artist." When he did, he ordered a number of Hall's enamels to sell in his various shops. He was also able to place some of Hall's enamels in the gift shop of the Museum of Modern Art. After this experience Kubinyi decided to devote more time to his enameling partnership with Hall. Kunbinyi described the collaboration in his private journal: "Control of color, design and most of the application of the enamel is done by Doris. I beat out the large sculptural forms, the metal forming, fabrication, ground coats, compounding of enamels, spraying and burning of undercoats. I take the brunt of the preparation."

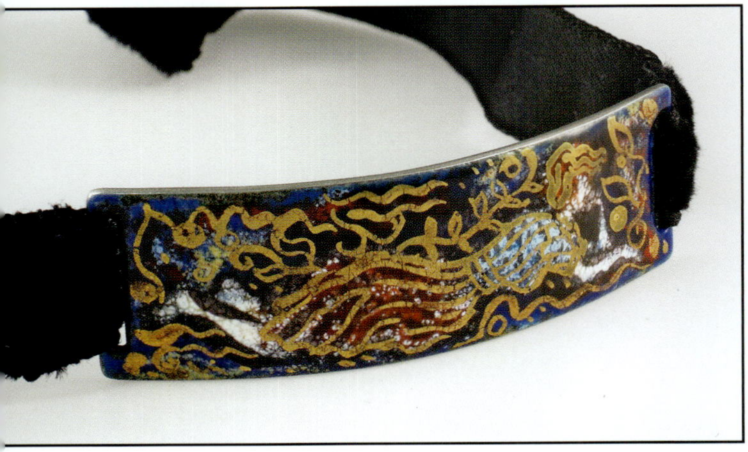

Doris Hall, choker, sterling silver, enamel, velvet ribbon, center plaque: 2-3/8" x ¾". *Collection of Marbeth Schon, photograph by Shirley Byrne.*

Due to an exhibition of Hall's enamels at the prominent New York showroom for Orrefors glass, museums and galleries throughout the country started to collect and exhibit her work.

In 1946 Hall was represented at the Syracuse Museum of Fine Arts' *National Ceramic Exhibition* and also began entering work in the Cleveland *May Show* on a regular basis.

In 1948 Hall's work was shown in an exhibition at America House in New York City, titled *Beauty in Enamels*. "The exhibition was one of the earliest to survey contemporary enameling in this country. "

In 1950 the Kubinyi's moved permanently to Gloucester, Massachusetts, where they opened a gallery and coffee shop on Rocky Neck to exhibit both paintings and enamels. Because they could now afford better materials, Kubinyi began to create enamel settings in sterling silver.

In 1951 the Kubinyis were employed by Robert Weaver as artistic directors of the Bettinger Corporation in Waltham Massachusetts. The firm produced enamel products for home and industrial use. Through Bettinger the artists had access to the technical resources and large kilns that allowed their work to expand to a monumental, architectural scale. Kubinyi believed that the medium was well suited to this scale--"Enamel is ideal for large outdoor mural purposes. Painting with fire on a grand scale is so very new compared to oil painting and other forms of art that it deserves to be seriously studied and seriously taught."

In 1952, at the May show, Hall won the coveted Horace E. Potter Memorial Award for Excellence in Craftsmanship and in 1953, she won first prize for two large panels titled *Ardito* and *Amoroso.*

In 1953 she received the New York Architectural league's silver medal in recognition of her accomplishments in the large-scale mural, *Daphnephoria.*

"One of the greatest collaborative works to emerge from this partnership is the twenty-eight-foot-diameter world globe that was commissioned by Babson College in Wellesley, Massachusetts and delivered in 1955. The maps of the various nations were enameled on steel and placed in their appropriate locations on the globe."

In 1959 the Kubinyi's purchased a home in the Beacon Hill section of Boston and opened a studio on Newbury Street. Also in 1959 Doris Hall was represented in the exhibition *Enamels* at the Museum of Contemporary Crafts in New York.

In 1963 Hall had to resign her position at Bettinger when she developed silicosis, a respiratory disease triggered by inhaling silica dust. That same year the Kabinyis moved to Stockbridge, Massachusetts where they renovated an older home to accommodate both living quarters and a retail shop that they named Cat and Drum. The shop specialized mostly in contemporary crafts.

In 1973 Kubinyi passed away from hepatitis contracted after heart surgery. Doris Hall, who never totally recovered emotionally from the death of her husband, eventually moved to New York to be close to her children where she lived until her death in 2000.

Doris Hall working at a furnace at Bettinger Corporation, Milford, Massachusetts, c. 1957, *Photograph by Will Rapport, courtesy of Lilyan Bachrach.*

Clifford Herrold

Clifford Herrold, following his being honored as a distinguished student of Central State College in Edmond, Oklahoma. *Photograph courtesy of Gerald L. Peterson, University Archivist, University of Northern Iowa.*

"My fascination with jewelry-making is maintained in the unlimited possibilities afforded for the design of exotic, sculptural forms." —Clifford Herrold

Clifford Herrold, brooch sterling silver and turquoise, 1-1/2" diameter. *Collection of Munir Meghji, photograph by Munir Meghji.*

Clifford H. Herrold (1913–1992) was born in Oklahoma. He studied at the Institute of Design in Chicago, and received his B.A. in 1939 from Central Oklahoma State College, his M.A. in 1947 from Colorado State College, and his Ed. D. in 1954 from Stanford University. [41]

He became an associate professor of art at Iowa State Teachers College, Cedar Falls, where he taught from 1947 to 1978. He traveled extensively, noting the following in his files: Canada, Mexico, Hawaii, Puerto Rico, Dominican Republic, Haiti, Jamaica, Cuba, Spain, Greece, Egypt.

Most of his work, which he sold from his studio, was done in sterling silver alone or in sterling combined with semi-precious stones and various woods. He died September 1, 1992.

Michael Higgins & Frances Higgins

Frances Higgins, necklace, glass, brass/red glass necklace, 15" circumference x 1-1/4" wide, *Collection of Joanne and Fred Doloresco, photograph by Fred Doloresco.*

Michael (1908 -1999) Higgins and Frances Higgins (1912 - 2004) were a husband and wife team who pooled their talents as artists to create their very successful enterprise, "higgins" glass. From the very beginning, their desire was to create useful glass objects that also had good visual appeal for the market, a blend of "utilitarian function and aesthetic appeal. Their production included "jewelry, bowls and plates, sculpture, screens, and roundelays," linked curtains of fused glass circles.[42]

Frances was born in Haddock, Georgia, in 1912. She graduated from the Georgia State College for Women, studied at Columbia and Ohio State Universities, and was assistant professor of Art at the University of Georgia.

Her experiments in glass began in 1942 when she tried "bending pieces in a kiln under high heat to create a plate." While studying under a Rockefeller

Foundation Fellowship at the Institute of Design, she met Michael Higgins who was Head of Visual Design. Michael, born in London, studied at Eton, Cambridge University, and the London Central School of Arts and Crafts before immigrating to the United States.

In 1948, after Frances and Michael were married, they left the Institute with the idea of making their living as designer-craftsmen. Originally planning to teach jewelry and weaving from their apartment, plans changed when they were asked to design a line of glass plates. They decided to try it, and not long after were filling orders for department stores like Marshall Field & Company. They began working incredibly long hours to keep up with the demand for their glass creations. "They made over one-hundred different types of trays, plates, bowls, and other accessories, many sold in complete sets for as little as five dollars."

In 1957 they became associated with Dearborn Glass Company of Bedford Park, Illinois and went into production with a consumer line of "reasonably priced and durable dinnerware and decorative items. Though this merger gave Higgins glass great public exposure, the tensions between the desire to produce products with handmade quality and the inherent difficulties involved with mass production were problematic enough for Michael and Frances to pull away and, except for two years with Haeger Potteries, they since operated an independent studio in Riverside, Illinois."

Michael Higgins died in 1999, and Frances died in 2004.

Joan Hurst & Jill Kingsbury

On very rare occasions you will find a piece of jewelry by Hurst & Kingsbury, two exceptional women designers who had a shop in New York in the 1940s and 1950s. The pair was Joan Hurst, a graduate of the Art Students League, and Jill Kingsbury, whose experience came from the art of the theatre and dance. Their work was constructed from cut biomorphic shapes. I have seen examples in silver, often with wire, sometimes with accents of wrapped wire and/or semi-precious stones such as moonstone or amber. Several examples are pictured in *Jewelry Making* by Kenneth Winebrenner, published in 1955.[43]

Hurst and Kingsbury, brooch, sterling silver, moonstone. 1-1/8" x 2-1/8". *Collection of Joanne and Fred Doloresco, photograph by Marbeth Schon.*

Ernesto Gonzales Jerrez

Ernesto Gonzales Jerrez , belt buckle, bronze, 2-5/8" x 4-3/8". *Collection of Joanne and Fred Doloresco, photograph by Fred Doloresco.*

Sculptor/jeweler Ernesto Gonzales Jerrez was born in Havana, Cuba, where he attended the Free School for Painters and Sculptors. In 1947, already gaining recognition for his art in his own country, the Cuban government awarded him a grant to study in the United States. He traveled to New York City where he began his studies at the Clay Club, a sculpture center in Greenwich Village. His first exhibit in the U.S. was a group show at the Whitney Museum of Art in New York City.[44]

During the latter 1940s Jerrez traveled widely in the U.S., becoming familiar with the people and witnessing the beginnings of modernism in American arts and crafts. He also discovered the oxyacetylene torch in which he saw the possibilities for use in his sculpture. "His use of this remarkable tool progressed so rapidly that he was soon able—with astonishing facility—to produce metal sculptures ranging from the minute to the monumental."

Jerrez worked with copper, steel, iron, random machine parts and bronze. He was the first (or one of the first) to fuse other metals with bronze. His large sculptures are monumental in size; for example, the groups he produced for the *Museo Nacional* (in Cuba) are each twenty feet long by ten feet high. Because of new techniques he developed that permitted him to "lessen sculptural weight without sacrificing monumental size," each weighs only fifteen hundred pounds.

His..."smaller pieces, which in their vitality and movement relate closely to the miniature sculptural arts of the archaic Greeks and Etruscans.... are created without the use of armature or pliers, they are created in three or four minutes: tiny animals of all kind—horses, bulls, unicorns; miniature human figures which take shape in a blaze of fire."

In the late 1940s Jerrez worked, exhibited and taught in New Milford Connecticut and later, in the 1950s and 1960s, did the same in Provincetown, Massachusetts.

In the late 1960s he moved to Palm Springs, California where he continued to work and exhibit his sculpture.

Michael Jerry

"I love the material. I still get excited when I go down and discover something new...teaching was ideal, because even though personally I wouldn't be working on all of those fronts, technically, it would constantly remind me of the potential of a lot of this stuff. So as I tried to excite students about working, I would also regenerate myself. I got as much out of it as they did."[45]

Michael Jerry. *Photograph courtesy of Michael Jerry.*

Michael Jerry was born in Grand Rapids, Michigan, in 1937. He first lived in Detroit where his father was Director of the WPA Art Project for the state of Michigan. The family later moved to Racine, Wisconsin, where his father was the first director of the Wustum Museum of Art (now the Racine Art Museum), and there Jerry made his first works of art.

He began his pursuit of a degree in metalsmithing when he saw an article in *The Saturday Evening Post* about the School for American Craftsman at the Rochester Institute of Technology in Rochester, New York. Armed with a National Scholastic Scholarship and some basic metalsmithing skills, he enrolled at the SAC and later continued his studies at Cranbrook Academy of Art with Richard Thomas. He returned to the School for American Craftsmen to earn both his B.F.A. and M.F.A. degrees under Hans Christensen. While studying with Christensen, he also worked as a production jeweler in the studios of both Ruth and Toza Radakovich, and Ronald Pearson – the four mentors who profoundly influenced his early jewelry and fine metal work.

In 1962 he was hired by Wisconsin State University where he taught three-dimensional design and developed a metals program. In 1970 he went to Syracuse University, accepting the metals professorship formerly held by John Marshall. At that time Jerry's work underwent a radical shift. After attending a blacksmithing conference organized by Brent Kington and Alex Bealer, he set up a blacksmithing facility at Syracuse University and experimented with iron and the combination of iron with other metals for nearly a decade. One of his pieces from this period, a hand-forged cooking pot, is in the permanent collection of the Metropolitan Museum of Art in New York City.

Jerry then turned his attention to making pewter vessels and to this day, he divides his time between the making of fine metals jewelry and pewter hollowware.

He has routinely exhibited in both national and international competitions and his work is in the permanent collections of the Museum of Arts and Design (formerly the Museum of Contemporary Crafts) and the Brooklyn Museum in New York, Yale University, the Racine Art Museum in Wisconsin, and the deYoung Museum in Los Angeles. He has been an awards judge for the Fulbright Foundation and the Ohio Arts Council, and he is a member of the American Craft Council and a charter member of the Society of North American Goldsmiths. His complete history can be found on the Smithsonian website of the *Archives of American Art*.

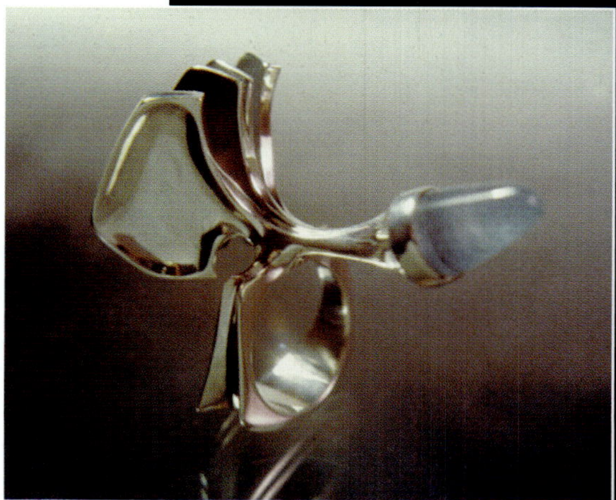

Michael Jerry, ring, sterling, aquamarine, 1-3/4" long x 1-3/4" wide x 1-1/2" deep, c. 1964. *Collection of Michael Jerry, photograph courtesy of Michael Jerry.*

Arthur King.

Arthur King

New York jeweler Arthur King (1921-1986) was a self-taught artist. He became interested in jewelry design during World War II when working with scrap metal in the United States Navy. After the war, he opened a gallery in Greenwich Village, where he became well known for his innovative jewelry designs. [46]

"Influenced by abstract painting during the 1960s, his jewelry incorporates the same sense of spontaneity and painterly gesture found in 'action painting." He worked in gold, precious gems, and baroque pearls and was a master at the technique of lost wax casting. His jewelry has an organic quality inspired by natural forms. He let his materials define the shapes of his objects and often used natural, unpolished stones.

He received numerous awards for his jewelry designs. His works are included in public and private collections around the world, including the Victoria and Albert Museum in London and the Stockholm Museum of Modern Art.

Arthur King, brooch, sterling silver, quartz, 2-1/8" x 2-1/8", *Collection of Joanne and Fred Doloresco.*

Sam Kramer

Sam Kramer at his workbench, *Photograph by Pedro E. Guerrero. Courtesy of The Sarah Bodine & Michael Dunas Archives of 20th Century Jewelry, Tyler School of Art, Temple University, Professor Stanley Lechtzin, Curator of Metals/ Jewelry Archives and Collections.*

"A jewelry craftsman, at first, tends to force his materials to fit his notions. Later he lets his ideas develop from the materials themselves, or the particular process in use, and when this happens he finds his expression growing more free and vital.

Personally, I am preoccupied with the emotional context of art. Jewelry, I feel, should express these same emotional conditions, sometimes subtly and sometimes with powerful impact and often in ways that are difficult to say. Pieces should make the observer feel and think." — Sam Kramer

Born in Pittsburgh, Pennsylvania, Sam Kramer (1913-1964) was the son of an unsuccessful produce merchant who disappeared when Sam was very young, never to return. His college education began at age of seventeen at Pittsburgh University, but he later transferred to the University of Southern California.[47]

Sam was an individualist from the very beginning. He had aspirations to be a writer together with a great deal of natural literary talent, but a fortuitous jewelry-making class with ceramist Glen Luckens, who praised his work, made a great impression on him.

His first shop was in Pittsburgh but he closed it within a few weeks because he said, "Pittsburgh was full of morbid industrialism," and "nobody there seemed to dig me." In 1938 he left his home in Pittsburgh for a nine-dollar a week room in New York City. He was able to enroll in a gemology course at New York University, but had to sell his stones and coins for food. Sam peddled his jewelry to everyone willing to look, but had few sales. "Everyone was spectacularly uninterested," he recalled.

In Greenwich Village he met the legendary landlord Papa Strunsky whose motto was "You aren't an artist if you pay your rent" and he was given a studio that had once been occupied by Eugene O'Neill. During that time he met and married Carol Enners. Later he and Carol moved the shop to a second floor walk-up at 29 West 8th Street, diagonally across from a Greenwich Village landmark called the Jumble Shop. For a while they lived a Spartan life style behind a screen in the rear of the shop. They cooked on a hot plate and slept on collapsible cots. Sam often waited on early morning customers in his pajamas.

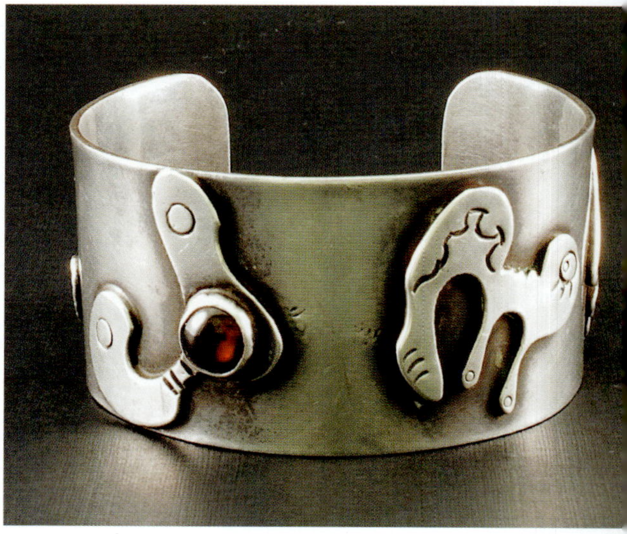

Sam Kramer, cuff, sterling silver, carnelian. *Collection of Jill Crawford, photograph by Shirley Byrne.*

When Kramer referred to his own work he usually used the words "modern" or "abstract." In his own words on a form filled out for the American Craft Council, he said, "I work in silver and gold and gems, and other metals and materials and curious objects. My work is abstract and personal, and experimental at times. It is more closely related to the areas of art than the field of design. All the pieces are entirely made by hand in our own studio-workshop. I have made pieces large enough to be called sculptures."

In an article from a 1959 Walker Art Center *Design Quarterly* Kramer said "he loved strange contrasts--paradoxes of form and texture... the shock of things that at first appear ugly, but immediately seem natural and quite beautiful." Although he appeared to be mainly interested in his own form of expression, he hoped that his ideas might play a roll in the development of public acceptance of jewelry and

Sam Kramer, Sterling ring with faceted ruby eye. Courtesy of Mark McDonald, 555 Warren St., Hudson, New York, photograph by Bill Hibbs.

Sam Kramer, brooch, *Panther,* sterling silver, 2-3/8" x 2". *Collection of Joanne and Fred Doloresco, photograph by Fred Doloresco.*

an art form. He believed that experimentation was the life flow of jewelry as a creative expression.

Kramer thought that the streamlined, unadorned, strictly modern jewelry of the early 1930s lacked vitality and sensuousness because of lack of color and that conventional jewels and stones, used in new ways as integral parts of design, were necessary for satisfactory compositions. The gems also facilitated the mysterious, symbolic qualities of design Kramer so enjoyed. Sam's love for rocks and stones was obsessive. His collection of stones included "jasper, oriental girasol, fluorite, malachite, chalcedony, and bloodstone, as well as ninety-odd other obscure ones identifiable mainly by mineralogists. "If it's a stone, I'll use it," he said.

Sam Kramer had a lifelong interest in primitive and ancient crafts and art. On an American Craft Council Questionnaire resume he lists: "Careful study of Navajo and Indian jewelry (in 1937); four trips to Mexico in the 40s for the Study of Mexican Art, archeology and jewelry and a 1952 tour of Italy and France, [for the] study of historical examples of craft, jewelry and art."

Sam Kramer died suddenly of a heart attack on June 9, 1964..."a part of the color of Greenwich Village died with him."

Earl Krentzin, brooch, *Balloon Man,* sterling silver, gold, stones, 3" x 3-1/2", *Collection of Marbeth Schon, photograph by Shirley Byrne.*

Earl Krentzin

Earl Krentzin was born in Detroit, Michigan, in 1929. There he attended Cass Technical High School, graduating with honors in 1948. Krentzin enrolled at Wayne State University, Detroit, for his undergraduate education, earning his B.F.A. in 1952. He enrolled at Cranbrook Academy of Art, Bloomfield Hills, Michigan, in 1952, where he later received his M.F.A. in metalsmithing. After Cranbrook, Krentzin took post-graduate studies at the Royal Academy of Art in London, where he studied silversmithing from 1952 through 1954. While in Europe he began a collection of delightful art objects—"primitive and folk art purchased at Europe's street markets and flea markets became the focus of his collection and inspiration for his own creations."[48]

Krentzin's techniques are rich and highly accomplished, closer to the complex work of European and Oriental craftsmen who made beautiful, unique presents for wealthy and titled persons, sometimes with an added touch of humor. Krentzin uses silver, 18-karat gold and semiprecious stones including amethyst, carnelian, onyx, agate, garnet, jasper, aventurine and malachite to create his pieces as well as other natural materials such as wood and ivory.

Krentzin says, "I'm not the kind of artist that has a message. I make these things because I like to make them. I like to let my works just speak for themselves." These days, he is mostly involved with small sculptures, not jewelry.

Krentzin's pieces are a humorous, sometimes satirical; "technological advances are satirized, occupations are romanticized, sports and other entertainment are whimsically interpreted.... he is able to assimilate his travel, teaching, collecting, researching, and profound interest in the life around him into a tiny joyous world that delights children even more than adults."

Krentzin has exhibited in numerous programs sponsored by the American Crafts Council, Michigan Silversmith's Guild, Michigan Council for the Arts, Wisconsin Designer-Craftsman Association and Cranbrook Academy of Art. He was awarded a Louis Comfort Tiffany Grant in Creative Metalwork in 1966 and a Fulbright Grant to study at the Royal Academy of Art. Mr. Krentzin, in developing a personal style of expression, amply proves that individuality is possible in all art forms and that such individuality is a worthwhile and logical goal. Without such personal interpretations of design elements, work in metal too easily becomes merely skillful technique, resulting in anonymity.[49]

Mary Kretsinger

"The Phoenix destroyed himself in a fire of his own making and rose fully vigorous out of the ashes... He recreated himself. This is the way the human spirit is meant to be." —Mary Kretsinger

Mary Kretsinger (1915-2001) was one of the most respected experimental enamellists of her generation. With successful teaching and art careers spanning more than fifty years, she dedicated her life to her art and the advancement of modernist philosophies in jewelry. She was accomplished in many art forms, including painting, printmaking, sculpture and ceramics, but it was through her unique contributions to cloisonné enameling on gold and silver jewelry and art objects that she gained international recognition.[50]

Mary was born in Emporia, Kansas, to William Kretsinger, a successful businessman involved in politics, and Rose Good Kretsinger, a renowned quilting artist, who co-authored an early definitive book on quilting, *The Romance of the Patchwork Quilt In America*. Encouraged by her mother, Kretsinger was exposed to arts and crafts at an early age, developing a variety of artistic skills. She received her BA in History at the University of Kansas, and her Masters in Art History and Design at the State University of Iowa. She continued her art studies in New York at Columbia University and the Craft Students League where she was strongly influenced by Adda Husted-Andersen. She also attended The Institute of Technology in Rochester, New York and the University of Indiana in Bloomington.

Through the 1940s and 1950s she taught art in elementary schools, intermediate schools and colleges in Arizona, Iowa, and Kansas, becoming an Associate Professor at Kansas State Teachers College (now Emporia State University) where she taught Craft Design and Ceramics. In the early 1960s she retired from professional teaching to pursue a career as a full time artist. Through gallery representations, patrons and commissioned works, she was successful, although she continued teaching art and silversmithing at facilities such as the Wichita Art Association, (now the Wichita Center for the Arts) Kansas and Worcester Craft Center, Massachusetts.

Mary Kretsinger, triptych ring, 18k gold, enamel, garnet, 2-1/2" x 1/8", *Courtesy of the Josephine A. Wallace Trust, photograph by Sheila Pamfiloff.*

Always a proponent of craft as art, she was the President of National Craftsmen's Guild, held memberships in the Kansas Art Educators Association, Kansas State Federation of Art, American-Swedish Historical Museum, Central States Craftsmen's Guild and American Craftsmen's Educational Council, lecturing throughout the Mid-west to art and jewelry associations.

By the very early 1950s she was an established member of the American modernist crafts movement with many exhibitions and awards to her credit. During her career, she was invited to exhibit in over eighty shows in galleries, art centers, and museums

Her earliest jewelry was primarily in brass, formatted in ribbons of metal in maze-like configurations with jagged edges, or flat metal pieces that were hammered, gouged and fused, creating rugged moonscape-like surfaces. Later she tamed some of the wildness with more subtle nuances, preferring to work in fine silver and 18k or 24k gold. Her surfaces are vigorous and intricate with no detail, front or back, left unattended; every closure and hinge is meticulously handmade.

Mary Kretsinger in her studio. *Courtesy of the Josephine A. Wallace Trust.*

Unique to her cloisonné work is her treatment of wire and enamels. The top wire surfaces are textured, often in a saw-tooth fashion, or the wire is soldered in loops and knots, folding the wire on itself, creating subtle high and low points and thick and thin divisions; every metal surface received her attention. Edges on boxes and jewelry have metal beading and some flat surfaces have granulation--hammered flat like nail heads, creating shiny planes. Tiny metal discs hang off of edges in random areas acting as light reflectors or embellishments. A master of multiple transparent glazing, her colors are rich and powerful, incorporating the new iridescent glazes to design advantage. She used jewel-toned enamels in small irregular shapes, floating independently in luminous backgrounds of silvery-grey, gold or pearl white, treating each bit of color as precious. Some *cloisons* were left slightly open, allowing colors to bleed into one another.

This one-of-a-kind jewelry reflects a playful wit containing surprise elements in the design; pendants, bracelets and rings may have double and triple hinges, often hiding some clever treatment on the back surface, or may have convertible parts and removable pieces that serve dual purposes. This same wit took a serious direction as she applied these techniques to her commissioned ecclesiastical works, creating processional crosses, baptismal font covers, altarpieces and devotional objects for churches and temples, including the Catholic Chapel at Brandeis University.

Although, Mary Kretsinger had a passion for travel, touring in Europe and Asia on many occasions, she chose to live the majority of her life in the family home. She passed away in 2001, at age 86, in her hometown, Emporia, Kansas, among familiar streets and memories. It is said of her that she had a bold and amazing wit. She was never embarrassed to share her thoughts, living her life following her own internal compass, which was reflected in the whimsical treatment and themes of her work.

Mary Kretsinger, double sided pendant, sterling silver, 18k gold, enamels, 2-3/4" x 3", c. 1985. *Courtesy of the Josephine A. Wallace Trust, photograph by Sheila Pamfiloff.*

Ibram Lassaw

Ibram Lassaw, standing among sculptures in his studio, Duke University, 1963. *Photograph by Charles Lewis, courtesy of the Miscellaneous Photograph Collection, Archives of American Art, Smithsonian Institution.*

Ibram Lassaw (1913 - 2003) was one of the first artists to intentionally create "sculpture to wear." One of America's leading Abstract Expressionist sculptors, his work in welded bronze is in permanent collections of most of the major museums in the United States and abroad.

For fifty years Lassaw created miniature abstract expressionist sculpture for the body. He called them "Bosom Sculptures." The Kootz Gallery in New York City sold them from 1951 until 1965. Among the early collectors of these small bronzes was Nelson A. Rockefeller who purchased eight pieces in 1951. Lassaw also sold them through other galleries, gave them to friends, and sold them from his studio. In the 1960s and 70s he began plating his pendants with silver or gold. A number of his "Bosom Sculptures" are in museum collections.[51]

Ibram Lassaw was born in Egypt. His parents left the Ukraine and stayed with relatives in Alexandria while putting together funds in order to travel to the United States. The advent of World War I delayed their emigration until 1921 when Lassaw was eight years old.

The family became established in New York and some time later, Lassaw discovered the Brooklyn Children's Museum and began a clay class taught by Dorothea Denslow. He studied classical sculpture at the Beaux Arts Institute of Design from 1930-31, and also attended City College of New York.

By 1933 Lassaw had moved to Greenwich Village where he lived a Bohemian life style moving from place to place learning how to create what he needed from whatever he could find. "He was a part of a growing group of young artists who knew each other from the Clay Club, the Art Students League, the Beaux Arts Institute or just from the Village neighborhood. Many of them, such as William de Kooning, Balcomb Green and Philip Pavia became friends for life."

Between 1933 and 1942 Lassaw worked on numerous federal arts projects: the Public Works of Art Project, the Civil Works Authority and the WPA Federal Art Project. He helped to found "American Abstract Artists" in 1936, and became president of the same from 1946 to 1949.

Lassaw observed that "art" adapted to the latest technologies and materials before the general population and realized that human thought was being redirected into the discovery of space and the character of nature. It is his open space welded sculptures in bronze, nickel silver, phos-copper, silicon bronze, steel and other alloys that he is most well known for, though he simultaneously worked with other media such as works on paper and canvas with inks and acrylic, lithographs, and welded bronze-gold plated jewelry.

Lassaw did not begin selling his work until 1951 when he was invited by Samuel Kootz to be represented by his New York gallery. Sales followed to Nelson Rockefeller, the Museum of Modern Art, the Whitney Museum of American Art and other museums. He was also one of five American Artists to be included in the 1954 Venice Biennial in Italy.

Lassaw was the Benjamin N. Duke Professor at Duke University, 1962-63; taught at the University of California, Berkeley in 1965-66; Southampton College from 1966 to the mid-70's and spent a year as a visiting professor at Mount Holyoke College.

Lassaw's work is in the permanent collections of museums on four continents, including the Museum of Modern Art, New York City; The Israel Museum, Jerusalem; The Albright Knox Gallery; Museum of Modern Art, Rio de Janeiro, Brazil; the Metropolitan Museum of Art, New York City; The Guggenheim Museum, New York City and many others.

Sam Hunter, art critic, wrote: "Few artist have made more personal and poetic statements in sculpture out of the collective impulse of abstract expressionism than Ibram Lassaw."

Idella La Vista

"For me, jewelry making is a deeply personal matter. I feel the need to bring out to the full the latent qualities in the silver, gold and stones. The keenest pleasure, however, is to design the perfect piece—pendant, bracelet, ring, etc., for a specific person. People...are still the most important part of jewelry—for it is worn for adornment and must add beauty and interest and bring out the personality of the person wearing it. The metal, stones, forms and shapes are mingled in my mind with people living in 1953, their way of living and their way of dressing as well. The jewelry which I create is frequently simple, casual and uncluttered, becoming dramatic on the simple-lined clothes worn by so many women today." [52] —Idella La Vista

Idella La Vista, pendant, sterling silver, 3" x 1-1/2". *Collection of Sherrye Webster, photograph by Marbeth Schon.*

Idella La Vista, c. 1940s. *Courtesy of Reme Aldana.*

"Stones fascinate me—precious and semi-precious. I have no interest in the precious stones other than for their accent and loveliness, and so find no interest in working for people who buy diamonds and gold jewelry as a sure money investment. " —Idella LaVista

Tennessee native, Idella La Vista, was a talented and dedicated artist who created jewelry and owned a shop where she sold her work and promoted artists from other disciplines. In the 1950s she found a small space at 44 West 54th Street in New York City that she remodeled and made into her shop and studio. As well as making jewelry (sometimes for twelve to fifteen hours a day), she sold hand-wrought jewelry, apparel accessories and interior accessories. She held exhibits featuring the paintings of Anthony Buzelli, Irene Rice Perera, Rene Procopio and Robert Borgatta as well as sculpture by Nat Werner, Chaim Gross, Adollf Adorfer, Joseph Konzal and Isabel Case Borgatta.

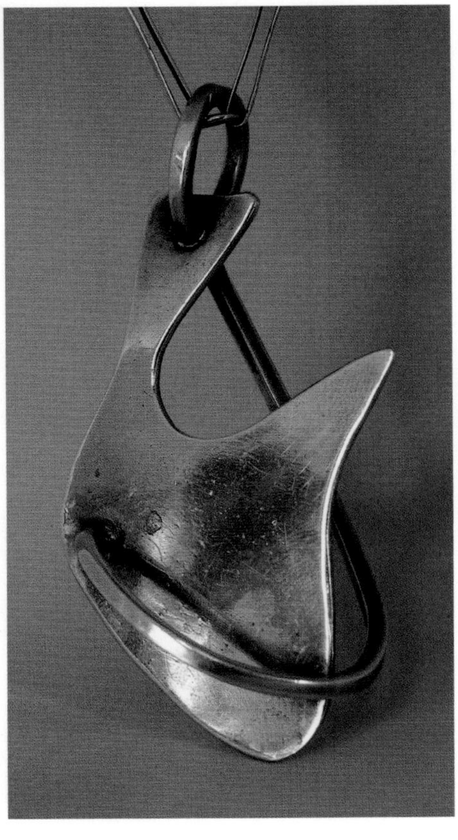

Idella LaVista in front of her shop in Greenwich Village, c. 1940-1950s. Courtesy of *Reme Aldana*.

"Friends...understand that my way of life is working in the little area behind the showroom," she explained, "which is my workshop for twelve, and frequently more, hours every day. It is a way of life, just as well as the butcher's, the carpenter's, the Wall Street broker's—the great industrialist's. I am happy to work and love to be surrounded in my shop by other beautiful crafts that other serious artists throughout the country are creating today...thus adding to and enriching our culture."

Her design inspirations came from many sources. "For me," she said, "everything that I see, touch, do, hear...provokes, stimulates, fills me with thought—whether I walk down a city street, a lonely country road—take a night flight—go to the theatre, or watch children play."

She worked along with her husband and though they came to jewelry along different paths—he through engineering and she through dance, their different experiences were mutually beneficial to the work they produced.

She spoke of the joy of making something by hand:

> We were a rugged people who did things actively a hundred years ago. We felled the forests and built our homes, made our furniture and most of our decorations. We were strong, courageous, and ingenious. Our country was young and the men and women who built it faced hardships and dangers. Today we have modern cities and beautiful farms. We watch baseball games, play canasta, sit cozily and watch television programs, see a film about once every week. And a subtle transformation has taken place in our lives that we may not even be aware of most of the time. We are passive and a little unhappy about it. We really have a great deal of fun when we do something ourselves, knowing that we are able to do it, and well, too, but not even thinking of ourselves in a professional capacity.

Idella La Vista studied at the Beaux Arts in France and worked with a goldsmith in Paris. She exhibited her work at Craft Exhibits in New York City and Wichita, Kansas.

Stanley Lechtzin

"We arise out of historic competence." —Stanley Lechtzin

Stanley Lechtzin was born and educated in Detroit, Michigan. His father owned a drug store and Lechtzin's first job was working behind the soda fountain. Early on he decided that the drugstore business was not to be his career choice— he said he did not want to "spend his life making pills."

He enrolled in Cass Technical High School in central Detroit, a school that still continues to offer technical training—at that time their curriculum included drafting,

Stanley Lechtzin at his workbench in 1968. *Photograph courtesy of Stanley Lechtzin.*

auto mechanics and even a foundry program. He took as many technical courses as he could and began thinking about beginning an apprenticeship in the tool and dye industry but could not gain access to the union, probably fortuitously, because he was offered a job by the father of one of his friends to do jewelry repair after school where he learned the basics of jewelry making. Though he had no plans for a career in jewelry, he decided as a lark to take a jewelry course at Cass where his innate artistic talents were quickly recognized by his teacher who linked him with Phillip Fike at Wayne State University.[53]

Stanley Lechtzin at his workbench in 1968, *Photograph courtesy of Stanley Lechtzin.*

Excited by the possibility of taking jewelry courses on the college level, Lechtzin applied and was accepted at Wayne State University where he was told that he would need to take basic art courses such as drawing and design before he would be able to work with Fike—news that motivated Lechtzin to "dive" into the art curriculum. While at Wayne he set up his own studio and began to receive awards and commissions for his work. Lechtzin's earliest work shows influences of the niello work of Phillip Fike.

He received his B.F.A. from Wayne and, in 1960, enrolled at Cranbrook Academy of Art where he studied metalsmithing with Richard Thomas. It was at Cranbrook that he first began to understand and respect the academic community and its goals; he developed a sense of the value of academic freedom and the importance of research. Lechtzin completed his master's degree at Cranbrook with a thesis on gold granulation.

At the time Lechtzin graduated from Cranbrook, in the early 1960s, universities were beginning to reestablish their metals programs and as he said, "there were many positions to choose from." Lechtzin chose Tyler School of Art at Temple University in Philadelphia where, after five years, he developed a graduate program in metals that, continuing under Lechtzin's leadership for over forty years, has become one of the most innovative and well respected programs of its kind in the world.

Lechtzin said that the research he did with Phillip Fike at Wayne State University provided an example of what one can do in a university setting that is "true research" and still meaningful in terms of art. This is probably what stimulated his idea to pursue electroforming. Electrochemistry was invented and developed in the 19th century, but, at that time, had only a short period of interest for the arts. The technical and research aspects of electroforming appealed to Lechtzin as well as its possibilities for the creation of large, lightweight forms.

In 1964 he volunteered to present his recently developed technology to the First World Congress of Craftsmen in New York City. In preparation for this and in order to see what types of visual statements other craftsmen could make with the process, he invited a group of metalsmiths, including Olaf Skoogfors, Phillip Fike, Earl Krentzin and Ron Pearson, to participate in a weekend workshop at Tyler. The group generated more than 30 pieces, all of which were shown at the metal symposium of the World Congress.

For the development of the processes of electroforming in making jewelry, Lechtzin has received numerous research grants from Temple University and a Craftsmen's Fellowship from the National Endowment for the Arts in 1973, 1976 and 1984.

Stanley Lechtzin, brooch , electroformed silver gilt, amethyst, 8-3/4" x 3" x 2". *Courtesy of Stanley Lechtzin.*

Lechtzin, who is more comfortable working directly with materials than creating sketches now uses the computer as one way of "working directly." In the late 1970s he started to look to computers and computer aided technologies as a new way of making jewelry. He believes that artists are the "cultural antenna" of society and in that role address the issues of contemporary society; unique objects have and will continue to maintain importance in society. Reaching into the future, he is engaged in an exploration of how metalsmithing and craft communities are changing to fulfill the continuing need for unique objects in society as well as what the objects will be and how they will be made."

Since 1958 Lechtzin's work has been exhibited extensively in the United States and abroad. Some of the most important exhibitions were: *Jewelry 1967 Trends, Invitational*, Schmuck-Museum, Pforzheim, West Germany; International Jewelry Exhibition, invitational, Tokyo, 1970 and 1973; *The Art of the Jewel*, Florence, 1973; *Twentieth Century Jewelry*, Electrum Gallery, London, England, 1985; *Masterworks of Contemporary American Jewelry*, Victoria and Albert Museum, London, 1985; *CRAFT TODAY: Poetry of the Physical*, American Craft Museum, New York, 1986; *The Eloquent Object*, The Philbrook Museum of Art Tulsa, 1987; and one-man exhibits at the Museum of Contemporary Crafts, New York, 1965, Goldsmiths' Hall, London, 1973, The Works Gallery, Philadelphia, 1984;The University of Pittsburgh Art Gallery, 1984.

Stanley Lechtzin received the *Young American Bronze Medal for Excellence in Design and Craftsmanship* and *Craft Horizons* magazine award in 1962, the *Hazelett Memorial Award for Excellence in the Arts in Pennsylvania* in 1984, and a Fellowship in Crafts, Pennsylvania Council on the Arts in 1987.

From 1984 until the present he has exhibited in countless National and International Exhibitions and won numerous awards for his distinguished career as an innovator in the field of metalsmithing and teaching.

Ed Levin at his workbench. *Courtesy of Ed Levin.*

Ed Levin

New York City was the birthplace of Ed Levin in 1921. He had a natural inclination for the arts and after spending his youth on Long Island, decided to enter Columbia University to study fine arts. His interest in the arts was diverse and was continued later at the Barnes Foundation, the New School for Social Research, private study with sculptor Chaim Gross and painting with Kurt Seligman and Paul Wieghardt and courses in ceramics at Alfred University.[54]

The Cuban-American metalsmith, Francisco Rebajes was one of the few modernist jewelers Levin could find in the 1930s when he went looking for an unusual gift for his mother. He purchased two of Rebaje's copper stylized cubist brooches. Levin began making his own jewelry in 1942, creating rings from lathe-turned steel.

Levin took the "less traveled path" during the war years as a pacifist and social activist working with the very beginnings of CORE, the movement for racial equality,

Ed Levin, brooch, sterling silver, 1" x 1-1/4". *Collection of Joanne and Fred Doloresco, photograph by Fred Doloresco.*

devoting some of his time to a ward for psychotic children in Chicago and, in 1943, co-founding a commune in a West Side Chicago slum.

When he returned to New York, Levin taught painting, ceramics, woodworking, and pottery at the 110th Street Community Center in Harlem. Levin still enjoys the roll of educator and is very proud that he has been able to teach hundreds of jeweler/artisans throughout the decades he has been producing jewelry in such places as Bennington, Vermont and Cambridge, New York.

While Levin was visiting Buenos Aires with his family after the war, around 1947, a seventy-year-old Florentine jeweler, Seňor Michi, had a profound influence on him. Seňor Michi worked in the Renaissance tradition and made some of his own tools by hand. Levin was fascinated by the hands-on production and decided to remain in Argentina with his brother who was living there. In order to support himself, he went to work for the elderly metalsmith. From Michi he learned to use gold and silver, to make his own alloys and to create innovative handmade objects that were self-expressed works of art and not mere adornment. "Every step in the process was done by hand, from processing the metals, to stretching it into wire, to polishing it into a miniature work of art." This training was paramount to Levin's later experiences as a studio jeweler. Levin's ability to make his own tools, developed from his experiences in Argentina and also from his skill as a machinist, is one of the reasons for the remarkably fine craftsmanship of his jewelry.

Returning to New York from Argentina about 1948, Levin began working as full-time craftsmen from his railroad flat beneath what is now Lincoln Center. Nostalgia for the country and the inspirations he found in nature drew him to rural Shaftsbury, Vermont in 1953 where he set up an attic studio with his wife, Ruth. He and Ruth worked alone until he hired Charles Thompson in 1958.

Levin's early handmade jewelry was made from silver in the constructivist tradition. Wire often intersected his designs sometimes holding pearls or semi-precious stones threaded or suspended creating interest and movement. Oxidation was used to emphasize forms and Levin, like Ed Wiener and Art Smith, was concerned with the use of negative space as an element of design.

The popularity of Levin's jewelry inspired him to seek a different location and in 1964, he decided to move to Bennington Village where his business would attract more customers. There, the demand for his work grew more rapidly and soon his shop "The Levin Arts Workshop" employed six artisans. The company was occupied with both wholesale and retail operations.

Levin's jewelry remained true to his respect for materials and good design. Originally one artisan was responsible for a particular piece from start to finish. "The apprentice would receive a "kit' which would include an original made by Levin and step-by-step instructions detailing the entire procedure in sequential order. Each piece, upon completion, would be personally inspected by Levin and approved before it could be sold."

In the 1970s, spurred on by the increasing market for handcrafted jewelry, and at the advice of an uncle, Levin decided to sell his business in Bennington to move to a larger facility in Cambridge, New York. His desire was to increase the quantity and cost-effectiveness of his production without jeopardizing the quality and spontaneity of his jewelry designs. Levin was able to accomplish this by developing a new, unique production operation.

Levin's business is now housed in a refurbished 19th century building in Cambridge, New York.

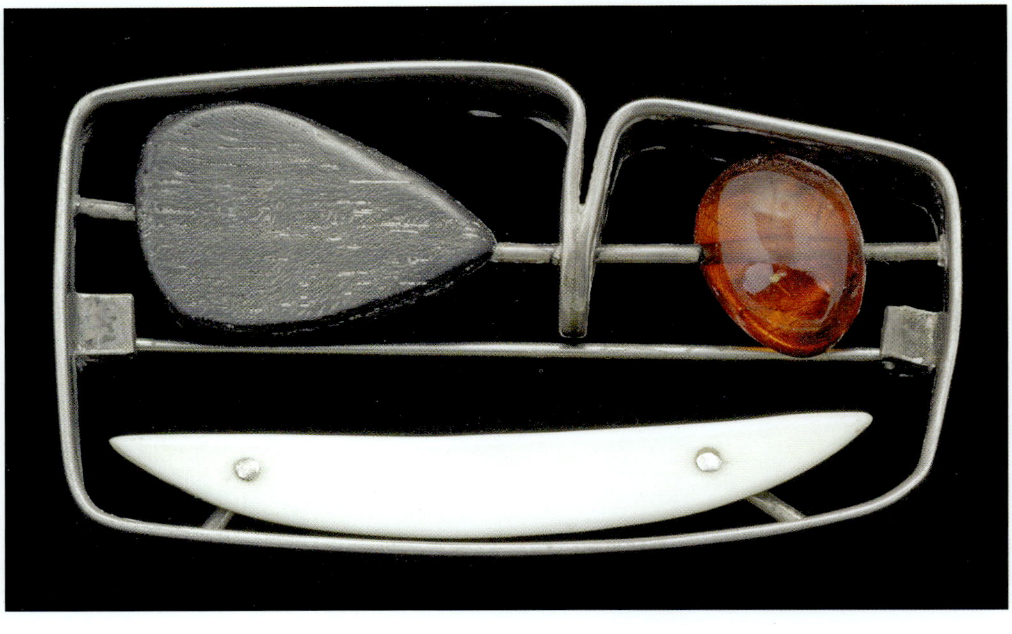

Ed Levin, brooch, sterling silver, ivory, ebony, 1-7/8" x 1-1/8". *Courtesy of Mark McDonald, 555 Warren St., Hudson, New York, photograph by Bill Hibbs.*

Esther Lewittes

Esther Lewittes received a degree from Columbia University's Teachers College in New York City where she also studied Industrial Design at the Art Students League and jewelry making with a staff jeweler at Cartier. In the 1950s she began creating her own jewelry and selling it at stores such as Georg Jensen and America House in New York City and Nanny's in San Francisco.[55]

After moving to California she became known as one of the most "colorful" jewelers working in the Los Angles area. About 1961 she opened a gallery on La Cienega Boulevard in Los Angeles and moved to Melrose Avenue about a year later. She carried her own jewelry as well as handmade pieces by other artists working in many different media.

Lewittes's forms were both forged and cast, mostly abstract constructed designs sometimes incorporating stones, wood or ivory.

Esther Lewittes, bracelet and earrings, sterling silver. *Collection of Steven Cabella, photograph by Geoff Turner.*

Paul Lobel

"Paul Lobel had small interest in fame or fortune. He was first and always an original and dedicated explorer in art."[56]

Romanian born Paul Lobel, (1899-1983) one of the most well-known of the mid-20th century modernist jewelers, was also a successful painter, cartoonist, sculptor, and designer of glass, furniture and silver hollowware. His life began modestly on Manhattan's Lower East Side. "Lobel's first venture into the industrial arts field was a hanging match holder made from a flattened tobacco (or sardine) tin, which he embellished with a pair of stiff calla lilies. This he created while a member of the P.S. 34 art club, where the group's mentor, Mr. Reich, reveled in training his young students to compete with the arts and crafts group of P.S. 62, 'The Snobs of Hester Street."[57]

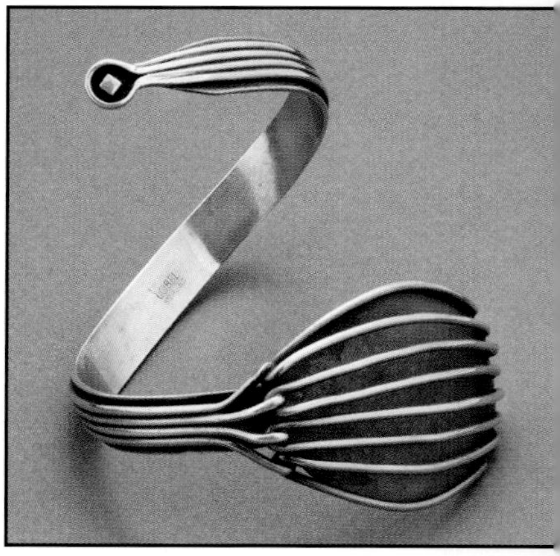

Paul Lobel, cuff, sterling silver, 3-1/4 x 2-1/2. *Courtesy of Mark McDonald, 555 Warren St., Hudson, New York, photograph by Bill Hibbs.*

As soon as he was old enough, Lobel began looking for employment. He worked at numerous odd jobs until, after studying mechanical drafting at the Mechanic's Institute, he was employed by the U.S. Rubber Co. as a junior draftsmen.

At the beginning of World War I Lobel signed up for the radio operator's course offered by the Marconi Communications Institute (later known as R.C.A.) The war was over when he received his operator's license so he joined the merchant marine where he could use his new skills.

When the merchant fleet was downsizing and his skills were in less demand, he enrolled in a commercial art course at Pratt Institute in Brooklyn, New York and studied illustration with cartoonist/painter, Boardman

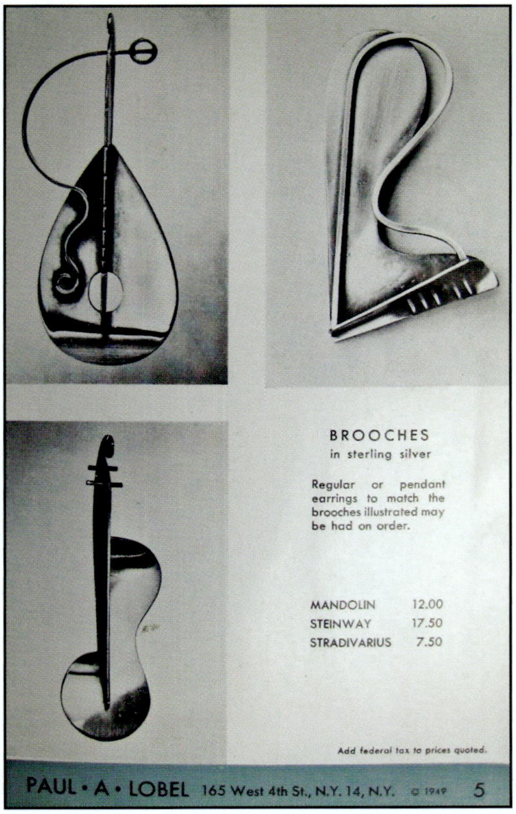

Paul Lobel brochure, c. 1949, Courtesy of The Sarah Bodine & Michael Dunas Archives of 20th Century Jewelry, Tyler School of Art, Temple University,Professor Stanley Lechtzin, Curator of Metals/Jewelry and collection.

Robinson at the Art Student's League. He was able to sell a series of drawings to Brooks Atkinson, editor of the Book Review Section of *The New York Times* and also made some decorative black-and-white sketches for the *New Yorker* magazine and *Collier's Weekly* as well as designing book jackets.

By 1925 he had put together enough money to go to Europe, and, fortuitously, arrived in Paris just in time for the *Exposition International des Arts Decoratifs et Industriels Modernes* where he saw what he perceived was a revolution in three-dimensional design. Soon after this experience, he began his first experiments with metal. A miniature-constructed bullring was one of his first projects and in less than a year, Lobel was exhibiting his artwork. In the summer of 1926 he showed 35 works including drawings, etchings, paintings, metalwork and sculpture in a one-man show at the *Grande Librairie Universelle* in Paris. The next year he traveled throughout Europe absorbing the arts of London, Rome, Florence, Rotterdam, Brussels, and Berlin. When funds ran out he returned to America where, by necessity, he went back into advertising.

Paris and the flourishing of modern design he had witnessed in Europe inspired him to borrow the money needed to open his first metalworking studio on New York's Lexington Avenue. Architect Eugene Schoen was opening a new gallery at that time in order to show modernist work by designers and craftsmen. Schoen's inaugural exhibition was a one-man show of works in brass by Paul Lobel who, as a result, gained several commissions for private estates and yachts. In 1928 he was able to exhibit his sculpture in the *Exhibition of Decorative Arts* of the National Arts Club, New York City, sponsored by R.H. Macy & Co.

From 1929 until the beginnings of World War II, Lobel was mostly involved with Industrial Design. One of Lobel's most famous discoveries, the Benduro process, developed from his experiments with bending glass. The Benduro line--textured glass in either a "diced" or "ribbed" pattern produced in several colors was made between 1935-1943. Offerings were informal well-designed wares including candlesticks, ashtrays, cocktail mixers, tables, magazine racks, bowls, dishes, boxes, mirrors, wastepaper baskets and vanities. This line won several awards including the Home Furnishings Silver Medal and the Ceramics and Crystal Works Bronze Medal of the *International Exposition of Decorative Arts* in Paris in 1937. Continuing to create objects in silver, Lobel exhibited in *Contemporary Industrial and Handwrought Silver* at the Brooklyn Museum in 1937 and in 1940 was included in *Silver: An Exhibition of Contemporary American Design by Manufacturers, Designers and Craftsmen* at the Metropolitan Museum of Art.

He continued to design in other materials, experimenting with individual transportation units for the New York World's Fair. He did a series of lamps for American Designs Inc. and Russell Wright and worked in the design of wooden furniture from wooden slats including screens, tables, trays, hampers and other household accessories.

Paul Lobel, pendant, sterling silver, 2-1/2" x 1-1/4". *Collection of Joanne and Fred Doloresco, photograph by Fred Doloresco.*

During World War II Lobel was one of the first (before either Sam Kramer or Art Smith) to open a studio/shop in Greenwich Village. Lobel's was at 165 West 4th Street and it was there that he began to create jewelry and small sculptures. Though modernist in construction, the sometimes-stylized themes of Lobel's jewelry tend to be reminiscent of earlier Art Deco pieces or show influences of American Regionalist art of the 1930s.

His abstracted musical instruments are often derivative of cubist motifs as in the work of Picasso or Braque. Lobel also used floral and animal themes regularly as well as creating more purely abstract constructed necklaces, bracelets, pendants, earrings, etc. His pieces were simple and unadorned and the influence of Lobel's background in industrial design is often apparent.

Sometime in the late 1950s Lobel closed his shop in Greenwich Village. He returned to industrial design and, in the 1960s and early 1970s, worked in plastics . His last experiments were with paper in what he called "paperteering" which was the creation of sculptures from newspaper. The sculptures were mostly influenced by African and Native American masks and they were shown in 1972 at the New York public Library's Donnell branch.

Paul Lobel passed away in 1983. His contributions to numerous facets of the decorative arts are significant. He is revered by those who own and collect his jewelry as one of the founding members of the movement that created "wearable art."

Lobel's accomplishments included a one-man show in Paris in 1925, two awards at the *International Exposition of Decorative Arts* in Paris in 1937, and exhibitions at the Museum of Modern Art in New York City.

Charles Loloma

Charles Loloma, cuff, sterling silver, turquoise. Collection of Jill Crawford, photograph by Shirley Byrne.

Charles Loloma (1921-1991) is known as "the most influential Native American jeweler of the twentieth century." His career in the arts began in high school, where he studied painting. In 1945 he moved away from the Hopi Reservation to study ceramics at the School for American Craftsmen in New York City. He then went to Arizona where he opened a ceramics studio at the Kiva Crafts center, and from 1954 – 1958 taught a ceramics course at Arizona State University. During that time Loloma changed from ceramics to a career in making jewelry. His lavish and groundbreaking way of setting and using stones, wood, ivory, and other materials made him an "undisputed master who personally broke down the barriers of regionalism and helped give contemporary Native American Art worldwide recognition." [58]

He established an international reputation and was featured in many magazines including *National Geographic, Arizona Highways, American Craft, and Metalsmith*. In 1973 he became a member of the Arizona Commission on the Arts and Humanities and in 1974 he was an artist in residence in Japan and Korea. In 1976 he was made a fellow of the American Craft Council.[59]

Daniel Macchiarini

Daniel and Peter Macchairini at their studio on Upper Grant Ave., San Francisco in 1998. *Photograph by Marbeth Schon*

"My first memories of the shop (the studio), was a space where my father and mother created and encouraged me in creating visual artwork. In the late 1950s and early 1960s, I would come to the shop every day during the summer, and every Saturday during the school year. I learned to both hard and soft solder when I was seven years old, and gas weld iron by the time I was nine. My father would have me focus on the projects I had designed and he insisted that I finish everything I started. He took time to teach me basic metal working...skills and art was always all around---integrated into my existence and consciousness. His opinions and direction were ever present."[60] — Daniel Macchiarini

Daniel Macchiarini (b. 1953) speaks of the rich experiences of his childhood in his father's shop in the hip section of San Francisco called North Beach:

> The shop was a center for a wide community of artists and iconoclasts who, along with customers, constantly came in to discuss art, sometimes buying, but always intellectualizing about modernism and art in general. Among them were people like Bufano, a regular visitor who would always critique my work. I remember Margaret De Patta and the wonderful discussions she had with my father about the work they were creating and his great grief on hearing of her death in 1963. The African-American sculptor and muralist Sargent Johnson was also an ever-present visitor to the shop; he lived on Telegraph Hill and frequented the New Tivoli Bar with my father along with a myriad of other artists for their nightly, early evening rendezvous. Johnson told great stories of Mexico, the women he knew, his life and art. Joe Rosenthal, the photographer who took the shot of the Marines raising the flag at Iwo Jima, was also among the regulars.
>
> So many others I can't remember. I was raised in the studio and at that bar, hearing about their strife and struggles as well as the great triumphs and joys they felt from their work. This was the scene and I took it for granted. I was not legally supposed to be at the bar but it was never questioned that I was allowed there. I didn't drink, but I "drank" in ...the ambiance of these characters of iconoclast intellect.... As a young boy I was totally accepted in the presence of these artists and mentored by them. It was...natural and I thought nothing of it ...even though now I consider my whole upbringing as an incredibly extraordinary education, unique, complete and positively exceptional.

Though Daniel Macchiarini continues to advance his father's explorations into design, techniques and materials, he is making his own unique contributions to the same. One in particular is his study of reversible designs like the bracelet, pendant and brooch below.

Daniel Macchiarini, reversible bracelet, sterling silver, copper, bras, bronze, ebony, ivory, 7-1/3" x 1/1/4" x 14", *Collection of Juliette Kontor. Photograph by John Kontor.*

Daniel Macchiarini, pendant (can be added to the bracelet below as an extra link), sterling silver, bronze, copper, bras, ebony, ivory, wood, 1-1/3" x 1". *Collection of Juliette Kontor. Photograph by John Kontor.*

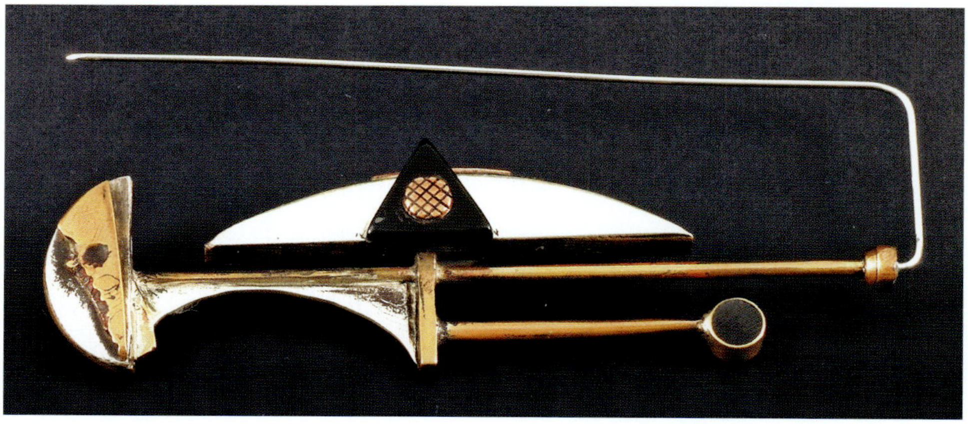

Daniel Macchiarini, reversible brooch, sterling silver, brass, copper, onyx, ebony, ivory, 4-1/2" x 3/4". *Collection of Jill Crawford, photographs by Shirley Byrne.*

Remaining true to his father's tradition of creating handmade jewelry from a studio where customers can participate in intellectual conversation while watching their pieces being made, Daniel Macchiarini is involving customers with the actual process of creating jewelry—they participate in a "casting event." When a piece requires the use of the "lost wax" centrifugal force casting process, Daniel invites the customer to put the metal for their piece into the crucible, then Daniel melts the metal and casts the work before their eyes. When they break the mold, they see their piece emerge in metal! Though, after the casting process, about eighty percent of the work in the actual metal is done by Daniel, these casting events further the integration of the artist with the people who buy and wear his jewelry.

Daniel's father, Peter Macchiarini, is considered one of the pioneers in the field of modernist sculpture and jewelry. Daniel defines himself as a neo-modernist. Staying within the traditions of the early modernists, Daniel creates pieces of enduring artistic value through serious study of form and design, but he also embraces elements of "post modernist" thinking which celebrates the greater involvement of artists with society and its influences on the creative processes of individual artists.

Though the Macchiarini Shop and Studio (now called Macchiarini Creative Design and Metalworks Gallery) has moved a few times, always within a few blocks of the orginal North Beach lovation where Peter Maccharini became established many years ago. It is one of very few metal studios (if not the only one) that has continued as a working studio from the 1930s to the present day.

Peter Macchiarini at his work bench in 1970. *Photograph courtesy of Daniel Macchiarini.*

Peter Macchiarini

"At any price, the product of an artist is in itself a major contribution to society as a whole."

"Creative spontaneity cannot be bridled to a machine." —Peter Macciarini

Peter Macchiarini (1909-2001) was born to Italian parents on the Wohler Ranch, a hopyard and vineyard spread on the Russian River near Santa Rosa, Sonoma County, California. He attended grammar school and high schools in Sonoma County until the age of fourteen, at which time his parents returned to Italy. In Italy, Macchiarini took preliminary courses in the Italian language and after deciding on an artistic career, took entry examinations for the Art Academy Pietrasanta, Province of Lucca, and was accepted. At the Academy he received basic training in marble carving, clay modeling, architectural drawings, and general sciences. [61]

Peter Macchiarini, brooch, sterling silver, brass, iconel, ivory, 4-5/8" x 1-5/8". *Courtesy of Mark McDonald, 555 Warren St., Hudson, New York, photograph by Bill Hibbs.*

Peter Macchiarini, pendant, carved ivory, bronze, silver, copper. *Courtesy of Daniel Macchiarini, photograph by Leslie W. Rabine.*

In 1928 he returned to the United States where he was employed as a stone carver with several San Francisco Bay area firms. He continued his art studies by taking night courses in San Francisco at the California School of Fine Arts. In 1936 he worked on projects under Beniamino Bufano and Ralph Stackpole.

His first jewelry was made in 1936, but he was not able to open his own business and devote himself full time to making original contemporary jewelry until the end of World War II.

Macchiarini helped organize the first San Francisco outdoor Art Festivals in Hotaling Place and the Ferry Building in 1939, 1940 and 1941. During the 1952 and 1955 six-week summer sessions at Mills College, Oakland, California, he taught jewelry and metal sculpture and in 1953 he conducted a jewelry course in Lafayette, California.

His sculpture and jewelry are represented in the permanent collections of the State of California, the Oakland Museum, the City and County of San Francisco, the Walter Benisek Gallery, the Montreal Museum, the Metal Arts Guild (of which he was one of the original organizers) and many private collections.

Peter Macchiarini, brooch, wood, silver, brass, copper, 3-1/4" x 2-1/8". *Collection of Joanne and Fred Doloresco, photograph by Fred Doloresco.*

Peter Macchiarini, *Amazon* sculpture, bronze on mahogany base, 20" high, c.1965, *Collection of Daniel Maccharini, photograph by Leslie W. Rabine.*

Peter Macchiarini's location at 1529 Grant Avenue was, like Sam Kramer's studio in New York City, a center for intellectual discussion as well as a studio/shop. Artists like sculptor Beniamino Bufano, The African-American sculptor and muralist Sargent Johnson, and jeweler Margaret De Patta were regular visitors whose presence guaranteed intense conversations about modernism.

Macchiarini's pieces were made from various metals often used in combination including silver, nickel silver, copper, brass and iron. Other frequently used materials were ivory and ebony along with natural and synthetic stones. Like Margaret De Patta, Macchiarini called on San Francisco lapidary Francis Sperisen for special cuts for specific design problems. Macchiarini's work was always handcrafted.

peter macchiarini

YU6-5847 1415 GRANT AVE SAN FRANCISCO 11, CALIFORNIA

BROOCHES	1 silver	$ 35.00
	2 silver and bronze	35.00
	3 silver and bronze with pearl	30.00
	4 silver with onyx	30.00
	5 bronze and silver	30.00
	6 silver	25.00
	7 silver	25.00
	8 silver	45.00
	9 silver, bronze, and copper with green-sulphate areas	25.00
	10 silver with quartz	25.00
	11 bronze with green-sulphate areas	25.00
	12 sterling silver and copper	30.00
PENDANTS	13 sterling silver and copper with green-sulphate areas	25.00
	14 bronze with green-sulphate areas	25.00
	15 bronze with green-sulphate areas	25.00
	16 sterling silver and copper with green-sulphate areas	25.00
	17 bronze with green sulphate areas	25.00
	18 sterling silver with green-sulphate areas	25.00
	19 bronze with green-sulphate areas	25.00
RINGS	20 pinky, sterling silver	20.00
	21 sterling silver with cultured pearl	35.00
	22 man's size sterling silver	40.00
	23 wedding bands, sterling silver . each	28.20
	or gold . each	40.00
	24 pinky, sterling silver	20.00
	25 wedding bands, gold . each	40.00
	26 wedding bands, sterling silver . each	20.00
	or gold . each	40.00
CUFF LINKS	27 sterling silver	20.00
	28 sterling silver	17.50
	29 sterling silver	17.50
	30 sterling silver	12.50
	31 sterling silver	12.50
	32 sterling silver	20.00
EARRINGS	33 sterling silver	20.00
	34 bronze and sterling silver with green-sulphate areas	10.00
BELT BUCKLES	35 bronze	20.00
	36 sterling silver and copper with green-sulphate areas	35.00
BRACELETS	37 bronze and copper with green-sulphate areas	100.00
	38 bronze and copper with green-sulphate areas	100.00

Peter Macchiarini Studio brochure, *Courtesy of Daniel Macchiarini.*

Peter Macchiarini, brooch, silver, copper, brass, ebony, ivory, 1-1/8" wide x 2-3/8" inside diameter, 4"high x 3-3/8" wide. *Collection of Jill Crawford, photograph by Shirley Byrne.*

Peter pioneered centrifugal force casting with modern centrifuge processes as early as the 1930s and used it, not for mass production, but to create one-of-a-kind pieces sometimes constructed from both forged and cast elements. He advocated that all art and, in particular, jewelry should be labeled in any retail setting as to its origins: as individually hand crafted and custom made or mass produced so the public could have an honest view of the character of the work.

Peter Macchiarini was a well-loved member of his community, known for his humanity as well as his artistic achievements. He held the unofficial title of "Mayor of Upper Grant Street" and on his 90th birthday in September of 1999, the city of San Francisco honored him by naming the steep set of steps on Kearny Street, in North Beach where he had his very first studio in 1933, "Peter Macchiarini Steps."

Macchiarini passed away in 2001, but his legacy continues through his extraordinary sculptures and wearable works of art.

Peter Macchiarini using his centrifugal casting machine, c. 1956, *Courtesy of Daniel Macchairini.*

Peter Macchiarini, brooch, silver, copper, brass, ebony, ivory, 1-1/8" wide x 2-3/8"(inside diameter) x 4"high x 3-3/8" wide. *Collection of Jill Crawford, photograph by Shirley Byrne.*

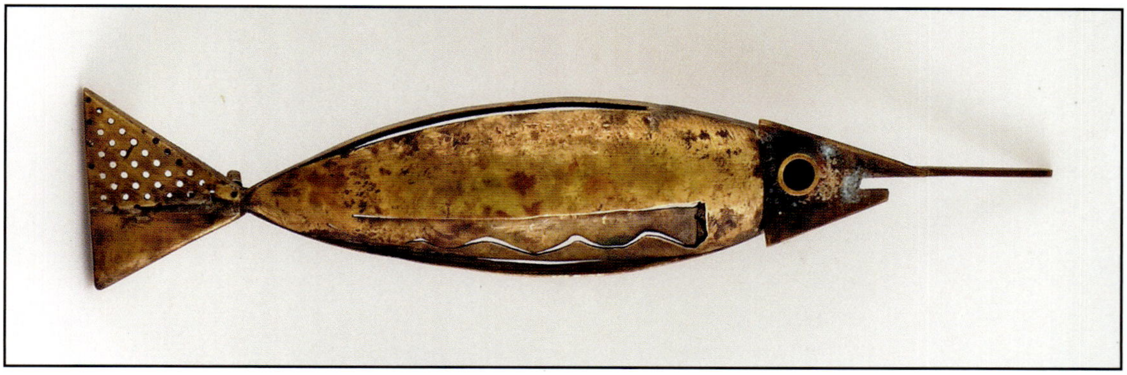

Peter Macchiarini, brooch, brass, copper, silver, patinated copper, ivory, 5-7/8" x 1-1/8". *Collection of Jill Crawford, photograph by Shirley Byrne.*

Everett Macdonald

"Giving each piece real individuality is the jeweler's toughest problem...individual statements are rare among jewelers today because copying yourself is still copying." —Everett Macdonald

Everett Macdonald opened a shop in Laguna Beach, California in 1947. He was mostly self-taught through his mother, who was a crafts instructor at Fullerton High School, first introduced him to metalworking.[62]

Macdonald initiated the use of nylon monofilament--strung between the negative spaces of his pendants and earrings recalling the work of sculptors Henry Moore and Naum Gabo. He worked in silver, gold, ebony and ivory.

His pieces were primarily one-of-a-kind though he sometimes produced very small limited editions of certain designs. Macdonald exhibited nationally and won several awards though his recognition was basically regional.

Everett Macdonald, brooch, sterling silver, 1-3/4" x 1-5/8". *Collection of Joanne and Fred Doloresco, photograph by Fred Doloresco.*

John Paul Miller

"Well, I mean...there's no question that I wanted it to be beautiful...I didn't want it to be kinky or unique particularly or something that was avant-garde or anything. I wanted it to be beautiful, and it was -- and I always felt that jewelry reflected the taste of the person that was wearing it and should sort of, in some way, enhance your relationship when you saw the piece, the way you reacted to them as a person." [63]—John Paul Miller

John Paul Miller at the Renwick's Founding Metalsmith Conference. *Courtesy of The Sarah Bodine & Michael Dunas Archives of 20th Century Jewelry, Tyler School of Art, Temple University, Professor Stanley Lechtzin, Curator of Metals/ Jewelry Archives and Collections.*

John Paul Miller (b. 1918), one of the leading goldsmiths in the U.S., is best known for reviving the ancient Etruscan technique of granulation—that of embellishing a gold surface with infinitesimal spheres of gold, some as tiny as 1/200 of an inch in diameter.

He was born in Huntington, Pennsylvania. When he was old enough, he took classes at the Cleveland Institute of Art's Saturday Program. Kenneth Bates was one of his early teachers. After high school graduation, he enrolled at the Cleveland Institute of Art majoring in Industrial Design with a minor in ceramics. Frederick Miller was a classmate and John Paul credits him with teaching him the fundamentals of working with silver jewelry.

He began making rings and brooches in his basement. "I built a small kiln from fire brick," Miller said, "with two elements from coffee makers as the heat source. I bought some Thompson enamels, and did an ash tray and a few brooches with enamels in a bezel setting." In 1941,one year after graduating with a Bachelor of Fine Arts Degree, Miller enlisted in the United States Army where he remained for four and a half years. The army made use of his artistic talents—first his painting skills to create a nativity scene for a base church and murals for a recreation hall and later his expertise in drawing when assigned to the Training Literature Department of the Armored Forces--a group of writers and illustrators that produced illustrations and maps for the tactical uses of tanks.

John Paul Miller, pendant/brooch, Hermit Crab, c.1981, 18k gold, enamel, Courtesy of The Sarah Bodine & Michael Dunas Archives of 20th Century Jewelry, Tyler School of Art, Temple University,Professor Stanley Lechtzin, Curator of Metals/ Jewelry and collection, photograph by John Paul Miller.

After the war Miller received a position at the Cleveland School of Art to teach various subjects and at the same time began making some jewelry in gold. Fred Miller, who had returned to work as chief designer for a fine jewelry and hollowware store in Cleveland, took over the silversmithing department at the school. Miller was able to obtain a supply of unused European enamels from the store; the previous owner had been a well-known jeweler/enamellist working in the early part of the 20th century.

Miller, who is considered the originator of the art of granulation in America, has inspired a generation of jewelers who now work in that technique. His designs are mostly based on animal or crustacean forms; he created an exquisite "menagerie of beetles, moths and snails" from 18-karat gold with elegant surfaces, a combination of granulation and enameling.

Examples of Miller's work can be seen in the Smithsonian Institution's Renwick Gallery. He received the American Craft Council's Gold Medal for Excellence in 1994. Miller's work has been shown extensively in such prestigious exhibitions as the 1958 Brussels World's Fair and the 1962 London Jewelry International. His many one-man shows have included those at the Art Institute of Chicago and the Museum of Contemporary Crafts, New York.

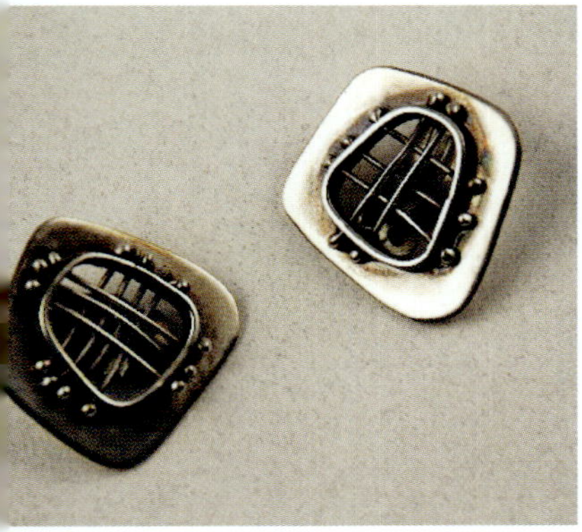

Frank Miraglia, earrings, sterling silver, 1" x 1". *Collection of Joanne and Fred Doloresco, photograph by Fred Doloresco.*

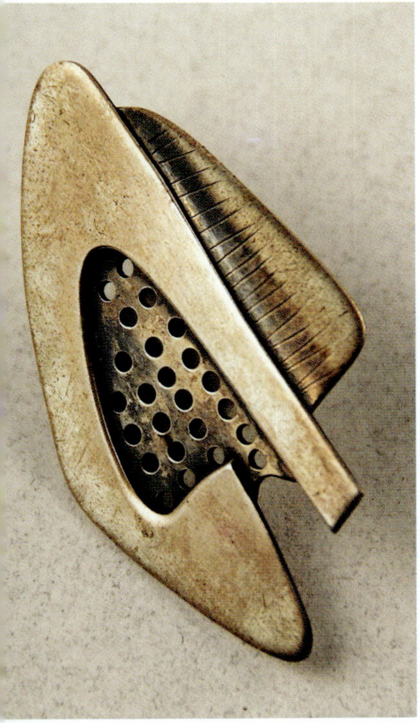

Frank Miraglia, brooch, sterling silver, 2" x 1-1/8", *Collection of Joanne and Fred Doloresco, photograph by Fred Doloresco.*

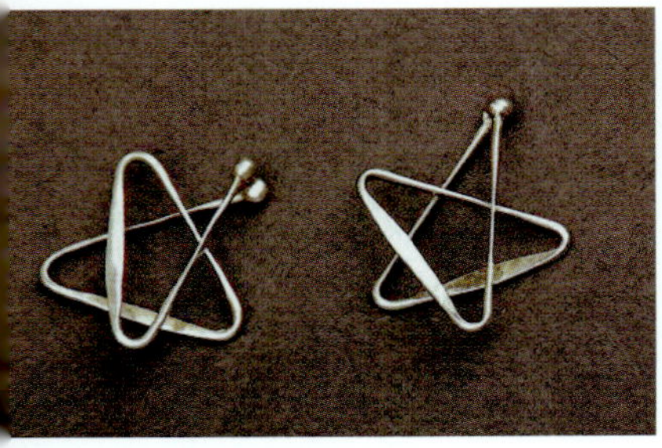

Philip Morton, earrings, sterling silver, 1-1/2" x 1-1/8". *Collection of Joanne and Fred Doloresco, photograph by Fred Doloresco.*

Frank Miraglia

Frank Miraglia was a studio jeweler in New York during the mid-20th Century. His designs were derivative and sometimes copies of the work of his contemporaries, however he created unique designs as well and he is highly regarded as an accomplished modernist jeweler. [64]

Phillip Morton

Philip Morton (1911-2001) wrote two books, *Contemporary Jewelry, a Studio Handbook* and *Contemporary Jewelry, a Craftsman's Handbook, that* are invaluable resources for collectors, jewelers, and students who wish to learn about the history of the modern studio jewelry movement and its design principles, materials, and techniques.[65]

Born in Utah, Morton spent his childhood there and received a scholarship to attend the University of Utah, where he studied sociology and psychology. In the 1930s he was attracted to jewelry design when his wife took a course at a WPA sponsored art project. During World War II Morton moved his family to Berkeley, California where he worked as a plant foreman. It was during this period that he opened a workshop in his basement and began to make jewelry. His study of contemporary art movements was done on his own.

Philip Morton, brooch, sterling silver, approximately 2-/12" x 4-1/2". *Collection of Jan Krenke Southern, photograph courtesy of Tom Muir, photograph by Keith Meiser. According to Jan Krenke Southern, this brooch by Morton is a replica (he made several) of the first piece of jewelry he created.*

Morton's jewelry was sold successfully at many of the leading shops in the San Francisco area and by 1946 he was also producing his own line of contemporary silverware. In 1947, because of his success as a metalsmith and designer, he was invited to teach design at Alfred University at the School for American Craftsmen. A year later he took a position with the newly formed art department at the University of Minnesota where he taught three dimensional design, jewelry making and sculpture. In 1951 he established the first bronze foundry in any American university art program. His own work over the next few years was devoted to bronze sculpture and jewelry making.

His work was widely exhibited and received international attention in the Swedish magazine *Form* in 1951, in the Italian publication *Esempi di Decorazione Moderna di Tutto il Mondo* by Aloi in 1954 and in the first *International Exhibition of Modern Jewelry 1890-1961,* held at the Victoria and Albert Museum in London.

In 1956 Morton began to study the works of Carl Jung. Because there were no Jungians in New York City to help to record and analyze his dreams he moved to Jackson Hole, Wyoming where he sold his jewelry, worked as a land surveyor and designed houses. He wrote his book *Contemporary Jewelry, A Studio Handbook* at that time.

He moved many times in the 1970s: teaching art at the University of Utah, working as a goldsmith at a community college in Toronto and opening an apprenticeship program in metalwork and jewelry in Bowling Green, Ohio, from 1970 to 1974. In 1974 he went back to Chicago to work in the training of Jungians while working toward a Masters Degree in clinical work. He received his M.A. in 1976 in Rehabilitation Counseling after which he moved back to Bowling Green to open his own psychotherapy practice. In 1980 he moved to Montana to live in a house he had designed and built, to practice psychotherapy, and to offer workshops in dream analysis.

Philip Morton passed away in March of 2001.

Philip Morton, ring, 18k gold, stone. *Collection of Stephanie Frank, photograph courtesy of Tom Muir, photograph by Keith Meiser.*

Jack Nutting

Jack Nutting made and sold jewelry in Northern California in the 1950s and 1960s. His work is carefully constructed and modernist in style. He also designed furniture and interiors and had a jewelry shop in San Francisco.

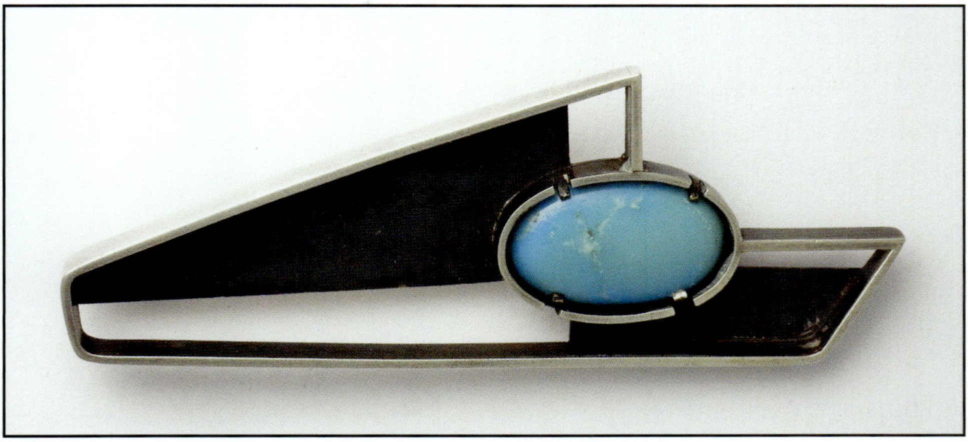

Jack Nutting, brooch, sterling silver, turquoise, 2-7/8" x 1". c. 1953, *Collection of Steve Cabella, photograph by Geoff Turner.*

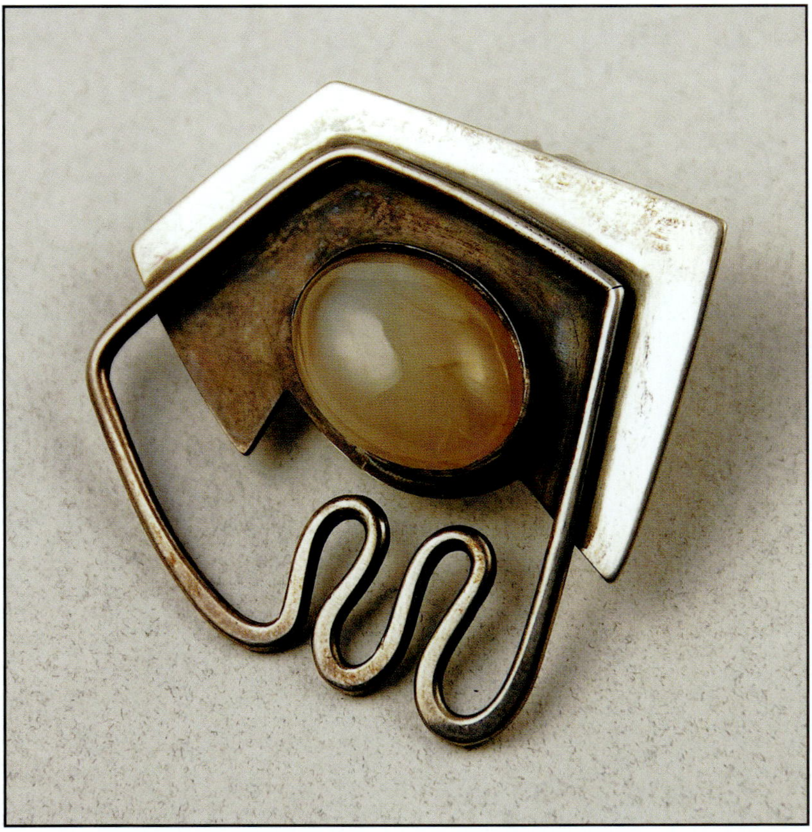

Jack Nutting, brooch, sterling silver, agate, 2" x 2", c.1953. *Collection of Joanne and Fred Doloresco, photograph by Fred Doloresco.*

Albert Paley

Albert Paley (b. 1944) began his career in metalworking in the early 1960s. He was engrossed with bringing together fine and applied arts—to blur the line between arts and crafts. His jewelry was made with that in mind.

Paley realized from the beginning that jewelry making is challenging and takes a great amount of discipline. His work was imbued with symbolism, often including historical aspects from the Greeks, Romans and Etruscans."[66]

Paley studied with Stanley Lechtzin at Tyler School of Art, receiving his degree in 1969. Halfway through his studies, he went to Europe where he visited major metalsmiths and returned with an advanced and mature view of the roll of the meatalsmith in society.

In 1970 Paley became intrigued by the plasticity of iron. He notes that, "When it is hot, iron is extremely plastic and fluid. It is very submissive and yielding to a cause-and-effect response, a directness and spontaneity. The paradox is that one is able to visually record all this in a very hard, rigid and permanent material." Paley has become famous for his whip-like forms in furniture and also large-scale sculpture.

His works are included in some of the most prominent art collections in the world including The British Museum; Metropolitan Museum of Art; Museum of Fine Arts Boston; Victoria and Albert Museum; and, the White House. Albert Paley is the first metal sculptor to receive the coveted *Lifetime Achievement Award* from the American Institute of Architects, the AIA's highest award to a non-architect.

Commissioned by both public institutions and private corporations, Paley has completed more than fifty site-specific works. Some notable examples are the Portal Gates for the Renwick Gallery of the Smithsonian Institution in Washington, DC; the Portal Gates for the New York State Senate Chambers in Albany; a plaza sculpture for AT&T in Atlanta, Georgia; a sculpture and plaza designed for Adobe Systems in San Jose, California; major entrance rotunda gates for the State Courthouse in San Francisco; the main entrance gates for the Naples Museum of Art, Naples, Florida; as well as a sixty-five-foot sculpture for the entry court of Bausch and Lomb's headquarters in Rochester, NY.

Recently completed works include a pair of entrance sculptures for the Columbia Public Library, Columbia, Missouri; exterior archways for the town of Perry, Iowa; *Sentinel*, a monumental plaza sculpture for Rochester Institute of Technology (which is his largest work to date) and *Animals Always*, a ceremonial archway in Forest Park for the Saint Louis Zoo.[67]

Paley has a working studio in Rochester, New York.

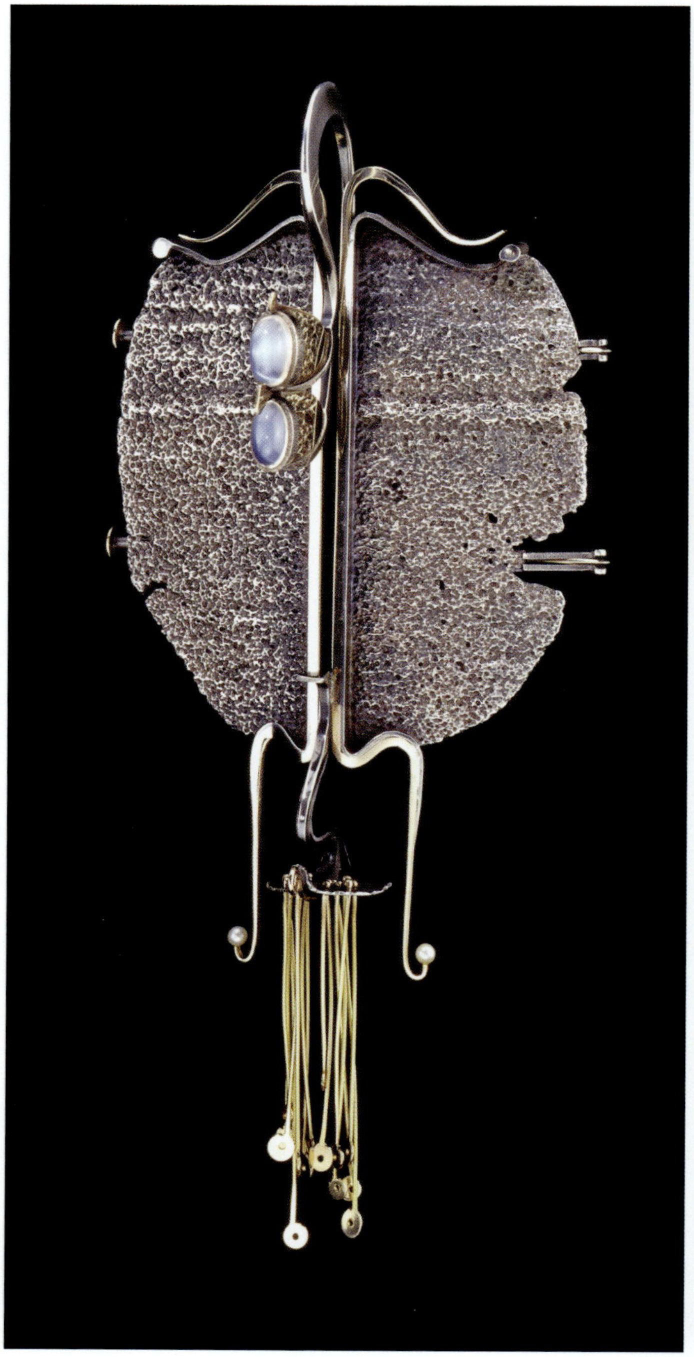

Albert Paley, *Sectional* brooch, silver, gold, moonstones, pearls, forged and fabricated, oxidized silver, 3-1/4" wide x 7" high x 1-2/3" deep. *Courtesy of Albert Paley, The Paley Archive, Rochester, New York.*

Earl Pardon in 1955. *Courtesy of Tod Pardon.*

Earl Pardon

Earl Pardon (1926-1991) was first and foremost an artist who transferred ideas back and forth between the fine and plastic arts and was involved with both large-scale sculpture and jewelry, joining his love of painting and metalsmithing through his colorful enamel work.[68]

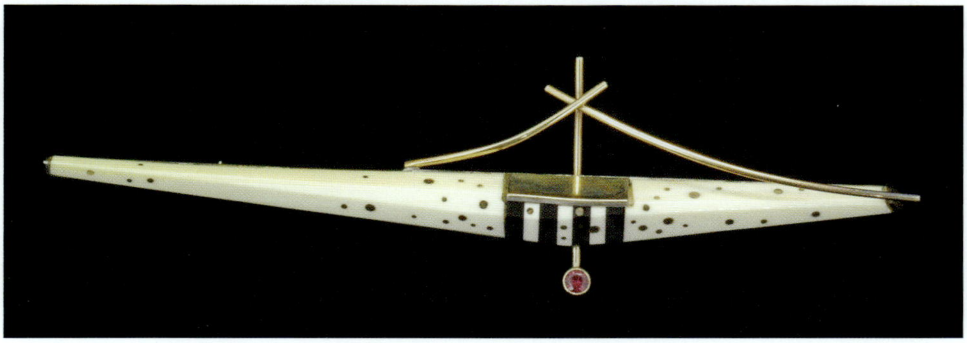

Earl Pardon, brooch, brass, ivory, 5-1/2" x 1-1/2". *Courtesy of Mark McDonald, 555 Warren St., Hudson, New York, photograph by Bill Hibbs.*

Pardon was born in Memphis, Tennessee. He served in Germany during World War II. Pardon received his Bachelor of Fine Arts degree at the Memphis Academy of Arts in 1951 and his M.F.A. in painting at Syracuse University in Syracuse, New York in 1959. While still in college, Pardon began exhibiting his jewelry and was awarded a scholarship to the 4th National Silversmith's Conference sponsored by Handy and Harman. As early as 1951 he was teaching art at Skidmore College and teaching painting at Union College, Schenectady, New York.

Between 1954 and 1955 he was a designer for the Towle Silversmiths, Newburyport, Massachusetts, but returned to Skidmore later in 1955 where he continued metalsmithing in his own studio.

Pardon's early pieces are abstract and playful and often combinations of silver with wood, ivory or enamels.

Earl Pardon, brooch, sterling, ebony. *Collection of Munir Meghji, photograph by Munir Meghji.*

Earl Pardon, brooch, sterling and ebony, 2-1/8" high, c. 1958. *Collection of Munir Meghji, photograph by Munir Meghji.*

Pardon worked for Towle Silver Company in the mid-1950s where he designed elegantly modern holloware in silver and enamels.

Pardon continued to show his work nationally after 1955 in numerous museum and gallery shows. He exhibited jewelry in *American Jewelry and Related Objects* at the Huntington Galleries—a three-year traveling exhibit sponsored by the Smithsonian Institute in Washington, D.C. where he was awarded a purchase prize. In 1957 he exhibited painting, sculpture, jewelry, and enamel work at the Museum of Contemporary Crafts in New York.

His later jewelry designs and large installations were mostly works in enamel and silver or enamel with a combination of other metals such as bronze and copper. Pardon's perfectionism is especially apparent in his enamel work; many of his pendants are reversible so that each side is as beautifully designed and crafted as the other. Pardon uses surprise as an element in his jewelry; his "portable pieces of art," as Pardon refers to them, often have hidden stones—colored beads on the back of a pendant or black pearls on the underside of a ring—known only to the two partners in the artistic contract."

Pardon worked with a combination of techniques including cloisonné, fabrication, and inlay. Instead of exhausting an idea until all the secrets were known, Pardon went back and forth between his past ideas and techniques, reworking them in new ways. "I have a tendency to make pieces that are organic in feeling," he said, "when I tire of that, I go after more graphic, sharper-edged effects--they balance each other out."

In the late 1950s Pardon exhibited his enamel work at the Museum of Contemporary Crafts' Enamels Invitational in New York and in 1959 was commissioned to create a wall sculpture in enamels for the main lobby of the building owned by the Prudential Insurance Company in Newark, New Jersey. The ten by seventeen foot screen was constructed of three layers of geometric metal shapes in brass, bronze, nickel and copper designed parallel to each other and to the curved wall of the building.

Between 1962-1964, photographs of his screen were included in a traveling exhibition sponsored by the Architectural League of New York. In 1965 his jewelry was exhibited at the Gallery of the Society of Arts and Crafts in Boston, Massachusetts and in 1970 he was commissioned by Green Mountain College in Poultney, Vermont to create an eight by ten foot sculptural metal wall in brass, bronze, and copper.

In 1975 he had a one-man show in sculpture, jewelry and enamels at the Hawthorne Gallery at Skidmore and a two-person show with his wife, Eunice Norton Pardon.

The October/November 1982 issue of *American Craft Magazine* featured an article by Ettagale Lauré about Pardon's show at the Aaron Faber Gallery in New York that same year.

In 1984 Pardon's work was included in the group show, *Structure and Ornament, American Modernist Jewelry from 1940-1960* at the Fifty/50 Gallery in New York City. The Montreal Museum of Decorative Arts purchased his work in 1989 and between 1991-93 Pardon's jewelry was part of the traveling exhibition sponsored by the same museum called *Design 1935-1965: What Modern Was*.

Earl Pardon passed away in May of 1991. In 2002 he was posthumously honored with *A Tribute to Earl Pardon* at the Connell Gallery in Atlanta, Georgia. "Fourteen select former students exhibited their work as a tribute to a man whose life was an embodiment of grace, imagination, and good humor."

Pardon's work is in the permanent collections of over fifteen museums including the Renwick Gallery in Washington, D.C. and the Metropolitan Museum of Art in New York.

Earl Pardon, brooch, sterling silver, ebony, garnet, 4-3/4" x 1/4" x 1/2", c. 1965. *Courtesy of Mark McDonald, 555 Warren St., Hudson, New York.*

Earl Pardon, brooch, sterling silver, brass, ebony, ivory, 1-9/16" x 3/16", c. 1950s. *Collection of Munir Meghji, photograph by Munir Meghji.*

Tod Pardon

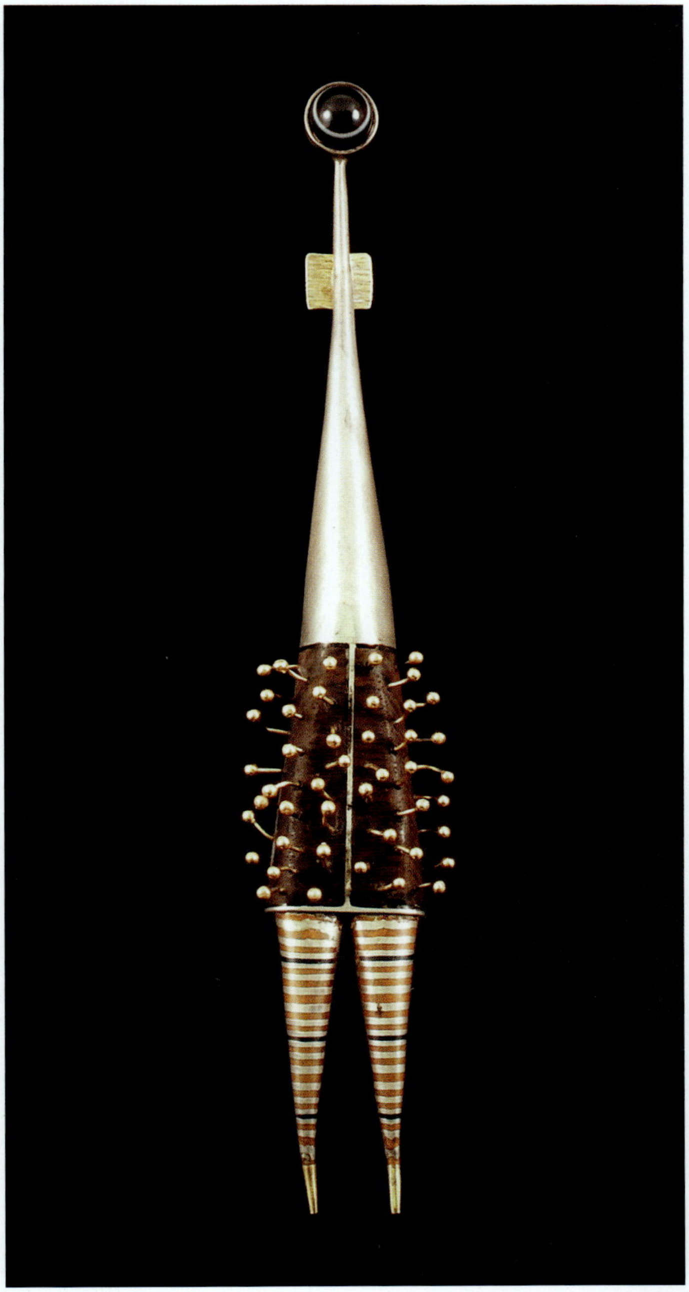

Tod Pardon, brooch, *Uro*, sterling silver, 14k gold, wood, agate, 6-1/8" x 2-1/8". *Collection of Jill Crawford, photograph by Shirley Byrne.*

"Over the past ten years the content in my work has been influenced by many elements that are vast, varied, and personal. I see it as an expression of life's inherent duality and instability.

"There are contradictions of anxiety and humor, good and evil. The humor and color play an important role in contrast to the sometimes-screaming pieces. Much like the Balinese Barong dance of good versus evil. The character I'm drawn to most is Rangda, Queen of the Leyaks. A bloodthirsty, child-eating, witch-widow mistress of black magic. She is feared and nasty but is portrayed and acts in a comical way. Without humor the anxiety we face cannot really be interpreted; without shadow, we can't see form. It's like you can't see the light without the dark. Or as Rabindranath Tagore, the well-known poet from India says, "truth in her dress finds facts too tight, in fiction she moves with ease."
—Tod Pardon

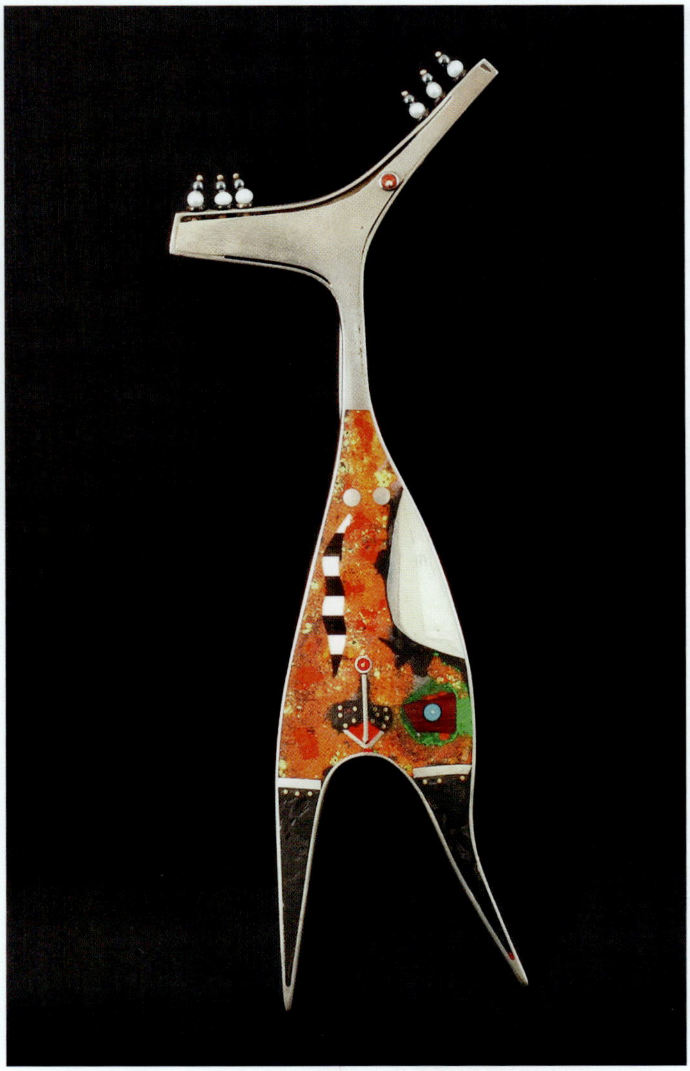

Tod Pardon, brooch, *Temptoria,* sterling silver, enamel, ivory, ebony, pearls, red bead, 6 x 2-3/4". *Collection of Jill Crawford, photograph by Shirley Byrne.*

Tod Pardon was born in August of 1952. He attended Haystack Hinkley School of Crafts in 1969, Skidmore College (Summer Six Program) in 1970, received his B.F.A. in painting and drawing at the School of Art & Design in Syracuse in 1974, and his M.F.A. in painting at the same school in 1977.

His pieces are fabricated from sterling silver and 14k gold. The inlay is a mixture of a variety of materials including bone, woods, pigment, glass, ivory and metal. The pieces are built up using a cold setting binder and then sanded and polished smooth. Pardon says that this is an additive and reductive process that relates to his background in painting and drawing.

"The underlying structure of my work is totemic to a large degree," he says, but can be viewed in many ways. Again quoting Tagore, 'What seems to be coming at you is really coming from you."

His work is sold at galleries in New York City; Atlanta, Georgia; Santa Fe, New Mexico; Charlottesville, Virginia; and San Diego, California and has been included in numerous exhibitions throughout the United States. Two recent exhibits include: *What Lies Beneath*, Patina Gallery Invitational, Santa Fe, New Mexico, 2007 and *Attitude and Action: North American Figurative Jewelry*, Society of North American Goldsmiths, curated by Gail Brown, Birmingham, England, 2000.

Pardon's work is in many museum collections including the Museum of Art and Design, New York City; the Renwick Gallery of the Smithsonian National Art Museum, Washington, DC; The Arkansas Arts Center Decorative Arts Museum, Little Rock, Arkansas; The Hyde Collection Museum, Glens Falls, NewYork; and Samuel Dorsky Museum of Art, SUNY at New Paltz, New York.

Tod Pardon, brooch, Simoza Memories, sterling silver, 14k gold, enamel, ivory, 4-5/8" x 3/4". *Collection of Jill Crawford, photograph by Shirley Byrne.*

James Parker

"A silversmith of the heavy, bold school in his rings, he is [also] capable of considerable delicacy using conventional jewelry techniques... Parker is a member of the active Allied Craftsmen of San Diego one of the few craft associations in the West promoting the activities of community artists working in all media in the plastic arts." [69]

James Parker, brooch, sterling silver, 1-3/4" x 1-3/4". *Collection of Joanne and Fred Doloresco, photograph by Fred Doloresco.*

James Parker (1914-1987) taught English at Brossmont High School, San Diego, and possibly other classes in art, general crafts, ceramics, and photography. He was a mostly self-taught metalsmith—teaching himself to make jewelry after only one adult education class in the subject.[70]

His designs are unique statements of subtlety mixed with boldness. The linear elements of his designs almost always curve or circle around his forms creating a feeling of vitality. He used enamels extensively, often with a whimsical juxtaposing of colors. Parker also used vibrantly colored stones, many times incorporating synthetic varieties for their unusual hues.

Parker was an avid collector of enamel work by other artists, including plates and jewelry by Ellamarie and Jackson Wooley (also of San Diego) and pieces by Barney Reid, Hazel Bray and David Andersen, among others. After his death in 1987, the entire collection was donated to the Wichita Art Association (renamed Wichita Center for the Arts in 1991).

Parker, who was elected president of the Allied Craftsmen of San Diego in 1951, continued to be active with the organization until the 1970s.

He was invited to submit work for consideration in the Brussels World's Fair and was represented in *Craftsmanship in a Changing World*. In 1967 the Oakland Museum acquired his unique two-sided pendant with nine enamel plaques suspended within a silver frame. A necklace of sixteen white enameled silver nuggets was exhibited in *California Design Ten* in 1968 at the Pasadena Art Museum.

James Parker, brooch, sterling silver, 3-1/2" x 2". *Collection of Jill Crawford, photograph by Shirley Byrne.*

James Parker, ring, sterling silver, stone, top: 7/8" diameter. *Collection of Jill Crawford, photograph by Shirley Byrne.*

Ronald Hayes Pearson

"The hammer is our tool. In skilled hands, it will shape malleable metal into simple or complex fluid forms. There seem to be no end to what one can achieve and it is the chance to explore new terrain that makes this work so exciting." —Ronald Hayes Pearson

Ronald Hayes Pearson in 1982, at the symposium, *American Metalsmithing and Jewelrymaking in the 1940s and 1950s, sponsored by the Renwick Gallery and the Archives of American Art. Courtesy of The Sarah Bodine & Michael Dunas Archives of 20th Century Jewelry, Tyler School of Art, Temple University, Professor Stanley Lechtzin, Curator of Metals/Jewelry Archives and Collections.*

Ronald Hayes Pearson (1924-1997) lived his entire adult life as a full-time producing artist. His father, Ralph M. Pearson, was an artist, teacher and writer who had his own art school in New York City.[71]

Pearson attended the University of Wisconsin after which, during World War II, he served in the Merchant Marine Corps. In 1947, after being discharged from the service, Pearson enrolled at the School for American Craftsmen in Alfred, New York to study metals with Philip Morton.

Though they both stayed only one year, Morton's encouragement to develop his skills in metal into a career and his offer to teach Pearson at his studio for a month made a great impact upon his future.

He set up his first studio in a former chicken coop " complete with an old spinning lathe, tools, chucks and several hundred pounds of sheet bronze." For a year he worked by himself making a series of spun-bronze bowls, ashtrays, candleholders and desk accessories. Several of his bowls were included in the *Good Design* shows organized by the Museum of Modern Art in New York City.

In the early 1950s Pearson moved to Rochester, New York where he became involved with other creative craftspeople including silversmith Jack Prip, woodworker Tage Frid, ceramist Frans Wildenhain and jewelers Ruth and Svetozar Radakovich. It was an especially fertile time for crafts; programs sponsored by the American Craftsmen's Educational Council (now the American Craft Council) and by regional craft organizations brought artists together to discuss mutual issues regarding competitions, exhibitions, shops and galleries, marketing opportunities, techniques, etc. "The relatively small size of the craft community across the country meant that artists often knew each other personally as well as professionally and welcomed opportunities to be involved in mutually beneficial activities on a regular basis."

Prip, Frid, Wildenhain and Pearson recognized a need for a retail shop owned by practicing craftsmen where unique and limited production craft items could be purchased. They opened Shop One in Rochester, New York after which Pearson became a full-time studio artist working principally with forged or cast metal, creating both small one-of-a-kind gold and silver jewelry and large iron and copper accessories.

The simple modern forms that Pearson created look as if they grew directly out of the forging process--he was a consummate craftsman. Whether cast or constructed, his forms exemplify his complete control of the metal—"Surface qualities enhance form and details of function have been perfectly analyzed."

Ronald Hayes Pearson, brooch, sterling, baroque pearl, 1-3/4" x 1-7/8". Collection of Marbeth Schon, photograph by Marbeth Schon.

Pearson developed ways of doing business that would insure a stable income for himself and his family and also remain compatible with his artistic goals. He set up systems of limited production that took as little of his time as possible to operate and monitor. Pearson enjoyed each stage in the development of new pieces that included designing, creating, finishing, and deciding how to repeat the form effectively and efficiently.

Pearson also designed his own line of flatware for the Kirk Steiff Company and was commissioned by several institutions and churches to execute various projects.

Pearson never isolated himself from his local community or the larger community of artists. He never joined academia, but often taught in schools such as Haystack and Penland as well as in his own studio. He participated in a government program of job training for several years in which he worked with young people from his area in an apprenticeship program. He continually welcomed other artists to his workshop such as J. Fred Woell and John Prip who were there for long periods of time working on their own or in studio production. The same hospitality was extended to the many Haystack students who visited him every summer.

Pearson was a founding member of the Society of North American Goldsmiths, served on the board at Haystack Mountain School of Crafts, and during certain periods, was a board member of the Louis Comfort Tiffany Foundation, Boston University's Program in Artisanry, the Maine Crafts Association and America House.

From the very beginning of his career Pearson participated in national exhibitions. His work has been included in such prestigious shows as *Goldsmith '70*, *Craft Today: Poetry of the Physical*, *Silver in Service* and most recently, *Silver, New Forms and Expressions* and *Art that Works: The Decorative Arts of the Eighties, Crafted in America.*

Pearson received many grants, prizes and awards over the years. "His lifetime of achievement was honored in 1976 when he was elected a Fellow of the American Crafts Council, and in 1987 when he received an Honorary Doctor of Laws degree from the Portland School of Art for his valuable contributions to American jewelry design and for his 'quiet conviction, sensitivity and unending commitment to excellence."

Ronald Hayes Pearson passed away in August 1997. He left a lasting impression in the metals community through his work and many contributions. "He was a prominent figure in the metalsmithing field, and one that is dearly missed."

Miriam Smith Peck

Miriam Smith Peck attended Western Reserve University and the Cleveland Institute of Art. Her jewelry is mostly abstract compositions in enamel on fine silver. She also painted watercolors.[72]

Miriam Peck, brooch, enamel on copper, 2-1/4" x 2-1/4". *Collection of Joanne and Fred Doloresco, photograph by Fred Doloresco.*

Miriam Peck, brooch, enamel on copper. 2" diameter. Collection of Munir Meghji, photograph by Munir Meghji

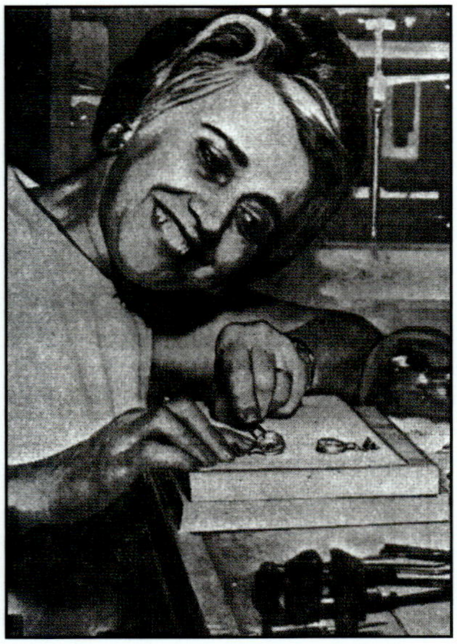

Coralyn Pence in her studio. *From Metalsmith Never Does Anything Twice by Dorothy Brant, Women's News, Seattle Times, August 18, 1966, Courtesy of The Sarah Bodine & Michael Dunas Archives of 20th Century Jewelry, Tyler School of Art, Temple University, Professor Stanley Lechtzin, Curator of Metals/Jewelry Archives and Collections.*

Coralyn Pence, earrings, sterling and stone. 1" x 3/4". *Collection of Joanne and Fred Doloresco, photograph by Fred Doloresco.*

Ruth Penington. *Courtesy of The Sarah Bodine & Michael Dunas Archives of 20th Century Jewelry, Tyler School of Art, Temple University, Professor Stanley Lechtzin, Curator of Metals/Jewelry Archives and Collections.*

Coralyn Pence

Coralyn Pence was born in Oregon. She attended Chouinard Institute, Los Angeles, and the University of Washington and taught at Edison Technical School, Seattle, Washington.[73]

Pence spent the summer of 1956 traveling in Europe, believing that a designer needs to travel for inspiration and perspective. She designed with sheet gold and silver, often with precious and semi-precious stones. Pence used a torch like an artist uses a pencil to draw, becoming more proficient with time. She believed that design and technical skills should be kept on the same development level—one as important as the other. She maintained a full-time studio workshop, designing and executing jewelry for individuals on commission only.

Her work was included in many national exhibits such as *Jewelry and Related Objects*, Smithsonian Institution, 1955- 1956; *Designer-Craftsmen of the West*, De Young Museum, San Francisco, 1961; *Designer-Craftsmen of the Far West*, Museum of Contemporary Crafts, New York City, 1961; *American Jewelry Today*, Everhart Museum, 1963; World Craft Council Exhibit, New Zealand, 1966; and others.

She won several awards for her jewelry including a Theta Sigma Phi Merit Award from the American Craftsmen's Council.

Ruth Penington

"You've got to see it, be with it, be a part of it." —Ruth Pennington (speaking about art), 1974

Ruth Penington (b. 1905) was born in Colorado Springs, Colorado. Her early education included Columbia Teachers College in 1929, the Carnegie Summer School at the University of Oregon in 1931 – 1932, studies with Gilbert Rhode in New York City in 1944 and a Handy and Harman workshop with William Bennett at the Rhode Island School of Design in 1947. In 1952 she worked in the shop of A. Michaelson in Copenhagen.

She received her B.F.A. and M.F.A. from the University of Washington, Seattle and taught at the University of California in the 1940s and at the University of Alaska in the 1950s. In 1955 she established her own Fidalgo Summer School of the Allied Arts in La Conner, Washington and in 1959 she became Professor of Art at the University of Washington.

Penington also operated her own studio. She created jewelry that was often monumental in scale—"so much that her work was sometimes juried out of competitive exhibitions because it was too big to wear, though it was often very comfortable and actually quite wearable." Penington's influences were many—Byzantine, Viking, pre-Columbian, Native American, etc. In 1962 she had a solo exhibition at the Henry Art Gallery in Seattle. At that time, her mentor, painter Henry Isaacs wrote to her, "It is if metal were clay in your hands. You have risen above the difficulties of the craft and have reached expression."

Penington was a founding member of many organizations with the purpose of helping artists and craftsmen. In recognition of her long years of service to the American Craft Council, she was made Trustee Emeritus and Fellow in the 1970s.

John Prip

"For me, coming to the United States from Denmark during the post-war years was, to quote a cliché, a perfect case of being in the right place at the right time. The American craft movement, as we know it, did not exist. The work being done then was not impressive by today's standards. The network of organizations, schools, museums, shows, galleries and collectors that we now take for granted were not even imaginable at the time. But the people attracted to this field were special. They were dedicated and enthusiastic with an almost fanatical belief in their work. Working as a craftsman was a way of life, with few exceptions of making anything but a modest living. They were 'true believers' and looking back, I am glad to say that I was one of them." —John Prip

John Prip was born in New York City of Danish parents. When he was ten his family returned to Denmark. His introduction to metalsmithing began with his family—both his father and grandfather were silversmiths. He remembered playing in silver factories when he was a child; his father owned a small flatware factory that employed forty to fifty people. When he was fifteen Prip apprenticed to a silversmith in Denmark and in 1942 he completed his journeyman's piece. [75]

In 1948 he returned to the United States with his wife and his son to begin teaching at the School for American Craftsmen in Alfred, New York. When the school moved to the Rochester Institute of Technology he, together with Ronald Pearson and others, became involved with the retail crafts outlet, Shop One.

In 1957 Prip resigned from his teaching position at the School for American Craftsmen. He became a designer in residence for Reed & Barton silver company where several of his unique designs were put into production. It was at Reed and Barton that he was introduced to a low temperature metal known as white metal and explored the possibilities of working with white metal and pewter. In 1960 Prip reduced his commitment to Reed & Barton and began teaching at the School of the Museum of Fine Arts in Boston, Massachusetts. By the 1960's Prip had begun to incorporate different metals into his work as well as granite and other stones. His later work was done in the Scandinavian style and involved the seaming and interlocking of forms.

His work is in permanent collections nationwide and in 1992 he was the recipient of an American Craft Council Gold Medal. Prip has received numerous other awards and honors and is recognized as a prominent figure in the field of metalsmithing.

Ruth Radakovich & Svetozar Radakovich

Toza and Ruth Radakovich, c.1958. *Photograph by Terry S. Lindquist, Rochester, New York, courtesy of Jean Radakovich.*

"In a world in which people are concerned with what they shouldn't do, art is an oasis without any real should-nots. There are no absolutes, no wrongs: there isn't one thing, one way, a right way. The only limits are those you impose on yourself. The things you like and respond to all your life become a part of you and emerge in your art." —Ruth Radakovich

"Work I have done in the past and the work I do now is my statement. It comes as a result of my philosophy, knowledge, perceptiveness, understanding, beliefs and my skills. I like to give what information I think is necessary and leave room for the viewer's imagination to be part of the seeing... It is a great feeling, understanding that whatever I do, I am the only judge of what I do, and how, from the very beginning to the finish of the work. I am interested, naturally, in the final results, but without going through the process of creating it, I would be left incomplete." —Toza Radakovich

The story of two exceptional artists, Svetozar and Ruth Radakovich, is one of commitment, courage, dedication, and brilliant creativity.[76]

Ruth (1920-1975) was born in Winnetka, Illinois, and spent her 18th summer in Scandinavia with the "Experiment in International Living Program." Afterward, she toured England, Whales, Scotland, and Ireland by bicycle. In 1949 she received her M.A. in art and anthropology from the University of Michigan, Ann Arbor. She began her studies in 1938 at Sarah Lawrence College in Bronxville, NY, majoring in journalism and political science.

World War II interrupted her studies and she joined the war effort working in Ford's bomber factory in Detroit, Michigan. She learned to fly but was kept out of the military for health reasons.

She continued to augment her education, attending a number of summer courses at various institutions including Mills College in Oakland, California and the Experiment in International Living in Brattleboro, Vermont. During 1950 and 1951 she attended the School for American Craftsmen, both at Alfred University and at Rochester Institute of Technology, New York where she studied metalwork with Jack Prip and later with Hans Christensen.

Svetozar (Toza) (1918-1998) was born in Belgrade, Yugoslavia, where he graduated from the Royal Art Academy with an M.F.A. in 1939. He won awards and was internationally recognized for his work as a graphic artist for the United Nations Relief and Rehabilitation Administration's publication. From 1949 to 1953 he worked for Yugoslavia's prestigious national art magazine, *Jugoslavia* as a graphic artist and art editor. During WWII he fought in the Yugoslav and Russian armies and became a survivor of prison camps and political tyranny..."his duties as a frontline foot soldier, near starvation, severe illnesses, Nazi prison camps and daring escapes caused nightmares... that would haunt him the rest of his life."

He met Ruth in Belgrade in 1946 when they were both working with the United Nations Relief and Rehabilitation organization. In 1947 Ruth had to leave Yugoslavia because the government suspected that she was trying to help Toza flee the country. In 1953, when Toza finally managed to escape from Yugoslavia after seven years of writing to each other via miniature letters rolled up and stuffed into vitamin capsules or hidden under watercolor paintings, they were reunited in Paris. They lived in Paris and Copenhagen for the next two years while awaiting permission to marry and immigrate to the United States.

Between 1954 and 1955 Toza and Ruth studied metalsmithing with Mogens Bjorn Anderson in Denmark. They were married in Paris in 1955, after which they went to Italy to study filigree metalwork before coming permanently to the United States to Rochester, New York where Toza and Ruth began teaching at The School for American Craftsmen at Rochester Institute of Technology and at the Memorial Art Gallery at the University of Rochester. There they became part of a groundbreaking community of like-minded artists at Shop One, founded by Jack Prip, Tage Frid, Franz Wildenhain and Ron Pearson. Shop One was one of the first venues for Designer-Craftsmen to show and sell their own work

In 1959 the Radakoviches relocated to the charming seaside town of Encinitas, California where they began to establish themselves as Designer Craftsmen and Toza became an American citizen.

Ruth believed that jewelry should have an overall shape and unity and be uncluttered in form, but also be interesting enough to get the feeling that "you have to see more of it -- that you hadn't seen all when you first looked at it; she spoke of a piece of jewelry made by her husband in which she was always able to find something new she hadn't seen before--that (to her) was a sign of a good piece.

The Radanovich's did not believe in invention (novelty) for the sake of being different. The "realization" of the piece was most important. Ruth was particularly sensitive to the natural world and her work was organic in form and design. Toza's work was reflective of old-world armor. Serbian design also came into play along with his love for the sea. There were often hidden aspects to his designs, influenced by his delight in discovering surprises in nature.

Toza was constantly intrigued with the nature of materials and how things were put together. He often seemed less concerned with the finished piece than with the process of making something with his hands, while Ruth's focus was on the intellectual stimulation and conceptual aspects of her work. Like the evolution of any process, as they discovered different media and their inspirations changed, their work also changed but remained recognizably unique.

Although Toza was best known for his innovative jewelry and metal sculpture, he worked in many media. His carved wooden doors, forged iron gates and stained glass windows are a treasured part of many homes.

In the 1960s Toza taught sculpture at San Diego State University where he created a course in bronze casting. He also taught jewelry at the Southwest Indian Art Project through the University of Arizona. In the 1970s he taught jewelry casting at Palomar College in San Marcos.

The Radakovich's participated in numerous exhibitions throughout the United States.

Because they are remembered as two of the most accomplished modernist artist/jewelers to have entered and established themselves in that medium, they have been included in almost every major publication on the history of modern metalworking in the mid-20th century.

Ruth Radakovich, necklace, sterling silver, Mexican opal in matrix, 5-1/4" wide x 9-1/4" high. cast and forged, c. 1950s. *Collection of Jean Radakovich, photograph by Jean Radakovich.*

Francisco Rebajes

Francisco Rebajes (1907-1990) was a brilliant, energetic man who overcame incredible odds to make a name for himself as an artist/craftsman. He obtained financial success and left a legacy of good design for decades to come. He was the first studio jeweler we know of to open an actual shop in Greenwich Village.[77]

Francisco Rebajes, brooch and earrings, sterling silver, brooch: 3-5/8" x 1-1/2 ". *Collection of Joanne and Fred Doloresco, photograph by Fred Doloresco.*

His life began humbly in the town of Puerto Plata in the Dominican Republic. He was born to the family of shoemaker, Francisco Torres. (He later took his mother's last name, Rebajes.) When Rebajes was still a very young man, his father, Señor Torres, was able to send him to study in Barcelona, Spain. He stayed for a short time, finding interest in very little except the architecture of Antoni Gaudi. In 1922, at the age of 16, he left by himself for the United States.

Arriving in New York with a little over three hundred dollars, Rebajes said he passed immigration by "removing my hat, speaking good English, and showing my cash." He worked several different odd jobs to support himself in New York; he panhandled and sold apples during the depression on the corner of 44th Street and Sixth Avenue. His friends were the bohemian artists, writers, poets and intellectuals from Harlem. In 1932, at a party in Greenwich Village, he met a New York girl named Pauline Schwartz, whom he married later that year. Rebajes was homeless at the time so they "spent their wedding night on the subway, riding the Coney Island local back and forth."

Conditions did not improve for the couple right away. Having nowhere else to go, Rebajes rented an austere, tool-filled basement apartment in Greenwich Village from his friend Julio Avendano for $10 a month. As well as the couple's home, the "apartment" became Rebajes' first studio/workshop—the place where he began to create his first metal sculptures: whimsical animals cut and formed from tin cans and scrap metal. These he displayed in 1932 at the Washington Square outdoor art festival where they came to the attention of Juliana Force, the first director of the Whitney Museum of American Art. She purchased the entire collection for the sum of thirty dollars, enough in those days to allow Rebajes to open his first shop, a small space with a dirt floor between two buildings on West 48th Street. Frank and Pauline slept on piles of newspapers on the dirt floor. He had very few tools and his first sale, an aluminum ashtray that sold for thirty-five cents, was forged on a piece of stone. Rebajes began to make and develop his own special tools in order to create objects out of copper including his first jewelry examples.

Francisco Rebajes, aluminum ashtray. *Photograph courtesy of Patricia Riveron Lee.*

In 1934 Rebajes moved to a better location on West 4th Street. He was gaining acceptance by the art and design community; his work, including several silver-plated objects and some jewelry, was selected to be included in *Contemporary Industrial and Handwrought Silver: An Exhibition of Contemporary American Design by Manufactures, Designers, and Craftsmen*," at the Metropolitan Museum of Art. He received a bronze medal at the *Exposition Internationale des Arts et Techniques* in Paris in 1937 and a gold medal for his sculptures at the theater in the United States Pavilion at the 1939 New York World's Fair.

Francisco Rabajes, theatre designs at 1939 New York Worlds' Fair, *Photo courtesy of Patricia Riveron Lee.*

As well as jewelry Rebajes produced platters, boxes, bowls and candlesticks. Rebajes inherently followed the Bauhaus principles of social integration (which was of great philosophical importance to Margaret De Patta when she decided to mass produce her jewelry in the 1950s); he deliberately kept his prices low in order to provide items of good design for ordinary people.

Part of his oeuvre was one-of-a-kind primitive pendants and brooches with wire-wrapped stones in sterling silver and amoeba shaped pieces with moving parts. He may also have experimented, before or alongside Sam Kramer, with processes to produce the spontaneous jewelry made by the uncontrolled melting of metals. "In a letter published in the January/February 1968 issue of *Craft Horizons*, Rebajes alluded to sessions with Sam Kramer which took place at his own workshop in 1939...'(To) gether we worked—just for fun—on what we then called 'crazy' jewelry. With a powerful oxyacetylene torch I 'fussed (fused?)' many pieces. Sam was enchanted and continued these experiments in his shop. We decided to call it 'controlled melting."

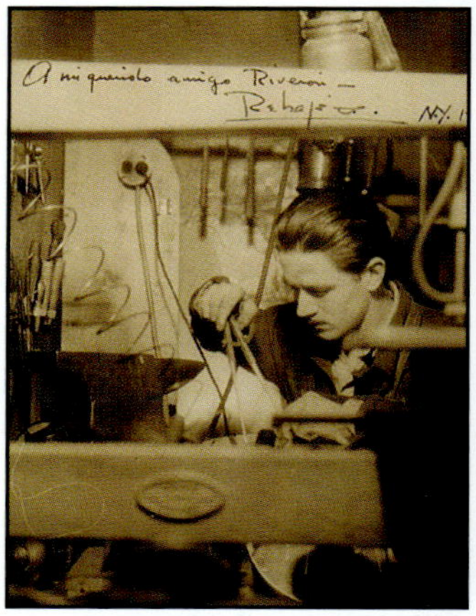

Rebajes in his workshop in 1939. *Photograph courtesy of Patricia Riveron Lee.*

In 1942 Rebajes moved from the Village to 377 Fifth Avenue, a space designed by Puerto Rican architect, José Fernandez. The Rebajes Jewelry and Gift Shop was an ultra- modern design with an "ingenious s-shaped shelf and showcase system which hung from thin steel rods attached to the ceiling. The shelves were glass and the showcases were faced in white plastic laminate. A dangling fixture which housed fluorescent lights followed the entire length of this curve." The interior was stunning in muted colors, gray marble, pickled oak and bronze trim. Blue leather covered the folding door separating the floor from the stock room.

Interior of Rebajes Jewelry and Gift Shop. *Photograph courtesy of Patricia Riveron Lee.*

Along with his retail outlet, Rebajes opened a workshop at 10 West 17th Street. He employed over 100 artisans, but he himself designed and made all the prototypes as well as the unique equipment required to produce the work. A few pieces were one-of-a-kind and handcrafted. The separate elements of each production piece were cast or die stamped and assembled by hand. Sometimes hammer marks were added to create a handmade look. Copper was used most often and was sometimes silver-plated. Sterling silver was used less frequently and mostly for constructed pieces, which could also contain enamel, semi-precious stones, pearls or found objects.

Rebajes jewelry and objects were sold all over the United States, advertised in fashion magazines such as *Glamour* and offered through outlets like Saks Fifth Avenue and hundreds of other stores and boutiques. In 1958 Rebajes sold his complete factory operation and original designs to his foreman Otto R. Bade who, after two years, moved the operation to New Hope, Pennsylvania where he continued to produce the designs under the "ORB" hallmark.

Francisco (Frank) and Pauline moved to Torremolinos, Spain in 1960, opening a small metal shop where he continued making some hand-crafted jewelry though he concentrated mainly on sculpture until his death in 1990.

merry renk

"...I like the line itself. It really attracted me. And in the beginning...I was very, very intuitive; I couldn't discuss them in words...I began with a bent wire which I then used twice to make the boomerangs, or three times, repeating the V shape three times on one ear(ing). And then I took that shape and put it together at the center with three shapes...and so the forms began to build up. And the training that I had at the ID (Institute of Design) was to work nonobjectively, so that I...wasn't making flowers. I was making structures. If you put things together, they make a certain pattern, but they were reflective of nature, because nature works like that. It works with one form being repeated and repeated and repeated and repeated, so that they were natural forms, but at the same time they were nonobjective to me."[78]
—merry renk

merry renk in her studio pounding "boomerang" earrings, c.1976, *Photograph by Frank Clancy, courtesy of merry renk.*

merry renk brooch and earrings, sterling silver, brooch: 2-1/2" diameter x 3/8" deep, earrings: 1-1/2" diameter x 1" deep. *Collection of Steve Cabella, photograph by Geoff Turner.*

merry renk (b. 1921)(who decided in Chicago that capitals and serifs were non-essential so even her hallmark is in lower case) is a delightful person whose art is evocative of her wit and appreciation for life. She is also an extraordinarily skilled metalsmith whose highly structural designs continue to change form, but consistently possess the fundamental principles of "good design" taught by László Maholy-Nagy at the Institute of Design in Chicago where renk studied during 1946 and 1947.[79]

During the time she was studying at the Institute of Design in Chicago, renk opened a gallery called the 750 Studio with two fellow students. They sold paintings, sculpture, photographs and crafts and lived in the rear of the shop. The shows they held at the 750 Studio were quite successful and they managed to get prominent artists to exhibit their work. renk said that they were unique in that they were one of the only galleries showing nonobjective art.

Using the experimental approach learned at the Institute of Design, renk began to work with enamels on metal and not too long after started to work with wire, forming simple shapes into designs for jewelry. Her "Boomerangs" design from 1947, made with a bent wire "V," became an essential element which she developed and repeated throughout her career.

In 1948 renk moved to California where she worked full time making jewelry. Her "Atoms" pieces from the 1950s were made of either oxidized silver or gold.

merry renk added crowns and hair ornaments to her repertoire. She made them out of silver and gold in bent wire, folded metal, and interlocking metal. Some are embellished with gems, pearls and enamel. Her *Folded Crown* of 1954 was made from folded thin silver sheet, which has the sculptural (light and shadow) quality of folded paper together with the added visual interest of the reflective metal. merry said it was very light and comfortable when she wore it in her long hair. In 1968, she created her famous *White Cloud Wedding Crown* for the exhibit *Objects: USA* that opened at the Smithsonian in 1969. The crown was made from interlocking rings of repeated shapes in 14k yellow gold with cultured pearls on ends of wires that emerged from within the form like the flower, Baby's Breath.

By the 1950s interlocking forms were an integral part of renk's designs. Earrings from 1958 are made from 14k gold sheet that was sawed and the pieces "interlocked." The sections of the earrings "fly" in space like a flock of birds and the form is reminiscent of a Calder mobile.

In 1959 merry renk married ceramist Earle Curtis. An original watercolor shows renk with her new baby Bonnie in a sling around her neck while she saws gold to make her interlocking wedding bands.

renk had a fondness for tiny diamonds which she used in necklaces and crowns, usually mounted at the ends of wires. She used stones more as accents than focal points.

In 1967, after losing focus in her right eye, renk turned adversity into a constructive force by shifting her concentration from jewelry to large interlocking sculptures-some as high as seven feet and cut with a torch from rusted sheet iron, copper or brass that she would patinate in different ways. She went back to jewelry later when she was able to adjust to her partial loss of vision.

In 1974 renk received a National Endowment of the Arts Craftsman Award to work a year in her favorite enamel technique, *plique-à-jour*.

renk had solo exhibitions at the San Francisco Museum of Art in 1954; the M.H. De Young Memorial Museum in San Francisco in 1971; the Smithsonian Institution, National Museum of History and Technology, Washington, D.C. in 1971; and a retrospective at the California Crafts Museum in Palo Alto in 1981.

After twenty-five years of adhering to the nonobjective ideas of the Institute of Design, her desire is now to express memories of family and more complex political ideas using realism. She is curently involved with painting watercolors.

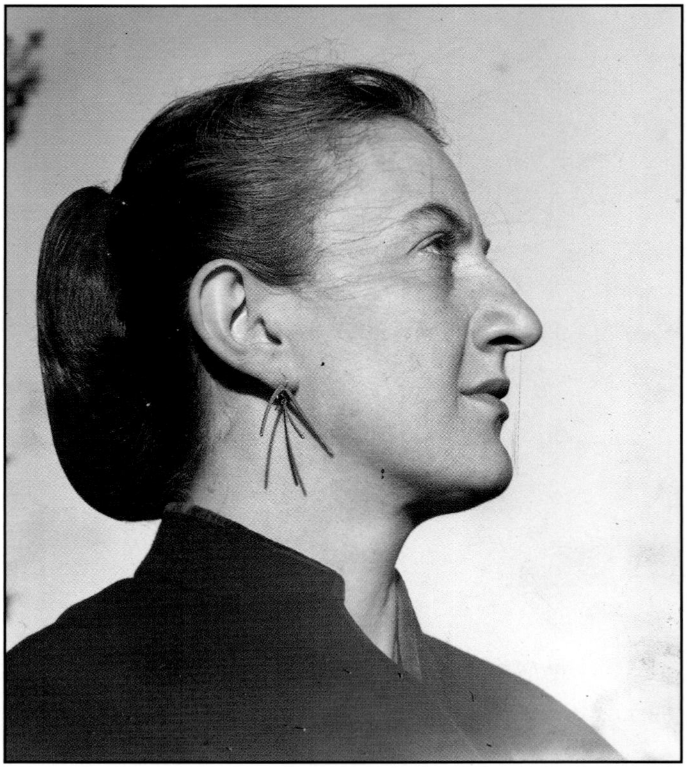

merry renk in San Francisco, c. 1952. *Photograph by Dan Grae, courtesy of merry renk.*

Barney M. Reid

Barney M. Reid (d. 1992) was a versatile and talented craftsman who worked with jewelry, ceramics, wood and screen-printed textiles. He attended Arizona State College and the State University of Iowa. His jewelry was enamel and copper or wood in combination with silver.[80]

Reid was one of the original members of an organization founded in 1947, the Allied Craftsmen of San Diego, formed to foster cooperation among craftsmen and stimulate interest among the community in contemporary crafts. He became president of the organization in 1953. Harry Bertoia, who was residing in San Diego at the time, was one of the most famous members. Reid, who shared a studio with Bertoia, exhibited his jewelry with Allied Craftsman in 1951 and that same year, won second prize for jewelry at the San Diego County Fair.

Reid exhibited at the Wichita Art Associations *Decorative Art and Ceramics* Exhibition in 1953 and in 1955 and in the Contemporary Jewelry exhibit of at the Walker Art Center in Minneapolis, also in 1955. That same year he also participated in *American Jewelry and Related Objects* in Huntington, West Virginia. His work was included in the 1956 *Craftsmanship in a Changing World* exhibition at the Museum of Contemporary Crafts in New York City and he received an invitation to submit work for consideration in the American Pavilion of the 1958 World's Fair in Brussels.

Reid's work of the 1960s was mostly sculpture constructed from enameled copper and brass panels "arranged in flowerlike formats atop attenuated brass stalks, reminiscent of Bertoia's sound sculptures form the same period."

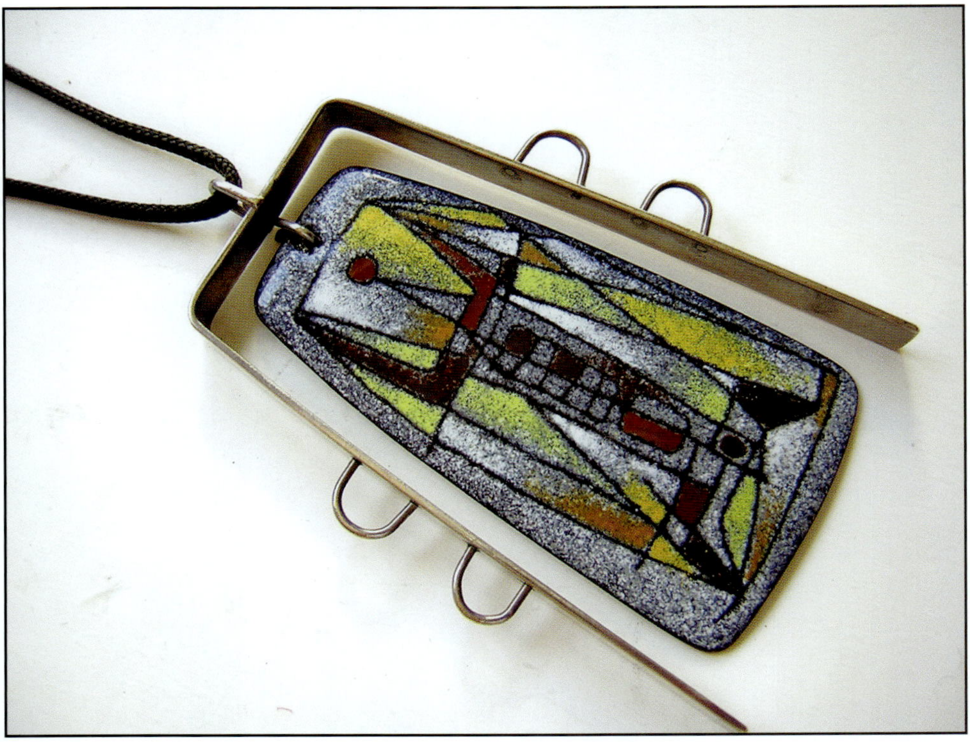

Barney Reid, pendant, enamel on copper with sterling silver, 3" x 2", c. 1956.
Collection of Munir Meghji, photograph by Munir Meghji.

Florence Resnikoff

Florence Resnikoff, pendant, gold, pearls, blue spinel (cut by Francis Sperison), 3-1/2" x 1-1/2". *Collection of Joanne and Fred Doloresco, photograph by Fred Doloresco.*

Florence Resnikoff (b. 1920) first made jewelry in 1949 while attending the Ox-Bow Summer School of Painting at Saugatuck Michigan. The school was affiliated with The Art Institute of Chicago. Robert von Neumann, who was teaching jewelry at the University of Illinois at that time, offered a workshop at Saugatuck. She made a round silver pin with a cutout cat shape, an applied head and wire eyes. Her second articulated silver cat pendant followed. "This was the beginning," she said.[81]

Resnikoff's work has progressed through the mastery of many difficult techniques including electroforming, anodizing, *plique-a-jour, keum-boo*, and *makume gane*. She has worked with gold, silver, platinum, pewter, copper, bronze and refractory metals such as titanium and niobium.

In 1951, when she moved to the West Coast, The San Francisco Metal Arts Guild and the influences of distinguished member Margaret De Patta were major stimuli to Resnikoff's career as a metalsmith. The interaction among members brought her out of isolation and into discussions with other metalsmiths. It was De Patta's "emphasis on structural conceptualizations and the systematic probing of materials" that most affected Resnikoff. She also studied casting for a short time with Bob Winston, whose approach to design was less structured than that of Margaret De Patta.

Resnikoff's early pieces were cast or constructed designs that adhered to the principles of the modernists; materials and function were allowed to define the character of the form, though her work rejected the Spartan simplicity of modernism--it was her nature to enrich and ornament surfaces.

By the mid-1960s Resnikoff's jewelry appeared in numerous national shows and was being shown at galleries and at exhibits on the West Coast and Midwest. At this time she began exploring the possibilities of other metals and larger forms such as bronze sculpture. Part of the impetus to begin formal training in sculpture was a prestigious exhibition award she received in 1962 for a cast bronze sculpture. She wanted to strengthen her work with new materials and forms. "I found myself becoming anxious to break out of the precious metals, precious stones format. I wanted to become a metalsmith, to develop a personal image become part of a new wave..."

Florence Resnikoff, pendant, sterling silver, turquoise, 2 -1/8" x 5/8". *Collection of Joanne and Fred Doloresco, photograph by Fred Doloresco.*

In 1963-1964, because of her husband's academic career, Resnikoff moved to Chicago. Her experiences with the Midwest Designer Craftsmen organization helped her to establish connections to craftsmen and universities in the Midwest and allowed the interest in her own work to become widespread nationally. In 1965 she moved back to California and resumed her education, receiving her B.F.A. in sculpture from the California College of Arts and Crafts, Oakland in 1967 and, in 1973, an M.A. from San Jose State University. That same year she received a fellowship from the National Endowment for the Arts to study electroforming techniques and their application to jewelry and metalsmithing. She enrolled in a graduate workshop conducted by Stanley Lechtzin at the Tyler School of Art. She then set up her studio to probe the potential of electroforming with the related processes of electrotexturing.

Resnikoff's jewelry of the 1970s is filled with energy and exploration. For a while she discontinued the use of stones while she concentrated more and more on metal in combinations of bronze (the metal of choice for her sculpture) with silver, silver with copper, and chrome plating over silver with copper. In the 1970s she began using the Japanese technique of *makume gane.*

In 1973 she began teaching at the California College of Arts and Crafts in the Jewelry Metal Arts Program, becoming Program Head in 1980. Around that same time she began experiments in anodizing highly refractory metals. This technology brought new dimensions in color and material to her work.

Resnikoff's studio contains machines that replace some of the traditional hand processes and equipment to work with highly refractory metals. She does not believe that this negates her identity as a creative artist producing unique objects.

Color, a necessary element of composition in most of the fine and applied arts, is not foremost in the discussion of modernist jewelry, however Florence Resnikoff "delights in the use of color--vibrant, glowing shades of purple, rose, peacock, blue, and green and gold or clouding of blue gray--the expanded palate she achieves with anodized titanium or niobium."

Her search for color began in the 1950s; first in her experiments with enamel using the ancient techniques of *plique-a-jour* and *champleve* to bring the richness of color to silver jewelry and then in her densely patinated silver, gold and alloyed pins. Color experimentation continued with dyed cast resins, which she introduced in the 1960s, and in the "subtle variations of patina she obtained by patinating various plated or electroplated metals." Her skillful handling of color is also apparent in her radical mixtures of different metals and gemstones. The depth of Florence Resnikoff's oeuvre is truly amazing. She continues to explore innovative, fresh ways to express herself in metals.

In 1989 Resnikoff retired from the California College of Arts and Crafts as Professor Emerita and has been honored by having a student scholarship named for her. She is an honorary member of The Society of American Jewelry Historians and has lectured on such topics as *The Background Of Early Decorated Man*, and *Factors And History Of Our Contemporary Art Jewelry*.

She has exhibited her work extensively in the United States and abroad.

Walter Rhodes

Walter Rhodes was born in New York City. He received his art education at the Cooper Union and the Art Students League, studying jewelry making under Adda Husted-Andersen and silversmithing under Peter Muller-Monk and Lauritz Eichner. He worked as a studio artist/jeweler in Tappan New York. His jewelry was mostly abstract, constructed of cutout biomorphic silver shapes and wire with a conservative use of stones. He only worked in one-of-a-kind pieces or very limited editions, which he sold from his workshop.[82]

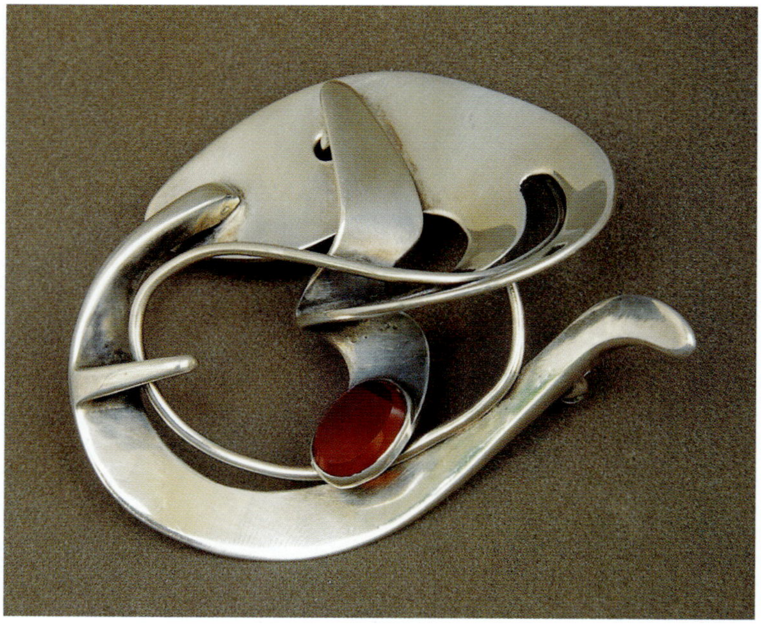

Walter Rhodes, brooch, sterling silver, 2-3/4" x 1". *Collection of Joanne and Fred Doloresco, photograph by Marbeth Schon.*

Rima

Rima (d. 2001) was a sculptor, jeweler, and designer as well as a teacher. She studied at the Art Students League, the Pratt Institute, the Museum of Modern Art School, the Sculpture Center, the Educational Alliance and Preferred Casting of New York City. Her work was widely exhibited and publicized in magazines and newspapers such as *Vogue, New York Magazine, The New Yorker, the New York Times,* and *Interiors Magazine.* Her jewelry was mostly cast. She taught at Parson's School of Design in New York and the Jewelry Institute of Providence.[83]

Rima taught wax casting at the Jewelry Workshop and Gallery of New York and at the Abbey School of Jewelry Design in New York City. She also gave workshops in the "foil" method of stained glass making at Tiffany's in New York, as well as teaching clay and wax modeling, mold making and plaster.

Her sculptures were mostly nonrepresentational abstract works sometimes in a geometric cubist style and other times biomorphic, however she also made representational pieces. Rima was commissioned to design and make jewelry for manufacturers, stores and industry. Clients included the Metropolitan Museum, Cartier, Katram, Jad Jewelry and others. Some of her special sculpture commissions included relief portrait medallions of President John F. Kennedy, Robert Kennedy, Martin Luther King, Jr. and a Mother of the Year Award Sculpture. Rima created a commemorative plaque for the Anti-Defamation league, which was presented to Eleanor Roosevelt and President Truman.

Rima, brooch, sterling silver, 1" x 2-3/4". *Collection of Joanne and Fred Doloresco, photograph by Fred Doloresco.*

Ruth Roach

"My aim...seems to be to help Iowans and the Midwest to become aware of these good things. This business of people saying 'I know what I like', when they really mean 'I like what I know' is nearly an obsession with me. Awareness, appreciation and education seem to be the answers...maybe I can help." —Ruth Roach

Ruth Roach (1913-1979) was an extraordinarily multitalented artist/craftsman who made an improbable but significant impact on the art world during her relatively short career. She was also an avid collector and patron of the arts.[84]

She was born Ruth Schirmer in Chisholm, a small mining town in the center of the Mesabi Iron Range in northeastern Minnesota. The Schirmer family moved from Chisholm to Chicago, and later to Cedar Rapids, Iowa. It was in Cedar Rapids, in the early 1930s, that Ruth met her future husband, James L. Roach. They were both students at the University of Iowa where Ruth was taking courses in nursing. After their marriage, Ruth and Jim Roach settled in the small rural Iowa community of Plainfield on the Cedar River.

Roach first studied art in Chicago during the depression, after her family moved there from Chisholm. She took painting classes at the Chicago Art Institute and also studied with William Henry Watson. Much later, during 1946 and 1947, she went back to school at Iowa State Teachers College in Cedar Falls with plans to become a potter. Throughout her life, she won several awards for her pottery and was capable of throwing very large pieces. One of her works was a baptismal font for the Plainfield Methodist Church—a beautiful, large hand-thrown font that still stands within an iron frame placed against an inner wall.

In 1948 Roach took her first jewelry course with Harriet Larkin, and in 1954, inspired by classes with studio jeweler Robert von Neumann, she decided to concentrate almost entirely on jewelry.

In 1954 Roach's first one-woman show was held at the Des Moines Art Center, Des Moines, Iowa, and in 1955 her work was accepted in national competitions at museums in Wichita, New Orleans, Huntington, West Virginia, and St. Paul, Minnesota. That same year, as well as participating in the exhibition *Contemporary Jewelry* at the Walker Art Center in Minneapolis, she had two one-woman shows: one in Salem, Oregon, and the other in Mason City, Iowa. And photographs of her work appeared in the May/June issue of *Craft Horizons.*

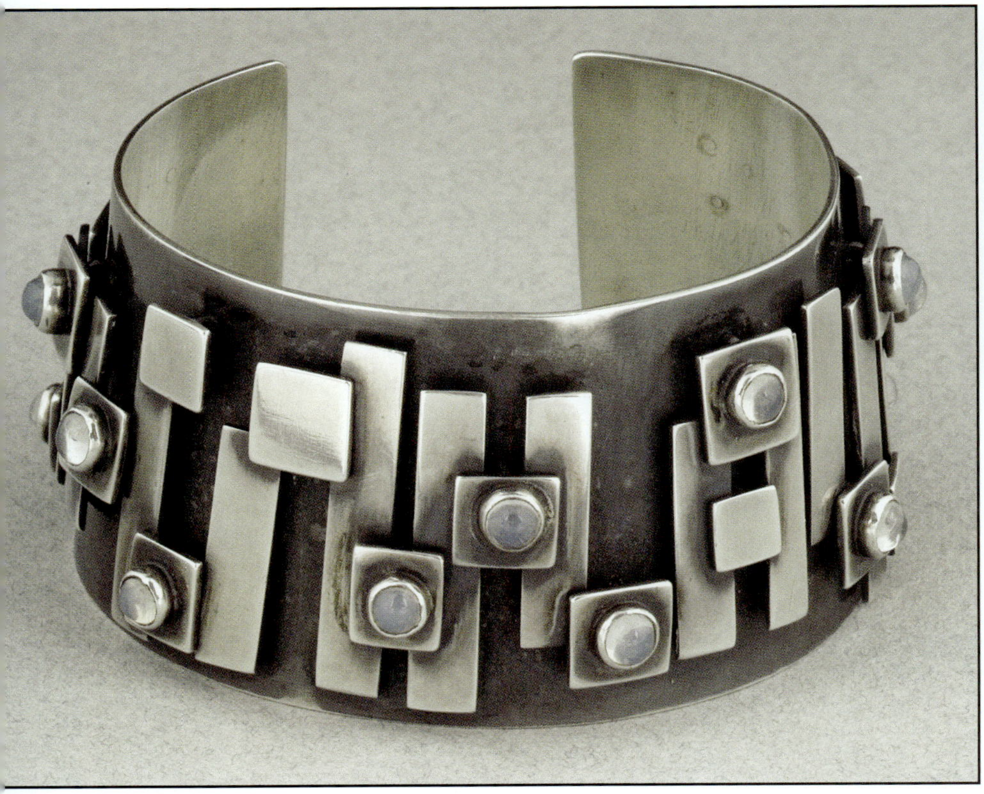

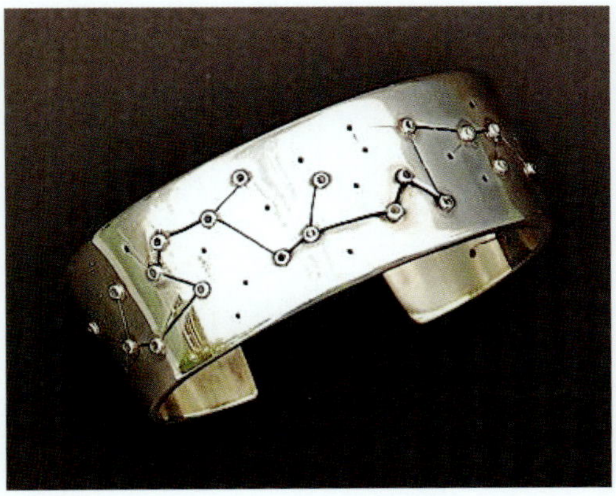

Ruth Roach, cuff, sterling silver, 5-1/2" (inside diameter) x 1" wide. *Collection of Joanne and Fred Doloresco, photograph by Fred Doloresco.*

Ruth Roach, cuff, sterling silver, moonstone, 2-1/2" x 2-1/4". *Courtesy of Mark McDonald, 555 Warren St., Hudson, New York, photograph by Bill Hibbs.*

From 1956 through 1959, Roach won many prizes for her jewelry including an award from *American Jewelry, and Related Objects* at the Memorial Art Gallery, in Rochester, New York (circulated by the Smithsonian Institution); an award for two pieces from the *10th Annual Iowa Artists Show*, Des Moines Art Center, Des Moines, Iowa; and an award from the *Midwest Designer Craftsmen*, Joslyn Art Museum, Omaha, Nebraska (also circulated by the Smithsonian Institution). Photographs of her jewelry appeared in *Craft Horizons*, in February of 1957; *Art in America*, Issue #2, 1959; and *Jewelry Making,* a textbook by Murray Bovin.

Ruth Roach, *Clarinet key* bracelet, sterling silver, ebony. *Courtesy of Mark McDonald, 555 Warren St., Hudson, New York, photograph by Bill Hibbs.*

In 1960 her work appeared on *The Today Show* with David Garroway. The same year she exhibited at the Museum of Contemporary Crafts in New York, and her jewelry was pictured in *Design Quarterly*, issues 45-46, Walker Art Center, Minneapolis and in *Craft Horizons*.

From 1961–1965 she continued to receive accolades for her jewelry; she was offered a one-woman show at the Minneapolis Institute of Art and was featured in *Cross Country Craftsman.*

Roach's studio was in the basement of her home. She used part of the space for her workshop and the rest for a salesroom and gallery where she showed jewelry collected on world travels with her husband and pieces by other American jewelers. She was also a collector of fine art and pottery. Her ceramics collection included work by Harvey Littleton, Clyde Burt, Clarence Alling, Toshiko Takaezu, the McKinnels, Gerald Williams, Secrest, the MacKenzies, etc.

One of Roach's dearest friends was Minnesota studio jeweler Christian Schmidt who would visit her in Plainfield bringing beets and other vegetables from his garden. Roach and Schmidt would spend hours in the studio trading secrets about new techniques and tricks each had learned.

Roach worked both in sterling and gold using many semi-precious stones. Each piece was well planned so that the clasps and chains become integral parts of the designs and many pieces had moveable parts. "I make one-of-a-kind jewelry only," she said, "although there are similarities.... for instance, while working on one piece, the idea for another invariably crops up. This is the area in which my craft becomes exciting. I enjoy using planned textures, either by fusing or soldering. There seems to be no limit of possibilities."

In 1966 Roach had a retrospective exhibit at *L'Atelier Galerie* in Cedar Falls, Iowa. She was also part of *Art of Personal Adornment*, National Invitational, Museum of Contemporary Crafts, New York City, and was featured in *Pageant Magazine*. Ruth's work is part of permanent collections at Huntington Galleries, Huntington, West Virginia; Memorial Art Gallery, Rochester, New York; Brooks Memorial Gallery of Art, Memphis, Tennessee; and North Iowa State University, Cedar Falls, Iowa.

In 1968, after the death of her husband, Roach moved from Iowa to Naples, Florida, where she opened a gallery in the Landmark building on 5th Avenue.

In 1969 she had a one-woman show at the Sheldon Art Gallery, University of Nebraska in Lincoln. The Sheldon purchased one of her pieces for their permanent collection. She also exhibited in *OBJECTS USA* whose sponsor, the Johnson Wax Collection, purchased a work by Ruth titled *Amber Tea Party* for their permanent collection.

Ruth lived her last 10 years in Naples. She died at the age of 66.

Roach is remembered not only for her remarkable creative output, but also for being a tireless proponent of arts and crafts in Iowa. She acted as the President of the Iowa Designer Craftsmen guild and was in great demand as a speaker across the state for her enthusiastic demeanor and quick wit.

Ruth Roach, brooch, sterling silver, opal, 2-1/4" x 7/8". *Collection of Joanne and Fred Doloresco, photograph by Fred Doloresco.*

Caroline Gleick Rosene

Peripatetic jeweler Caroline Gleick Rosene studied at Washington University in St. Louis, Radcliffe College in Cambridge, Massachusetts, and *L'Institute d'Art at d'Archeologie* in Paris. She also studied with Isami Doi in Honolulu, Adda Husted-Anderson in New York City, and Marian Hartwell in San Francisco. She was the director of the City Art Museum in St. Louis and the Art Center at Fitchburg, Massachusetts.

Rosene was a studio jeweler with her own shop and participated in numerous national exhibitions. In the late 1940s or early 1950s, Irena Brynner studied under Rosene in San Francisco. Rosene was also an instructor at the College of San Mateo in California.

Most of the work I've seen by Rosene has been in silver, always constructed—either abstract or based on natural forms. She also worked with gold, wood and coral and sometimes included stones.[85]

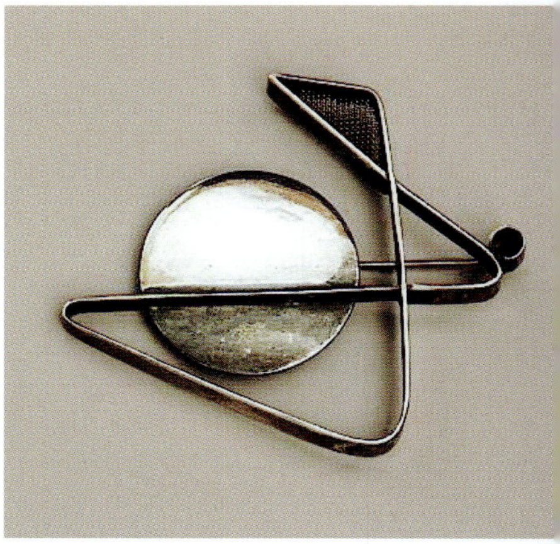

Carolyn Rosene, brooch, sterling silver wire, mesh, 2-7/8 x 3 ¼. *Collection of Joanne and Fred Doloresco, photograph by Fred Doloresco.*

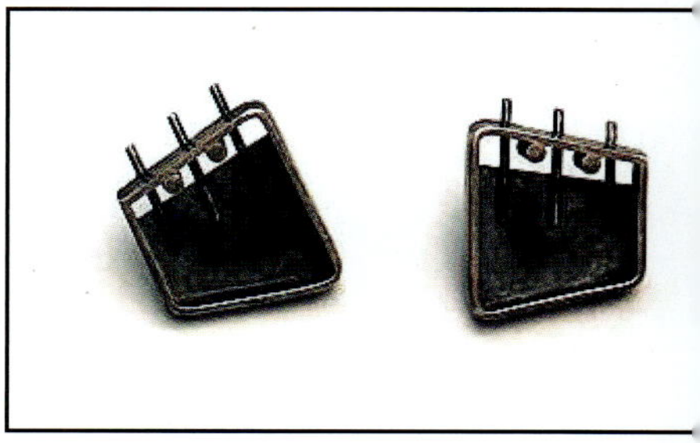

Carolyn Rosene, brooch, sterling silver, 7/8" x 3/4". *Collection of Joanne and Fred Doloresco, photograph by Fred Doloresco.*

George K. Salo

"Design must be an organization of many elements: space, line, texture, chiaroscuro, planes and forms." —George Salo

George K. Salo attended the Whitney Art School in New Haven, Connecticut and the Chicago Art Institute. He worked in pewter and silver in both in hand constructed and cast forms and his pieces were modernist in style and mostly abstract.[86]

George Salo, brooch and earrings, sterling silver, turquoise, brooch: 2" x 2-3/4", earrings: 1" x 7/8". *Collection of Joanne and Fred Doloresco, photograph by Fred Doloresco.*

Zahara Schatz

Zahara Schatz (1916-1999) was a native of Palestine. Her father founded the Bezalel Art School and Museum in Israel. She graduated from the *Eccole Nationale Superieure Des Arts Decoratifs* in Paris and came to the United States shortly after, in 1937.[87]

Schatz was a recognized painter and sculptor whose jewelry was a small part of her total output. Her fascination with plastics began in the late 1940s and early 50s when she began making small Plexiglas pendants and wide bracelets with arrangements of miniature metal shapes. She later worked with trays, bowls, lamp bases, screens, murals, layer paintings and sculpture. Her work was done exclusively in Plexiglas, a thermoplastic substance (polymethyl methocrylate) that retains its shape after being molded with heat.

Zahara Schatz, cuff, Plexiglas, copper, brass, wire, Lurex thread, 1-7/8" x 5-1/4". *Collection of Joanne and Fred Doloresco, photograph by Fred Doloresco.*

To make her plastic jewelry or other small objects, Zahara Schatz would start by cutting a piece of Plexiglas from a standard 3 x 4 sheet with a hand or electric saw. She then painted the background design in metallic pigments using bronze, gold and aluminum powders after which she applied and arranged a collage of collected items which might include both metals and leaves in as large a variety as possible of shapes, colors, and textures.

Metal compositions included very fine silver wire and thin sheeting of aluminum, copper, brass, steel and possibly small pieces of fine or coarse copper mesh or shapes of silver screen. Schatz also used small objects like washers or discs "(sometimes both together for a positive-negative effect), wire raveled from screening, tiny glistening beads and dots and improbable odds and ends salvaged from workshops." Lurex (a type of yarn) was also snipped and sometimes sprinkled like "thistledown" in the background of the composition. When she was satisfied with her composition she laminated the piece by covering it with another transparent or lightly tinted Plexiglas sheet and joining the two sheets. This was accomplished by coating the top layer with a solvent such as acetone or ethylene dichloride and clamping the two layers together between sheets of metal or plywood until the solvent set.

Another joining method was the use of heat, which was more difficult but more interesting because the plastic would flow like thick paint around and through the design. Schatz would heat the sheets separately for about ten minutes at about 250° to 300° in an ordinary kitchen oven. The sheets were joined and pressed using the same method until set. When the Plexiglas was hot, it could be shaped by hand or put into molds to create bowls, plates, trays or lamp bases. Practice was required for the molding process because too much pressure would crack the material and overheating produced bubbles and crystal effects. Part of the "fun", however, was controlling those very effects to create artistic variations.

When the laminated pieces were set, Schatz filed, scraped, sanded, buffed and polished the pieces by hand and trimmed them into asymmetrical, often biomorphic shapes.

Schatz was excited about the components she couldn't completely control. Her collages created space and new textures of their own when pressed by the lamination process. Plastic sculptures, because of their transparent qualities, would change when the light shone through or on them at different angles.

Schatz strove to create abstract designs out of the natural materials she collected; an exercise she admitted was extremely difficult. Schatz worked as an artist and industrial designer. Her work has been exhibited in the United States and Israel.

Mary Schimpff

Mary Schimpff's jewelry was shown alongside that of Margaret De Patta, Bob Winston, Paul Miller, and Robert von Neumann in 1954, in an article titled *Five Contemporary Jewelers,* published in *American Craft Magazine* that was concurrent with an exhibit at American House.

Mary Schimff, on the radio program, *The Voice of America* after receiving the *Diamonds International Award* in the late 1950s. *Courtesy of Mary Schimpff.*

Mary Schimpff's work compares favorably with the best of mid-20th century modernist jewelry. Like De Patta, Schimpff is a perfectionist and a modernist whose designs are based on the integration of form and function. [87]

From earliest childhood, Schimpff was precise. "When I was three," she related, "I took an art class and we had to make a coil pot and I was so upset because I couldn't roll out the coil evenly...I wanted things to be right." Her first experience with jewelry was an introductory course at prep school. When she returned home with her work to show her mother, she was surprised to find out that she had a full set of equipment stored in the attic. "I didn't know she'd ever made jewelry!"

Schimpff's mother Frances began as a fine arts student in the 1920s; she attended the Art Institute of Chicago, The Chicago Academy (with notables such as Walt Disney), the Kalo shop, and Pratt in New York City.

Mary attended the Peoria Art Institute and the Illinois State University and throughout her career studied privately with various jewelry technicians, stone setters, stonecutters, toolmakers and enamelists.

In the 1950s Mary and Frances began to make jewelry together. They both worked in abstracted naturalistic themes. Neither did any casting of pieces—everything was hand constructed.

Like their modernist counterparts, the Schimpff's challenged conventional ideas and were among the first to use precious stones informally, pairing them with semi-precious stones. At the same time, they created unique mixes of materials such as matching gold with platinum.

Mary's constant flow of ideas, many inspired by her natural surroundings, were sketched on envelope backs, napkins and newspaper margins to be stored later in one of her many boxes of design notations.

Schimpff's husband, Bruce Webb, began making jewelry shortly after they were married--a background in the linen business and weaving prepared him for the intricacies of working with metal and stone. Desiring to learn to cut their own stones, they traveled together to Germany where they were inspired by master stonecutter, Bernd Munsteiner. Mary wanted to be able do unusual cuts in stone to enhance the designs she made in metals.

Schimpff worked with many materials and techniques including wood, colored gold, bronze, semi-precious stones, silver, and enamels as well as married metals and the ancient Korean technique *keum-boo* (pure gold file adhered to a silver surface). She has also worked with black iron and has exquisitely combined iron with baroque pearls.

Lately she has turned to designing perfume bottles inspired by trees shaped by the ocean breezes, silver fountains and intricate figural boxes.

Mary Schimpff has achieved international recognition for her work that has been exhibited in such places as American House and the Metropolitan Museum in New York City; *"Tendenzen"* at the *Schmuckmuseum* in Pforzheim, Germany; the Brooklyn Museum of Art; and Georg Jensen Inc. in New York City. Her work is in the permanent collection of the Smithsonian Institution of Art, Washington, D.C.; Honolulu Academy of Arts, Honolulu, Hawaii and the Museum of Arts and Sciences in Daytona Beach, Florida.

When Adlai Stevenson was leaving office, he commissioned Frances and Mary Schimpff to design small silver boxes and letter openers bearing the seal of the state of Illinois that he gave as parting gifts to his staff.

She won many international awards including four De Beers Diamonds-International awards.

Mary Schimpff is a past president of the North East Chapter of the Florida Society of Goldsmiths, a group co-founded by Schimpff and her late husband.

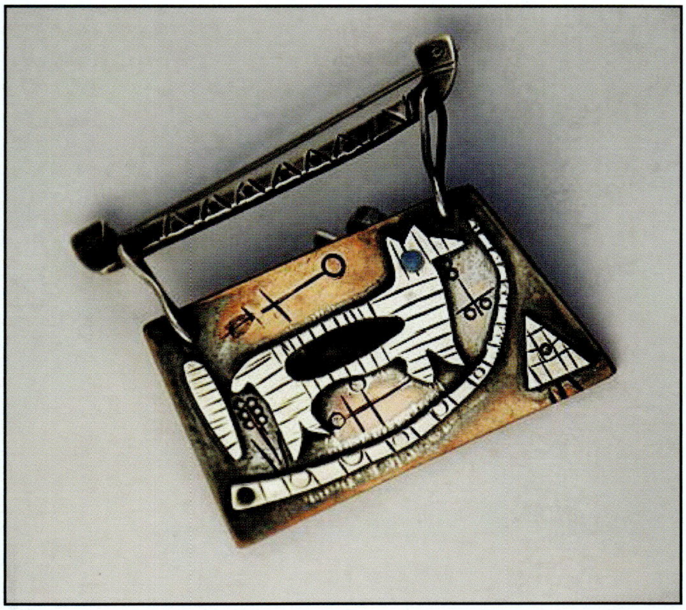

Howard Schleeter, brooch, sterling silver, 2 1/4" x 2 1/2". *Collection of Joanne and Fred Doloresco, photograph by Fred Doloresco.*

Howard Schleeter, necklace, sterling silver, 4" x 3". *Collection of Joanne and Fred Doloresco, photograph by Fred Doloresco.*

Howard Behling Schleeter

Howard Schleeter (1903-1976) was born in Buffalo, New York, in 1903. The son of a commercial artist, he began his studies at the Albright Art School in Buffalo, though his studies there were brief and he was mostly self-taught.[89]

In 1929 he and his wife settled permanently in New Mexico. In the 1930s Schleeter studied under Brooks Willis and worked in several media including gouache, watercolor, oil, scratchboard and engraving. Jewelry was probably a small percentage of his output. During the Depression Schleeter was at times forced to dig ditches to make ends meet. In 1936 his financial status improved when he received the first of several commissions from the Works Progress Administration (WPA). Although he worked primarily in abstraction, the five murals he completed for a WPA commission in the Melrose Public School library are realistic depictions of the American West.

From 1936 to 1942 he worked on several more New Deal commissions in locations including Santa Fe, New Mexico and Washington D.C. During 1938 and 1939 he also taught art classes at a Las Vegas, New Mexico gallery.

In 1945 the *Encyclopedia Britannica* referred to Schleeter as "an artist's artist." He received local attention when he became one of the first artists chosen by Peter Hurd and Jane Mabry for significant contributions to New Mexico's art. Schleeter taught at the University of New Mexico from 1950 to 1951 and in 1954. He was a member of the Art League of New Mexico and exhibited his work at numerous museums throughout the United States.

Christian Schmidt

Christian Schmidt's art was a personal statement; his philosophies regarding procedure, design, and subject matter were uniquely his own and derived from the totality of his life experiences, especially those related to nature. He was a perfectionist who strove to communicate his ideas through his writing, photography and jewelry.[90]

Schmidt received his B.S. in Art Education from the University of Minnesota. He taught art and design for eleven years at the secondary and college level. His jewelry designs in gold, silver, ebony and natural stones are mostly interpretations of natural forms.

He created both structurally complex forms and simple modernist pieces and regularly applied textures to create surface interest and/or to create a more naturalistic look, though he also left many surfaces undecorated. Like a sculptor, he contrasted surface texture with highly polished surfaces or solid areas with pierced areas. He also combined cast and hand constructed techniques, integrating gems and stones to work with a particular idea or form.

Schmidt's designs evolved gradually; he often created sequences of the same idea. He strove to develop and refine all the possibilities or variations that were suggested by a certain material, technique or specific tool, exhausting all the design possibilities before moving on to the next form.

Schmidt was one of twelve jewelers whose work was selected for exhibition at the Brussels World's Fair. In addition to his activities as a panel speaker and juror at art competitions, he exhibited in numerous one-man and group shows throughout the country.

Sadly, he gave up jewelry making shortly after 1969, when his book *Encounter with Art* was published. He moved to Alaska where he died at a relatively young age.

Christian Schmidt in 1969. *Photograph by Janet Schmidt, courtesy of The Sarah Bodine & Michael Dunas Archives of 20th Century Jewelry, Tyler School of Art, Temple University, Professor Stanley Lechtzin, Curator of Metals/Jewelry Archives and Collections.*

Pearl Shecter

Pearl S. Shecter received her M.F.A. at Columbia University. She studied abstract painting at the Hans Hoffman School of Fine Arts, New York and also attended the Chicago Bauhaus School of Moholy-Nagy. Her interest in jewelry was furthered by studies in enameling and metalsmithing with Adda Husted-Andersen in New York City. Shecter maintained a studio in New York for many years while also teaching at New York University and directing the art department at the Little Red Schoolhouse High School.[91]

Shecter's jewelry was mainly abstract and constructed, not cast. She mostly worked with silver and sometimes wire which she wrapped around rough-cut stones or used to create fluid, linear definition around or within her compositions. She made hair combs and ankle bracelets as well as more common jewelry forms.

Pearl Shecter, brooch, sterling silver, 1-1/4" x 2-1/4". *Collection of Joanne and Fred Doloresco, photograph by Fred Doloresco.*

Helen Shirk

Helen Shirk (b. 1942) is Professor of Art (Emerita) and Head of the Jewelry/Metals program at San Diego State University where she has taught since 1975. In 1963 she received her B.S. from Skidmore College, where she took her first jewelry course with Earl Pardon. She studied with Alma Eikerman at Indiana University in Bloomington, Indiana, where in 1969, she received her M.F.A.

Helen Shirk, *Courtesy of Helen Shirk.*

Shirk's jewelry from the 1960s falls within the constructivist tradition; it is assembled, three-dimensional, abstract and architectural--suggesting something much larger.

In the 1970s she began creating hollowware vessels that freed her from the necessities of function inherent in jewelry. Her later work, especially of the 1990s, is more related to natural forms.

From 1971 to 1973 Shirk taught at Indiana University and from 1973 to 1975 at the Des Moines Art Center before going to San Diego State University. In 1963 she received a Fulbright Grant to study in Denmark and, in 1978 and 1988, she was the recipient of National Endowment for the Arts Fellowships. In 1999 she was made a Fellow of the American Craft Council.

Exhibitions include the National Gallery of Australia, Canberra; Gold Treasury Museum, Melbourne, Australia; Schmuckmuseum, Pforzheim, Germany; Goldsmith's Hall, London, England; Museum of Art and Design, Helsinki, Finland; Danish Museum of Decorative Art, Copenhagen, Denmark; National Museum of Ireland, Dublin; Vestlandske Kunstundustri Museum, Bergen, Norway.

Shirk's work is in many public collections, among them the *Schmuckmuseum* (Pforzheim), National Museum of Modern Art (Kyoto), Victoria and Albert Museum (London), the Mint Museum of Craft and Design, the Museum of Art and Design, Cooper-Hewitt National Design Museum, the Houston Museum of Fine Arts, the Carnegie Museum, Indianapolis Museum of Art, and Oakland Museum.

Shirk's work has been featured in numerous magazines and books, including *Women Designers in the USA 1900-2000* (Bard), *Color on Metal* (Guild), *International Dictionary of Jewelry* (Edition du Regard), *Modern Jewelry 1955-1999* (Arnoldsche), *Product Design 4* (PBC International), *Jewelry of Our Time* (Thames and Hudson), *International Crafts* (Thames and Hudson), *Jewelry Concepts and Technology* (Doubleday), *Metalsmith* and *American Craft.* [92]

Helen Shirk, brooch, sterling silver, amethyst, c. 1968. *Courtesy of Helen Shirk*.

Olaf Skoogfors

"The challenge now is to extend myself further, to re-evaluate rather than do the same thing [for] ever. I approach jewelry less as a jeweler than as a creative person. I'm concerned more with imagery than with technique or tradition. I don't just want a variation on a theme. I want new themes. This is slow—to struggle with these images and make an evaluation of what I'm doing. I am concerned now with an incongruity—a balance of organic and geometric. As the play between the two becomes clearer, the statements are becoming stronger. I'm imposing more restrictions on the organic; therefore the pieces are starker. I'm working on the idea of richness." —Olaf Skoogfors

Olaf Skoogfors. *Courtesy of The Sarah Bodine & Michael Dunas Archives of 20th Century Jewelry, Tyler School of Art, Temple University, Professor Stanley Lechtzin, Curator of Metals/Jewelry Archives and Collections.*

Skoogfors (1930-1975), whose surname means "forest stream," was born Gustav Olaf Jansson in Sweden in 1930, in a small backwoods iron center. (Sometime in his life, he changed his name.) "When he was four, his family emigrated from Sweden to the United States, settling in Philadelphia. Skoogfor's father had been an engineer in Sweden, and for a while Olaf tried working as a mechanical draftsman, but quickly became dissatisfied. He said that he wanted to design with his hands, to make something he could "see and hold." [92]

By 1959 Skoogfors had opened an independent studio in Philadelphia after which he was hired to teach at Philadelphia College of Art, Philadelphia, Pennsylvania. He made production and special-order jewelry, hollowware and ecclesiastical metalwork in addition to awards and plaques for industry and institutions.

Skoogfors was primarily concerned with technique. He created assemblages using natural forms for inspiration and his textures and surfaces evoke landscapes or sensual human forms. He often added moonstones and/or pearls as embellishments. Many of his more sculptural forms were made using the lost wax casting process, introduced to him by Ruth and Svetozar Radakovich. He often added reticulation and chasing and sometimes fused textures.

A man ahead of his time, Olaf Skoogfors was able to take an infatuation with the technique of casting and the dripping wax designs of the 1960s, left over from abstract expressionism, and make strong yet sensitive visual statements. He was a master of the textured wax module with simple, very subtle variations. His work suggests an awareness of the best work of European jewelers such as Hermann Junger and Reinhold Reiling; he absorbed much from his European trips, two of which he made with Stanley Lechtzin with the expressed purpose of meeting and viewing the work of European jewelers. Skoogfors' strength was in the subtle surprise of his compositions and the juxtaposition of smooth and textured forms. He used stones and pearls as exclamation points in visual statements.[93]

Gail Roeshman-Selig (a student at the Pennsylvania College of Art from 1974 to 1977), spoke about her first classes with Skoogfors:

> Still the most vivid memory I have of him is walking into my first "jewelry design" class. Olaf had written on the board, "May the sewers of Calcutta back up into your breakfast." He said this was the worst curse he could visualize. We had an active discussion for the next hour about different cultures' ideas of curses, and then our homework was to come up with an even more awful curse. When we came back the next week for the class, he had arranged the chairs in a circle with a record player in the center with the music of Bela Bartok playing. For almost forty-five minutes we sat and listened to the music and then for fifteen minutes he discussed Bela Bartok and his theories and evolution of modern classical music. It wasn't until five or six weeks into the course that he ever mentioned jewelry, but by then our young minds had been opened to a world of creativity.

Skoogfors died suddenly at the relatively young age of forty five. His students, colleagues and friends felt a great loss.

Nancy Sherwood

Nancy Sherwood received her B.F.A. from the University of Kansas where she majored in textile design. She started making jewelry as a hobby in 1953, working in silver and also using some gold. [94]

Nancy Sherwood, brooch, sterling silver, 2 1/4" x 1/2". *Collection of Joanne and Fred Doloresco, photograph by Fred Doloresco.*

Noble (Shirley) Smith

Noble Smith was the "pen name" of Shirley Smith, an extremely talented silversmith who graduated from high school in 1946 and then attended the Boston Museum School in the early 1950s. A classmate from the Boston Museum School, jeweler Phyllis Allen, believes that Noble was Shirley's mother's maiden name.

Her work is seen in the market place with the mark of "Noble Smith" and is usually constructed from silver in abstract designs.[95]

Noble (Shirley) Smith, brooch, sterling silver, 2-1/2" x 5/8". *Collection of Joanne and Fred Doloresco, photograph by Fred Doloresco.*

Art Smith

"I see myself as someone who does this thing. This is me. This is what I do...." —Art Smith

Art Smith, necklace, sterling silver, 10" x 8-1/8". *Courtesy of Mark McDonald, 555 Warren St., Hudson, New York, photograph by Bill Hibbs.*

Art Smith, *Modern cuff*, sterling silver, 2-1/2" x 2" x 2-1/2". *Collection of Munir Meghji, photograph by Munir Meghji.*

Art Smith (1917-1982) had wit, a self-effacing personality and dedication to the craft that gained him success despite incredible odds. These are qualities that emanate from the many interviews, articles and books about him. He seems approachable, magnetic—a truly great personality.[96]

Arthur Smith was of Jamaican heritage but born in Cuba. His father, James Smith was a Garvey militant and his mother, Mary Smith was a tiny spirited woman of barely five feet tall who kept the Caribbean community of New York City together by always "keeping in touch." Art was her first boy after two older sisters. His niece remembers, "Arthur had a capacity to deal with all the senses to the fullest-- the ears for the music, the eyes for observing beauty, the hands for making it.

He was always interested in drawing and coloring as a child. The only opportunity for art in high school was an extracurricular painting class in which he enrolled and spent sitting on the grass painting at the park. On weekends he would sit in the window at home and create landscapes of the backyard that he would enter at competitions like the ASPA animal poster contests. Because he was black and came from the ghetto, Art Smith's early opportunities were limited. His mother and sister supported his desire to be an artist, but from everyone else, he was discouraged. "Well, as far as my mother was concerned," he said, "she told those people, you know this is my son. He wants to do this. I'm sure she must've been wringing her hands secretly thinking, Lord I wish there was something else he wanted to do more practical."

The Cooper Union was one of the few art schools at the time open to black students. Art heard about the school and was able to obtain a four-year scholarship.

His first experiences with jewelry did not happen at the Cooper Union, but when he took a part time job teaching crafts at the Children's Aid Society in Harlem. In the same building a young woman named Winifred Mason was teaching art classes. Mason, who was making copper jewelry in her studio at home and selling it to friends, was interested in finding a partner and opening a shop. Smith found this a great opportunity and worked with Winifred for four years in a shop at 133 West 3rd Street in Greenwich Village making and selling jewelry and keeping the shop. In the Village, Smith met and was influenced by other artists working there at the same time. Paul Lobel (who had once offered him a job), Sam Kramer, Arthur King and Rebajes were already there. A passionate jazz lover, Smith enjoyed going with friends to hear Billie Holliday sing in a club around the corner from the Third Street shop. He spoke of his early experiences in Greenwich Village in his autobiography, "It was a kind of marvelous place. It was a little Bauhaus in a way. We had a whole big establishment, a tremendous enthusiasm and an exciting group of people contributing to it. It was in the midst of compatible neighbors and friends; people like Bill Attaway, Charles Seabry, Talley Beatty, Ralph Ellison, Gordon Parks, Bill Stein, Archer Winston, the critic...They all knew Winnie and we got to know each other..."

Smith's second shop was on Cornelia Street in Little Italy where he was subjected to racial prejudice because of his color and public hostility because he was an artist. With financial backing from Craftsmen's Equity, an organization that he had joined when he was in the village and of which he was president, he was able to obtain a permanent studio at 140 W. 4th St. in 1948. That same year, he participated in the *Second National Exhibition of Modern Handmade Jewelry, Modern Jewelry under fifty dollars,* at the Walker Art Center in Minneapolis, an exhibit that helped reinforce his already mounting reputation as a master designer/craftsman.

More than any other modernist jeweler of his day, Art Smith was concerned with ornamenting the human form. His primitive-inspired biomorphic constructions are only truly understood in relation to the human structure. His jewelry was bold, but unlike Calder's primitivism which stood alone as art with disregard for the wearer, Smith's designs were each integral to the part of the body it was made to adorn; his jewelry, though sculpturally advanced, was not made to stand alone.

Model wearing Art Smith collar, c. 1950s. *Courtesy of The Sarah Bodine & Michael Dunas Archives of 20th Century Jewelry, Tyler School of Art, Temple University, Professor Stanley Lechtzin, Curator of Metals/Jewelry Archives and Collections.*

Like Calder, Art Smith used a direct approach to silver, copper, brass and wire; both worked with strong biomorphic shapes and twisted and/or hammered wire, though Calder preferred not to use solder, using rivets, twisting, and wrapping to attach sections of the design. Smith, who did use solder, was also a constructivist, layering and superimposing his amoeboid shapes, intersecting them with wire, adding three-dimensional elements such as spheres and, like Margaret De Patta and Peter Macchiarini, using negative space as a design element.

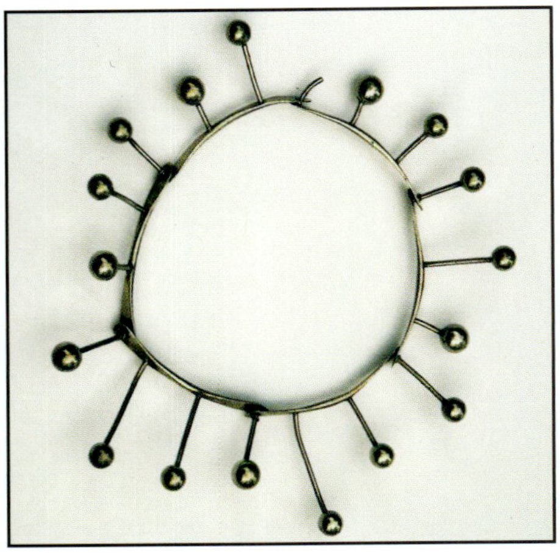

Art Smith, necklace, sterling silver. *Collection of Joanne and Fred Doloresco, photograph by Fred Doloresco.*

Art Smith designed jewelry for the dance troupes of Talley Beatty and Peal Primus. These pieces by necessity were large and dramatic but light enough not to be cumbersome, easy to put on and remove, and had to work with specific costumes, attributes that carried over into his general output. Many of his designs were grandiose, imbued with a sense of drama. Neckpieces became huge biomorphic collars, earrings often hung to the shoulders or below and rings were made to cover more than one joint or several fingers.

Art Smith received some recognition for his work during his lifetime. He was given a one-man show at the Museum of Contemporary Crafts (now the Museum of Arts & Design) in 1969 and included in *Objects USA, The Johnson Collection* in 1970. Many colleges, Universities and Craft centers such as Bennington College, Indiana University, Brookfield Craft Center, the Studio Museum in Harlem, and the Staten Island Museum of Arts and Sciences invited him to lecture and exhibit his work and, due to his inclusion in several traveling museum exhibitions, his work became nationally known.

Though several regional galleries and department stores carried his jewelry, he was much more interested in selling through his own shop and devoting the bulk of his time and energy to creating jewelry instead of managing a business.

When former customers talked about Art Smith, they remember interesting conversations in his studio at the back of the shop and the close friendships that developed, how he would always offer them a snack and how the radio was always playing jazz.

Smith remained at his shop on West Fourth Street until 1979, after which ill health forced him to close his doors; he passed away on February 20, 1982.

Art Smith Catalog. *Catalog photo credit: Lida Moser, courtesy of The Sarah Bodine & Michael Dunas Archives of 20th Century Jewelry, Tyler School of Art, Temple University, Professor Stanley Lechtzin, Curator of Metals/ Jewelry Archives and Collections.*

Henry Steig

Henry Steig, pendant, sterling silver with turquoise, 2-5/8" x 2-3/4". *Collection of Munir Meghji, photograph by Munir Meghji.*

Art Smith and Ed Wiener acknowledged jazz as inspiration, but from 1922 to 1932, Henry Steig (1906-1973) actually made his living for a time as a musician, playing saxophone and clarinet in New York dance bands.[97]

Steig's parents were both artists, though not by occupation until their children were grown. His brother, William was a cartoonist for the *New Yorker* magazine and also illustrated children's books.

Steig spent three years at the City College in New York City after which he attended the National Academy of Design studying painting and sculpture. From 1932 to 1935 he worked as a cartoonist and commercial artist for *Life* and the *New Yorker* signing his drawings with the pseudonym "Henry Anton" so they wouldn't be confused with the work of his brother William."

The *Saturday Evening Post, Esquire, Colliers*, and the *New Yorker* published Henry's stories about jazz and growing up in the Bronx. He was also published in the *Saturday* with illustrations by his brother William. In 1941his novel, *Send Me Down*, the story of brothers who became jazz musicians in the 1920s, was published and the same year he arrived in Hollywood to write screenplays for the movies. Due to the bombing of Pearl Harbor, his time in Hollywood was cut short and he returned to New York and worked as a writer until about 1947 when, in order to produce a steady income, he tried his hand at manufacturing artists' colors with his brother Arthur. The company, Steig Products, failed to produce enough income for two so Henry decided to try something else--jewelry seemed the right pursuit.

Henry Steig was a largely self-taught metalsmith whose earlier training in art and sculpture is evident in his sophisticated design vocabulary. His early work was mostly silver, both primitive, such as his Calder-like hammered silver pendants with wrapped wire and biomorphic like his curling, undulating bracelets. Steig was a constructivist--layering his silver shapes, piercing or joining them with wire, and using negative space as a design element.

In 1949 he had his first jewelry exhibition and sale in his apartment on West Ninth Street. About 1950 he opened a store in Manhattan on 51st Street and First Avenue and another in Provincetown, which like Ed Wiener and Jules Brenner, he operated only during the summer months. About five years later he moved his New York location to 590 Lexington Avenue and remained there until 1963 when he and his wife moved permanently to Provincetown where he continued to work as a jeweler and painter.

Steig's later jewelry was mostly done in gold, which he had cast commercially. These pieces were delicate with openwork and sometimes applied granulation.

In 1972 he sold his shop in Provincetown and the rights to his designs to Chicago jeweler Jan Dee.

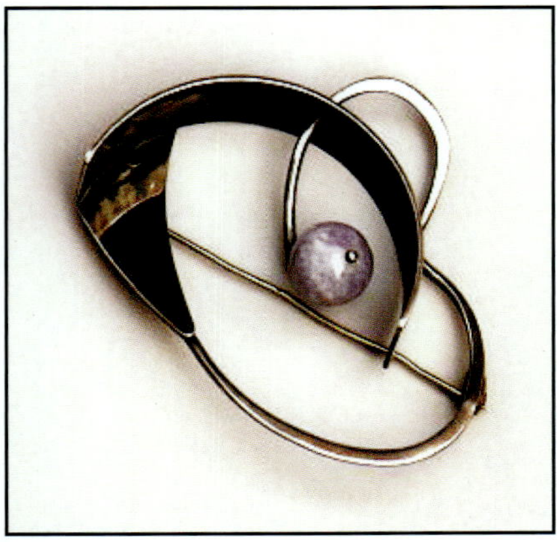

Bill Tendler, brooch, sterling silver, stone, 2-1/8" x 2-1/4". *Collection of Joanne and Fred Doloresco, photograph by Fred Doloresco.*

Bill Tendler

Though not much is known about the life of Bill Tendler (1924-1981), his work appears quite often in the marketplace. Between 1952 and 1981 he owned shops with various names and locations in New York's Greenwich Village, including Bill Tendler Gifts at 20 Christopher Street in 1952, 169 West Fourth Street in 1955, and in 1963, Bill Tendler Jewelry at 179 MacDougal Street.[98]

His jewelry appears in many different styles, but always within a modernist tradition. He worked with constructed abstract forms sometimes adding wire or wood in the style of Ed Levin. Like Paul Lobel, he created abstracted animal forms, though Tendler's are slightly more stylized, less cubist, and more three-dimensional.

His work also appears in cast form; he worked with the technique of fused casting like Kramer though on a smaller scale.

Bill Tendler, brooch, sterling silver, ebony, 1-1/2" x 2". *Collection of Joanne and Fred Doloresco, photograph by Fred Doloresco.*

Paul Voltaire

Paul Voltaire, c. late 1960s. *Courtesy of Alice Seymour.*

Paul Voltaire (1917-1979) gave up a flourishing career as a metallurgical engineer to become a full-time artist. He studied at the Institute of Technology in Austria, first concentrating on chemical engineering then shifting his emphasis to electronics. In 1936 he immigrated to the United States and worked in Boston theatres as a stage lighting technician and motion picture projectionist before going on to New York City in 1940 to begin a career in electronics and mechanical engineering. In the early 1940s he became a citizen and aided the Allied war effort as a research assistant to the prominent powder metallurgist and fellow Austrian émigré, Dr. Paul Schwarzkopt.[99]

After World War II Voltiare turned his attention to the arts. He was one of the founding members of Craftmen's Equity in New York City.

On December 10, 1949, after studying at the Art Student's League, Voltaire opened a small shop in Greenwich Village where he designed and made jewelry. Working directly with a variety of metals including silver, brass, gold, copper and even steel (often without sketches), he created jewelry that was beautiful, comfortably wearable, and always contemporary in feeling—most pieces were one-of-a-kind.

Paul Voltaire, tie bar, sterling silver, 2-1/4" x 7/8". *Collection of Joanne and Fred Doloresco, photograph by Fred Doloresco.*

Voltaire was an "odd bird" (in his own words) who brought scientific principles into play in the designs of his mostly abstract jewelry, photographed by Look, Vogue, Glamour and other fashion magazines. "For some reason," he said, "engineers and artists seem to be a diametrically opposed--engineers, as a rule, score very low on tests measuring artistic ability and they generally have no interest in or understanding of art. And artists, on the other hand, seem to be afraid of science and math—afraid, perhaps, that it will stultify their expression. The two seem to meet only in architecture and, if I had to do it over again, I believe I'd be an architect."

Because he understood the scientific properties of the materials with which he worked (usually gold or sterling), Voltaire found it easy to shift from one medium to another.

In the latter 1950s Voltiare and his wife Alice began to notice a change in the atmosphere of the Village and when a coke bottle came sailing through their skylight, they decided it was time to leave.

Successively, the Voltaire's had shops in New Hope, Bucks County, Pennsylvania, and Woodstock, New York. In 1956, while looking for a new location, they found and purchased a small log cabin in New Milford Connecticut. Voltaire designed and built a two-story addition and the enlarged cabin became a studio and a gallery where art and fine crafts were sold. Voltaire's became nationally known and artists and craftsmen who exhibited there remember it as one of the finest of its kind in the country.

Paul Voltaire, *Owl* brooch, 4-3/16" high. *Photograph courtesy of Alice Seymour.*

Lois Franke Warren

Lois E. Franke Warren received her B.A. in art from the University of Los Angeles in 1947 and her M.A., with a thesis in Forged Jewelry, from California State College in Los Angeles. She is the author of the book *Handwrought Jewelry*, published in 1962 by McKnight & McKnight, Bloomington, Illinois. The book is a "how to" handbook for studio jewelers which contains photographs of the work of twenty-six studio jewelers who were working at the time, many of whom have become well-recognized modernist jewelers.[100]

In 1950 Warren studied silversmithing and ceramics with Carleton Ball at Mills College, Oakland, California as well as ceramics with Laura Andreson at the University of California, Los Angeles. In 1951 she learned silversmithing with Hudson Roysher at Chouinard Art Institute and was one of only twelve in the U.S. to be chosen to work under Baron Erik Fleming at the Fifth Handy and Harman Silversmithing Conference.

Between 1955-1960 Warren studied enameling with master enamellist Atzie Schiff in Los Angeles and in 1957 was given sabbatical leave to research historical jewelry and silversmithing in Europe. Between 1963 and 1964 she studied gemology through the Gemological Institute of America, becoming a Graduate Gemologist and being awarded a Fellow Diploma from the Gemological Association of Great Britain. In 1976 she studied diamond setting with Grant Alford in Los Angeles.

Warren prefers the technique of forging, working directly with gold and silver and allowing the tools to partially dictate her forms. She is remarkably versatile. During the 1950's she created demonstration pieces to illustrate various working techniques and methods to show students different approaches to creatively designing jewelry. Much of this work became illustrations in her book; some of the most striking is reminiscent of later work by Scandinavian designers such as Grete Pritz Kittlesen-- openwork abstract forged silver pendants enhanced with mobile enamel disks. A forged silver abstracted fish pin from 1957 has mobile blue enamel "scales." An earlier work, from 1951, in sterling silver and stainless steel screen, is very much like the Constructivist work of Margaret De Patta.

Lois Franke Warren taught jewelry, gemology, ceramics, design, art history and humanities. She does not desire to create for the retail market, preferring instead to work on private commissions for one-of-a-kind pieces of which, from 1947 to the present, she has completed several hundred in sterling silver and 14k gold.

In addition to working on gold and gemstone jewelry, she has been involved over the last few years with the creation of crystal wine goblets in silver and gemstones, woven copper foil and enamel gift boxes as well as with other enamel experiments that she expects to explore further over the coming years.

Warren has had extensive teaching experiences, including working for the Los Angeles City School District as Chairman of the Art Department and Teacher of Art, Art Crafts, Jewelry and Ceramics from 1947 to 1967. During that period she lead many workshops and seminars dealing with jewelry and crafts. From 1967 to 1971 she was Professor of Art History and Humanities at Los Angeles Southwest College and from 1971 to 1993 she was employed as Instructor of Art History and Humanities for the Los Rios Community College District. She exhibited her jewelry and lectured widely between 1951 and 1999.

Lois Franke Warren, *Fire and Ice*, pendant and neck ring, 14k gold, peridot, orange zircon, quartz crystal, pendant: 2-3/4" x 1-1/4", neck ring: 16-1/4" circumference. *Collection of Marbeth Schon, photo by Shirley Byrne.*
About the design of the above pendant, Lois Franke Warren said, *"The design of the pendant and the choice of materials with which it is made has meaning to me beyond being just a pretty ornament. The crystal cluster in matrix was chosen to represent the earth wherein lovely gems are discovered. The faceted gems, Peridot and Zircon, tell us of the creativity of the jeweler and skill of the gem-cutter. The cast gold backing of the crystal cluster reminds us of gold nuggets and the 49ers of the Gold Rush, while the hammered gold framework represents the refining process that makes the lovely jewelry possible."*

Ed Wiener

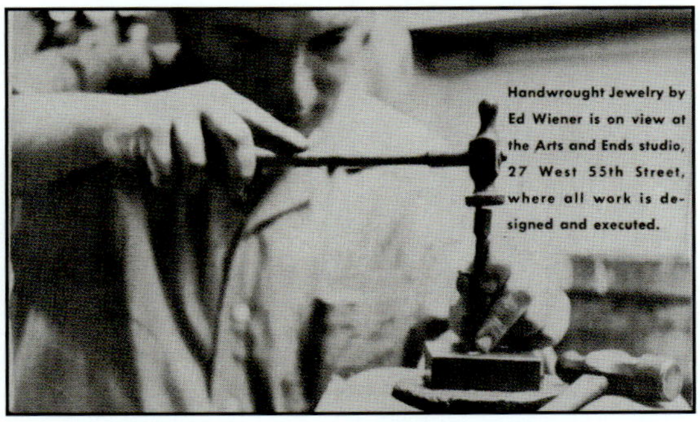

Ed Wiener in his studio, c.1950s, from *Arts & Ends* Catalog. *Courtesy of Michele Wiener*.

Perhaps none of the modernist jewelers working in New York after World War II was so well loved and respected as Ed Wiener (1918-1991). Though almost entirely self-taught, he possessed a magnificent appreciation of form, line, and color together with an amazing ability to uniquely apply the ideas and principles of modernism to his life's work. He was also a transitional figure-very much an inspiration and teacher to the next generation.[101]

Wiener was born and raised in New York City. His father was a butcher and Wiener worked in his shop until the beginning of World War II when his job assembling radios facilitated the discovery of his manual skills. He was married in 1944 and in 1945, a friend, Shirley Gorelick "dragged" him and wife Doris to a general crafts class at Columbia University which met once a week for a semester. Wiener's innate skills as an artist/craftsmen and educator were immediately apparent and he all but "took over" the class from the start. His first piece of jewelry was "a huge woman's belt buckle with a wire-drawn face."

Ed Wiener, *Abacus* brooch, silver, baroque beads, 2-3/8" x 2". *Courtesy of Mark McDonald, 555 Warren St., Hudson, New York. photograph by Bill Hibbs.*

Wiener had no plans for a career in jewelry making at that time but realized he needed a means to make a living. He and his wife hitchhiked to Provincetown where he worked for a sandal maker and absorbed the ambience of Provincetown, already an important art colony. Between 1947 and 1964 Wiener had a variety of shops in Provincetown.

When he returned to New York Wiener used his kitchen stove for a makeshift studio, creating "initial" and "name" pins out of twisted wire for their friends and making just enough money to invest in tools. Encouraged by that experience, Wiener realized that jewelry making might be a way to bring in a second income. In the fall of 1946 Wiener rented a studio on Second Avenue and 2nd Street in what is now the East Village. In the winter of 1947 he opened his first New York store on 55th Street between Fifth and Sixth Avenues, a few steps below street level on the ground floor of an old brownstone. He called his shop "Arts and Ends" because there was another "Ed Wiener" who had a jewelry business in New York. Wiener remained in that location until 1953.

Friendships with modernist jewelers already working in Greenwich Village were of significant influence when he was still trying to decide what direction his life should take. The unconventional jewelry forms of Sam Kramer who became his mentor especially inspired him. Initially Wiener was more comfortable thinking of himself as a craftsman than an artist but, as he became more enthusiastic about his own creations, the label seemed more appropriate to him.

Wiener worked from the "outside in." He would begin with designing very complex forms, which he would then simplify by selecting one or two sections to use for the single piece. The leftover sections were isolated to be recombined with new or existing pieces. He worked in geometric and biomorphic forms, finding inspirations for them everywhere—he stretched wire through space, like sculptors Henry Moore and Naum Gabo, and used oxidation to emphasize form.

His first experiments in creating texture began in 1949 after speaking with Ward Bennett about handmade surface textures made by hand rubbing the metal with pumice or planishing it with a hammer. The "square spiral" on which he pounded some areas flat with a ball peen hammer was a break-through design for Wiener, helping him to understand the character created by affecting design through the natural results of hammering.

Wiener credits Calder with giving him "profound insight" through his wire drawing of a sow which he saw exhibited at the Museum of Modern Art and spoke of as "one of the wittiest wire drawings extant." He admired the economy of Calder's use of space and the energy and intensity of his creations. Wiener, however, was always concerned with designing for the human body—Calder's designs did not share that concern and were oversized and "larger than life." Wiener designed his pieces so that every part that touched the body would feel comfortable to the wearer and he enjoyed seeing his pieces being worn.

In 1953 Wiener moved his shop to 46 West 53rd Street closer to the Museum of Modern Art. He began to use a material called Carvex. Casting with wax or Carvex gave him the ability to create free-form sculptural pieces and fascinating textures. Even Wiener's cast pieces were consistently one-of-a-kind and he made certain that the "hand of the artist" was apparent. In 1966 Wiener moved to Madison Avenue at 69th Street and from 1976 to 1981 his store was located in the fashionable area of 57th Street and Madison Ave.

Until 1966 Ed Wiener created most of his jewelry from silver though he also worked in gold. He used few stones except for pearls, which he said "were complete when found." Opals held a fascination and he said that the "floating, refracting, changing color forms," reminded him of Abstract Expressionist paintings.

Under the influence of a myriad of new influences, the mid-1960's brought about important stylistic changes for Wiener. His trips with his wife Doris to India exposed him to Asian art. And he also saw the medieval reliquaries in the Cluny Museum in Paris. Fascinated by the warmth of the metal, use of multicolored stones, and the explosion of color in these works he began designing in eighteen-karat gold with colored stones and bezel settings. What differentiated Wiener's work from the pieces that inspired him was the infusion of abstract expressionistic sensibilities into this ancient aesthetic. He worked to create beautifully textured cast surfaces while his work remained large, bold, and now, more colorful.

Wiener's final reprise was a reiteration of his of earlier ideas; now conceptualized as large flat hammered shapes. The final works were heavily weighted towards the spiral. With every other development and evolution of his work they contained the esthetic of movement, everything in balance but not in complete symmetry. He didn't go backwards-his intellectual challenge was to create beauty through the simplest forms by applying the principles of design he had learned and passed on throughout his life and had spent long hours discussing with artist friends in Provincetown--on the decks where the "talk" was his school and in Greenwich Village in the 1950s with his mentor Sam Kramer.

In 1988 the Fifty/50 Gallery in New York staged a retrospective of his jewelry and his work was included in the 1991 traveling exhibition, *Design 1955-1965: What Modern Was*, organized by the *Musée des Arts Décoratifs* of Montreal.

Ed Wiener passed away on July 21, 1991. Wiener said jewelry was a "gift of love." His gift was his genius coupled with constant searching, experimenting, and arriving, through much concentration and hard work, at the most beautiful solutions possible.

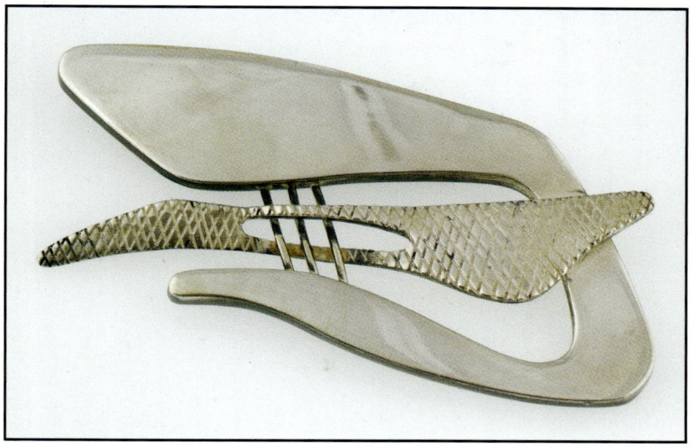

Ed Wiener, brooch, sterling silver, 3-1/2" x 2-1/4". *Courtesy of Mark McDonald, 555 Warren St., Hudson, New York, photograph by Bill Hibbs.*

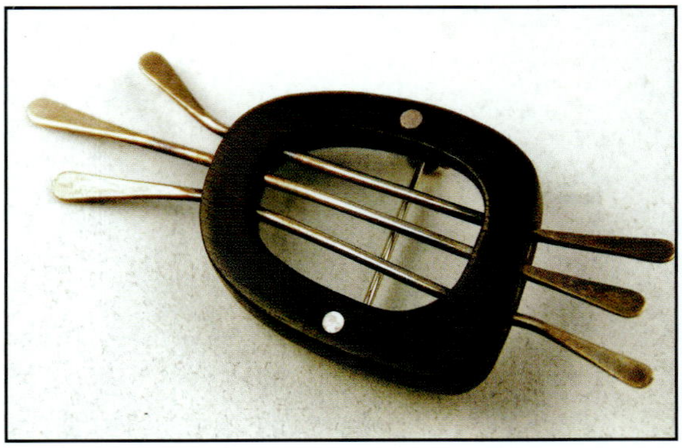

Ed Wiener, brooch, sterling silver, ebony, 1-1/8 x 2-1/2". *Collection of Joanne and Fred Doloresco, photograph by Fred Doloresco.*

Byron Wilson

Byron Wilson, a mostly self-taught metalsmith, was a native of Oakland, California. After high school graduation in 1936, he worked as an illustrator. About 1940 he became very interested in working in three-dimensional forms with metals and began making jewelry on his own. Finding it difficult to find a program that taught metalsmithing techniques, he eventually learned to cast from a dental technician and became familiar with the use of jeweler's tools and soldering techniques from various jewelry repairmen with shops in Oakland.[102]

In the latter 1940s Wilson was introduced to the work of Margaret de Patta and other founding members of the Metal Arts Guild in which he began to participate. He was amazed at the similarities between his own jewelry and that of De Patta. Though Wilson felt he owed De Patta a great deal of gratitude for her inspiration, his work is actually much richer in natural materials, heavier and more layered. He combined ivory, wood, and bone with silver to create forms that are abstract but also borrow from primitive and pre-Columbian motifs and symbols.

Margaret De Patta and her husband Eugene Bielowski were set up for limited production through lost-wax casting at their farmhouse in Napa, California and would hold Sunday open-house sessions to discuss metalsmithing and techniques related to casting. Wilson, who had helped to set up their casting operations, was there for many Sunday discussions. Both de Patta and Wilson agreed that jewelry making could become a viable business and Wilson was unrelenting in seeking outlets to sell his own work.

In the early 1950s Wilson was already becoming a significant influence in the California studio-jewelry movement and was included in and receiving awards at numerous exhibitions and fairs in the West as well as in national shows such as Fiber, *Clay, and Metal* at the St. Paul Art Gallery, St. Paul, Minnesota in 1953 and 55; *American Jewelry and Related Objects* at the Memorial Art Gallery, University of Rochester, Rochester, New York in 1956; the Inaugural Exhibition at the Museum of Contemporary Crafts, New York City in 1956; and *Craftsmanship in a Changing World*, Smithsonian Institution Traveling Exhibitions in 1956 and 57.

In 1956 Wilson was hired to teach metalsmithing at the California College of Arts and Crafts. His ingenuity in creating a metal sculpture foundry from mostly "scavenged materials" permitted, for the first time, the casting of large metal sculptures at the College. For many years after, Wilson and his students continued to improve the furnaces until the college could afford a modern facility for large-scale castings. Wilson had little time for his own work because he taught full time while holding down a second job with the railroad.

In an article for a 1992 issue of *Metalsmith Magazine* titled "*The Gadget Man*," Toni Lesser Wolf wrote, "The picture of Byron Wilson drawn for me by his many admiring students was of a modest, warm, giving and caring teacher who never imposed his own style but allowed each student to develop his or her own esthetic sense... he was such an infusive instructor most students took Wilson's class over and over again."

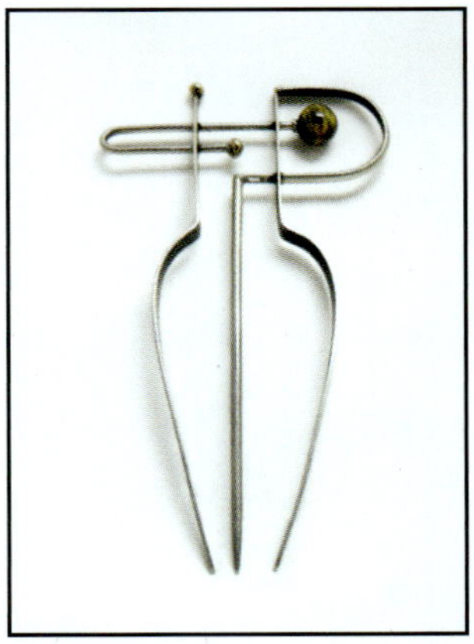

Byron Wilson, Hair ornament, sterling silver, 18K gold, Tiger's eye, 4-1/2" x 1". *Collection of Joanne and Fred Doloresco, photograph courtesy of Mobilia Gallery, Cambridge, Massachusetts.*

Byron Wilson, brooch, sterling silver, 2 1/8" x 3 1/2", c.1940s. *Collection of Joanne and Fred Doloresco, photograph by Fred Doloresco.*

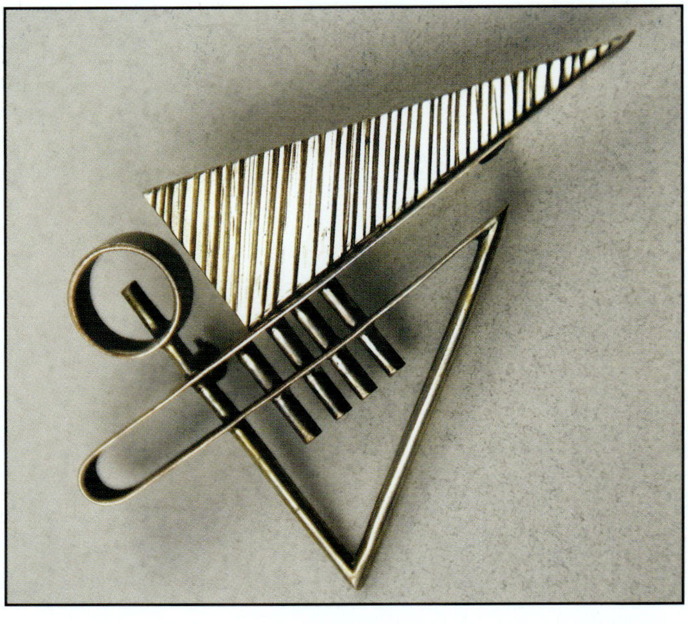

Winfield Fine Art in Jewelry

Armand G. Winfield (b. 1919) is internationally known for his innovations in plastics. Originally a student of anthropology and geology, he was awarded an undergraduate fellowship in 1939 to teach geology at Franklin and Marshall College and serve as Assistant Curator of the College Museum where he worked on the preservation of specimens which involved molds, impressions, lattices, etc. He began experimenting with plastics after a trip to New York City where he saw an exhibit by the DuPont Company of amethystine crystals suspended in acrylics.[103]

After graduation, in 1941, Winfield attended the Graduate School of Anthropology at the University of New Mexico in Albuquerque where his studies were cut short by the attack at Pearl Harbor shortly after which he was drafted into the army. He returned to civilian life in 1944 and decided to continue working for museums—this time in plastics. In 1945, he invented the first process to mass-produce embedments in clear acrylics.

In 1946 he and his brother Rodney assembled a group of art students and teachers from the Cooper Union in New York City to produce unique jewelry by embedding the artists' work in acrylics. From the very beginning, the jewelry attracted much attention and sales were strong enough for Armand and Rodney to consider finding their own space. They pooled their own meager resources, borrowed from interested friends, and rented a small shop at 184 West 4th Street in Greenwich Village. They called their business, Winfield Fine Art in Jewelry.

As more and more people became aware of Winfield Fine Art in Jewelry and business increased, newspapers and magazines also took note. The March 1947 issue of *Cosmopolitan Magazine* featured the gallery in an article titled *Floating Fashions*. Authors, Raymond Rosenthal and Bernard Wolfe wrote:

> ...there is a chic young woman around New York these days with two Peruvian postage stamps, both collector's items dangling from her earlobes. Another sports an iridescent Patagonian beetle--the genuine article. A third wears a dress clip in which curlicues of hair, a couple of fingernail parings and several baby teeth are arranged in an abstract design. Embedded in chunks of transparent plastic, such weird bits of feminine decor have converted some of New York's smartest women into walking natural history exhibits. No one is more disconcerted by these flamboyant oddities than their creator, twenty-six year old Armand Winfield. His modest idea, when he wandered into jewelry designing was simply to transform fashionable women into mobile art galleries, adorning them with the latest canvasses of well-known known modern painters. And later, in the article, You wouldn't think these women would have the nerve to actually wear some of the things they order. Winfield says with resignation, "I live in constant fear that the door may open at any moment and a woman will walk in with a pair of giraffe's eyebrows or a pet poodle's tail which she is determined to wear in a lavaliere around her neck.

Paul Lobel made some of the silver frames for Winfield's jewelry and the copper work was done by Pedro Pujol. Armand Winfield worked day and night embedding, shaping, and polishing to make the miniature paintings and sculptures into "wearable art." Nighttime visits by Pedro Pujol were common because his shop was a few doors away." Pedro was a coppersmith," Armand remembers, "Spanish, with a marvelous sense of humor and a twinkle in his eye. He loved rum for breakfast and since I was the only one around who was up, we often shared a cup before the workday began."

Winfield Fine Art in Jewelry, brooch, Ruth Patsy Klein, watercolor on paper, encased in acrylics, sterling silver frame by Paul Lobel, 2" x 1-3/4", c.1946 or 1947. *Collection of Armand Winfield,photo by Shirley Byrne.*

Winfield Fine Art in Jewelry closed at the end of 1947. Winfield credited long hours, high commissions, overhead, untrained help, and a general lack of business training and experience for the his physical collapse at that time as well as the closing of his workshop/gallery.

Bob Winston

Bob Winston (b. 1915) attended the University of California, Berkeley, where he received his Bachelors Degree in art with a minor in history. In 1943 he earned his M.A with a minor in art history. In the late 1930s he began making jewelry as well as teaching evening classes in jewelry making at Berkeley High School between 1937 and 1938. In 1942 he began teaching at the California College of Arts and Crafts in Oakland, and in 1943 became one of the first jewelers to experiment with the lost-wax method of casting by centrifuge. By 1945 this process had become an integral part of his teaching program and he was chiefly responsible for the implementation of the lost-wax method by such artist-jewelers as Irena Brynner, Robert Dhaemers and many others.[104]

The lost-wax casting course created a great deal of interest; it was the first time the subject had been included in the curriculum of an institution of higher learning. The emphasis of the course was on developing designs that were possible only with the lost wax casting technique.

In 1959 Winston left the California College of Arts and Crafts to concentrate on his own career as a designer/craftsman. He moved to Scottsdale, Arizona, but (as Winston said, "once a teacher, always a teacher") he ended up teaching in the Extended Education Department in one of Arizona's three universities. During this time he also worked on a textbook on the lost wax casting technique en*titled Cast Away* that was published in 1970.

Winston's jewelry designs are fluid, highly sculptural, and textured forms that appear to be carved and modeled directly in metal. Each piece is unique; he never cast in multiples. His earliest pieces, however, were constructed abstract shapes in silver with forged and bent silver wire.

As well as exhibiting at the Walker Art Center in Minneapolis in 1948 and 1955, his work was exhibited at the Seligman Gallery in New York City and the Raymond and Raymond Gallery in San Francisco.

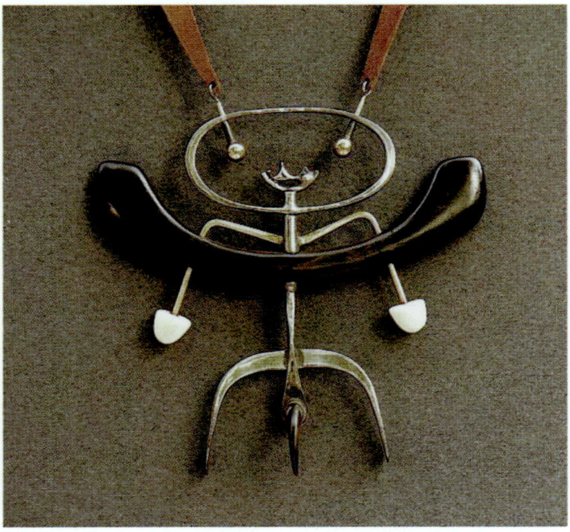

Bob Winston, pendant, sterling silver, ebony, claw, ivory, brass, leather cord, pendant: 5-3/4" x 5-3/4". *Collection of Joanne and Fred Doloresco, photograph by Fred Doloresco, Illustrated in Design Quarterly #33, 1955, pg. 12.*

Part IV
MACCHIARINI

Portrait of Peter Macchiarini, c. 1960.

CHAPTER 9
Sculpture by Peter Macchiarini

Photographs shown below are courtesy of Daniel Macchiarini and taken by Leslie W. Rabine.

Abstract, silver, copper base, 1-1/4″ high x 3″ wide x 2-1/2″ deep, c. 1957.

Standing Man, bronze, turquoise, patina, wood base, 13-1/2″ high x 2-1/4 wide x 2″ deep, c. 1961.

Arrow, brass, copper, bronze, scrap metal base, 14″ tall x 7-1/2″ wide x 6-3/4″ deep, c. early 1960s.

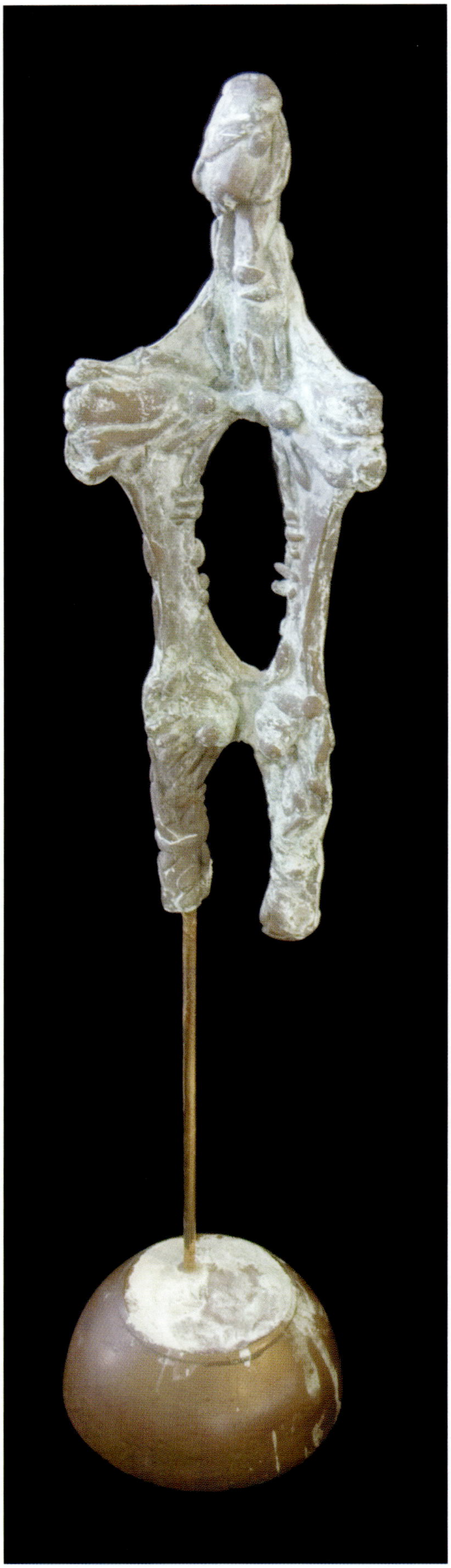

Abstract Mobile, bronze, copper, brass, stainless steel ball, mahogany base, 17-1/2" high x 8-1/4" wide x 8-1/4" deep, c. 1980.

Abstract Figure, bronze with green patina, copper stem, copper base, 13-1/2" tall x 3" wide x 3" deep, c. 1978.

Cubist Venus II, bronze, red/brown patina, wood base, 18-1/4″ high x 5-1/4″ wide x 4″ deep, c. early 1990s.

Cubist Venus I, working maquette, plaster, plasticine clay, plaster of paris, 14-1/2″ high x 7-1/2″ wide x 10-1/4″ deep, c. 1986-1987.

Architectural Abstract, 9-1/4″ high x 4″ wide x 4-1/4″ deep, c. 1998.

CHAPTER 10
Jewelry by Peter Macchiarini

Photos below are courtesy of Daniel Macchiarini and taken by taken Leslie W. Rabine.

Earrings

Earrings, nickel silver, ebony. 3" x 1-1/4", c. 1937-1938.

Bracelets

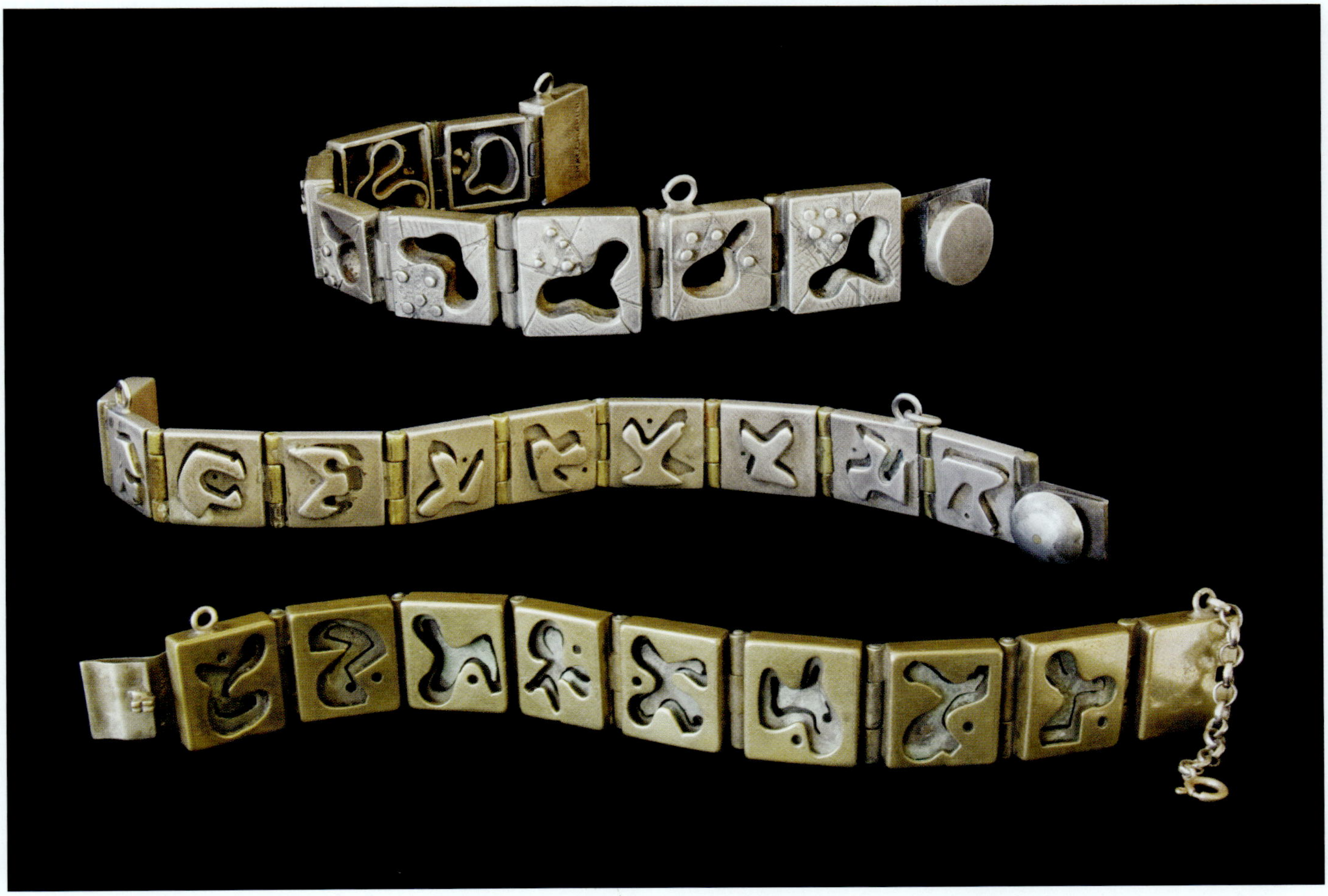

Three bracelets, silver, brass, bronze inlay, copper hinges, nickel silver. c. 1948.

Brooches

Seed Pod clip, iron exterior, copper interior, brass clip, 3-1/2" diameter, c. 1960s.

Brooch, bronze, silver with ebony and ivory inlay, 3-1/2" x 2-1/2", c. early 1980s.

Pod brooch, bronze exterior, copper interior, ivory flash, 3-1/2" x 3-1/4". c. 1970.

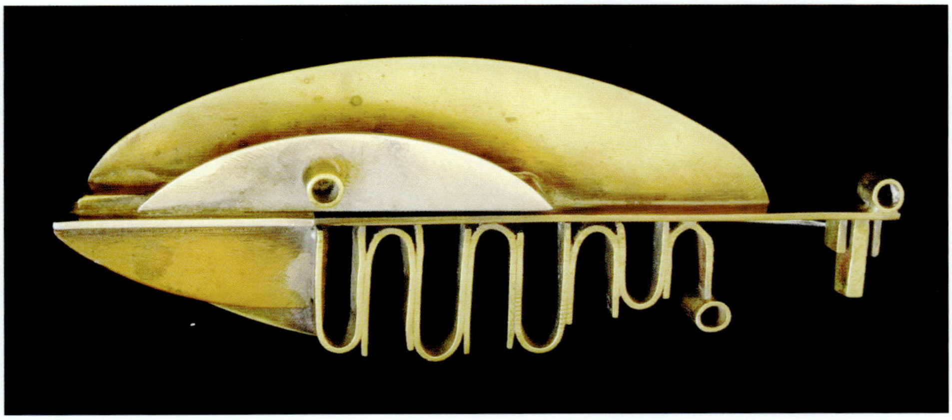

Fish brooch, silver, bronze, 1-3/4" x 4-3/4", c. 1980s.

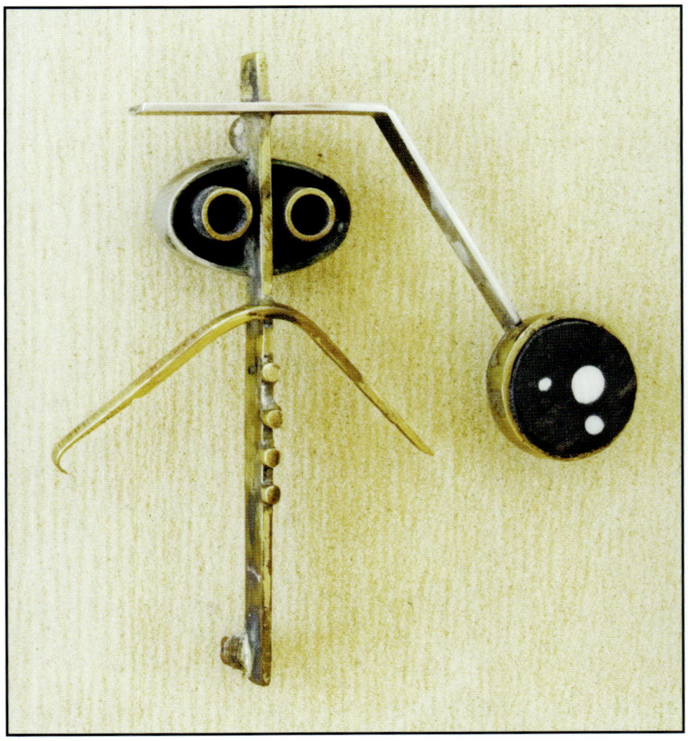

Alien brooch, copper, silver, bronze, 3" x 3", c. 1989.

Teapot by Peter Macchiarini

Peter Macchiarini with teapot. *Photograph courtesy of Daniel Macchiarini.*

Cream Pitcher, silver, ebony, 3" x 3-1/2", c. 1955.

CHAPTER 11
Jewelry by Peter & Daniel Macchiarini

Peter and Daniel Macchiarini in the 1970s. *Photograph courtesy of Daniel Macchiarini.*

Bracelets and Cuffs

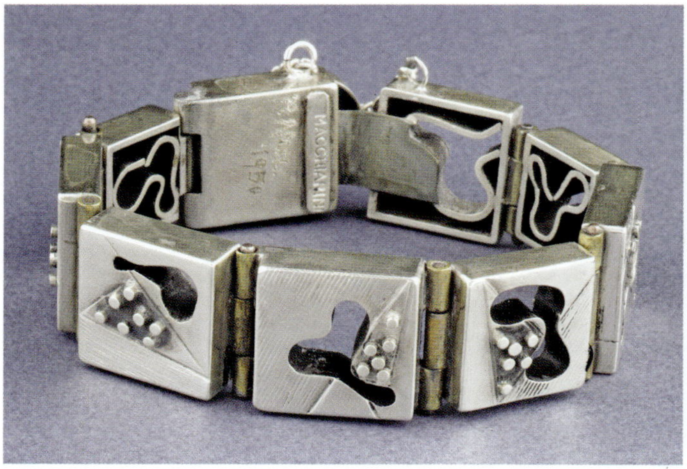

Peter Macchiarini, bracelet, sterling silver, 4-5/8" x 2-1/4". *Courtesy of Mark McDonald, 555 Warren St., Hudson, New York, photograph by Bill Hibbs.*

Daniel Macchiarini, cuff, sterling silver, copper, brass, ebony, 15/16" wide x 3" inside diameter.
Collection of Jill Crawford, Photograph by Shirley Byrne.

Daneil Macchiarini, bracelet, sterling silver, copper, ebony, ivory, 3" x 3" x 3" x 1/4" wide. *Collection of Jill Crawford, Photograph by Shirley Byrne.*

Daniel Macchiarini, cuff, sterling silver, copper, brass, moonstone, 7/8" wide x 2-5/8" (inside diameter). *Collection of Jill Crawford, Photograph by Shirley Byrne.*

Earrings

Peter Macchiarini, earrings, sterling silver, brass, 1-1/2" x 1". *Courtesy of Mark McDonald, 555 Warren St., Hudson, New York, Photograph by Bill Hibbs.*

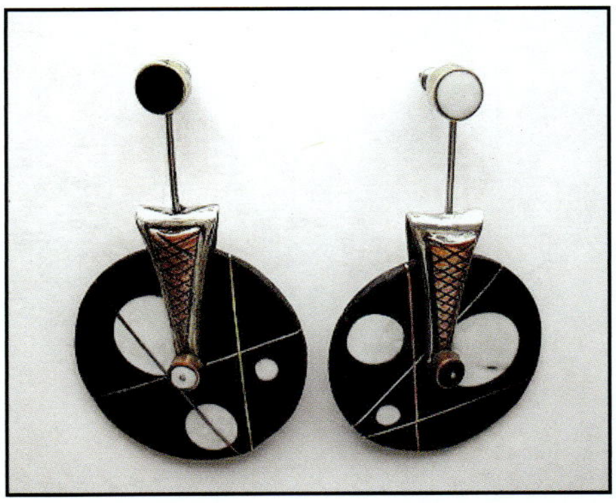

Daniel Macchiarini, *Pizza Cutter earrings*, sterling silver, copper, brass, bronze, ebony, ivory, 2-1/4" long, disk: 1-1-/4" (diameter). *Collection of Juliette Kontor, photograph by John Kontor.*

Rings

Peter Macchiarini, *Sculpture* ring, sterling silver, brass, ivory, ebony, 1-1/8" high, 7/8" top diameter, *Courtesy of Historical Design, Inc., photo ©HD, Inc.*

Peter Macchiarini, ring, sterling silver, brass, onyx, top: 1-1/4"x 5/8", *Collection of Jill Crawford, Photograph by Shirley Byrne.*

Peter Macchiarini, ring, Sterling silver, brass, wood, ivory, top: 1-3/8"x 5/8". *Collection of Jill Crawford, Photograph by Shirley Byrne.*

Daniel Macchiarini, ring, sterling silver, wood, brass, ivory, top: 1-1/8"x 3/8", *Collection of Jill Crawford, Photograph by Shirley Byrne.*

Peter Macchiarini, ring, sterling silver, brass, wood, ivory, top: 1-3/8"x 5/8". *Collection of Jill Crawford, Photograph by Shirley Byrne.*

Brooches

Peter Macchiarini, brooch, copper, patinated copper, 2-1/2" x 1-1/8". *Collection of Jill Crawford, Photograph by Shirley Byrne.*

Peter Macchiarini, brooch, sterling silver, brass, 4-1/2" x 1-1/2". Collection *of Jill Crawford, photograph by Shirley Byrne.*

Peter Macchiarini, brooch, sterling silver, copper, brass, ivory, ebony, 5-1/8" x 1-1/2". *Courtesy of Historical Design, Inc., photo ©HD, Inc.*

Peter Macchiarini, brooch, copper, silver, brass, ivory, 5" x 1-5/8". *Collection of Jill Crawford, photograph by Shirley Byrne.*

Peter Macchiarini, brooch, sterling silver, copper, brass, ivory, 4-3/8" x 1-3/8". *Courtesy of Historical Design, Inc., photo ©HD, Inc.*

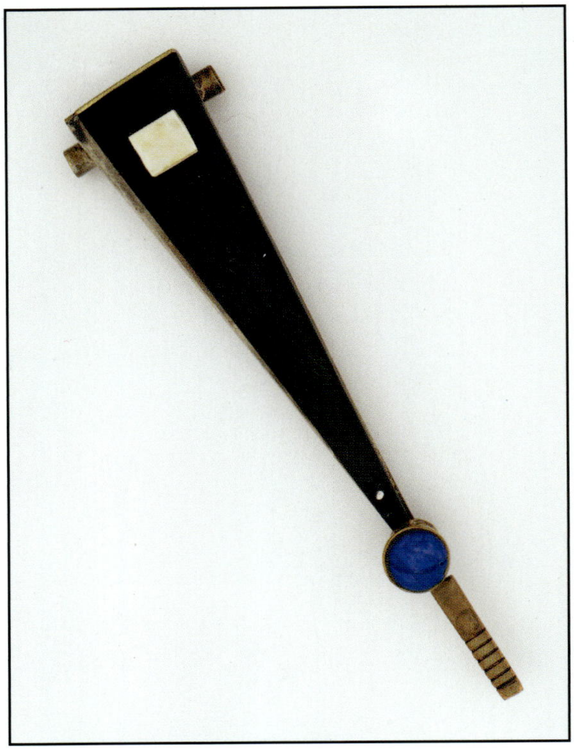

Peter Macchiarini, brooch, sterling silver, brass, copper, ebony, ivory, lapis lazuli, 3-3/4" x 1". *Courtesy of Historical Design, Inc., photo ©HD, Inc.*

Daniel Macchiarini, brooch, sterling silver, copper, brass, ebony, ivory, 4-1/2" x 1-1/2", *Courtesy of Historical Design, Inc., photo ©HD, Inc.*

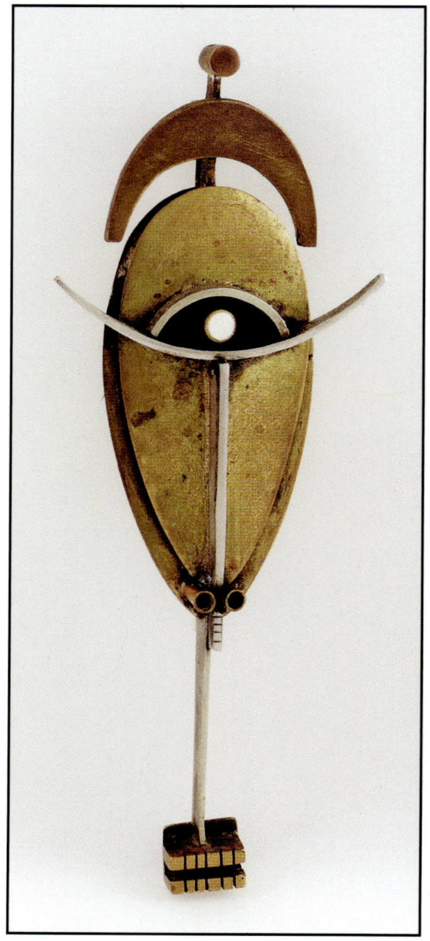

Peter Macchiarini, brooch, sterling silver, brass, copper, ebony, ivory, 4-7/8" x 1-3/8".

Peter Macchiarini, brooch, sterling silver, copper, brass, ivory, 3-5/8" x 1-3/8". *Courtesy of Historical Design, Inc., photo ©HD, Inc.*

Peter Macchiarini, brooch, sterling silver, brass, copper, ivory, 4"x 1-3/4". Collection of Joanne and Fred Doloresco, photograph by Fred Doloresco.

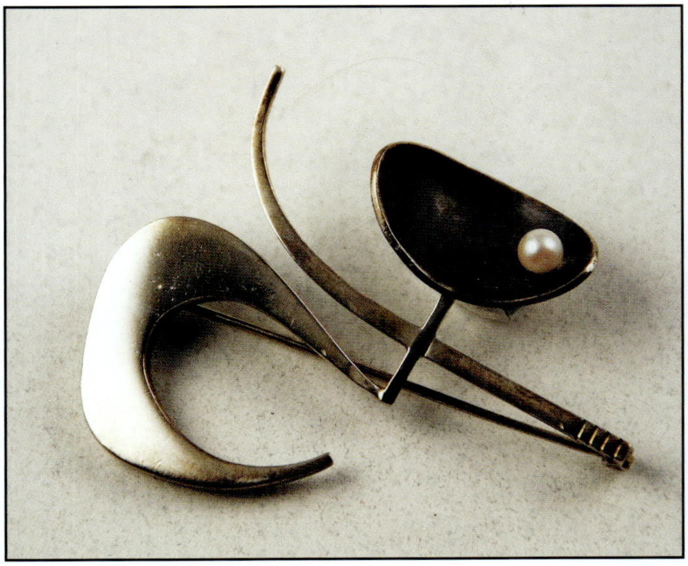

Peter Macchiarini, brooch, sterling silver, pearl, 2" x 2-3/8". *Collection of Joanne and Fred Doloresco, photograph by Fred Doloresco.*

Peter Macchiarini, brooch, brass, silver, copper, stone, 4-7/8" x 2". *Collection of Jill Crawford, photograph by Shirley Byrne*

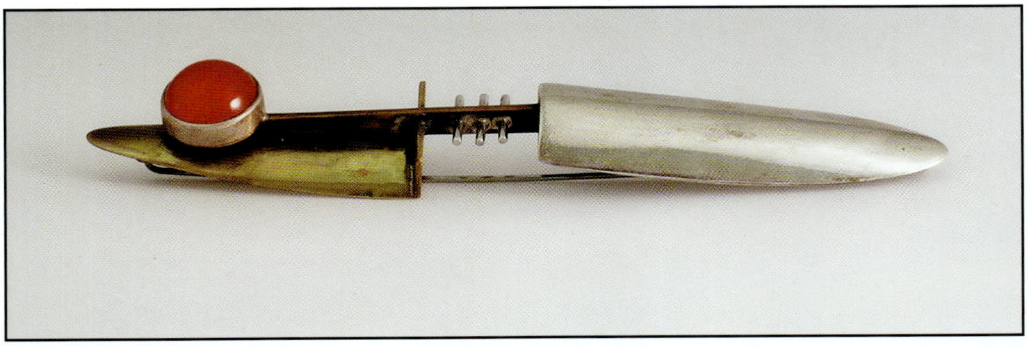

Peter Macchiarini, brooch, silver, brass, copper, carnelian, 5-5/8" x 15/16". *Collection of Jill Crawford, photograph by Marbeth Schon.*

Peter Macchiarini, brooch, silver, brass, copper, wood, 6" x 3/4". *Collection of Jill Crawford, photograph by Shirley Byrne.*

Peter Macchiarini, brooch, brass, copper, silver, patinated copper, ivory 5-7/8″ x 1-1/8″. *Collection of Jill Crawford, photograph by Shirley Byrne.*

Peter Macchiarini, brooch, brass, silver, copper, ivory, ebony, 4-3/8″ x 1-5/8″. *Collection of Jill Crawford, photograph by Shirley Byrne.*

Peter Macchiarini, *Butterfly* brooch, silver, brass, ebony, ivory, 3-1/4″ x 2-1/8″. *Collection of Jill Crawford, photograph by Shirley Byrne.*

Peter Macchiarini, brooch, copper, brass, moonstone, screen, 2-1/8″ x 1-3/4″. *Collection of Jill Crawford, photograph by Shirley Byrne.*

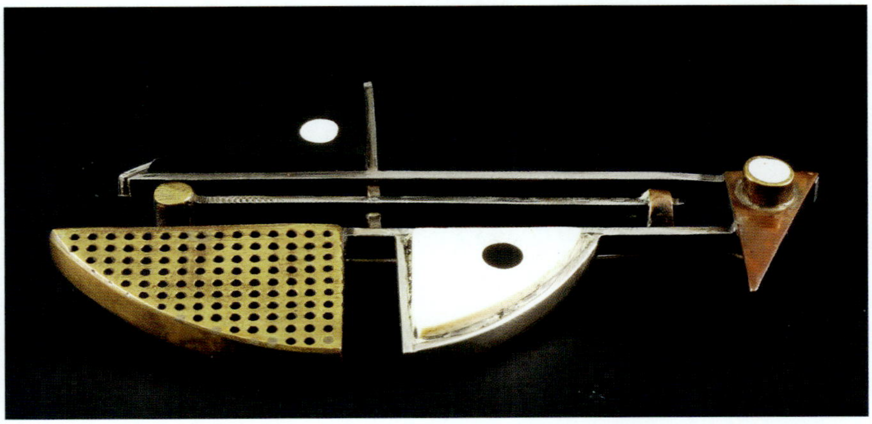

Peter Macchiarini, brooch, brass, silver, copper, wood, ivory, ebony, 3-3/4" x 2-1/8". *Collection of Jill Crawford, photograph by Shirley Byrne.*

Peter Macchiarini, brooch, brass, silver, copper, wood, ivory, ebony, 3-3/4" x 2-1/8". *Collection of Jill Crawford, photograph by Shirley Byrne.*

Pendant

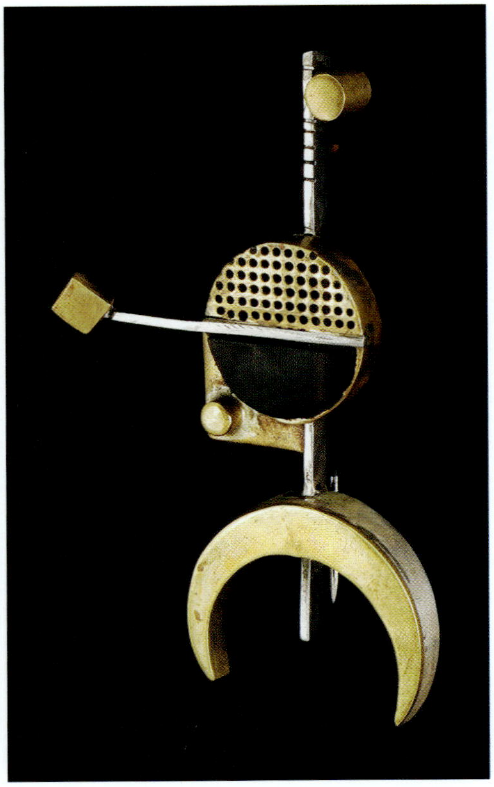

Peter Macchiarini, *Samurai* brooch, brass, silver, wood, 2-1/2" x 1-3/8". *Collection of Jill Crawford, photograph by Shirley Byrne.*

Peter Macchiarini, Pod Pendant, sculpted copper, silver, brass, 2-1/4" diameter. Courtesy of Historical Design, Inc., photo ©HD, Inc.

Part V
MAKERS' MARKS

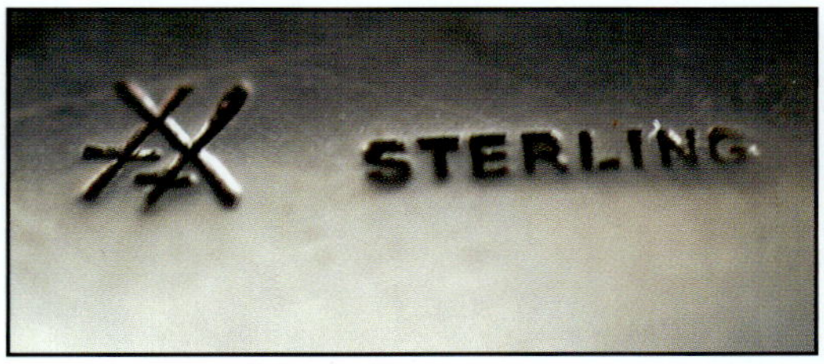

Adda Husted-Andersen

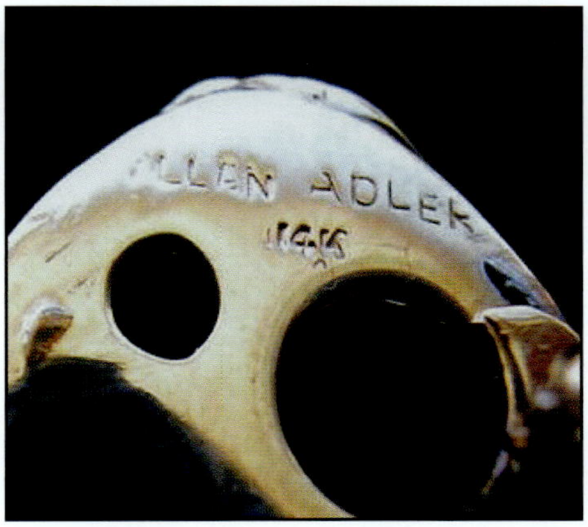

Allan Adler

Lilyan Bachrach

Mildred Ball

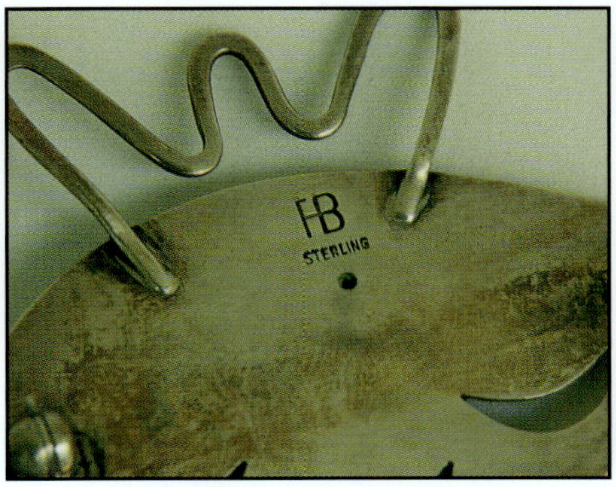

Frances Holmes Boothby

Jules Brenner

Irena Brynner

Irvin and Bonnie Burkee

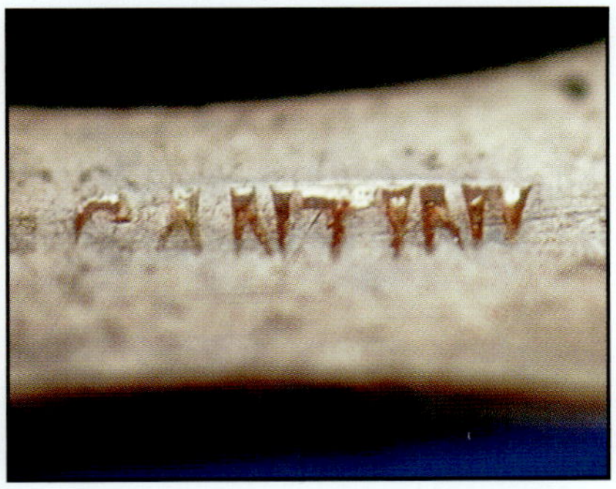
Virgil Cantini

Milton Cavaganaro

Betty Cooke

Margaret De Patta

Karl Drerup

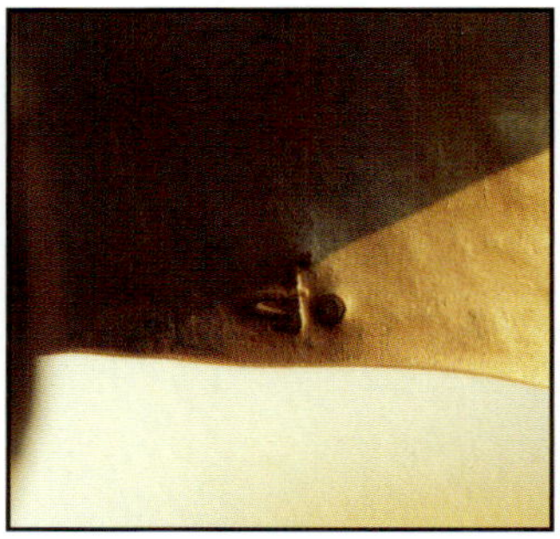

Claire Falkenstein

Lois Franke Warren

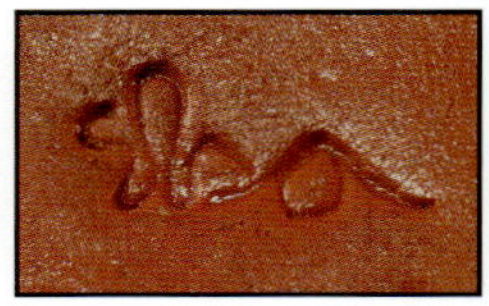

Elsa Freund

Doris Hall

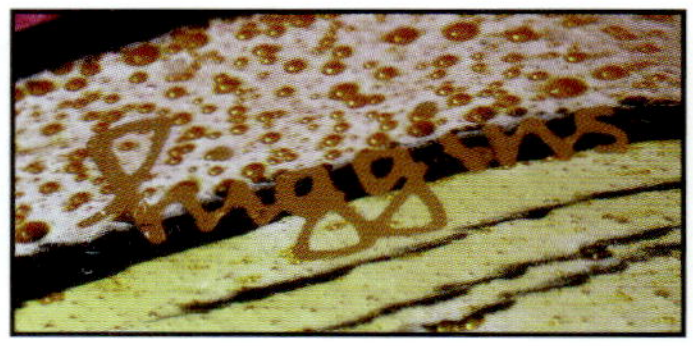

Higgins

Arthur King

Hurst & Kingsbury

Sam Kramer

Earl Krentzin

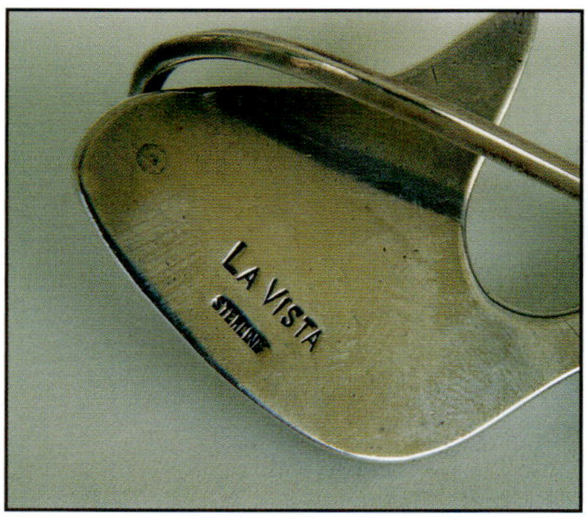

Idella La Vista

Ibram Lassaw

Ed Levin

Paul Lobel

Esther Lewittes

Charles Loloma

Peter Macchiarini (script)

Daniel Macchiarini and Peter Macchiarini

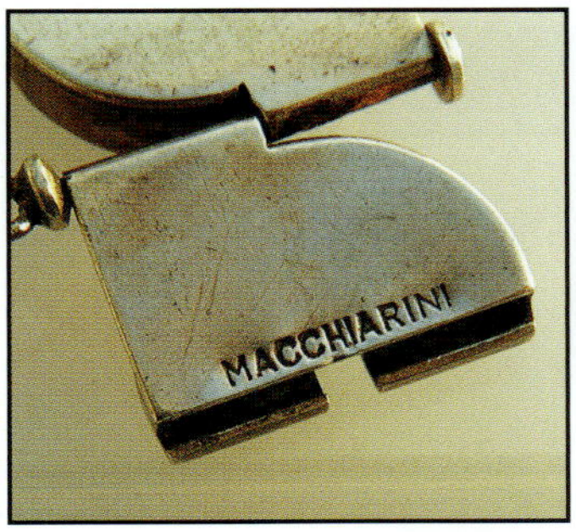

Everett Macdonald

Frank Miraglia

Philip Morton, double strike.

James Parker

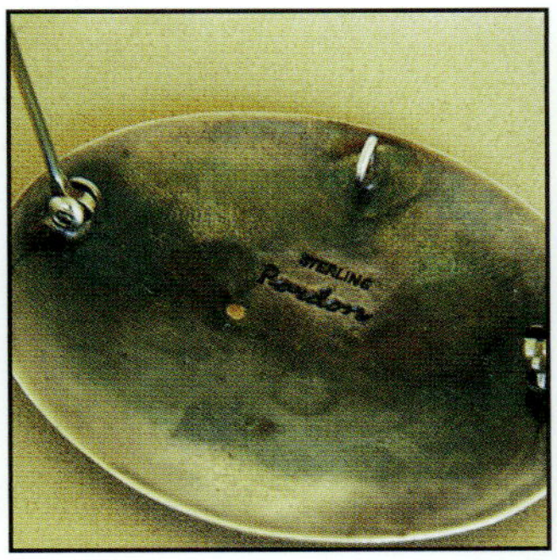

Earl Pardon

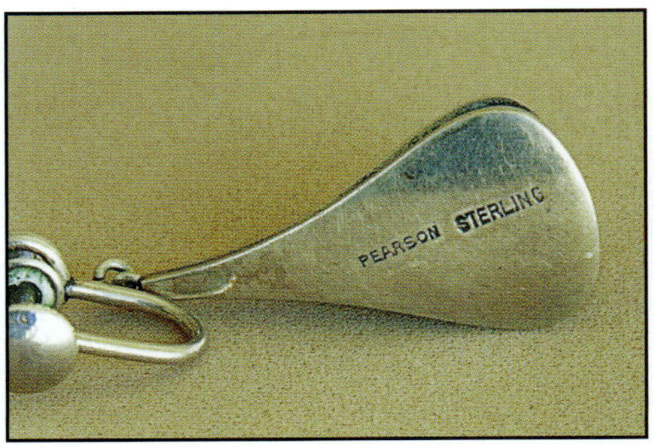

Ronald Hayes Pearson

Francisco Rebajes

merry renk

Walter Rhodes

Ruth Roach

Carolyn Rosene

George Salo

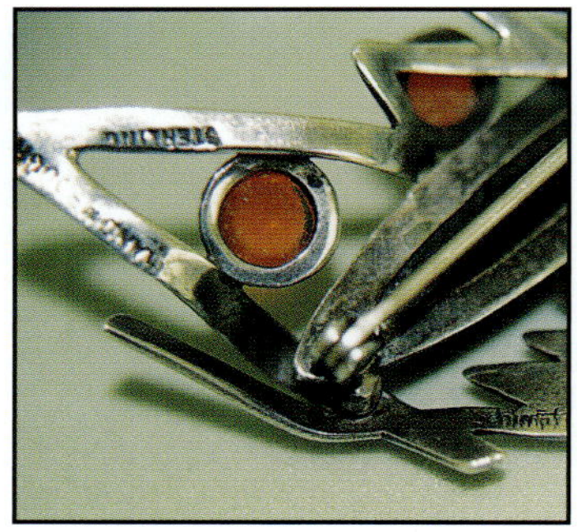

Mary Schimpff

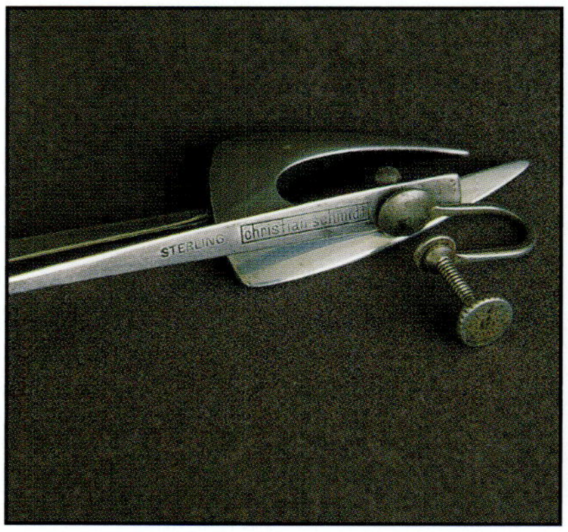

Christian Schmidt

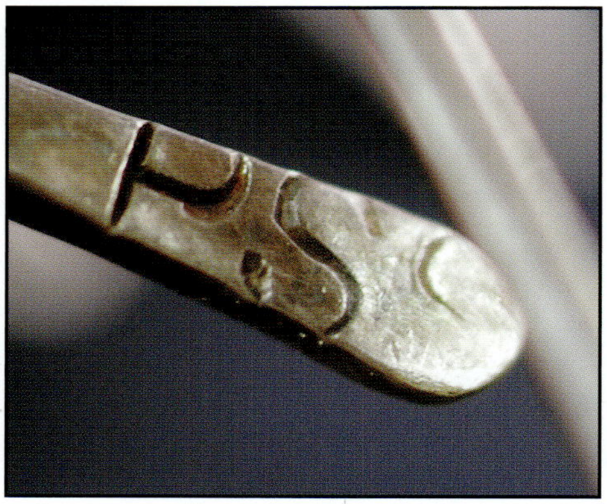

Pearl Shecter

Noble Smith

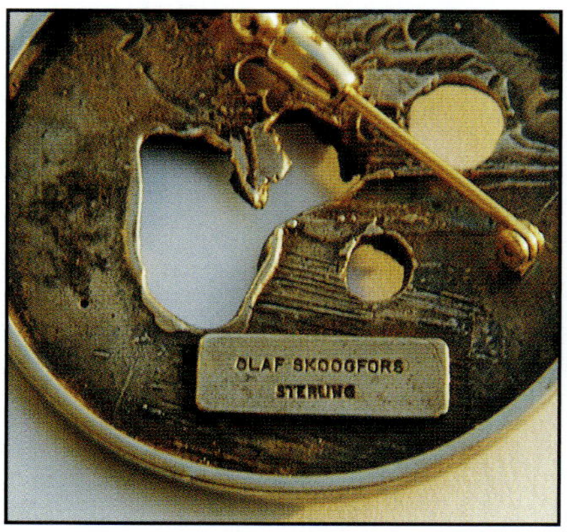

Olaf Skoogfors

Art Smith

Henry Steig

Bill Tendler

Ed Wiener

Byron Wilson

Winfield Fine Art
in Jewelry

Notes

Part I: American Crafts Revival in Metalwork

Chapter 1

1 Cecelia Beaux, *Is there an American Art?* February, 1922.

2 Martin Eidelberg, *Design 1935-1965, What Modern Was*, Musée des Arts Décoratifs de Montréal, New York, Abrams, p.22.

3 Ibid.

4 Ibid.

5http://www.pbs.org/wnet/americanmasters/database/black_mountain_college.html

6 Yohsiko Uchido, *The Jewelry of Margaret De Patta, a Retrospective Exhibition*, Oakland Museum of Art, 1976, pg. 14.

7 www.cranbrookart.edu/site/about_history.html

8 Aileen O. Webb, *American Craftsmen's Council/ 1964, The International Era*, Craft Horizons, v. 24, 1964.

9 Deborah Norton, *A History of the School for American Craftsmen + conversation with John Prip*, Metalsmith, Winter, 1985, pp. 15 - 21.

10 Ibid.

11 Ibid.

12 Marbeth Schon, *Interview with Margret Craver Withers*, 2001, and Margret Craver, speech at conference *"American Metalsmithing and Jewelrymaking in the 1940s and 1950s"*, sponsored by the Renwick Gallery and the Archives of American Art.

Chapter 2

13 Susan Lewin, *One of A Kind, Art Jewelry Today*, New York, Abrams, 1985, page. 34.

14 Jazzar and Harold B. Nelson, *Painting with Fire, Masters of Enameling in America, 1930 – 1980,* California, Long Beach Museum of Art, 2006, page 21.

15 Ibid. pp. 119-120.

16 Philip Morton, *Contemporary Jewelry*, New York, Holt, Rinehart and Winston, 1976,page 39.

17 Marbeth Schon, *Interview with MargretCraver Withers*, 2004.

18 Byron Wilson, letter, The Sarah Bodine & Michael Dunas Archives of 20th Century Jewelry, Tyler School of Art, Temple University, Professor Stanley Lechtzin, Curator of Metals/Jewelry Archives and Collections.

19 Deborah Norton, *History of the School for American Craftsmen + conversation with John Prip*, Metalsmith, Winter, 1985 pg. 15 – (the following two paragraph are also from this source).

20 Paul Voltaire, *Notes on Greenwich Village*, courtesy of Mrs. Alice Seymour.

21 Deborah Norton, *A History of the School for American Craftsmen + conversation with John Prip*, Metalsmith, Winter, 1985, pp. 15 - 21 (The following three paragraphs are also taken from this source.

22 Sharon Church, *Interview with Arline M. Fisch*, Archives of American Art, Smithsonian Institution, July 29 and 30, 2001.

23 Magret Craver, speech, symposium *American Metalsmithing and Jewelrymaking in the 1940s and 1950s*, Renwick Gallery and the Archives of American Art, 1982.

24 Sharon Church, *Interview with Arline M. Fisch*, Archives of American Art, July 29 and 30, 2001.

25 Deborah Norton, *A History of the School for American Craftsmen + conversation with John Prip*, Metalsmith, Winter, 1985, pp. 15-21 (The following seventeen paragraphs are also from this source.)

26 Jan Yager, *Interview with Fred Fenster*, Archives of American Art, Smithsonian Institution, August10, 2004.

27 Robert Cardinale, Metalsmith, Fall-1980, pg. 23.

28 Jan Yager, Interview with Fred Fenster, Archives of American Art, Smithsonian Institution, August 9 and 10, 2004.

29 Julie Hall, "A Conversation with Richard Thomas, master metalsmith," *Metalsmith*, Spring, Summer 1982.

30 Marbeth Schon, *Interview with Stanley Lechtzin*, May, 2008.

Chapter 3

31 Mrs. Aileen Vanderbilt Webb, speech for the opening of the World Crafts Council, Craft Horizons, V. 24, 1964, page 9.

32 Helen W. Drutt English and Peter Dormer, *Jewelry of Our Time, art, ornament and obsession*, New York, Rozzoli, pg.8.

33 Jamie Bennett, "Jewelry Meditating Jewelry," *Metalsmith*, Winter 1998, page 27.

34 RalphTurner, *Jewelry in europe and america new times, new thinking*, New York, Thames and Hudson, Ltd. page 12.

35 Martin Eidelberg, *Design 1935 – 1965, What Modern Was*, Musée des Arts Décoratifs de Montréal, New York, Abrams, page 302.

Part II. What Is Jewelry?

1 Renée S. Neu, *The Artist as Jeweler,*. Art in America, Nov. Dec. 1967, pg.111.

Chapter 4

2 Bruce Metcalf, *On the Nature of Jewelry*, Metalsmith, Winter 1993, page 23.

3 Ralph Turner, *Contemporary Jewelry, A Crtical Assessment 1945-1975*, New York, Van Norstrand Reinhold Company, pg. 16.

4 Renée S. Neu, *The Artist as Jeweler,*. Art in America, Nov. Dec. 1967, pg.110.

5 John D. Willenbecher, *Harry Bertoia: A Monograph*, Unpublished Honors Thesis, Providence, Brown University, 1958.

6 *For the Metalworker Experiments Lead to Success*, Craft Horizons, Vol. 8, No. 18, August 1947.

7 Pearl Shecter, Walker Art Center, *Design Quarterly*, 1959, pg. 60.

8 Long Beach Museum of Art, *The Modernist Jewelry of Claire Falkenstein*.

9 Mark Foley, *Sam Kramer, Fantastic Jewelry for People Sho are Slightly Mad*, Metalsmith, Winter 1986, pg. 16.

10 *Craft Horizons*, pg. 21, Sept/October 1956.

11 Marbeth Schon, *Modernist Jewelry, 1930 – 1960, The Wearable Art Movement*, pg. 63

12 Paul Cummings, *Interview with Art Smith*, Archives of American Art, Smithsonian Institution, 1971.

13 Irena Brynner, *What I Remember*, Irena Brynner, 2002, pg. 164.

14 Rose Slivka, *Irena Brynner*, Craft Horizons, V. 19, 1959, pg.33.

15 Helen W. Drutt English and Peter Dormer, *Jewelry of Our Time, Art, Ornament, and Obsession*, New York, Rizzoli, 1995, pp.20-21.

16 Rose Slivka, *Radakovich Interview,* Craft Horizons, Sept.1958, pg. 28.

17 Deborah Norton, *A History of the School for American Craftsmen + conversation with John Prip, Metalsmith*, Winter, 1985, pg. 15 - 21.

18 Ibid.

19 Sharon Church, *Interview with Arline Fisch*, Archives of American Art, Smithsonian Institution, July 29 and 30, 2001.

20 National Gallery of Art, *Alexander Calder, 1898-1976,* http://www.nga.gov/exhibitions/calder/realsp/room2a-1.htm

21 Ibid.

22 Yohsiko Uchido, *The Jewelry of Margaret De Patta, a Retrospective Exhibition*, Oakland Museum of Art, 1976, pg. 18.

23 Margaret De Patta Bielowski , *From the Inside*, notes, The Sarah Bodine & Michael Dunas Archives of 20th Century Jewelry, Tyler School of Art, Temple University, Professor Stanley Lechtzin, Curator of Metals/Jewelry Archives and Collections.

24 Joan Pearson Watkins, *Opulent and Organic, The Jewelry of Merry Renk*, American Craft, V. 41, 1981

25 Rean Schilling, *Designing ladies*, More, The News Observer, Section B, Jan 29, 1978.

26 Denise Lassaw, unpublished biography of her father Ibram Lassaw (the following two paragraphs are also from this source.

27 Charlotte Streifer Rubenstein, *American Women in the Arts*, Avon, 1982, pp.314-316,

28 Ibid.

29 Daniel Macchiarini, *Daniel Macchiarini Speaks, Macchiarini on Macchiarini*, Modern Silver Magazine, June/July, 2000.

30 Daniel Macchiarini, *"Daniel Macchiarini Speaks, Macchiarini on Macchiarini," Modern Silver Magazine*, June/July, 2000.

31 Peter Macchiarini, "Peter Macchiarini Speaks, Macciarinin on Macchiarini," *Modern Silver Mahgazine*, June/July, 2000.

32 Margaret De Patta Bielowski, *From the Inside,* notes, The Sarah Bodine & Michael Dunas Archives of 20th Century Jewelry, Tyler School of Art, Temple University, Professor Stanley Lechtzin, Curator of Metals/Jewelry Archives and Collections.

33 *The Artist and the Cleavland School of Art*, pg. 5

34 Reid Hastie and Christian Schmidt, *Encounter with Art*, New York, McGraw Hill, 1969, pg. 142. (the next three paragraphs are also from this source).

35 La Mar Harrington, *Ruth Penington, Pioneer in 20th Century Metal and Modernism*, Archives of American Art, Smithsonian Institution, July 8, 1983.

36 www.iconicinteriors.col.uk/bauhaus.shtml

37 Marbeth Schon, *Interview with Betty Cooke*, Modern Silver Magazine, June 13, 2001

38 Yohsiko Uchido, *The Jewelry of Margaret De Patta, a Retrospective Exhibition*, Oakland Museum of Art, 1976, pg. 15.

39 Ralph Turner, *Jewelry in europe and american, new times, new thinking*, pg.7

40 Adolph Gottlieb, *Art in New York,* Broadcast WNYC radio, interview with Mark Rothko

41 Sam Kramer, *Creating Spontaneous Jewelry*, Design Magazine, 1951.

42 L.J. Walstein, Profile, *The World of Earl Krentzin.*

43 Yohsiko Uchido, *The Jewelry of Margaret De Patta, a Retrospective Exhibition*, Oakland Museum of Art, 1976, pg. 12.

44 www.exampleessays.com/viewpaper/82870.html

45 Toni Lesser Wolf, *"Ed Wiener's Arts & Ends," Metalsmith*, V.8, 1988, pg. 28

46 Phillip Morton, *Contemporary Jewelry, A Studio Handbook*, New York, Holt, Rinehart and Winston, Inc, 1970. pg. 34

47 Mark Foley, *Fantastic Jewelry for People who are Slightly Mad*, page. 15, Metalsmith, Winter 1986)

48 Sam Kramer, *Design Quarterly*, Walker Art Center, Minneapolis, 1959.

49 Sam Kramer, *Creating Spontaneous Jewelry*, Design Magazine, 1951.

50 Ibid.

51 Kevin L. Stayton, *Vital Forms, American Art & Design in the Atomic Age* (Introduction), New York, Harry N. Abrams, Inc. 2001, pg. 52.

52 Toni Lesser Wolf, *Goldsmith, Silversmith, Art Smith*, pg. 125.

53 Martin Eidelberg, *Design 1935-1965, What Modern Was*, Musée des Arts Décoratifs de Montréal, New York, Abrams, p. 302.

54 Sarah Bodine and Michael Dunas, *Reviving the Studio Image, Design Vision, International Directions in Glass, American Jewelry, and Metalwork*, Australia, 1992, pp.78-79

55 Reid Hastie and Christian Schmidt, *Encounter With Art,* McGraw-Hill, 1969.

56 Smithsonian American Art Museum, *The Jewelry of Robert Ebendorf: A Retrospective of Forty Years*, Resource Library Magazine, provided by the. www.tfaoi.com/aa/3aa/3aa598.htm

57 Denise Lassaw, unpublished biography of her father Ibram Lassaw.

58 La Mar Harrington, *Ruth Penington, Pioneer in 20th Century Metal and Modernism*, July 8, 1983, Archives of American Art, Smithsonian Institution (the following four paragraphs are also from this source).

59 Ettagale Lauré, *"The Jewelry of Earl Pardon," American Craft*, V. 42, 1982.

60 Reid Hastie and Christian Schmidt, *Encounter with Art*, New York, McGraw Hill, 1969, pg. 142.

61 Ed Wiener, *Jewelry by Ed Wiener*, New York, Fifty-50 Gallery, 1989, pg. 18

62 Theresa D. Parker, *Religious Art in America Today*, Art in America, Fall, 1957, pp. 16,17.

63 La Mar Harrington, "Ruth Penington, Pioneer in 20th Century Metal and Modernism," *Archives of American Art*, Washington, D.C., Smithsonian Institution, July 8, 1983.

Chapter 5

64 Yohsiko Uchido, *The Jewelry of Margaret De Patta, a Retrospective Exhibition*, Oakland Museum of Art, 1976, pg. 13.

65 Ibid. pg. 15. (the following three paragraphs are also from this source).

66 Margaret De Patta Bielowski , *From the Inside*, notes, The Sarah Bodine & Michael Dunas Archives of 20th Century Jewelry, Tyler School of Art, Temple University, Professor Stanley Lechtzin, Curator of Metals/Jewelry Archives and Collections.

67 *Biography of Allan Adler,* The Sarah Bodine & Michael Dunas Archives of 20th Century Jewelry, Tyler School of Art, Temple University, Professor Stanley Lechtzin, Curator of Metals/Jewelry Archives and Collections.

68 Sam Kramer, *"Gems In New Contexts," Craft Horizons*, Vol. 12, No. 5, 1952.

69 Toni Lesser Wolf, *Goldsmith, Silversmith, Art Smith*, pg. 125.

70 Toni Lesser Wolf, *Ed Wiener's Arts & Ends*, pg. 29

71 Nancy Ukai Russell, *"Modern Jewelry Pioneer, Elsa Freund," Ornament Magazine*, V. 15, 1991-1992, pp. 50-55 and 87-88. (The following paragraph is also from this source.)

72 Douglas Steakley, "Charles Loloma, 1921–1991," *Metalsmith,* Volume 12, 1992.

73 Rose Slivka, *"Radakovich Interview," Craft Horizons*, Sept.1958, pg. 25.

74 Bernard N. Jazzar and Harold B. Nelson, *Painting with Fire, Masters of Enameling in America, 1930 – 1980*, Long Beach Museum of Art, 2007, page 71.

75 Lee Nordness, Mary Kretsinger, *Objects: USA*, New York, Viking Press, pg. 72.

76 Margaret De Patta Bielowski, *From the Inside*, notes, The Sarah Bodine & Michael Dunas Archives of 20th Century Jewelry, Tyler School of Art, Temple University, Professor Stanley Lechtzin, Curator of Metals/Jewelry Archives and Collections.

77 Marbeth Schon, "Winfield Fine Art in Jewelry, a fusion of art and scientific discovery," *Modern Silver Magazine,* April/May, 2003. (The following six paragraphs are also from this source.)

78 Margaret Anderson, *"An Artist Works in Plastic," Craft Horizons*, V. 12, 1952, pp. 8-12. (The following paragraph is also from this source.)

79 Donald-Brian Johnson, *"Frances Higgins' House of Glass," Modernism* magazine, spring 2003.

80 Donald Brian Johnson, *"The Higgins Touch, Artistry in Modern Glass," Echoes*, Fall 1997.

Chapter 6

81 Robert Dhaemers, "Northern California, A Center for Experimental Jewelry, *Craft Horizons*, v. 16, 1956.

82 "Robert Cardinale," *Metalsmith*, Fall 1980, pg.23.

83 John Coyne,Ed., *The Penland School of Crafts Book of Jewelry Making*, North Carolina, Penland School of Crafts, pg. 116.

84 Sarah Bodine and Michael Dunas, *Reviving the Studio Image, Design Vision, International Directions in Glass, American Jewelry, and Metalwork,* Australia, 1992. (The following paragraph is also from his source).

85 Robert Cardinale, *Metalsmith*, Fall 1980, pg. 23 (the following paragraph is also from this source).

86 Jan Yager, "Phillip Fike, American Metalsmith, 1927-1997," *Metalsmith*, Spring 1998.

87 PJM archives, http://www.professionaljeweler.com/archives/articles/1998/mar98/0398pm1.html. (The following paragraph is also from this source.)

88 Lee Nordness, *Objects: USA*, New York, Viking Press, pg. 200.

89 Marbeth Schon, *Interview with Margret Craver Withers*, 2004.

90 *Biography: Stanley Lechtzin*, The Sarah Bodine & Michael Dunas Archives of 20th Century Jewelry, Tyler School of Art, Temple University, Professor Stanley Lechtzin, Curator of Metals/Jewelry Archives and Collections (The following paragraph is also from this source.)

91 Hazel Bray, *Probing the Potential of a New Esthetic*, Metalsmith, Fall 1987, pp.15-18.

92 Yohsiko Uchido, *The Jewelry of Margaret De Patta, a Retrospective Exhibition*, Oakland Museum of Art, 1976, pg. 15.

93 Daniel Macchiarini, *Unpublished Notes on Mass Production*, 2002.

94 Idella LaVista, *The Craftsman in the Modern World*, pg. 3.

95 Robert Engstrom, letter, The Sarah Bodine & Michael Dunas Archives of 20th Century Jewelry, Tyler School of Art, Temple University, Professor Stanley Lechtzin, Curator of Metals/Jewelry Archives and Collections.

96 Robert Cardinale, *Metalsmith*, Fall 1980, pg. 29.

97 Christian Schmidt, "From the Craftsman's Forum, Some Remarks on Limited Editions."

98 Daniel Macchiarini, *"Daniel Macchiarini Speaks, Macchiarini on Macchiarini," Modern Silver Magazine*, June/July, 2000.

99 John Coyne,Ed., *The Penland School of Crafts Book of Jewelry Making*, North Carolina, Penland School of Crafts, pg. 114.

Chapter 7

100 Bruce Metcalf, "On the Nature of Jewelry," *Metalsmith*, Winter, 1993.

101 Susan Grant Lewin, *One of A Kind, American Art Jewelry Today*, Abrams. New York, pg. 14.

102 Ibid, pg. 13-14.

103 Sarah Bodine and Michael Dunas, *Reviving the Studio Image, Design Vision, International Directions in Glass, American Jewelry, and Metalwork*, Australia, 1992, Page 78.

104 Sam Kramer, *Design Quarterly,* v. #48-49, 1960.

Part III. Artists' Biographies

Chapter 8

1 *Biography of Allan Adler*, The Sarah Bodine & Michael Dunas Archives of 20th Century Jewelry, Tyler School of Art, Temple University, Professor Stanley Lechtzin, Curator of Metals/Jewelry Archives and Collections (Biography of Allan Adler is mostly from this source.)

2 Edan Hughes, *"Artists in California, 1786-1940"* Interview with the artist or his/her family. (Biography of Vera Allison is mostly from this source.)

3 *Design Quarterly*, Walker Art Center, Minneapolis, 1959.

4 Marbeth Schon, *"Lilyan Bachrach, Enamelist/Author," Modern Silver Magazine*, June/July 2003. (Biography of Lilyan Bachrach is mostly from this source.)

5 Marbeth Schon, *Modernist Jewelry, 1930 – 1960, The Wearable Art Movement*, Atglen: Schiffer Publishing, 2004, pg. 121.

6 Ibid, pg.21. (Biography of Harry Bertoia is mostly from this source.)

7 Al Munir Meghji, *Conversation with Robert and Esta Blood.* (Biography of Robert and Esta Blood is mostly taken from this source.)

8 Marbeth Schon, *Modernist Jewelry, 1930–1960, The Wearable Art Movement*, Atglen, Schiffer Publishing, 2004, pg.124. (Biography of Frances Holmes Boothby is mostly from this source.)

9 Ibid, pp.184-185. (Biography of Jules Brenner is mostly from this source.)

10 Ibid, pp. 126-132. (Biography of Irena Brynner is mostly from this source.)

11 Ibid, pp.222-225. (Biography of Irvin and Bonnie Burkee is mostly from this source.)

12 Ibid, pp. 20-21. (Biography of Alexander Calder is mostly from this source.)

13 Ibid, pp.133-134. (Biography of Eleanor Caldwell is mostly from this source.)

14 Bernard N. Jazzar and Harold B. Nelson, *Painting with Fire, Masters of Enameling in America, 1930–1980,* California: Long Beach Museum of Art, page 71. (Biography of Virgil Cantini is mostly from this source.)

15 Biographical information on the Cantanzaro sisters provided by Catherine Koenig.

16 Marbeth Schon, *Modernist Jewelry, 1930–1960, The Wearable Art Movement*, Atglen: Schiffer Publishing, 2004, pg. 228. (Biography of Milton Cavagnaro is mostly from this source.)

17 Ibid, pp. 46-50. (Biography of Betty Cooke is mostly from this source.)

18 Marbeth Schon, *Interview with Margret Craver*, 2005.

19 Marbeth Schon, *Modernist Jewelry, 1930–1960, The Wearable Art Movement*, Atglen: Schiffer Publishing, 2004, pp. 43-46. (Biography of Margret Craver Withers is mostly from this source.)

20 Ibid, pp. 25-28. (Biography of Magaret De Patta is mostly from this source.)

21 Ibid, pp. 137-138. (Biography of Robert Dhaemers is mostly from this source.)

22 Ibid, pp. 94-95. (Biography of Jose de Rivera is mostly from this source.)

23 Bernard N. Jazzar and Harold B. Nelson, *Painting with Fire, Masters of Enameling in America, 1930–1980*, Long Beach Museum of Art, 2007, pp. 69-81. (Biography of Drerup is mostly from this source.)

24 Marbeth Schon, *Modernist Jewelry, 1930–1960, The Wearable Art Movement*, Atglen, Schiffer Publishing, 2004, pp 139-141.

25 Jazzar and Harold B. Nelson, *Painting with Fire, Masters of Enameling in America, 1930 – 1980,* California: Long Beach Museum of Art, pg. 266.

26 Pieces of Eight, *ECU artist combine precious and the non-precious materials*. http://www.news.ecu.edu/poe/poeonline/MARCH2003/ebendorf.html.

27 Joh Coyne, ed., T*he Penland School of Crafts Book of Jewelry Making,* page 114. (The following paragraph is also from this source.)

28 Tacey Rosolowski, "Interview with Robert Ebendorf," *Archives of American Art,* Washington, D.C.: Smithsonian Institution, 2004.

29 Marbeth Schon, *Modernist Jewelry, 1930–1960, The Wearable Art Movement*, Atglen: Schiffer Publishing, 2004, pg. 188.

30 *Biography of Alma Eikerman*, The Sarah Bodine & Michael Dunas Archives of 20th Century Jewelry, Tyler School of Art, Temple University, Professor Stanley Lechtzin, Curator of Metals/Jewelry Archives and Collections *(*the following four paragraphs are also from this source).

31 Marbeth Schon, *Modernist Jewelry, 1930–1960, The Wearable Art Movement*, Atglen: Schiffer Publishing, 2004, pp 142-143. (Biography of Robert and Audrey Engstrom is mostly from this source.)

32 Ibid, pp 98-101. (Biography of Claire Falkenstein is mostly taken from this source.)

33 Louis Stern, Claire Falkenstein (1908-1997), www.louissternfinearts.com.

34 Jan Yager, "Interview with Fred Fenster," *Archives of American Art*, Washington, D.C.: Smithsonian Institution, 2004. (Entire biography of Fred Fenster is from this source.)

35 Marbeth Schon, *Modernist Jewelry, 1930–1960, The Wearable Art Movement*, Atglen: Schiffer Publishing, 2004, pp 144-145. (Biography of Phillip Fike is mostly from this source.)

36 Sharon Church, "Interview with Arline M. Fisch," *Archives of American Art,* Washington, D.C.: Smithsonian Institution, 2001. (Entire biography of Arline Fisch is from this source.)

37 Marbeth Schon, *Modernist Jewelry, 1930–1960, The Wearable Art Movement,* Atglen: Schiffer Publishing, 2004, pp 189-194. (Biography of Elsa Freund is mostly from this source.)

38 *"J. Arnold Frew, Jewelry for the movie stars," Craft Horizons,* Jan. – Feb. 1958, Vol. XV111, No. 1. (Biography of Arnold Frew is mostly from this source.)

39 Marbeth Schon, *Modernist Jewelry, 1930–1960, The Wearable Art Movement*, Atglen: Schiffer Publishing, 2004, pp 194-195. (Biography of Richard Gompf is mostly from this source.)

40 Bernard N. Jazzar and Harold B. Nelson, *Painting with Fire, Masters of Enameling in America, 1930 – 1980,* California: Long Beach Museum of Art, pp. 119-131. (Biography of Doris Hall is mostly from this source.)

41 Information courtesy of Gerald L. Peterson, Rod Library—Special Collections, University of Northern Iowa.

42 Marbeth Schon, *Modernist Jewelry, 1930–1960, The Wearable Art Movement,* Atglen: Schiffer Publishing, 2004, pp. 235-236. (Biography of Michael and Francis Higgins is mostly from this source.)

43 Ibid, pg. 236.

44 Jules Perel, *"The Welded Sculpture of ERNESTO," American Artist,* May, 1960. (Biography of Ernesto Jerrez is mostly from this source.)

45 Jan Yager, *Interview with Michael John Jerry*, Archives of American Art, Smithsonian Instutition, 2004.

46 Orlando Museum of Art*, About the Artists in Treasured Jewelry, Arthur King*. http://www.omart.org/pressreleases/about_the_artists.html. (Biography of Arthur King is mostly from this source.)

47 Marbeth Schon, *Modernist Jewelry, 1930 – 1960, The Wearable Art Movement*, Atglen, Schiffer Publishing, 2004, pp 30-33. (Biography of Sam Kramer is mostly from this source.)

48 Ibid, pp 194-195. (Biography of Earl Krentzin is mostly from this source.)

49 Robert Von Neuman, *The Design and Creation of Jewelry*, 1961, page 75.

50 Biography of Mary Krentinger is courtesy of Sheila Pamfiloff, www.glitterbox.com.

51 Biography of Ibram Lassaw is from an unpublished biography of her father by Denise Lassaw.

52 Idella LaVista, *The Craftsman in the Modern World*, speech.

53 Marbeth Schon, *Modernist Jewelry, 1930–1960, The Wearable Art Movement*, Atglen: Schiffer Publishing, 2004, pp 237-238. (Biography of Stanley Lechtzin is mostly from this source.)

54 Ibid, pp 76-81. (Biography of Ed Levin is mostly from this source.)

55 Ibid, pp 238-240. (Biography of Esther Lewittes is mostly from this source.)

56 Ellie Conason, *American Craft,* Dec. 3, 2004.

57 Marbeth Schon, *Modernist Jewelry, 1930–1960, The Wearable Art Movement*, Atglen: Schiffer Publishing, 2004, pp 57-60. (Biography of Paul Lobel is mostly from this source.)

58 Martha Hopkins Struever, *LOLOMA, Beauty is his Name*, Santa Fe, New Mexico: Wheelwright Museum of the American Indian.

59 Douglas Steakley, *"Charles Loloma, 1921–1991," Metalsmith*, Volume 12, 1992.

60 Daniel Macchiarini, *"Daniel Macchiarini Speaks," Modern Silver Magazine*, May, 2000.

61 Marbeth Schon, *Modernist Jewelry, 1930–1960, The Wearable Art Movement*, Atglen: Schiffer Publishing, 2004, pp 34-39. (Biography of Peter Macchiarini is mostly from this source.)

62 Ibid, pg. 240. (Biography of Everett Macdonald is mostly from this source.)

63 Jan Yager, *Interview with John Paul Miller*, Archives of American Art, Smithsonian Institution, 2004. (Biography of John Paul Miller is mostly from this source.)

64 Marbeth Schon, *Modernist Jewelry, 1930–1960, The Wearable Art Movement*, Atglen, Schiffer Publishing, 2004, pg. 118.

65 Ibid, pp. 105-106 (Biography of Philip Morton is mostly from this source.)

66 Robert Cardinale, *Metalsmith*, Fall, 1980. (Biography of Albert Paley is mostly from this source.)

67 www.albertpaley.com

68 Marbeth Schon, *Modernist Jewelry, 1930–1960, The Wearable Art Movement*, Atglen, Schiffer Publishing, 2004, pp. 105-106. (Biography of Earl Pardon is mostly from this source).

69 *Craft Horizons*, Sept/October, 1956, pg. 21.

70 Marbeth Schon, *Modernist Jewelry, 1930–1960, The Wearable Art Movement*, Atglen: Schiffer Publishing, 2004, pp. 243-244. (Biography of James Parker is mostly from this source.)

71 Ibid, pp. 202-205 (biography of Ronald Pearson is mostly from this source).

72 Ibid, pg.156.

73 Ibid, pg. 156. (Biography of Coralyn Pence is mostly from this source.)

74 La Mar Harrington, *Ruth Penington, Pioneer in 20th Century Metal and Modernism*, Archives of American Art, Smithsonian Institution, July 8, 1983. (Biography of Ruth Penington is mostly from this source.)

75 *Biography of John Prip*, The Sarah Bodine & Michael Dunas Archives of 20th Century Jewelry, Tyler School of Art, Temple University, Professor Stanley Lechtzin, Curator of Metals/Jewelry Archives and Collections.

76 Marbeth Schon, *Modernist Jewelry, 1930–1960, The Wearable Art Movement*, Atglen: Schiffer Publishing, 2004, pp. 206-210. (Biography of Svetozar and Ruth Radakovich is taken mostly from this source.)

77 Ibid, pp. 51-55. (Biography of Francisco Rebajes is mostly from this source.)

78 Arline Fisch, *Interview with Merry Renk*, Archives of American Art, Smithsonian Institution, 2001.

79 Marbeth Schon, *Modernist Jewelry, 1930–1960, The Wearable Art Movement*, Atglen: Schiffer Publishing, 2004, pg. 158-163. (Biography of merry renk is mostly from this source.)

80 Ibid, pg. 158. (Biography of Barney Reid is mostly from this source.)

81 Ibid, pg. 164-166. (Biography of Florence Resnikoff is taken mostly from this source.)

82 Ibid, pg. 93.

83 Ibid, pp. 107-108. (Biography of Rima is taken mostly from this source.)

84 Ibid, pp. 166-172. (Biography of Ruth Roach is mostly from this source.)

85 Ibid, pg. 108.

86 Ibid, pg. 108.

87 Ibid, pp. 109-110. (Biography of Zahara Schatz is mostly taken from this source.)

88 Ibid, pp. 210-215. (Biography of Mary Schimpff is mostly from this source.)

89 Biography of Howard Schleeter is from David Cook Galleries, LLC.

90 Marbeth Schon, *Modernist Jewelry, 1930–1960, The Wearable Art Movement,* Atglen: Schiffer Publishing, 2004, pg. 173-176. (Biography of Christian Schmidt is mostly from this source.)

91 Biography courtesy of Helen Shirk.

92 Marbeth Schon, *Modernist Jewelry, 1930–1960, The Wearable Art Movement*, Atglen: Schiffer Publishing, 2004, pg. 249. (Biography of Olaf Skoogfors is mostly taken from this source.)

93 Robert Cardinale, *Metalsmith*, Fall 1980.

94 Marbeth Schon, *Modernist Jewelry, 1930–1960, The Wearable Art Movement*, Atglen: Schiffer Publishing, 2004, pg. 210.

95 Biography of Noble Smith courtesy of Phyllis Allen.

96 Marbeth Schon, *Modernist Jewelry, 1930–1960, The Wearable Art Movement*, Atglen: Schiffer Publishing, 2004, pp. 69-76. (Biography of Art Smith is mostly from this source.)

97 Ibid, pp. 85-87. (Biography of Henry Steig is mostly from this source.)

98 Ibid, pp 82-83. (Biography of Bill Tendler is mostly from this source.)

99 *"Contemporary Workshop Reflects Skill in Science, Art, In the Touch of Paul Voltaire," New Milford Times*, December 10, 1963.

100 Marbeth Schon, *Modernist Jewelry, 1930–1960, The Wearable Art Movement*, Atglen: Schiffer Publishing, 2004, pp. 233-235. (Biography of Lois Franke Warren is mostly from this source.)

101 Ibid, pp. 60-69. (Biography of Ed Wiener is mostly from this source.)

102 Ibid, pp. 182-183. (Biography of Byron Wilson is mostly from this source.)

103 Ibid, pp. 110-114. (Biography of Winfield Fine Art in Jewelry is mostly from this source.)

104 Ibid, pp. 114-115. (Biography of Bob Winston is mostly from this source.)

Works Cited

Albert Paley Studios, www.albertpaley.com.

Alexander Calder, 1898-1976. National Gallery of Art http://www.nga.gov/exhibitions/calder/realsp/room2a-1.htm.

American Masters, *Black Mountain College*, PBS, http://www.pbs.org/wnet/americanmasters/database/black_mountain_college.html.

Anderson, Margaret. *An Artist Works in Plastic.* Craft Horizons, V. 12, 1952.

Bennett, Jamie. *Jewelry Meditating Jewelry*, Metalsmith Magazine, Winter 1998.

Bielowski , Margaret De Patta. *From the Inside*, notes, *The Sarah Bodine & Michael Dunas Archives of 20th Century Jewelry*, Tyler School of Art, Temple University, Professor Stanley Lechtzin, Curator of Metals/Jewelry Archives and Collections.

Bodine, Sarah and Dunas, Michael. *Biography of Allan Adler.* Archives of 20th Century Jewelry, Tyler School of Art, Temple University, Professor Stanley Lechtzin, Curator of Metals/Jewelry Archives and Collections.

___. *Reviving the Studio Image, Design Vision, International Directions in Glass, American Jewelry, and Metalwork*, Australia, 1992.

___. *Biography: Stanley Lechtzin.* Archives of 20th Century Jewelry, Tyler School of Art, Temple University, Professor Stanley Lechtzin, Curator of Metals/Jewelry Archives and Collections.

___. *Biography of Allan Adler*, Archives of 20th Century Jewelry, Tyler School of Art, Temple University, Professor Stanley Lechtzin, Curator of Metals/Jewelry Archives and Collections.

___. *Biography of Alma Eikerman. Archives of 20th Century Jewelry*, Tyler School of Art, Temple University, Professor Stanley Lechtzin, Curator of Metals/Jewelry Archives and Collections.

___, Archives of 20th Century Jewelry. *Biography of John Prip.* Tyler School of Art, Temple University, Professor Stanley Lechtzin, Curator of Metals/Jewelry Archives and Collections.

Bray, Hazel. *Probing the Potential of a New Esthetic*, Metalsmith, Fall 1987.

Brynner, Irena. *What I Remember*. Irena Brynner, 2002.

Cardinale, Robert. *Metalsmith Magazine*, Fall, 1980.

Beaux, Cecelia. *Is there an American Art?* February, 1922.

Church, Sharon. *Interview with Arline M. Fisch*. Archives of American Art, Smithsonian Institution, July 29 and 30, 2001.

Conason, Ellie. American Craft, Dec. 3, 2004.

"Contemporary Workshop Reflects Skill in Science, Art, In the Touch of Paul Voltaire." New Milford Times, December 10, 1963.

Coyne, John, Ed. *The Penland School of Crafts Book of Jewelry Making*. North Carolina: Penland School of Crafts.

Cranbrook Academy of Art, www.cranbrookart.edu/site/about_history.html.

Craft Horizons, Sept/October 1956.

Craver Margret. Speech at *American Metalsmithing and Jewelrymaking in the 1940s and 1950s*, sponsored by the Renwick Gallery and the Archives of American Art.

Cummings, Paul. *Interview with Art Smith*. Archives of American Art, Smithsonian Institution, 1971.

David Cook Galleries, LLC. *Biography of Howard Schleeter*.

Design Quarterly, Walker Art Center, Minneapolis, 1959.

Eidelberg, Martin. *Design 1935-1965, What Modern Was*. Musée des Arts Décoratifs de Montréal, New York: Abrams, p.22.

English, Helen W. Drutt and Dormer, Peter. *Jewelry of Our Time, Art, Ornament and Obsession*. New York: Rozzoli.

Engstrom, Robert. Letter.*The Sarah Bodine & Michael Dunas Archives of 20th Century Jewelry*, Tyler School of Art, Temple University, Professor Stanley Lechtzin, Curator of Metals/Jewelry Archives and Collections.

Example Essays.com. *Abstract Expressionism.* www.exampleessays.com/viewpaper/82870.html

Foley, Mark. *"Sam Kramer, Fantastic Jewelry for People Who are Slightly Mad," Metalsmith*, Winter 1986.

"For the Metalworker, Experiments Lead to Success," Craft Horizons, Vol. 8, No. 18, August 1947.

Frew, J. Arnold, "Jewelry for the movie stars," Craft Horizons, Jan. – Feb. 1958, Vol XV111, No. 1.

Gottlieb, Adolph. *"Interview with Mark Rothko." Art in New York*. Broadcast WNYC radio.

Hall, Julie. *"A Conversation with Richard Thomas, master metalsmith," Metalsmith Magazine*, Spring, Summer 1982.

Harrington, La Mar. *Ruth Penington, Pioneer in 20th Century Metal and Modernism*. Archives of American Art, Smithsonian Institution, July 8, 1983.

Hastie, Reid and Schmidt, Christian. *Encounter with Art.* New York: McGraw Hill, 1969.

Hughes , Edan. *Artists in California, 1786-1940.* Sacramento, California: Crocker Art Museum.

Jazzar, Bernard N. and Nelson, Harold B. *Painting with Fire, Masters of Enameling in America, 1930–1980*, Long Beach Museum of Art, 2007.

Johnson, Donald-Brian. *"Frances Higgins' House of Glass," Modernism Magazine,* Spring, 2003.

___. *"The Higgins Touch, Artistry in Modern Glass," Echoes*, Fall, 1997.

Kramer, Sam. *"Creating Spontaneous Jewelry," Design Magazine*, 1951.

___. *Design Quarterly,* Walker Art Center, Minneapolis, 1959.

___. *"Gems In New Contexts," Craft Horizons,* Vol. 12, No. 5, 1952.

___. *Design Quarterly,* #48-49, 1960.

Lassaw, Denise. *Unpublished biography of her father, Ibram Lassaw.*

Lauré, Ettagale. *"The Jewelry of Earl Pardon," American Craft,* Vol. 42, 1982.

LaVista, Idella. essay, *"The Craftsman in the Modern World".*

Lewin, Susan. *One of A Kind, Art Jewelry Today*. New York: Abrams, 1985.

Macchiarini, Daniel. *"Daniel Macchiarini Speaks, Macchiarini on Macchiarini," Modern Silver Magazine*, June/July, 2000.

___. *Unpublished Notes on Mass Production*, 2002.

Meghji, Al Munir. *Conversation with Robert and Esta Blood*.

Metcalf, Bruce. *"On the Nature of Jewelry," Metalsmith*, Winter, 1993.

Morton, Philip. *Contemporary Jewelry*. New York: Holt, Rinehart and Winston, 1976.

___. *Contemporary Jewelry, A Studio Handbook*. New York: Holt, Rinehart and Winston, Inc, 1970.

Neu, Renée S. *"The Artist as Jeweler." Art in America,* Nov. Dec. 1967.

Nordness, Lee. *"Mary Kretsinger," Objects: USA*. New York: Viking Press.

Norton, Deborah. *"A History of the School for American Craftsmen + conversation with John Prip," Metalsmith*, Winter, 1985.

Orlando Museum of Art, *About the Artists in Treasured Jewelry, Arthur King*. http://www.omart.org/pressreleases/about_the_artists.html

Parker, Theresa D. *"Religious Art in America Today," Art in America*, Fall, 1957.

Perel, Jules. *"The Welded Sculpture of ERNESTO," American Artist,* May, 1960.

Pieces of Eight, ECU artist combines precious and the non-precious materials. http://www.news.ecu.edu/poe/poeonline/MARCH2003/ebendorf.html.

PJM archives, http://www.professionaljeweler.com/archives/articles/1990/mar98/0398pm1.html

Rosolowski, Tracey. *"Interview with Robert Ebendorf, "* Archives of American Art, Smithsonian Institution, 2004.

Rubenstein, Charlotte Streifer. *American Women in the Arts*. Avon, 1982.

Russell, Nancy Ukai. *"Modern Jewelry Pioneer, Elsa Freund," Ornament Magazine*, Vol. 15, 1991-1992.

Schilling, Rean. *"Designing Ladies." The News Observer*, Section B, Jan 29, 1978.

Schmidt, Christian. *"Some Remarks on Limited Editions,"* from the Craftsman's Forum.

Schon, Marbeth. *Interview with Margret Craver*, 2001.

___. *Interview with Stanley Lechtzin*, May, 2008.

___. *Modernist Jewelry, 1930–1960, The Wearable Art Movement.* Atglen, Pennsylvania: Schiffer Publishing, 2004.

___. *"Interview with Betty Cooke," Modern Silver Magazine,* June 13, 2001.

___. *"Winfield Fine Art in Jewelry, a fusion of art and scientific discovery," Modern Silver Magazine*, April/May, 2003.

___. *"Lilyan Bachrach, Enamelist/Author," Modern Silver Magazine*, June/July 2003.

Shecter, Pearl. *Design Quarterly*, Walker Art Center, 1959.

Slivka, Rose. *"Radakovich Interview," Craft Horizons,* September, 1958.

Slivka, Rose. *"Irena Brynner," Craft Horizons,* Vol. 19, 1959.

Stayton, Kevin L. *Vital Forms, American Art & Design in the Atomic Age*. New York: Harry N. Abrams, Inc., 2001.

Steakley, Douglas. *"Charles Loloma, 1921–1991," Metalsmith,* Vol. 12, 1992.

Struever, Martha Hopkins. *LOLOMA, Beauty is his Name*, Santa Fe, New Mexico: Wheelwright Museum of the American Indian, 2005.

"The Bauhaus Story." www.iconicinteriors.col.uk/bauhaus.shtml.

"The Jewelry of Robert Ebendorf: A Retrospective of Forty Years," Resource Library Magazine, provided by the Smithsonian American Art Museum, www.tfaoi.com/aa/3aa/3aa598.htm.

The Modernist Jewelry of Claire Falkenstein. Long Beach, California: The Long Beach Museum of Art.

Turner, Ralph. *Jewelry in Europe and America, new times, new thinking*. New York: Thames and Hudson, Ltd.

___. *Contemporary Jewelry, A Crtical Assessment 1945-1975*, New York: Van Norstrand Reinhold Company.

Uchido, Yohsiko. *The Jewelry of Margaret De Patta, a Retrospective Exhibition*. Oakland Museum of Art, 1976.

Voltaire, Paul. *Notes on Greenwich Village* courtesy of Mrs. Alice Seymour.

Von Neuman, Robert, *The Design and Creation of Jewelry*, 1961.

Walstein, L.J. *"Profile,The World of Earl Krentzin."*

Watkins, Joan Pearson. "Opulent and Organic, The Jewelry of Merry Renk," *American Craft,* Vol. 41, 1981.

Webb, Mrs. Aileen Vanderbilt. *"American Craftsmen's Council, 1964, The International Era," Craft Horizons*, Vol. 24, 1964.

___"Speech for the opening of the World Crafts Council," *Craft Horizons*, Vol. 24, 1964, page 9.

Wiener, Ed. *Jewelry by Ed Wiener*, New York: Fifty-50 Gallery, 1989.

Willenbecher, John D. *"Harry Bertoia: A Monograph,"* Unpublished Honors Thesis, Providence: Brown University, 1958.

Wilson, Byron. Letter, *The Sarah Bodine & Michael Dunas Archives of 20th Century Jewelry*. Tyler School of Art, Temple University, Professor Stanley Lechtzin, Curator of Metals/Jewelry Archives and Collections.

Wolf, Toni Lesser. *"Ed Wiener Arts & Ends," Metalsmith*, Vol. 8, 1988.

___. *"Goldsmith, Silversmith, Art Smith," Metalsmith*, Fall, 1987.

Yager, Jan. *"Phillip Fike, American Metalsmith,1927-1997," Metalsmith*, Spring, 1998.

Yager, Jan. *Interview with Michael John Jerry*, Archives of American Art, Smithsonian Instutition, 2004.

___. *Interview with John Paul Miller*, Archives of American Art, Smithsonian Institution, 2004.

___. *Interview with Fred Fenster*. Archives of American Art, Smithsonian Institution, August 10, 2004.

Index